Choctaw Genesis 1500-1700

INDIANS OF THE SOUTHEAST

Series Editors
Theda Perdue, University of Kentucky
Michael D. Green, University of Kentucky

Advisory Editors
Leland Ferguson, University of South Carolina
Mary Young, University of Rochester

Choctaw
Genesis
1500-1700

Patricia Galloway

University of Nebraska Press
Lincoln and London

© 1995 by the University of
Nebraska Press. All rights reserved
Manufactured in the United
States of America. ☉ The paper in
this book meets the minimum
requirements of American National
Standard for Information Sciences –
Permanence of Paper for Printed
Library Materials, ANSI z39.48-1984.
Library of Congress Cataloging-
in-Publication Data
Galloway, Patricia Kay.
Choctaw genesis 1500–1700 /
by Patricia Galloway. p. cm. —
(Indians of the Southeast) Includes
bibliographical references and index.
ISBN 0-8032-2151-7 (cl : alk. paper)
1. Choctaw Indians — History. I. Title.
II. Series. E99.C8G35 1995
973'.04973 — dc20 95-1659 CIP

In Memory of
Samuel Belton Galloway
1918–1989
and
Charles Betts Galloway
1911–1983
for whom science and art
were two songs for the
same melody
and
with thanks to
Mary Kay Miller Galloway
who taught me what a
typewriter
was for

Contents

Illustrations

Tables

Tables

Series Editors' Foreword

Students of Southeastern Indian History have long been frustrated by the century between 1550 and 1650. Spanning the period between Soto and the return of European observers, this "black hole" of Southern Indian history obscures our understanding of the aftermath of the first extended contacts between Native Americans and Europeans. We know massive changes occurred during that period because the chiefdoms Soto saw and described were gone one hundred years later when Europeans returned to the South to stay. Recent scholarship on European epidemic disease and their effects on "virgin soil" populations suggests a cause for the collapse of southeastern native political systems and attendant social and economic upheavals, but few have dared to carry that insight into the "black hole" to recover the story. In this book Patricia Galloway not only does that, she also describes how she did it. Using an extraordinary array of traditional and nontraditional sources, approaches, models, and theories, Galloway presents her conclusions on the ethnic origins of the Choctaws and explains how and where they lived before they experienced sustained contact with Europeans. Part ethnohistorical interpretation, part methodological guidebook, this volume takes a proud place in the Indians of the Southeast series.

Theda Perdue and Michael D. Green

Note to Readers

Because we cannot today be certain what early writers and mapmakers actually referred to when they wrote down Indian tribal names and names of places, when I use documents and maps as sources I use the spellings found in those sources. There are many variants in these spellings, but to gloss over them by standardizing to one spelling would be to imply that we knew that the names were equivalent, and I argue throughout this book that we rarely know any such thing. Until long-term European settlements were established, the names we read today applied at best only to what the original observer saw.

Acknowledgments

This book, which dwells on the margins of several disciplines, would clearly have been impossible without the assistance of numerous friends and colleagues, too numerous to list them all here. Not least, I thank them for their respect, which scholars not based in academia often find hard to come by.

I list the archaeologists first, since so much of the evidence I had to depend on is recent, unpublished, and difficult to locate. James Atkinson, Jeffrey Brain, Sam Brookes, Sam McGahey, and Vincas Steponaitis have helpfully provided access to materials on the archaeology of Mississippi. Chris Peebles, Marvin Jeter, and Jay Johnson have sent me books, put up with a lot of strange ideas, and patiently explained anthropological complexities. John Blitz, Baxter Mann, Jerry Voss, Ken Carleton, John O'Hear, and Tim Mooney have shared their new data on the archaeology of the Choctaw homeland; sometimes the data were so new I had to wash the pottery myself. Ann Ramenofsky and Marvin Smith have willingly debated ideas about this difficult postexploration, precolonial period. David Morgan, then keeper of the Mississippi state site files, has been unfailingly helpful.

Among historians, I have learned from working with and being edited by Robert Weddle. David Henige and Paul Hoffman have both encouraged my unorthodox ideas about Spanish explorers, but neither is to blame for those ideas. Clara Sue Kidwell has shared her wide knowledge of Choctaw history and culture. LeAnne Howe has given me some truly remarkable insights from an artist's view of growing up Choctaw in the modern world. Julie Smith did a fine job of preparing my synthetic maps.

I would also like to thank the National Endowment for the Humanities, which provided funding for research on Choctaw landholding in the eighteenth century, and the Hermon Dunlap Smith Center for the History of Cartography at the Newberry Library, without whose fellowship chapter 6 would not have been written. Appointment to the Choctaw Heritage Council of the Mississippi Band of Choctaw Indians over a decade ago played a part in forming my determination to treat the subject. My own institution, the Mississippi Department of Archives and History, allowed me a year's leave of absence to write chapter 2 and has been supportive of this project in many different ways.

Last but not least I would like to thank my mechanic, Eddie Russell, who during the twelve long years of its genesis never failed to ask how my book was coming along.

Contemporary scholars have demonstrated again and again that, in penetrating the culture of a neglected group, historians often find more than they bargained for. What looked like a group becomes an amalgam of groups; what looked like a culture becomes a series of cultures. – Lawrence Levine, "The Unpredictable Past"

CHAPTER ONE

Source Materials and Methodologies

Ask simple questions, because the answers to complicated questions probably will be too complicated to test and, even worse, too fascinating to give up. – Alfred W. Crosby Jr., *Ecological Imperialism*

[H]istory is the privileged place where the gaze becomes unsettled, even if it is only that. – Michel de Certeau, *Heterologies*

The presence of the Choctaw Indians in the Euro-American history of the southeastern United States is comfortably familiar: they were some of the "Good Indians," one of the Five Civilized Tribes, led by their near-mythic chief Pushmataha to the aid of Andrew Jackson in the Battle of New Orleans. After that not much more is said; the Cherokees got most of the press and the pity for the Trail of Tears to Oklahoma, although the Choctaws were the first victims of Removal. Modern Mississippians point to their tolerance of these loyal Indians, using as their example Greenwood LeFlore, the French-Choctaw mixed-blood who was instrumental in arranging for Removal and ended as a rich planter in the Mississippi Delta, sitting in the state legislature and building a mansion called Malmaison. But Greenwood LeFlore was not the only Choctaw who remained. Hundreds of others, not so powerful or lucky, clung grimly to scraps of their homeland as the backwoods of east-central Mississippi were infiltrated by white settlers in the nineteenth century, to emerge in the twentieth as the reconstituted Mississippi Band of Choctaw Indians more than seven thousand strong, still speaking Choctaw, still not melted in the pot.

All these Choctaws are as much image as reality, however, and what is familiar is only the end of the story, after the missionaries had done their work and American political hegemony had reduced the Choctaws to a marginal existence. During the colonial period they were a populous and powerful people, holding with the Creeks the balance of power in the interior Southeast. When the French could barely muster a few thousand colonists, the Choctaws numbered as many as twenty thousand

I

(Wood 1989). Powerful enough to fear no significant threat from any neighbor once the French had armed them with guns (which they also used in the colonial deerskin trade), they were courted throughout the eighteenth century first by the French and British, then by the Spanish and British, and finally by the Spanish and Americans. They were a major power east of the Mississippi during the eighteenth century, the period in which they flourished (Crane 1956; White 1983; Foret 1990; Usner 1992).

Eighteenth-century Choctaws were a confederation of forty to fifty autonomous villages gathered in four groupings on the rivers that meet in what is now east-central Mississippi (figure 1.1; see also figure 2.2). The western Choctaws lived at the head of the Pearl River (Riviere aux Perles), in the vicinity of the "mother mound" of Choctaw legend, Nanih Waiya. The eastern Choctaws inhabited the Tombigbee River's western tributaries that interdigitated with the Pearl, chiefly the Sucarnoochee. The Sixtown Choctaws lived south of the western Choctaws, east of the Pearl and on the streams that flowed into the Chickasawhay River. The Chickasawhays, finally, lived somewhat south of the main body of Choctaw villages, on the Chickasawhay River. Each of these groups consisted of a number of villages, each led by a chief and several assistants, aided by a council of elders. Each village also had or could appoint a "red" or war chief when the occasion demanded. The groups, in turn, were usually led by one of their prominent village chiefs. The Choctaws did not generally heed an overall leader, in spite of French attempts to favor one, but the colonial period saw the French name a "Great Chief," and from the turmoil of the contest for empire a tribal war chief eventually also emerged.

Genealogical relationships ordered the social lives of eighteenth-century Choctaws, in matrilineal and matrilocal family groups. The head of a household was the brother of the woman whose household it was; her husband was a guest rather than a relative, and the children belonged to her lineage. The matrilines controlled the agricultural land that was important to a subsistence regime also dependent upon gathering by women and hunting by men. As the deerskin trade grew in significance during the eighteenth century, subsistence activities had to be altered to accommodate it, and it strengthened the importance of men to the support of their families.

Like other southeastern Indians, the Choctaws were crosscut by a great organizing principle, the moiety ("half"), an anthropological term denoting an additional division of the tribe into halves reaching throughout all villages. Marriage had to cross moiety boundaries, and members of each moiety performed ceremonies (such as for annual renewal and mourning) for members of the opposite moiety. Moiety allegiances inevitably had political importance, too, since civil chiefs came from one moiety and war chiefs from the other.

Because the Choctaws were so powerful during the eighteenth century and their good graces so crucial to the safety of European settlers, a good deal was written

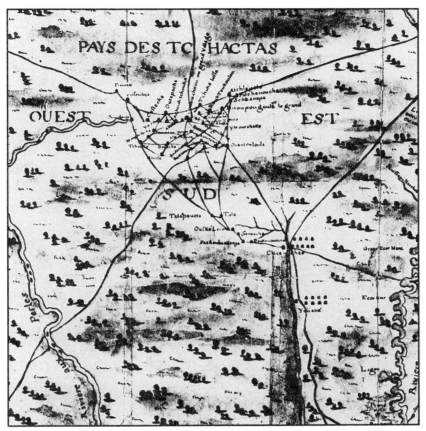

1.1. Choctaw towns in the eighteenth century. A portion of Baron de Crenay's *Carte de partie de la Louisiane* . . . , 1733, Dépot des fortifications des colonies, Louisiane 1A. Courtesy of the Archives Nationales, Centre des Archives d'Outre-Mer, Aix-en-Provence. All rights reserved.

about them by all their European suitors. It is not so easy to find out where they came from and what their story was *before* the Europeans' arrival. Not until 1660 or 1675 did the Choctaws appear under that name and in their general historical location in the writings of Europeans, nearly two hundred years after the coming of Europeans to the hemisphere. Their own origin legends focus on a homeland around the headwaters of the Pearl River, but, except for that one small region, the eighteenth-century homeland of the Choctaws was deserted in the late prehistoric period. I was struck by the failure of both history and archaeology to account for the presence of such a large group until so late, and it was not hard to discover why all serious study of the Choctaws had virtually ignored the conflict. The answer is a name, John R. Swanton, who almost single-handedly wrote the entire ethnography of the southeastern Indians between 1926 and 1946.

The opening page of Swanton's influential work on the Choctaws sums up his research with these words: "The feeling of a student for the Choctaw . . . might be described as of a powerful indefiniteness" (Swanton 1931:1). The weight of this opinion is one reason for the disappointing state of affairs observed by John Peterson (1972:178) forty years later: "The first area requiring further work is a more adequate description of traditional Mississippi Indian societies and their transformation following white contact. . . . Until the archaeologist and the ethnohistorian can describe the original inhabitants of Mississippi within a dynamic framework, it will be impossible for the historian to do other than follow their example." The authority of Swanton's work has led many later writers on the Choctaw (e.g., Debo 1961; DeRosier 1970; McKee and Schlenker 1980) to summarize the earliest period of Choctaw contact with Europeans briefly and to begin their works with a static portrayal of Choctaw society in the "ethnographic present" of some vague "aboriginal" period, portrayals strongly influenced by Swanton. Similar generalizations mar the wider-ranging works of Charles Hudson (1976) and J. Leitch Wright (1981).

In opposing Swanton's views on the predominance of matriliny in southeastern North America, William Willis (1963:251) pointed out that Swanton's belief in the stability of native institutions under the conditions of culture contact had led him to base much of his description of the southeastern tribes on nineteenth- and even twentieth-century materials. Swanton's (1931:3) outline of source materials for description of the Choctaws listed only two French sources as early as the eighteenth century (even though the French were closely associated with the Choctaws for some sixty years), and in addition to these he appears to have used only a small scattering of other French documents and only one English source for the early colonial period. Certainly Swanton was not in the business of writing ethnohistory; his "Historical Sketch" of the Choctaws fills little more than one page. This was not a failing of Swanton only but rather the product of the ethnographic approach common to American social sciences of the early twentieth century (Trigger 1983). Yet it is ironic that the Choctaws in particular should have borne Swanton's misleading label of cultural poverty and immutability for so long, since the Choctaws have undergone as much change from prehistory to the present as any other native group of the Southeast but have simultaneously retained the Choctaw language and cultural practices with a success that cannot be explained if their culture had no particular substance of its own.

PURPOSE OF THE INVESTIGATION

Since Swanton's time not only has little been done to reexamine Choctaw history and social change through the period of earliest European contact, but no effort has been made to project the evidence of that early contact history backward into the precontact period. The questions of who the Choctaws were and how and where they lived in prehistory have barely been asked, let alone answered satisfactorily, although as research on the late prehistory of the Southeast has proceeded, it has become increasingly clear that the answers will be complex. No study of Choctaw adaptation to the European presence, either before or after the Removal period, can be complete without a consideration of what went before; this study attempts to fill that gap.

The substantive evidence to be examined here is of three distinct kinds: archaeological, documentary, and cartographic. Some scant evidence from oral tradition and linguistics can also be called cautiously into play. The diversity of source materials is reflected in the diversity of scholarly methods to be applied, for in each case the adequacy of the evidence must be judged in the context of other evidence of the same kind and with the tools of the appropriate discipline. Once all evidence has been reviewed critically in its own terms, it can be combined under the joint aegis of ethnohistory and cultural anthropology, with the hope that the synthetic methods of these two disciplines will enable the formulation of meaningful answers to the questions of identity and origins.

Using these different kinds of evidence, this work develops hypotheses falling under two headings: those regarding the various kinds of dislocation to which the proto-Choctaw and early historic Choctaw peoples were subjected, and those regarding the social effects of these dislocations.

The first, demographic, dislocation may have been the most serious, but it is also the most complex to assess, since several causative factors seem to have been at work, resulting in different kinds of demographic disturbance. Some of the mound-building Mississippian chiefdoms were already in a state of decline and dissolution when the expedition of Hernando de Soto gave the earliest extant European view of the interior Southeast in 1539–43. Some researchers have suggested that this "Mississippian Decline" was a natural phase of the cyclical social evolution of tribes, but as yet there have been no firm theoretical underpinnings for such an argument for the Southeast.

Nor is it likely that a "Mississippian Decline" was solely responsible for the serious depopulation that was important in the formation of the historic tribes; European disease was the most significant factor. Three systematic studies have attempted to assess the disastrous effects of the wildfire spread of European disease in various regions of the Southeast near time of contact (Dobyns 1983; M. Smith 1987; Ramenofsky 1987; see also Thornton 1987), but the database for such a study of the area of interest, the Mississippi-Alabama region, is still poor. In addition, the possible effects of depopulation due to European aggression must be examined. Another, better-documented European contact that resulted in depopulation, the slave-raiding promoted by the English colonists of South Carolina toward the end of the seventeenth century (Wright 1981), probably exacerbated previous demographic changes. Because depopulation was probably the single most important factor in the formation of the Choctaw confederacy, all its facets must be examined carefully.

The impact of disease, death, and slave-raids was probably felt not only in terms of population: archaeological evidence, as well as some cartographic material and documentary accounts, suggests that a physical dislocation of constituents of the Choctaw confederation was another substantial result of both the decline of chiefdoms and of these alien phenomena. The geographic shift is obvious in the Choctaw case; what we do not know is precisely when it occurred.

An additional change, evidenced as European settlers of the early eighteenth century searched in vain for the splendid chiefdoms described by the publicists of the early explorers, was in basic social structure: hierarchical chiefdoms had somehow become egalitarian tribes and confederacies during the "dark" seventeenth century. Certainly this change was in some way a consequence of demographic dislocations, and because it made a dramatic difference in how Indian groups viewed themselves and each other, it also affected how they would deal with permanent European settlers. One task here is to propose a model to account for this sociopolitical dislocation.

The final dislocation considered here took place in intertribal relations. There has been a great deal of discussion of endemic warfare in the Southeast before the advent of Europeans (Larson 1972; Gibson 1974; Hudson 1976:239–57), but even after European pressures began to demand intertribal war, and down through the whole of the colonial period, southeastern Indians in general did not tend to prosecute client warfare with much enthusiasm. The southeastern region in the late prehistoric period was a network of connections between polities, connections that seem to have been stronger than the territorial imperatives of competing chiefdoms, and mechanisms to maintain this network must have existed. With the dislocations of the early contact period, these mechanisms had to adapt to the new sociopolitical reality, and interpolity relations must have changed accordingly, not discarding the workable substrate of tradition, but perhaps altering the qualifications required to become a player in the game.

Because these four kinds of dislocation – population diminution, locational shift, changes in sociopolitical organization, and alterations in interpolity relations – were the result of ongoing native social process as well as the effects of European contact, this study examines proactive as well as reactive responses to change. In the remainder of the present chapter I present an overview of available source materials and a discussion of methodological principles. Chapter 2 is a presentation of the archaeological evidence for the florescence and decline of agricultural chiefdoms in the Mississippi-Alabama area and their distribution and variation across the region. The theory of cyclical chiefdom development and decline is examined as a prelude to

6

chapter 3, in which I begin the examination of the documents from sixteenth-century European exploration of the interior Southeast with a detailed look at early Spanish coastwise reconnaissance, followed by an examination of the Hernando de Soto expedition's documents for what they can tell us about the "natural" cyclical process of development and decline. Chapter 4, which deals with the remaining expeditions of the sixteenth century – most importantly that of Tristán de Luna – concentrates on evidence for catastrophic demographic disaster due to European disease. These two chapters also examine the existing evidence for the beginnings of historic tribe formation through these two processes.

Chapter 5 continues the examination of early contact documentation through the seventeenth century, concentrating on the evidence for serious geographic and demographic dislocations that contributed to the settlement of the Choctaws in the country later to be considered their immemorial homeland. Chapter 6 looks at early European maps, showing what they can reveal about tribal locations and settlement patterns in the sixteenth and seventeenth centuries. Chapter 7 explores the question of ethnicity by analyzing evidence from two aspects of material culture, pottery types and mortuary practices, taken from late prehistory to the beginning of sustained contact in the early eighteenth century, with a focus on the Choctaws and their immediate neighbors. The examination continues in chapter 8 as I look at documentary evidence for ethnicity in patterns of intertribal relations, language and dialect distributions, and migration legends. In the final chapter I evaluate Choctaw social change during the protohistoric period as a response both to the natural evolution of sociopolitical systems under conditions of environmental alteration and to the problems presented by the new European element in the Southeast, summarizing the proposed hypothesis for the formation of the Choctaw confederation of the eighteenth century.

ARCHAEOLOGICAL EVIDENCE

The problems I want to address cannot be tackled without the evidence of archaeology; late prehistory is, after all, defined as the period just before documentary evidence begins, and the earliest documents are singularly uninformative about ethnic identification. Even after the first unsustained forays of Europeans usher in the "protohistory" of 1500–1700, archaeology remains the most important source for the geographical and temporal distributions of material cultural attributes crucial to the interpretation of the meager documentation.

The first difficulty in using relevant archaeological evidence lies in deciding what is figure and what is ground. The evidence has been variously partitioned spatially and temporally by its students on the basis of perceived patterns of interest to them, such as the co-occurrence of several pottery types or the distribution of settlement

7

patterns and mortuary practices. Only in exceptional cases have archaeologists been willing to attach an ethnic name to a specific pattern with any conviction. Yet this is what I must try to do, with more than one name. For as the Choctaws emerged from a series of dislocations in the protohistoric period, so also did the other named historic tribes who would become their neighbors, and perhaps only the fleeting signatures of pottery styles and burial preferences can tell us who was where and when.

In the study of archaeology it has become abundantly clear that the archaeologist's model of social process is likely to bias the very evidence that is recovered simply by dictating sampling strategy, and to bias the interpretation of that evidence by determining what shall be recognized as material correlates of specific social, political, and ideological activities. In this study I shall try to pay attention to the effects of such research biases.

Before the archaeological evidence can be evaluated or even identified, it will be necessary to look at the political geography of the Southeast between the Mississippi and Alabama/Tombigbee river systems in the period defined as late prehistory: ca. A.D. 1100–1500. This was the period of florescence and decline of the great Mississippian cultures of the Southeast, characterized by political/ceremonial centers with distinctive large flat-topped mounds. Because these mounds are such impressive features in the landscape and have long attracted scholarly interest, quite a lot is known about them and the people who built them (a modern summary in B. Smith 1978b), although these impressive mound sites represent only the iceberg-tip of the society that supported them, and clearly more research is needed to establish the details of agricultural and other settlement in the hinterlands of these sites. This evidence is also frustrating, however, since absolute dating of Mississippian cultures and their transformation into the historic tribes known to European colonists is not yet firmly established (Sheldon 1974; Lankford 1977; Curren 1976, 1984b; Peebles 1986), nor is it always clear which of the historic tribes they became.

Archaeological work in the Mississippi Valley has long been dominated by the work and research focus of the Lower Mississippi Survey, whose surveys and limited excavations in the Yazoo Basin have provided much of what is now known of the spread of Mississippian culture in that region (Phillips, Ford, and Griffin 1951; Phillips 1970; Williams and Brain 1983; Brain 1988, 1989). The LMS has also been responsible for the delineation of the Coles Creek–Plaquemine culture sequence that will be of greatest interest here in the valley south of the Yazoo (Ford 1936; Phillips 1970; Neitzel 1965, 1985; Steponaitis 1974; Brain 1978a; Williams and Kidder n.d.). The approach of the LMS throughout has been aimed at reconstructing pottery sequences, however, and they have carried out relatively little excavation with the purpose of uncovering evidence for political systems or subsistence regimes.

More excavation has taken place on the Tombigbee/Alabama river system. The region benefited from the WPA projects of the 1930s, concentrated on the great Moundville site near Tuscaloosa (Peebles 1974, 1979a, 1979b). The late 1920s and early 1930s also saw the intensive work carried out on the large protohistoric/historic town sites of the Montgomery region by the relic collectors of the Alabama Anthropological Society (Sheldon 1974). The Moundville material remained unanalyzed until recently, however, while the cemeteries unearthed near Montgomery were simply massively looted, so the provenience can be precisely determined for very little of the enormous resulting artifact collection. Recent archaeological activity in the region has had a more professedly scientific slant, as lock and dam construction by the U.S. Army Corps of Engineers on the Tombigbee poured large amounts of money into contract work (e.g., Peebles 1983b; Jenkins 1981) and universities undertook long-term projects, working under the positivist paradigm of the "New Archaeology" of the 1960s. Several areas have benefited from research designs aimed at discerning the structure of late prehistoric polities (Peebles 1978; Steponaitis 1978; Bozeman 1983; Welch 1991) as well as their ceramic sequences (Steponaitis 1983).

Archaeologists specializing in the study of the late prehistoric period along both the Mississippi and the Tombigbee/Alabama drainages are far from agreement on the social process that characterized the protohistoric transition and on the material evidence that should mark such a process. But the major obstacle to a solid use of this archaeological evidence is the quality of the database, which is at best uneven and frequently poor. Although several long-range projects have led to excellent data recovery, in other crucial areas even survey is nonexistent. Thus the evidence from this period is abundant but far from complete, and some speculation will be necessary to suggest the cultural context before European explorations.

Archaeological evidence is biased not only by the questions it was excavated to answer but by the discourse in which its reporting is embedded. The work of the LMS, while nominally culture-historical, has manifested itself most characteristically as a Linnaean genealogy of pottery types, based on materials gathered largely from surface collection in a region where the surface has been reworked naturally and artificially more extensively than anywhere else. Sites have been discovered by luck and educated guess, and survey was rarely designed to recover a representative sample. Cultural reconstructions made on the basis of this work, therefore, are severely limited by the nature of the evidence and in any case have tended to be based on an implicit model of capitalist expansionism.

This particular culture-historical model seems to have influenced some researchers working in the Tombigbee region, but many more are guided at least nominally by the "processual" model, ushered in with the "New Archaeology" of the 1960s, which takes environmental issues more seriously and is more likely to study pre-historic settlement as a systemic phenomenon. In some circles a model of social evolution based on the work of anthropologists Elman Service and Morton Fried is assumed, but although this model has been used to explain observed phenomena, proximate causes for evolutionary social change have never been adequately addressed.

The archaeology of Choctaw sites is even less well understood. Although the locations of several historic-period Choctaw settlements have been known archaeologically for more than half a century, very little evidence attests clearly to the early Choctaw and proto-Choctaw peoples; until very recently, scientific excavation had not been carried out on a Choctaw site to establish even the historical sequence. Although Henry Halbert identified some sites in his study of two European maps (Halbert 1899a, 1902), he never reported on any artifactual evidence. Henry Collins (1926), in connection with his anthropometrical work on living Choctaws, conducted brief and ill-reported excavations of what appear to have been several ossuary mounds, but he apparently secured no evidence for establishing dates. Following Halbert's locational suggestions, Collins also identified and collected from several sites; that collection, now in the Smithsonian Institution, was the basis of Collins's definition of the Chickachae Combed pottery type as diagnostic of historic Choctaw sites (Collins 1927). Archaeologists using this type as such have recognized several sites over the years (Ford 1936; Phillips 1970; Penman 1977, 1978; Tesar 1974; Atkinson 1976; Chambers 1932–35; Voss and Blitz 1983, 1988; Blitz 1985), and the type received formal definition by Haag (1953), also drawing upon the collections of Chambers (1932–35; see also Chambers 1980; Baca 1989). Collins (1977:14) has confirmed, however, that the sites he collected from were those identified by Halbert, and Halbert's writings reveal that he himself depended heavily upon informants whose memories of site locations could not have dated before the middle of the nineteenth century (Halbert 1902; Peterson 1985). There is also good reason to believe that the Chickachae Combed type is a colonial-period development (Galloway 1984). Therefore, for most sites so far identified, we can only be certain that they were occupied around the time of Removal in the 1830s.

Some collections were made in connection with surveys conducted by the National Park Service for the Natchez Trace Parkway, but this material has been neither published nor studied, and its whereabouts are now uncertain. After a long period of indifference, legislation and federal programs have led to archaeological activity for several federally funded projects. Again, though this material has been analyzed to the extent necessary for the required reporting, most of the existing reports reflect only surface collection (Atkinson 1976; Atkinson and Blakeman 1975; Tesar 1974; Penman 1977, 1978). Penman's (1983) interest in the material has led to a recent reanalysis of the Collins collection and the refinement of the Chickachae Combed type into several constituent varieties, but Penman (pers. comm. 1982) himself has observed that none of the European material in the Collins collection dates from as early as the French period.

In addition to this professional activity over the years, there has been a good deal of amateur interest in the collection of Choctaw ceramics. An extensive collection from the Nanih Waiya mound and its environs, which would now be invaluable because of subsequent deep plowing and destruction of features on the site (Brown 1926; Chambers 1932–35; Wailes 1852), was made around the turn of the century by W. A. Love, but this collection may now be lost (Ward, pers. comm. 1982). Collections from the Meridian area and from Neshoba and Kemper Counties have not yet received detailed study. Ward (1984) has prepared a report of collections that include Chickachae Combed ceramics from the West Point area, but his interests center on nineteenth-century sites. Further amateur collections may exist (for example, WPA n.d.), but fortunately for the student of Choctaw history, the early historic-period burial practice did not include grave goods, since treasure-hunters have thus not been tempted to pillage sites.

Still, most of the work mentioned has been guided by the presence of Collins's Chickachae Combed pottery type. Solid evidence has recently come to light that plausibly supports the assertion that Chickachae Combed pottery is a late historic type. The site of the French Fort Tombecbé near modern Epes, Alabama, was excavated in the summer of 1980, and the French levels were found to be sealed under later English and Spanish occupations, thus offering a clearly stratified collection of Choctaw ceramics dated securely to the 1736–63 period (Parker 1982). This collection of pottery is characterized by some decorative motifs very similar to those that appear on the Chickachae Combed varieties, but the decoration is applied with freehand incising or engraving techniques rather than combing. The implications of this evidence are significant: other site collections may well have to be reevaluated and new types defined with different chronological indicators. Indeed, recent surveys and studies by Blitz (1985) and Voss (Voss and Blitz 1983, 1988) have shown that these new types are prominent in the Choctaw assemblage when surveys do not depend on the Chickachae Combed type to define Choctaw cultural affiliation.

More evidence for the proto-Choctaw period may have come from the recently excavated Lubbub Creek site near Aliceville, Alabama. Originating as a small cere-monial center in early Mississippian times – around A.D. 1000 – this site seems to have been occupied into the late seventeenth century, when populations of Indians east of the Tombigbee River may have been depleted by the English-inspired slave raids carried out by Upper Creek tribes (Peebles 1983a). The site is identified as proto-Choctaw in its later phases by means of its burial ritual, which included ossuary interment of previously defleshed bones. The Lubbub Creek site is especially significant because it may allow us to establish continuity from the Mississippian period through the protohistoric Burial Urn period into historic Choctaw culture; its implications will be discussed more thoroughly in chapters 2 and 7.

These two recently excavated sites suggest the revolution in understanding that may come with excavation of multiperiod sites in what is understood as the Choctaw homeland in the historic period, between the Pearl and the Tombigbee Rivers. Even without excavation, a great deal of potential evidence from long-sustained surface collecting rests in the hands of amateurs (Goldman, pers. comm. 1980; Willis 1985), and systematic study of these collections and the sites they represent, presently under way, may yet lead to earlier sites. The recent appointment of a tribal archaeologist by the Mississippi Choctaws holds even greater promise; he has already carried out some survey work and has directed limited excavations in the Choctaw "homeland" area that have yielded significant new pottery evidence (K. Carleton, pers. comm. 1992). Nevertheless, the archaeological evidence for early Choctaw settlement in east-central Mississippi is so far the weakest, and one of the tasks of the current study is to suggest hypotheses about settlement patterns, social structure, and subsistence base that can be tested through excavation. In addition, the new pottery evidence and the restudy of the old may yield much information about cultural sequence in the areas now seen as later Choctaw. Settlement in that area may well have been sustained since the early historic period (Galloway 1982b; Galloway and Kidwell 1990); if such is the case, many sites now yielding Chickachae Combed ceramics in surface collection may upon excavation yield earlier ceramics and evidence of social change over two centuries.

Apart from the two excavations just cited, no scientific excavation of any Choctaw site of any period has been properly reported (but see Mooney 1991, 1994); furthermore, one of those two covers only the extreme early limit of our interest, and the second is not an aboriginal site. Survey around the Tombecbé fort site during the summer of 1981 failed to identify any nearby Choctaw settlement (Parker, pers. comm. 1981), but French testimony indicates that toward the end of the French period the nearest Choctaw village was a bow-shot from the fort. Further south near Demopolis, Alabama, a site has been investigated that is identified by ceramics as Choctaw (Parker, pers. comm. 1984). Mitigation work on the Pearl River to be carried out for Corps of Engineers projects may lead to the identification of sites, but this work lies in the future. Coordinated projects of site survey in Kemper and Lauderdale Counties have been conducted by two university teams (Voss and Blitz 1983; R. Marshall, pers. comm. 1981), and already this work has yielded useful reexaminations of Choctaw pottery types (Blitz 1985; Voss and Blitz 1988; Voss and Mann 1986; Mooney 1991); ideally, some excavation will follow.

The apparent definitiveness of Collins's work, added to the "powerful indefiniteness" claimed by Swanton, has seemingly operated to limit archaeological interest in the Choctaws until very recently. Furthermore, the archaeology carried out in the Alabama-Mississippi region suffers from its own problems of structural bias of which we must be aware, as archaeologists themselves question the ideological models underlying their discipline.

One of the main thrusts of the present study is to advance hypotheses that can be tested by survey and excavation, in the hope that sufficient scientific interest may be generated to warrant such work. The Choctaws were one of the great tribes of the Southeast, yet archaeological interest in the less populous Chickasaws has been more pointed and sustained (Jennings 1941; Atkinson 1979, 1985; Stubbs 1982b; Johnson, Galloway, and Belokon 1989; Johnson et al. 1991). This disproportion in attention may exist because European evidence for the Chickasaw is mostly written in English, and it includes the brilliant efforts of the Chickasaws' friend James Adair. Apart from the so-called Anonymous Relation (Swanton 1931), the Choctaws had no directly comparable French exponent (other than nineteenth-century novelist Chateaubriand) to romanticize them.

DOCUMENTARY SOURCES AND GENRES

European colonial documents contain important material for Choctaw ethnohistory during the protohistoric and early contact periods. Nevertheless, the history that can be reconstructed with their help alone is most emphatically an "external" history; one must be far more critical when using these documents than when consulting histories written by participants in the culture described (Brain, Toth, and Rodriguez-Buckingham 1974). In the documents of European observers, two levels of bias appear. First, as is always the case, the truth must be disentangled from the web of personal biases. In addition, the complex of Western ideological prejudices – the conceptual frame through which European colonists viewed aboriginal societies – makes the task all the more difficult, because most modern Americans share this tradition to some degree.

The impact on the European world-view of the discoveries of new continents and peoples in the fifteenth and sixteenth centuries was profound. The notion of a new world was not just an idle phrase. The philosophical excitement engendered by the discovery of this populated Eden led in two directions: to the church, it represented a vast new field for conversions, whereas to the new spirit of secular political philosophy it represented a brand-new population of case studies for the testing of theory. To most, however, from the exponents of mercantilist economic theories to the pragmatic government ministers and businessmen who financed colonial projects, the population of the New World was incidental; exploitation of the new lands' rich resources dominated the motivations of the vast majority of those who became involved with colonial ventures.

We must assume, then, that the exploitative intentions of the colonizers underlie the attitudes of writers who reported on the aboriginal societies they encountered. Rationalization of this exploitation, as it concerned both the existing populations and the resources they commanded, rested upon notions of the superiority of the "civilized" over those whose societies did not manifest the same kind of organization, from which notion flowed the conviction that the right to this new world belonged to the forces of Western civilization (Berkhofer 1978:115–26). Nor should we forget that, except for the very earliest ephemeral coastal landings, the dealings of Europeans with the peoples of southeastern North America were conditioned by prior experience with other American peoples: in the case of the Spanish, with those of South and Central America; in the case of the French, with those of northeastern North America. These prior experiences substantially influenced European attitudes and behavior toward southeastern Indian groups by setting up specific expectations.

Hernando de Soto and his party, nearly the earliest and certainly the most important among the Spanish explorers, were veterans of campaigns against the chiefdoms and states of Mesoamerica and Peru. Soto's manifest intention was plunder (Sauer 1971), and his dealings with the southeastern tribes reflected tested practice: subjugation of a populace by subjugation of its leaders. This mode of action was so ingrained that the expedition did not abandon it even when it proved disastrously unworkable; the expedition, with the captive chief Tascaluça, was ambushed at Mabila. The Peruvian experience may also have conditioned the reporting of the expedition in a way that is more material to the purpose here. After the impressive masonry architecture of the Inca empire, even the considerable earthworks of such major ceremonial centers as Etowah or Moundville were unlikely to seem very important, and this myopic attitude (rather than the complete abandonment of such sites) may account for the failure of most of the expedition's narratives to describe them vividly (see Peebles 1971:89; Sheldon 1974:32); only the Inca, Garcilaso de la Vega (1951:170–71), mentions their ubiquity, although he never saw them.

The French experience with the peoples of northeastern North America had been different, and their expectations of the peoples of the Southeast differed accordingly. In Canada they had encountered some native groups whose subsistence depended primarily upon hunting and gathering and whose social organization was egalitarian and tribal as Service (1971a, 1971b) defines those terms, without hereditary elites. The efforts of French colonizers in Canada had been aimed in two contradictory directions: exploiting the hunters' skills for the benefit of the lucrative fur trade, and attempting to encourage centralized settlement and religious conversion as an aid to the introduction of farming and the eventual integration of a settled native population as part of the French colony (Jaenen 1976). In their Canadian experience, however, the French learned that the latter methods did not yield much success with hunter-gatherers. Also, as they moved further west and south in their explorations, they became acquainted with more sedentary tribes and thus were already aware, before their first complete descent of the Mississippi, that variety could be expected if not necessarily understood.

Finally, the English were to impinge only marginally upon the Indians of the interior west of the Appalachians during the period under consideration, even though that marginal contact was to have great effect. The English sent into what they called the "back country" not conquerors or colonizers but slavers and skin traders, and if these traders had an eye to anything it was to the pursuit of profit. They carried out whatever manipulations of native societies were necessary to maximize that profit. This pragmatic motivation made the English keen observers of a limited aspect of native society.

Besides these basic corporate viewpoints that must be considered in the pursuit of early Choctaw ethnohistory, the limited availability of documents also causes difficulties. For the period with which I am concerned here – up to 1700 – no known document describes the Choctaws as they appeared after 1700, nor is there even one that names them until 1675. To a certain extent this is a direct consequence of whatever administrative system backed the Europeans in question. In the case of the Spanish, the theme of exploration and confrontation is paramount, and the accounts of individuals predominate. The disastrous failure of Narváez's expedition left only the Cabeza de Vaca account of that expedition's wanderings. A similar case obtains as a result of the Soto expedition's broken line of supply and failure at colonization, forcing us to rely on later official reports and second- and thirdhand memoirs of the journey. The Luna expedition left its documentary legacy in elaborate judicial quarrels, which impeded it at every step, and in hagiography, so that the brief glimpses of native peoples appear more as justification for Spanish actions than as accurate portrayals of Indian life.

Evidence obtained during the seventeenth century from the Spanish missions of Florida, the aggressive inland push by the newly arrived English colonists of Carolina, and the French explorers on the Mississippi comes in a much less epic package. The bureaucratic niceties of Spanish colonial administration and Franciscan missionary activities bury the notices of various tribes to the west of the Apalachee missions of north Florida in the lengthy reports of official *visitas* or embed them in the self-serving letters of military officials charged with the defense of the missionized areas. Reported British contacts in the interior are few and often inferential, requiring careful extraction from accounts that amount to adventure narratives. The accounts of the French explorers are similarly individual narratives, but the genre of reference is not the heroic romance but rather the individual diary, since the French accounts are provably far closer to their original authors than are the Spanish exploration accounts.

The "normal" historiographical caveats that beset the use of documentary sources, especially the significance of social context and individual motivation for the production of the document, must of course be attended to on a case-by-case basis. As part of my general critical stance with reference to such sources, I plan to consider their textuality. No matter how lucid and transparent a document may seem, it emerges from traditions of literacy and hence from a dialogue with other texts. The historian must thus understand the textual content of a document before attempting to judge its mimetic content.

Every document used in this study will have its evidentiary credentials assessed. In most historiography this process passes in silence: the historian is assumed to have made a good-faith effort to accumulate all the facts and to present them in as "unbiased" a way as possible. But since history is one way in which human societies make sense of their world, and since the very medium in which history is written is not value-free, this assumption is unwarranted, even when the historian in question has the best will in the world. Especially in ethnohistory, decisions regarding what shall be counted as fact need to be made explicit, since the mode in which the "facts" are presented is inevitably dictated by an alien culture whose interpretive metaphors differ from those of the culture that generated those "facts."

The process by which documents are assessed is directly related to the document's degree of transparency and varies depending upon the nature of the document: its communicative status, what it is set up to be or claims to be. In the strictest terms, every kind of document – diary, letter, inventory, court transcript – calls for a distinct approach to the assessment of its content. Fortunately for Euroamerican ethnohistorians dealing with the early contact history of the Southeast, the documents are European, facilitating the decision of what approach to take. Reasonably reliable institutional histories exist to characterize the function of most of the documents in their original contexts, enabling scholars to judge fairly well the value and relevance of their content, though of course each case still demands individual evaluation.

One class of document – unfortunately just the kind that dominates the period with which I am concerned – has rarely been accorded the same kind of rigorous treatment by ethnohistorians of the Southeast: the extended individual narrative intended as a history. Hayden White summarized the arguments of many authorities writing on historiography when he offered meticulous and voluminous arguments in favor of treating historical narrative by the methods of literary criticism, and though his arguments were addressed primarily to "modern" historical narratives, they are no less applicable to those of the past. According to White (1987:88), "historical narratives are not only models of past events and processes, but also metaphorical statements which suggest a relation of similitude between such events and processes and the story types that we conventionally use to endow the events of our lives with culturally sanctioned meanings" (cf. Culler 1975:189), and again, "interpretation in history consists of the provision of a plot structure for a sequence of events so that their nature as a comprehensible process is revealed by their figuration as a *story of a particular kind*" (White 1978:58; emphasis in original).

The narrative genre is by its nature both interpretive and seductive. Life as lived is not a dramatic unfolding of a unified and meaningful series of events but a complex interwoven skein of many often disconnected events. A narrative, on the other hand, represents a selection of events from one or a limited number of event sequences, with the criteria for selection varying according to different cultural norms and contexts of discourse. But the fact (or the illusion, when the narrative in question is entirely fictional) of selection is part and parcel of narrative, because its purpose is to persuade, because whatever power narrative has to inform or entertain rides on the hearer's acceptance of the narrative itself as true for the purposes of the occasion. The genre of the narrative – history, epic, novel, fairy tale – dictates only the degree of fictionality, not its presence.

Ever since Russian formalist literary critics applied the findings of linguistics to textual artistry, analysts of narrative have made a distinction between form and content. The point of this distinction is to isolate the form ("plot" or "discourse"), seen as carrying implications of its own independently of the content ("fable" or "story"), so that it may be analyzed. Since narratives are seen as communications, analysts have postulated that the "sender" of the communication wears three aspects: the real author, who is very difficult to know except by external evidence; the implied author, who is "implied" by the sum of his artistic decisions in creating the text; and the narrator – if there is one – into whose mouth the narrative is put. The activities of these three personages are seen as shaping the narrative so as to manipulate the responses of its (again implied) reader, and through analysis of the narrative in terms of form and content one can begin to see how this manipulation was accomplished (see Chatman 1980:15–42).

The methods of the comparatist should be primary in an analysis of these narratives: the rather prosaic source search should be the *sine qua non* of an evaluation of any extended text in order to determine just what materials were available to the shaping of its narrative. But ethnohistorians have not generally used such methods, presumably because they have been so deceived by authors' frequent adoption of the "amanuensis/translator" topos that they have never thought to search for sources other than those claimed for the information presented (Henige 1986a). These narratives, however, were written in the Renaissance and at a time when the spread of printing was creating a closer European community of letters, so that their authors participated in the lively interchange of literatures, periods, and traditions that made the era a golden age of European culture. As a literary and intellectual revival of classical learning, it made familiar the writings of classical authors, historians and fabulists alike. In addition, works written in the vernacular languages, as were all those of concern here, partook of a new mood that made their authors likely to be especially aware of similar works. As Ernst Curtius (1963:15) has succinctly said, "The 'timeless present' which is an essential characteristic of literature means that the literature of the past can always be active in that of the present." The content or story of these narratives needs to be analyzed in order that we may discern the echoes of "the literature" – fictional and historical – "of the past" (Galloway 1991a).

The second end to be pursued is the analysis of the form or plot imposed upon the narrator's materials. In framing the narrative, the author gives it meaning that is managed by the implied author and the narrator. Value judgments lie not only in the kind of overt commentary exemplified by that of the narrator in Gonzalo Fernández de Oviedo's *Historia general y natural de las Indias* but also in the sequential arrangement of events with its covert or overt implication of causality. The set of roles the author specifies for his plot also invites analysis, since these roles will inevitably partake of conventionalized characterization if not stereotype. In the examples to be studied, this latter problem is particularly striking in the portrayal of native behavior, which still manages to suffer from ethnocentric stereotyping in even the best modern anthropological fieldwork. Writers of exploration narratives had before them a set of behaviors that, even if not understood, nevertheless had to be explained to an audience as the proximate cause of the responses of the explorers – *in a story that portrayed the explorers as heroes.*

The argument for a preliminary textual analysis gains additional weight in view of the fact that when these narratives were written no special distinction was made between "literature" and written materials not now considered to bear any literary aspect. For the writing of history the rhetorical models were the histories of classical antiquity, but the plot types were derived from both the classical tradition of heroic epic and the popular epics and romances of contemporary Europe. Further, the purpose of history, derived from that of medieval saints' lives and heroic epics, was not only to inform of the facts but to provide an edifying set of examples for proper conduct. Narrative sources of the sixteenth and seventeenth centuries should thus be evaluated in this context.

One other issue, inseparable from consideration of the textual qualities of the narratives, must be made explicit here. David Henige's (1986c:307) characterization of translations as "no more than one genre of secondary source, never more than a series of low-grade interpretations, sometimes philological, sometimes rhetorical, sometimes ideological" was ruthless but true, and he demonstrated how perilous their use could be in his critique of Henry Dobyns's demographic conclusions based upon them. Whether all translations should be considered "low-grade" interpretations is not a matter to be debated here, but as a translator I regretfully recognize that their nature as interpretations is beyond argument. Since historical narratives are already preinterpreted secondary sources, their translations are tertiary, and analysis of such translations to discern their factual content becomes something like brain surgery carried out wearing gardening gloves. I have not used translations for primary access to sources in the documentary analysis that informs much of the remainder of this volume, although for the convenience of the reader existing translations will be cited.

A related issue is the spelling of names. Because of uncertainty about the interpretation and identity of most place names in the sources, I have, at the risk of confusion, given place names in the spelling used in the original documents, using the modern conventional spelling only when a name has been identified with certainty.

To conclude this discussion of documentary sources for early Choctaw ethnohistory I will now survey and characterize them briefly. For complete bibliographic details the reader may refer to the bibliography. An initial breakdown of the material can be done by period: Spanish exploration and attempted settlement, French exploration, and English trade. These divisions are not entirely arbitrary, since to a large extent they are reflected in the kinds of documents generated.

The Spanish exploration and settlement efforts, as they affected the Indians of the deep interior, can be limited to four distinct episodes. The first is that of coastwise explorations. Pineda's 1519 reconnaissance was reported in the brief royal *cédula* granting to Garay the lands Pineda had seen (*Colección* 1864–84); yet with the constant traffic of treasure fleets through the Gulf of Mexico and the normal necessities of obtaining wood and water, many other brief landings along the Gulf coast must have occurred, and Weddle (1985) has made a detailed study of early Spanish coastal contacts in this area. Narváez's expedition to found a settlement in 1527 was primarily reported in a long travel memoir written later by one of the few survivors, Alvar Núñez Cabeza de Vaca (Núñez 1542, 1972). Another account from Núñez and his two companions in survival was used by Oviedo in his *Historia general* (Núñez 1972:160–271) and by López de Gomara in a similarly titled work ([1552] 1932), but these do not amplify Núñez for the Gulf coast part of his journey. The second Spanish effort that approached the area of interest was the expedition of Hernando de Soto, reported in one eyewitness account by Luis Hernández de Biedma (B. Smith

1857), two secondary histories embodying the testimonies of Roderigo Ranjel and the mysterious Gentleman of Elvas (Oviedo y Valdés [1851] 1944; Elvas [1557] 1932; all three translated in Bourne 1922 and Clayton, Knight, and Moore 1993), and a fancifully embellished compendium of participants' memoirs, folklore, and literary allusions by Garcilaso de la Vega ([1605] 1982; translated in Garcilaso de la Vega 1951). Another account, known to have been written by one of the priests who accompanied Soto, is so far only known from a brief summary, but the account may someday turn up (Lyon 1993).

The third relevant Spanish effort, another abortive settlement attempt, was carried out under the command of Tristán de Luna in 1559–61. The papers of this expedition differ in character from those of the other two because of the participation of administrative personnel and because most members of the expedition survived to return and bring back all the documentary material that had been generated by quarrels and disputes over command and over the actions of the commander (Priestley 1928). There is an additional account of this expedition by the Dominican friar Agustín Dávila Padilla ([1596] 1955), who wrote of the glorious actions of the missionaries who accompanied it. Shortly afterwards, in 1565–66, Juan Pardo's exploration westward from the Santa Elena settlement that Luna had failed to establish did not reach further than western Georgia or eastern Alabama (Hamilton 1910: 520–27; B. Smith 1857:15–19; Hudson 1990). Finally, among the documents relating the foundation and progress of the Apalachee mission in northern Florida (see Hann 1988), two notable Spanish postscripts from the seventeenth century come in the form of a description of the Southeast by Bishop Calderón of Cuba in 1675 (Wenhold 1936:2–14), which mentions the Choctaws by that name for the first time, and a description of Marcos Delgado's 1686 expedition from the Apalachee mission westward in an attempt to locate La Salle's settlement (Boyd 1937:2–32; Swanton 1937:127–29).

With the beginning of French exploration of the lower Mississippi Valley, again we find the characteristic narrative accounts. The La Salle expedition down the Mississippi in 1682 encountered no Choctaw Indians but left several accounts useful in recording the position of many small tribes, some related to the Choctaws, along the lower river (Margry 1879–88; La Salle [1682?] 1898; Minet 1684–85; Weddle, Morkovsky, and Galloway 1987; Shea 1852; Galloway 1982d). The same is true of the account by a survivor of La Salle's ill-fated colony in Texas (Joutel [1684–88] 1906) and the 1691 account of the lower valley by Henri de Tonti, La Salle's lieutenant on the first expedition and his partner in the fur trade, who had navigated the river again later to search for La Salle in 1686 (Tonti 1684). Iberville's journals of the explorations he undertook as the first steps toward colonization from the Gulf coast in 1699–1702 offer similar information and considerably expand the French notice of the Choctaw (Brasseaux 1979; Iberville 1981). Several other early journals, by Sauvole ([1699–1701] 1969), Penicaut ([1723] 1953), and La Harpe ([1831] 1971), offer additional amplification of this information but still no direct observation of the Choctaw country; this came in 1702 with Tonti's mission to the Choctaws and Chickasaws, and though the complete accounts he sent to Iberville do not survive, there are extant abstracts of these letters made by the cartographer Delisle for his own use (Galloway 1982b).

The documentary legacy of Carolina, the first southern English colony to have real impact on Indians beyond and south of the Appalachians, is relatively rich, but not as regards our topic here. Apart from the early exploits of the physician Henry Woodward, most of the Carolinians' activities in the interior, especially the traffic in slaves that was the major focus of the earliest exploration journeys, was illegal and therefore remained undocumented. More helpful, if rather late, are the journals of Thomas Nairne's expedition into the deep interior as Indian agent in 1708 (Nairne 1988).

We will always wish that the sum of this evidence were greater, but drawing out of even these few sources the data that they really contain is an immense task. Subsequent chapters examine this material from several angles in an attempt to assemble those details into something more than the external history they obviously constitute.

CARTOGRAPHIC SOURCES

Another kind of documentary evidence comes from the maps generated by and in support of the colonial enterprise. A glance at any collection of early maps of the Southeast will show that they vary widely in accuracy and trustworthiness, and certainly this is the case with their information about tribal locations. Nevertheless, because from the time of earliest European contact knowledge of these locations was known to be crucial to European exploitation of southeastern North America, there is good reason to assume that at least the official government cartographers had a strong interest in doing the best job they could and that they were on the alert for the best new information they could obtain (Cumming 1958; Delanglez 1943b). Thus over time the accuracy of European maps of the Southeast improved.

The cycle that generally characterized map-making for newly explored areas elucidates how this improvement took place. Explorers went forth into the wilderness with only sketchy notions of what they could expect to find, assembled from whatever reports might be available from coastal landings or in some cases from Indian informants; the earliest had no maps of the interior to guide them. One purpose of exploration, however, was to bring back the information needed for the making of maps, usually in the form of narrative accounts including direction and distance estimates and sometimes sketch maps. This information would then be incorporated into a map that would be used and tested by the next explorer, who would often expand its limits. His information, in turn, would be used to amplify the accuracy of the map, and so on (Cumming et al. 1974:24–25).

The problem with this cycle is that it can only promise an increasing accuracy in the portrayal of topographic features, which remained relatively fixed. As mentioned above, however, archaeological and documentary evidence show that Native American populations in the Southeast, as in the rest of the continent, underwent population movements not only of a substantial kind (Smith 1987) but also in more minor seasonal cycles (Larson 1980). Thus, even if an explorer's evidence led to the relatively accurate location of a tribe or band he had encountered, there is no guarantee that the next explorer would find that same tribe on the same spot; in fact, this phenomenon may be at least partially responsible for some of the occasional "retrograde" developments in southeastern cartography, which are otherwise unexplained.

This problem may turn to an advantage, however, if other sources can identify the periods during which population movements were considerable, since maps that reflected information collected at those times might very well preserve an otherwise very fleeting fact. As for maps made during stable periods, their locational evidence improved over time in the normal way. A study of the cartographic evidence for any tribe in the Southeast, then, should take several clearly defined steps in tracing the map-making cycle, viewing it as a problem in the utilization of information resources. The first step is to identify what was known of the area and its inhabitants before explorers penetrated it: this information may be gleaned from documentary sources. Then the cycle should be traced as it unfolds, examining in each case the information available to the mapmaker (including earlier maps), the use he made of it, and the reliability of this information if such can be established on the basis of other documentary evidence. Following this process methodically may enable us to deal with such problems as the cartographic representation of several periods in a single map.

Nearly all the maps except those of the earliest period present some general problems. Explorers and travelers frequently depended upon watercourses for transportation; as a consequence, even though the watercourses themselves may be distortedly charted due to errors in directional observation, the relative placement of native settlements that lay near them is quite likely to be worthy of confidence (cf. Halbert 1902) if the watercourses can be remapped onto their true locations. A second problem is to be found in the settlement pattern the Choctaws apparently preferred by the beginning of the French colonial period: long narrow villages, frequently consisting of one central village and its dependencies, along the high ground next to watercourses. Explorers found it difficult to understand where one village left off and another began, so that sometimes several villages were lumped under one name (Rowland and Sanders 1927–32, 1:155–56). This factor complicates the task of deciding if the cartographic evidence can support hypotheses about village movement or abandonment, which also took place due to agricultural exhaustion of soils, and, at certain times, to intertribal and intratribal warfare.

A final but much more amorphous question to be addressed is that of the cognitive process at work in the transformation of narrative data into two-dimensional maps (Kuipers 1978). It is not my intention to explore cartographic methodology in any detail, but this problem is worth bearing in mind when considering what distant European cartographers were able to make of explorers' accounts.

The genealogical relationships among the colonial-period maps will be discussed in detail later as necessary; here I instead aim at a brief characterization of the kind of information available from maps through the period.

From the 1540s to the beginning of French contact around 1700 more than thirty European maps identify a location for the Choctaw tribe or its possible precursors. The evidence from these maps accords well with the previous description of the "map-making cycle" of progressive improvement in representation and specificity. On the basis of the information they provide, the maps dating from the periods of interest in this volume can be placed into two groups: a Spanish exploration group and a French exploration and early settlement group. The nature of the information portrayed is very much of a piece with the purposes implied by the period labels.

The maps in the Spanish exploration group are all more or less related to the so-called "De Soto Map" (Boston 1941). This map, dated to about 1544 (Cumming 1958:113), shows a Gulf coast seamed with rivers like the lines around an old person's mouth, and the Indian population clusters are set along them in accordance with the vague clues provided by the expedition accounts. Each group is represented by a conventionalized drawing of a fortified city, showing a wall with one or more towers rising above it. The rivers themselves, many of which had been observed by Soto, take rather strange courses and frequently flow from erroneous sources inland. The principal interest for this study is that all the maps in this group show a Tascaluça town, and some show a Pafalaya as well – both thought by Swanton to be Choctaw groups. In addition, the maps indicate towns later recognized as Chickasaw and Upper Creek. In no case, however, was there more than a single symbol for each nation of Indians.

The early part of the French exploration period, from the Marquette-Jolliet journey in 1673 until the Iberville settlement expedition in 1699-1700, continued to be characterized by this same mode of representation, but considerable improvements were made in the location and courses of rivers during these early few years (with one notable exception: see De Vorsey 1982; Wood 1984). Beginning with Delisle's "Iberville map" sketch of about 1700, however, a new representation technique took account of estimated population by marking the locus of a tribe's settlements with multiple town symbols. No individual towns were named, but in some cases the cartographer attempted to render the pattern of settlement, as, for example, when the towns were shown in a linear group along a watercourse (e.g., Delisle 1701, in Cumming 1958:170–71). Little-known tribes were represented as before, with a single fortified-town symbol, but each of the multiple villages was shown as a stylized sketch of a wattle-and-daub house. As knowledge of the interior improved, additional tribes came to be represented in this way.

On the basis of this summary, several preliminary observations may be made. First, European maps clearly cannot provide any detailed information for the earliest and most problematic period; only general locational information can be expected, and that may well suffer from extreme inaccuracy. Second, as information became more detailed, most of the maps seem to have become problem oriented. Nevertheless, a steady accumulation of detail is evident throughout the period of interest, and with close study it should be possible to glean some information about general settlement location in the very early historic period. Coordination of the cartographic evidence with the narrative materials from which it was mostly drawn should amplify its effectiveness. This information will need to serve until a more complete archaeological reconnaissance of the region has been performed.

ORAL TRADITION

I have not yet mentioned oral tradition, which would seem to be a vital source for the history of nonliterate peoples. Unfortunately, the early explorers apparently ignored the bearers of tradition, or the latter did not offer such information to the European newcomers; and even if the Spanish friars who followed them had been interested, disease had taken its toll in the interim, for they too recorded very little of the kind.

The Choctaws themselves did not seek European-style literacy early, and no documents indicate that they related anything of their historical traditions to the French who were their closest European allies in the eighteenth century (and those Frenchmen in a position to learn such things, having married into the tribe, were apparently loath to reveal what they knew). Traditional history going back into the Mississippian period is thus effectively lost, although something of the "protohistoric" sixteenth and seventeenth centuries may be preserved.

I will use the extant origin legends of the Muskogean groups in chapter 8 on ethnicity, but for reasons I will discuss there, including most obviously the fact that the legends were collected in the nineteenth century, they cannot be used except metaphorically to reconstruct what happened at the time of Choctaw tribe formation.

Source Materials and Methodologies

LINGUISTICS

If the language of a people is a strong part of its identity, then evidence from the language may be of use in showing something of its past. Mississippi Choctaws today maintain the Choctaw language as their mother tongue, and at the end of the eighteenth century it may have been spoken as a lingua franca across a broad swath of the Southeast (Crawford 1978; Drechsel 1979, 1992; Galloway 1989b). While language is not necessarily coincident with ethnicity, it is inarguably a strong promoter of community solidarity, and their language has continued to serve the Mississippi Choctaws in this way through most of the twentieth century. And while language cannot be retrieved from southeastern material culture, details of the difficulties of communication experienced by early European incomers can now be used to reconstruct the distribution of languages and dialects. This evidence is not complete, but it permits a broad sketch that may give clues to Choctaw origins.

Another factor to be considered is the inclusion in the nineteenth-century Choctaw language of words and concepts that may offer evidence of the historical experience of its speakers. If Choctaw words exist defining semantic fields for sociopolitical structures or ceremonial complexes not observed for the historic Choctaws, it may be possible to infer prior existence for such phenomena. In addition, the results of historical linguistic reconstructions and lexicostatistical analyses may suggest some large patterns of ethnic relationships in a more distant past than is accessible using any other kind of data (Haas 1978; Martin 1992).

ENVOI

The objective of this book is the kind of "internal" ethnohistory that attempts to reconstruct social change in long-term and medium-term sequences. The work of the processual archaeologist and that of the social historian are relevant here. For the protohistoric period of interest, a narrative of events would certainly be impossible: too few events were reported to allow more than a glimpse of any of the southeastern Indians, and few of those cases reliably indicate *who* was glimpsed. Calvin Martin's arguments (1987:3-26,192-220) for a mystical, mythopoetic historical vision as the truest representation of the American native's experience of history before the coming of Europeans may have validity, but I can no more reconstruct that than I can the sound of a tree's fall in my absence. Nor can anyone else, European or Indian, who was born after the demographic collapse that marked the triumph of European microbes over thousands of years of tradition. All anyone can now even pretend to recover from the maelstrom of the protohistoric period is precisely those larger patterns that figure in anthropological theory and the history of societies.

Still, the Indians of the protohistoric Southeast can be called "people without history" (Wolf 1982) only if their history is judged by the old standards of *histoire événementielle*. The sources, certainly, bear reliably only upon the material and some slight behavioral evidence. Although the view they offer is a limited one, it is at least possible to browbeat these witnesses to wring from them every last detail of their testimony. The strategy here, then, is to uncover the deep narrativity of social process by confronting the broken sequence of the material record with the brief flashes of vision embedded in the ramblings of braggart soldiers and earnest friars.

CHAPTER TWO

Prehistory, 1100-1500

The pyramidal hills or artificial mounts, and highways, or avenues, leading from them to artificial lakes or ponds, vast tetragon terraces, chunk yards, and obelisks or pillars of wood, are the only monuments of labor, ingenuity and magnificence that I have seen worthy of notice, or remark. . . . The mounts and cubical yards adjoining them, seem to have been raised in part for ornament and recreation, and likewise to serve some other public purpose, since they are always so situated as to command the most extensive prospect over the town and country adjacent. . . . I was not in the interior parts of the Chactaw territories, and therefore am ignorant whether there are any mounts or monuments there. – William Bartram, *Travels of William Bartram*

It is disheartening to consider how much archaeology is required in order to write one sentence of history. – Philip Phillips, *Archaeological Survey in the Lower Yazoo Basin, Mississippi, 1949–1955*

The Choctaws were among the heirs of the mound-building Mississippian cultures of the Southeast. While some of these cultures were already on the decline by the time the first Europeans arrived to observe them, others were in full working order, and the previously unknown diseases carried by those observers were responsible for the drastic and precipitate end of most of the remaining Mississippian cultures. In this chapter I examine the late prehistoric to protohistoric archaeological data for the region of interest in order to discuss the processes of social evolution and devolution that are supposed to have contributed to the development of the regional variations of Mississippian culture.

Because I want to show how the Choctaws as a people were born in the decline of these Mississippian cultures and the subsequent pandemic episodes set off by European entry into the Americas, I must first delineate the distinctive features of these cultures so that we may recognize their descendants. The issues here are whether the archaeological cultures of the region are, as I judge them to be, plausible candidates for ancestral Choctaws, and if so, which one or ones. This transformation, however, was complex and did not happen all at once, so it cannot be simply explained, and the processes by which it was effected must be considered separately. "Natural" or indigenous cultural devolution took place by definition before European contact, and the archaeological record is the only evidence for it.

Unfortunately, these cultures have not been examined in detail by theorists of culture change and evolution, who have instead sought the set pieces for their theories in better-known or more recently destroyed societies. As yet no one has developed a fully elaborated and clearly applicable model for the decline of chiefdoms – as the Mississippian social structure is classified – and thus it will be necessary to adopt theory developed from evidence from other regions. An examination of some of the models for the *emergence* of chiefdoms will be helpful; although modeling their decline is not merely a matter of reversing such a process, the argument that the process may be cyclical requires examination of the tribe-to-chiefdom transition that underlies the "rise of the Mississippian."

The concept of an archaeological culture used in this context is very limited, and failure to recognize its limits has been the source of far too many implicit claims about the ability of archaeologists to identify basic cultural phenomena from material evidence. Named cultures, or "phases" thereof, are in fact sets of artifact types and other physical remains (dwelling structures, settlement patterns, burial practices, and so forth) that occur together consistently over a definite spatial extent and – as far as can be determined – over a definite continuous time period. To whatever degree these sets of artifacts and other features can give rise, through their attributes or their systematic distribution, to inferences about behavior, the cultures may be conceived as articulating certain behavioral patterns. In this way we can often draw conclusions about subsistence activities, though not necessarily about the division of labor involved in carrying them out. Aspects of kinship and social structure may also be deduced where, for example, evidence about settlement layouts is ample, but the farther one moves from material activity reflected by the artifacts, the more intractable is the evidence and the more recourse must be had to ethnographic parallels drawn from the literature world-wide. Most difficult to encompass are the spiritual and ideological aspects of culture, although evidence of the treatment of the dead aids deduction of the former. Archaeology has always been by nature materialist, but as an interpretive science it has frequently struggled against this limitation, with more or less success as fashion favored one or the other approach (cf. Binford 1968; Clarke 1968; Renfrew 1982; Leone 1982; Hodder 1986).

The relevant archaeological evidence comes from sequences of late prehistoric "cultures" along the watersheds to the east and west of the later Choctaw homeland in east-central Mississippi. Most of the area where the Choctaws were met by the French in the eighteenth century and where they still live today apparently did not support a Mississippian population or indeed any significant population during the Mississippian period (Penman 1977; Blitz 1985). Since many Choctaws were thus incomers, search for their antecedents must extend to neighboring areas.

The archaeological literature for these areas represents two broad approaches. Research in the Lower Mississippi Valley has been carried out over many years under the aegis of the Lower Mississippi Survey (Phillips, Ford, and Griffin 1951; Phillips 1970), as a unified effort and in a unified style that has depended strongly upon artifact classification and ethnographic parallel to attempt to reconstruct a prehistory in the European sense (Trigger 1983). Research on the Tombigbee-Alabama, on the other hand, began in the same spirit but has most recently been conducted in a style that claims allegiance to the "New Archaeology," with its interest in archaeological evidence as the residue of social processes rather than in historically specific developmental sequences. This difference in approach would be insignificant except that it differentiates the choice of sites and the ways in which they are investigated. The data from research in these two areas are thus not entirely comparable but for one unfortunately shared aspect: a lack of attention to smaller sites (Ramenofsky 1982; Smith 1987). As a result, treatment of the two regions in this chapter differs also.

Contrary to legend, the Choctaws did not literally emerge from the earth of the Nanih Waiya mound; they were, like many other tribes of the Southeast, the successors to the Late Mississippian cultures of prehistory. The course of this prehistory is far from well known. Charles Hudson's (1976) synthesis of the ethnohistory of the Indians of the Southeast has so far offered the best general tracing of the trajectory from prehistory into history, but even his study suffers from overgeneralization and an unavoidable lack of the most recent archaeological evidence (Brain 1978b), which often resides in obscure reports to federal agencies that financed the relevant work. Before Hudson, John Swanton's pioneering ethnographic work on the various tribes of the Southeast (1911, 1922, 1928a, 1928b, 1931, 1946) suffered far worse from generalizations from the Creek evidence and from Swanton's conviction that the historic tribes as they were observed in the late nineteenth century were substantially the same as they had been at the first coming of Europeans and indeed prehistorically as well.

The general late prehistory of the Southeast is becoming more and more understandable – although it has not reached the level of synthesis that would permit a study of the Choctaws comparable to Bruce Trigger's 1976 study of the Huron – and at the same time more notorious for its complexity. Archaeological work financed by public funds, beginning in the 1930s and continuing with the extensive federal programs of recent years, has given rise to a vast acquisition of knowledge about the archaeology of limited parts of the Southeast, spanning temporal periods from the Paleoindian cultures of more than ten thousand years ago to the colonial period not three hundred years past. At the same time, major theoretical advances in cultural anthropology have been used to articulate this evidence into coherent pictures of functioning social systems and their evolution over time.

Two results have emerged from an increase in the variety of Mississippian sites excavated and the corresponding development of theoretical explanation of the chiefdom level of social organization represented by such cultures. The first is an increased awareness of the variety of cultural manifestations formerly subsumed under the rubric of Mississippian culture; the second is a recognition that this very variety is at least partly due to the continuity of Mississippian systems with the local cultural developments that preceded them. Because of this amplified understanding of the preceding Woodland period, it is now possible to work with a longer trajectory in analyzing the process of culture change that brought the people of the Mississippian-period chiefdoms into the historic period as the modern tribes of the Southeast. Studies in ecology and environmental adaptation have shown the importance of the physical context in which a society grows up and of the powerful influence of that context in maintaining a substrate of cultural continuity in the face of even the most drastic social changes (Steward 1955). Thus, some of the differences observed in the southeastern tribes of the eighteenth century were likely not of recent date; rather, some traits probably had a long history, leading perhaps as far back as these Woodland "dark ages" of the Southeast. What made the Choctaws distinct from their neighbors began before Hernando de Soto ever dreamed of Florida.

John Swanton's view of the location and culture of the antecedents of the Choctaws was, as set forth in his summary of work on the Soto expedition (Swanton 1939), based very clearly on linguistic evidence and on the modern locations of the tribes defined by such linguistic evidence. The subsequent enormous input of archaeological data has called some of Swanton's conclusions into question, merely by altering the questions being asked (Lankford 1977; Smith 1977, 1987). New archaeological and newly discovered documentary evidence have been responsible for opening up several lines of inquiry. The first is a search for the cause of the transition from Mississippian to historic cultures; it is no longer assumed that European influences were solely responsible for this transition. Second, an examination of discernible relationships among the different Mississippian cultures may elucidate the relationships among the later historic tribes. Third, better knowledge of population distributions during the Mississippian period enables a preliminary assessment of the effects of European disease on the Indians of the Southeast in general and on the antecedents of the Choctaws in particular.

Most of these questions may be approached fairly straightforwardly by juxtaposing archaeological evidence for the late Mississippian period with the observations of the Spaniards who broke in upon the remnants of the Mississippian world, which will be done in the following chapter. First, however, we seek a picture of the Mississippian world itself – a dynamic picture of that world as it developed in its variations over the part of the Southeast of interest here.

THE EMERGENCE OF MISSISSIPPIAN CULTURE

The real beginnings of the period of Mississippian cultural development in the Southeast are around A.D. 800–900, when Woodland horticulturists turned to maize agriculture in a significant way. This transitional period and its heritage are important to the development of later variations in Mississippian culture. By no means are all aspects of the Mississippian emergence well understood, as recent work has shown (Smith 1990). Still, the broad outlines of the developmental sequence can be sketched, even though quite a lot remains to be learned about the major sites.

This sketch begins with a brief definition of the core features of Mississippian culture. As further knowledge of the artifactual variation across this culture has become available, a more functional definition has seemed appropriate to capture an applicable generalization for the whole. The definition advanced by Bruce Smith (1978a) in a book surveying Mississippian settlement patterns focuses on the theme of an ecological/social adaptation:

> I would like to propose that the term "Mississippian" be used to refer to those prehistoric human populations existing in the eastern deciduous woodlands during the time period A.D. 800–1500 that had a ranked form of social organization, and had developed a specific complex adaptation to linear, environmentally circumscribed floodplain habitat zones. This adaptation involved maize horticulture and selective utilization of a limited number of species groups of wild plants and animals that represented dependable, seasonally abundant energy sources that could be exploited at a relatively low level of energy expenditure. In addition, these populations depended significantly upon an even more limited number of externally powered energy sources. . . . (p. 486)
>
> . . . Many, if not all, Mississippian populations could be generally characterized as having a settlement system consisting of dispersed farmsteads surrounding a local center, with this system representing a flexible compromise solution to the opposing pressures of optimum energy utilization and optimum social-cohesion–boundary-maintenance abilities. . . . (p. 491)
>
> . . . Taken together, these three factors: (a) adaptive niche; (b) settlement system; (c) structure and level of complexity of the sociopolitical organization can be used to define the boundary conditions of "Mississippian." (p. 494)

This definition offers more concrete referents for verification than the popular conception of the Mississippian, which depends upon old racist conceptions of vanished "Moundbuilder" supermen or new millennialist conceptions of Aztecs from space (Silverberg 1974; Williams 1991). It also has the advantage of having arisen as an explanatory model for observed phenomena. It is broad enough to encompass all the varieties of Mississippian culture in the area of concern, the Mississippi-Alabama region, and it makes no claims that cannot be verified by reference to the archaeological and documentary evidence. Three things mentioned in this definition will be discussed in turn: the subsistence base and its ecological adaptation, the ranked society of Mississippian chiefdoms, and the issue of economic redistribution as it relates to the ecological context.

Most students of Mississippian culture recognize that its rise bore an intimate connection with a thoroughgoing acceptance of maize agriculture as a subsistence base by horticultural or marginally agricultural Woodland-period hunter-gatherers. It is now recognized, however, that maize was not the sole staple for Mississippian societies; not only was it supplemented by beans and squash, echoing the Mesoamerican agricultural trinity, but Mississippian groups also apparently followed their Woodland predecessors in cultivating certain plants, now considered wild, that provided starchy and oily seeds in abundance (Struever 1968; Dobyns 1983:219–28). Nor did they depend solely upon cultigens; native fruits, berries, nuts, and other plant products continued to be harvested as they had been among the earlier Woodland peoples. The meat of deer, bison, and several smaller mammals and reptiles, together with that of fish and certain fowl (especially turkey and migratory waterfowl), continued to be important, and the hunt saw its own technological innovation: the bow and arrow, introduced at the end of the Woodland period. In fact, the Mississippian peoples seem simply to have added to the rich resources for subsistence in the Southeast that had been so well exploited in the Primary Forest Efficiency adaptation of the Archaic and Woodland periods (Caldwell 1958), thus creating additional protein and carbohydrate resources that had the advantage of being more controllable. This augmentation is confirmed by the environmental niche most Mississippian cultures selected for in the Southeast: floodplains suitable for cultivation but also situated to exploit multiple ecological zones where the variety of wild resources was maximal (cf. Peebles 1978).

The question of why agriculture arose in the Southeast is only a part of the larger question of why it arose at all. Marvin Harris (1978) has suggested that it had a similar cause but followed a different course in the Old and New Worlds. Generally, he argues, once the Pleistocene megafauna passed from the scene, the growing human population found obtaining adequate sustenance through hunting alone increasingly difficult. They therefore had to concentrate more seriously upon plants as food sources to supplement intensified hunting of smaller game. In the Americas, domesticable herd animal species were lacking, and many areas also lacked open country where wild grain could grow, so sedentarism was not developed along with herding and gathering as it was in the Old World. Instead, Late Archaic– and Woodland-period hunters followed game and collected foods from plants in a seasonal round, slowly developing adherence to specific areas for storage of supplies against winter food shortages. Population grew as dependence upon plants grew, and food plant cultivation in an incipient form (chenopod, marsh elder, knotweed, sunflower, and so forth) began.

Southeastern North America is unique, however, in that the cultivation of maize as a full-fledged subsistence base and the rise of chiefdom social organization seem to have coincided. The major cultigens – squash, corn, and beans – appear in the archaeological record in that order. Squash remains are known from sites as early as 2000 B.C., while remains of Tropical Flint corn (a small popcorn) are seen in Early Woodland Hopewell contexts in the Midwest ca. 200 B.C. plus or minus 100 years (Yarnell 1976). Hence both were available as part of a horticultural repertoire in the eastern woodlands long before they became important foodstuffs. Tropical Flint corn apparently dates rather later in the Southeast, but it was never adopted significantly as a cultigen (Byrd and Neuman 1978). Indeed, some have argued that the significant import was the larger Northern Flint variety of corn, which could be grown more widely and offered a better yield when grown together with the common bean, since without the latter as a companion planting, corn will eventually exhaust the soil in spite of flood-renewed fertility, thus vitiating a fixed settlement location. Both of these cultigens seem to have become available around A.D. 800, which coincides with the first emergence of the Mississippian culture, although beans have only been identified from southeastern sites dating several hundred years later (Yarnell 1976). I want to emphasize, however, that the "emergence of the Mississippian" represents not a total revolution but rather a new articulation of many of the cultural elements already present in the repertoire of the peoples east of the Mississippi, and that it also coincided with an upward trend in population, evidenced by more and larger sites.

Adoption of agriculture thus seems to have been "pushed" by population pressure in the Southeast. Population pressure, it is thought, led to subsistence stress, and subsistence stress demanded one of two strategies in the exploitation of the available subsistence base: intensification or diversification. Subsistence remains from Late Woodland sites suggest that hunting and gathering strategies were already maximally diversified, and in some areas population pressures seem to have been forcing predation on smaller species, so that the hunt was beginning to show diminishing returns. The opportunities offered by an intensification of existing horticulture to the level of full-scale agriculture – particularly as new cultigens became available – were too cost effective to be missed (Scarry 1980a).

With the adoption of agriculture and the choice of the environmentally circumscribed floodplains came an increased measure of sedentariness. Crops require attention on a seasonal basis, and a commitment to permanent settlement is necessary to watch over the crops and to claim the land in some sense. For this reason Mississippian culture is also a sedentary culture, a culture whose settlements moved only when they experienced problems with the exhaustion of the soil or of the surrounding forest resources, which only happened in a drastic way when the habitat had been poorly chosen in the first place.

Along with the process of a transition to permanent settlement came an apparent change in social organization. Nothing outside the archaeological record documents this change; it is inferred on the basis of the archaeological evidence of settlement system and mortuary ritual, along with analogy to past and present social organizations as observed by ethnologists. This evidence is arranged in a developmental sequence using models worked out by the proponents of cultural evolutionism, paramount among them Elman Service (1971a, 1971b), who drew on a model by Morton Fried to formulate the evolutionary sequence from egalitarian band to tribe to ranked chiefdom. Fried (1967) and Sahlins (1968) have further amplified this model; Friedman (1975) has explained it as a dynamic system exemplifying an ideal trajectory of social transformation; and Peebles and Kus (1977) have applied it to the archaeological evidence for Mississippian cultures. Bruce Smith (1986) has added additional detail. The following discussion draws on these sources.

The Woodland cultures in the Mississippi-Alabama area and their sequences are shown in figure 2.1. These cultures were far from uniform throughout the area, but they did have certain features in common that became fundamental to the concept of the Woodland period. Woodland peoples were primarily hunter-gatherers, although toward the end of the period some groups had begun to cultivate corn and most groups to cultivate some other plants in a small way. Their culture included mortuary observances consisting of more-than-perfunctory – and often elaborate – treatment of the bodies of some of the dead, which were sometimes buried within small round mounds erected for the purpose. They used the spear propelled by an atlatl (spear-thrower), and eventually the bow and arrow, to kill game. They had become proficient in pottery manufacture, permitting the introduction of new culinary methods such as stewing. Their settlements served as bases of operations situated in the most favorable location within the territory they hunted. During fall and spring hunts much of the population probably spread out into hunting camps where meat, fish, and shellfish would be procured and processed to be brought back to the permanent settlement. Gathering of nuts, berries, and seeds was similarly seasonally scheduled.

The specific components of the subsistence base obviously strongly influenced the kinds of variation seen in Woodland culture. On the coast, where fish and shellfish offered the most consistently available protein, settlement and food-gathering were oriented toward these resources, while in inland regions the white-tailed deer was the

	PERIOD	TRADITION	SOUTHERN YAZOO	NATCHEZ BLUFFS	TRADITION	UPPER TOMBIGBEE		WARRIOR	MOBILE
1600	Protohistoric		Russell	Natchez		Mhoon	Alabama River	Alabama River	Bear Point
1540		Mississippian	Wasp Lake	Emerald		Sorrells	Summerville III	Moundville III	
1400			Lake George	Foster	Moundville				
1300	Mississippian					Lyon's Bluff	Summerville II	Moundville II	Bottle Creek
1200		Plaquemine	Winterville	Anna					?
1100			Crippen Point	Gordon		Tibbee Creek	Summerville I	Moundville I	Tensas Lake
1000		Coles Creek						West Jefferson	
900	Emergent Mississippian		Kings Crossing	Balmoral		Miller III			McLeod / Tate's Hammock
800			Aden	Ballina	Miller-Baytown				
700			Bayland	Sundown					
600	Woodland	Baytown							
500									
400			Deasonville	Hamilton Ridge	Miller	Miller II			
300		Troyville							
200		Marksville	Issaquena	Issaquena		Miller I			Porter
100			Anderson Landing	Grand Gulf					
0									
100			Tchefuncte	Tuscola	Panther Lake	Alexander	Henson Springs		Bryant's Landing
200									

2.1. Woodland-Mississippian culture sequence in the Lower Mississippi Valley and Tombigbee-Alabama Valley regions.

focus of the hunt. In some areas stone for weapons and implements was easily available, while in others such tools were made of sharpened cane and fire-hardened wood or imported stone. Houses and other constructions could take advantage of forest resources in many places; in many others the easily available cane was more frequently used. The ceramic traditions of the two major river systems and the different regions within them clearly show that the cultures utilizing these various resources did in fact differ in style and texture, although communication certainly took place across the Pontotoc Ridge separating the Yazoo and Tombigbee watersheds in the north and along the Gulf coast in the south. There was, on the whole, a great deal more interaction over the area than might be supposed. Although the river courses seem to have retained primacy as routes of travel, especially in a downstream direction, the great diagonal spine that would become the Natchez Trace, running from the lower course of the Mississippi to the headwaters of the Tombigbee, seems to have been in active use as a trade route well before the Woodland period, and east-west trails were certainly also in use (Meyer 1928; Tanner 1989; see figures 2.2 and 2.3).

The best-known cultural development in eastern North America during the Woodland period was the Hopewell culture of Ohio and Illinois (cf. Struever 1968; Seeman 1979; Brose and Greber 1979). The major sites are located along the Ohio and Illinois Rivers and their tributaries, and they include elaborate mortuary mounds and other earthworks. Settlement excavation confirms the existence of horticulture

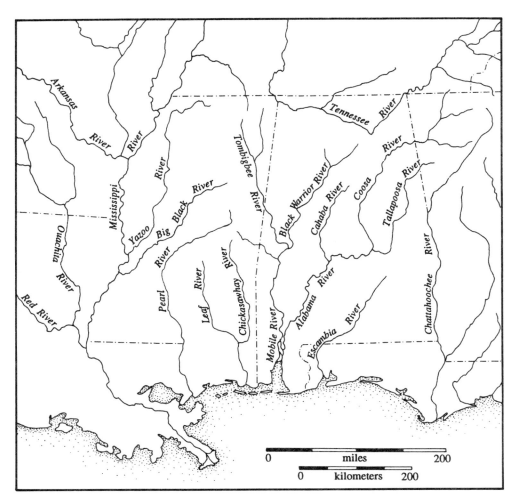

2.2. Major river systems in the Mississippi-Alabama region.

on at least some sites. Differential treatment of the dead indicates some social differentiation, and grave goods include objects of materials from distant sources, implying some form of long-distance trade. This cultural phenomenon is significant for
the Southeast, where such sites as Marksville in Louisiana, Helena Crossing in Arkansas, and Pinson in Tennessee, which indicate similar social complexity and cultural richness, have also yielded exotic craft objects and possibly mortuary ceremonialism, suggesting reciprocal long-distance connections with the Ohio Valley.

Like a dye injected into the southeastern arteries of trade and interaction, the
Hopewell culture traits cause those arteries to spring into visibility (see Seeman
1979:335). The distribution of those traits reveals that finished objects and not just
raw materials were circulating through the system; since a finished object implies
some agreement of its value on both ends of the trade, this evidence points to a

suddenly heightened degree of contact occurring over a broad area (Seeman 1979: 309). The social implications of these long-distance connections are less well understood.

A recent trend in speculation on the sociopolitical organization of archaeological cultures, drawing upon the evolutionary models mentioned above, has been to claim for one's favorite archaeological culture as much complexity as the evidence will bear. Although certainly this approach is more useful than considering everything before the development of Mississippian chiefdoms as undifferentiated savagery, it has little to do with an effort to seek the simplest explanation that fits the facts. Hopewell culture has not been exempt from claims of ranked social organization (Brose 1979; Struever and Houart 1972). More recently, Bruce Smith (1986) has developed a model, borrowing from Sahlins's (1968) discussions of segmentary tribal organization and Ford's (1979) arguments about subsistence resources, that fits the facts and also avoids the problems raised by interpreting the eventual disappearance of Hopewell as some catastrophic decline in social organization.

According to Smith, the settlement patterns, mortuary ceremonialism, and long-distance trade manifest in Hopewell culture can be adequately explained by postulating the rise of local leaders or "big-men" among segmentary tribes. They were leaders not by birth but because of their abilities to build a group of adherents through persuasion and reciprocal obligations. These adherents then aided the leader in intensifying food production or procurement in order to establish external connections that might function to ensure an additional source of food in times of shortage, defuse competition over circumscribed resource areas, and strengthen communal ethnic identity. Smith suspects that the exotic Hopewell artifacts spread spottily along major trails and river routes throughout the Southeast exhibit "the opportunistic and relatively sporadic movement (waxing and waning as specific community big men emerge, flourish to varying degrees, and die) of a limited volume of craft items between villages having weakly developed inter-community kinship ties" (Smith 1986:69; see also Braun and Plog 1982).

This activity took place among segmentary tribes, that is, political entities consisting of roughly equal-sized groups, bound by kinship ties, sedentarism, and certain ceremonies of community solidarity. These ceremonies included basically simple burial practices, except for a few exceptionally treated individuals who were probably the "big-men." Both settlement pattern – clustered, linear, or dispersed – and mortuary ceremonialism – ranging from completely egalitarian, without grave goods of any kind, to partially differentiated, with exotic grave goods and lengthy processing of selected remains – varied as the wide range of options for tribal organization was adapted to suit differing ecological conditions through different historical trajectories.

For years archaeologists assumed that the decline of Hopewell culture and its influence among Middle Woodland cultures generally resulted from some kind of regression that occurred in cultural development. As studies of settlement patterns and further site surveys began to indicate that the "good gray cultures" (Williams 1963) of the Late Woodland period (A.D. 450–750) were, in spite of the unspectacular material culture recovered through archaeological survey, ubiquitous, it became obvious that the period was one of steady population increase. Reexamining the evidence for subsistence, Smith (1986) has emphasized that during this time the existing horticultural repertoire, dominated by oily and starchy seeds, began to incorporate corn and to develop toward field agriculture. This gradual change in plant exploitation strategy supported population expansion throughout favorable river valley habitats.

The expansion was so gradual that no substantial change from the preceding tribal organization seems to have taken place, except for the one factor that makes this period seem artifactually colorless: the apparent disappearance of the big-men and their exotic objects and differential burial status. This change may have occurred as the increasing populations and growing dependence on horticulture of the Late Woodland tribal societies led to more modifications of the ecosystem, such that a failure of cultivated or gathered "crops" had more serious consequences. To maintain structural cohesion among larger numbers of more widely scattered tribal segments, authority positions began to arise within the lineages that held them together (Braun and Plog 1982).

Several new elements in the proto-Mississippian pattern could serve to fuel the further change from tribes organized by kinship relations to chiefdoms. The first element was the aforementioned sedentariness. The second was the surplus in subsistence supplies that probably accrued to agriculturally successful groups. Finally, we can infer that the variety of resources in the ecotone areas bordering the river valleys was a further subsistence asset. These three factors permitted a greater concentration of population and also could have led to diversification in the subsistence activities of groups settled in different corners of an area. On the material plane, then, the picture is of groups considerably larger than one extended family, living permanently in one place and enjoying the luxury of a surplus of sustenance but perhaps in no one case having access to every resource their cultural repertoire prepared them to exploit.

The motivating causes for the development of Mississippian culture are still not known with any certainty, and the question of whether maize agriculture or ranked social organization came first probably has several correct answers (see Welch 1990) and is in any case outside the scope of this study. How the culture developed, however, is no mystery. Maize agriculture was its base, and although Late Woodland developments had clearly prepared the way, a whole set of technological developments went along with it so obviously that the claim of a "revolution" in agricultural practice is not an exaggeration. Emergent Mississippian groups mastered the use of certain substances (alkali, salt) in processing maize for consumption, learned to store seed corn more carefully and securely (Morse and Morse 1983), and harvested substantial storable supplies of maize. The discovery of burnt shell as a tempering agent for pottery permitted a far more versatile and durable range of storage, cooking, and serving vessels (Steponaitis 1983). Settlement patterns showed a change, too, with a transition from villages to civic centers surrounded by hamlets and farmsteads, suggesting spatial adaptations to field agriculture as well. The "civic centers" are understood as such because they show the result of communal labor projects (the characteristic truncated pyramidal mounds) but were nevertheless not inhabited on a permanent basis by a large population. The evidence for the existence of a group of important people connected with centralization and communal labor also appears in the form of burials once more given special treatment.

Precisely how the change from tribal to chiefdom social organization took place is not known. Subsistence technology changes were gradual up to a threshold, beyond which lay actual agricultural revolution. In the past, archaeologists' efforts to explain a corresponding social revolution have led to invasion hypotheses and notions of Mesoamerican cultural missionaries (see B. Smith 1984). The current view, however, does not depend upon drastic cultural upheaval. Instead, principles of cultural evolution are applied to the archaeological evidence, with emphasis on the continuity of cultural development. Service (1971b:134–43), in his discussion of the tribe-to-chiefdom transition, emphasized the influence of increasing sedentarism in a region of differential access to resources, which then favors the development of some means of redistribution, further specialization, and finally the rise of a permanent leadership with the ability to organize the society for production and competition with outside forces. Morse and Morse (1983:202) have pointed to the irreversible nature of this process: once the constituent parts of a large tribe or several small ones begin pooling resources, there is increased incentive for production; this leads to irrevocable alteration of the ecological setting as field agriculture gains dominance; and this in turn supports population growth, which demands further efficiency of the central redistributive institution, as the need for long-term protection against crop failure becomes more pressing.

Fried (1967) views the evolutionary model somewhat differently and stresses the qualitative revolution in the transition from ranked (primarily "big-man") to stratified society, seen as a transition *from* egalitarian access to the requirements of subsistence *to* selective restriction of such access. According to this model, population pressure (in a context of successful sedentarism) makes the continued integration of society through kinship mechanisms and sodalities alone impossible, simply because the number of independent units and the area they cover grows too great for actions of benefit to the society as a whole to be coordinated solely by communication among local leaders. As dependence on agriculture increases, some mechanism for dealing with shortages is needed, requiring an authority to collect and manage surpluses. An effort to provide this integration probably causes an intensification of the formality and strength of kinship structures such as lineages, and as population grows and villages fission, the center of original settlement becomes the locus of the most senior lineages. The only step remaining is to recruit someone to undertake chiefly responsibility.

Fried turns to the classical example of irrigation agriculture as a paradigm for the kind of coordination required. In the river valleys of the Southeast, most particularly the Mississippi, increased cooperation and coordination could in many ways benefit the societies beginning full-scale field agriculture on the floodplains. A river-valley redistribution model, with the resources of environmental zones through which a river passes orchestrated into a redistributional system, has been developed for Mesoamerica (Flannery 1968), and it makes sense for the Mississippi's tributaries and other small river systems. For the Mississippi itself, however, nothing short of a state could begin to orchestrate the redistribution of its resources, and here there was apparently no such thing; nevertheless, the Mississippi did serve as a powerful avenue for the exchange of resources and information between chiefdoms.

Perhaps for this reason, the huge site at Cahokia, opposite modern St. Louis, long appeared to have been the center of the spread of this culture, and the Mississippi and its tributaries to have been the conduits. It is now apparent that Mississippian culture did not have one center – with population growth and transition to agriculture, the move to chiefdom organization probably happened in several places at once. Platform mounds seem to have proliferated early at Cahokia, but even these may have been adopted from people further south on the river. Yet there *were* connections with Cahokia to the east, south, and north along the rivers, and though its true role in this vast communication network is now unclear, Cahokia could have served as a clearinghouse for certain trade items such as Mill Creek chert for making hoes.

Rivers were not the only routes of communication or conduits for influence. Trails crossed and recrossed the Southeast and were the connection for Mississippian peoples seeking exotic artifacts across watersheds (Meyer 1928; Tanner 1989; see figure 2.3). Woodland-period big-men may have flourished at major crossroads and river junctures through which traffic in materials and goods had to flow, and there is no reason to assume that this traffic was less important in Mississippian times. On the contrary: conch shells from the Gulf, native copper from the Great Lakes, and other

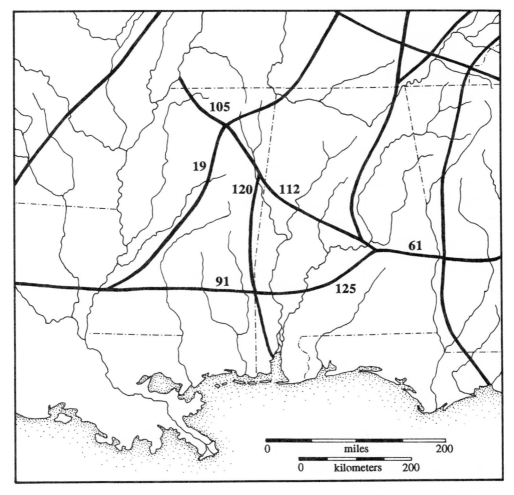

2.3. Principal Indian trails in the Mississippi-Alabama region; numbers refer to trail numbers assigned by William E. Meyer (adapted from Meyer 1928; Tanner 1989).

such luxury goods would grow in importance as social stratification intensified, bolstered by sumptuary regulation and the prestige goods trade that would enable chiefs to validate and reinforce their claims to leadership (Brown, Kerber, and Winters 1990). In fact, over time the popularity of particular trade items may be seen as an analogy for the ideas and knowledge that were circulating at the same time: early in the period, practical items such as Mill Creek chert hoes reflect technological advances in agriculture, while later on the distribution of status-related artifacts such as those bearing the symbolism of the "Southern Cult" (Peebles 1971; Waring 1968; Galloway 1989c) – among them the Mill Creek chert "maces" – suggests the development of ideological props for the new levels of control required for chiefdom cohesion.

Thus population migrations and forced ideological conversions no longer neatly explain the "rise of the Mississippian." The rather messier way of looking at the problem that stresses growing sedentarism and local cultural continuities all over the Southeast leads to a picture that makes rather more sense of the regional autonomy and disinclination to permanent alliances displayed by the tribes of the historic period.

As the numbers of people in the Southeast increased, they simply settled down in the river valleys and began to exploit first wild plants and then, when experience with domestication was widespread, imported cultigens. This process went on wherever the habitat was suitable, and as population and dependence on cultigens increased, social organization became more complex. Exchange of goods and information were constants, with evidence for them varying as leaders arose who saw advantage in taking a hand in systematizing either one. Perhaps population pressure on resources was not uniform, or some areas were quicker to feel such pressure, but where it was felt first leaders began to emerge who were capable of more broadly based organization that could enhance their societies' productivity and also their own importance and influence. The ideological revolution postulated by some seems to have been just as gradual as the agricultural one, again up to a threshold point. Beyond that point, according to Fried (1967), lay the full social stratification that led to two ends only: statehood or chiefdom collapse. Peebles (1979b; cf. Anderson 1990) has suggested the application of a cyclical model developed by Friedman (1975): increasing integration from tribe through chiefdom; then, when the chiefdom grew too large, took on enemies too powerful, or experienced serious crop failure, it would break up into "tribes" consisting of its major constituent lineages and begin the cycle anew. Hence the Southeast at the end of the Mississippian period was a patchwork of societies at various stages in this cycle and more or less dependent on increased social integration as they were more or less dependent on agricultural production.

With this general tracing of the cultural development in the Southeast as a background, the specific sequences of prehistoric cultures in the areas surrounding the historic Choctaw heartland can be examined. The physiographic characteristics of the area (see figure 2.4) have been influential in determining subsistence activities and communication routes. The eastern flank of the lower Mississippi Valley can be divided into two regions, the Yazoo Basin to the north and the Natchez Bluffs to the south. The Yazoo Basin, bordered on the east by the Yazoo River system, is a flat, ancient meander belt of the Mississippi River (Saucier 1974), crossed and recrossed by its tributaries and old channels. It benefited from the rich soils accumulated through millennia of riverine deposit as well as from rich aquatic wildlife resources and the larger game available in the mixed forest that once covered the area, but it was always subject to flooding. By contrast, the Natchez Bluffs are steep loess bluffs, well clear of flood danger, that border the Mississippi below the confluence of the

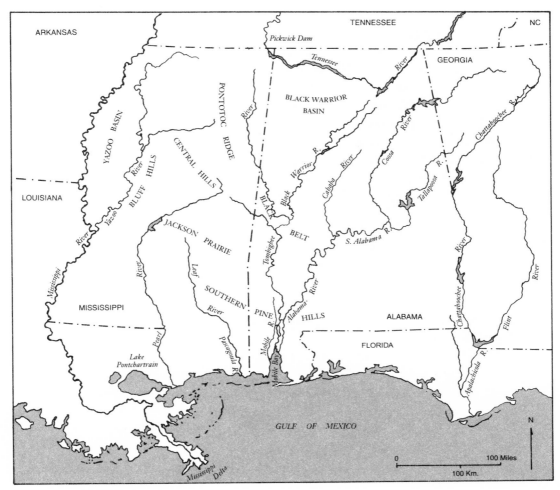

2.4. Physiographic map of the region.

Yazoo and continue northward alongside the Yazoo's eastern flank. The loess bluff strip is relatively narrow, but its loamy soils are very rich where not broken down by erosion, and bordering forests offered a good supply of upland wild game.

The valley of the Tombigbee is not so well provided with resources as that of the Mississippi; it is neither so large nor so old a river, and the redepositions of soil it has effected are not nearly so major. The land it cuts is more resistant to its actions as well. Together with the Alabama, the Tombigbee forms part of the river system that drains the southwestern end of the Appalachians, its tributaries flowing down from upland hills to join the larger rivers that meet as they cross the Gulf Coastal Plain to empty into Mobile Bay.

The Mississippi/Yazoo and Tombigbee drainages are separated in north central Mississippi by the hills of the Pontotoc Ridge, but as that ridge sweeps eastward and the loess bluffs sweep westward, each hedging off the drainage of a major river system, a broad wedge of land is left in south central Mississippi, with its base along the Gulf and its apex slightly east of central Mississippi. This wedge is drained to the south by two important river systems, the Pearl and the Pascagoula. Both take their rise in the eastward-swinging arc of the Central Hills region; both cross the Jackson Prairie and Vicksburg Hills before falling down into the piney woods of the Gulf Coastal Plain. But neither of these is a major river system like the Mississippi or even the Tombigbee/Alabama, and neither can compare with the latter in the width of their valleys or the richness of the habitat they offer.

ORIGIN OF THE PLAQUEMINIANS

The story in the Mississippi Valley suggests that horticultural people in a favorable environment could find that subsistence mode adequate to their needs for a long time. Significant influences from the north affected the Mississippi Valley twice as the cultures there evolved toward agriculture, and tracing what happened both times can convey a sense of the interdependency of the cultures of the Eastern Woodlands.

In the Mississippi Valley the embodiment of Woodland-period Hopewell influences, apparently connected with Havana Hopewell of the Illinois Valley, is identified as the Marksville culture (Toth 1988). Within the period of its development, differential distributions of pottery types define several phases, whose geographical distribution and relative dates suggest that the Hopewell influences "involved small, widely scattered communities which later drew together, forming a more compact interconnected system in the central and possibly southern portions of the area" (Phillips 1970:901). This "system" is manifested as the Issaquena phase (Greengo 1964), which dominated both sides of the Mississippi from the lower Yazoo Basin to south of Natchez. In terms of cultural practices, this late Marksville phase seems to have been marked by a "decrease in emphasis on mortuary ceremonialism . . . and increased dependence on agriculture" (Phillips 1970:901).

General archaeological opinion sees the succeeding Baytown period as more an interval between major cultural developments than a period marked by its own distinctive features. Although Baytown is not characterized by striking artifact types or unusual architectural features, there are other, less flashy considerations. First, Baytown was apparently a period of consolidation and population growth, a time of stability and of perfecting the adaptation to horticulture. Second, during this period the apparently "egalitarian" mortuary practices may indicate a growing importance of formal kinship organization, which would suppress the independent big-men and thus remove the exotic trade goods that gave evidence of their activity. Such a development toward increasing connectedness between neighboring localities could account for the stylistic uniformity of the Baytown ceramic assemblage as well (cf. Braun and Plog 1982).

The Baytown period lasted longer in the north than in the south. In the area south of the Yazoo Basin, the Troyville culture, expressed in the Hamilton Ridge phase, saw the introduction of pottery types from Gulf Coast sources and the use of mortuary platform mounds (Belmont 1982). In the Yazoo Basin, the sequent Deasonville-Bayland phases saw a stronger predominance of cord-marked pottery and introduced a distinctive pattern of shell middens on sites along the Yazoo River. It is generally assumed that Baytown-period cultures completely abandoned special mortuary practices, but this impression is probably due to the limited number of known single-component Baytown sites with burials; Phillips (1970) suggested, on the basis of a few burials in the mound at the multiperiod Thornton site, that Deasonville burials might have been laid out prone but with little or no accompaniment.

The Coles Creek culture represents an indigenous development of pyramidal mound-building and a modestly hierarchical settlement system in the lower end of the Mississippi Valley. No corn remains are known from any pristine Coles Creek occupation (Neuman 1984:213). Archaeologists, however, have looked at the apparent mound center–farmstead settlement pattern of Coles Creek sites, observed their location on rich river-bottom soils, and simply assumed that their subsistence base had to include corn agriculture (Brain n.d.). Lately, however, evidence for earlier periods has shown that corn agriculture was not necessary to support the kind of social organization that built the mounds and earthworks found on the impressive Hopewell sites of the Ohio Valley, thus suggesting that it may not have been necessary for Coles Creek peoples either. There is no disputing, however, that Coles Creek was an indigenous development and was restricted to the lower Mississippi Valley, from the southern Yazoo Basin south and from the Natchez Bluffs westward to take in the Tensas Basin. The authenticity of its indigenousness is supported by the frequent difficulty in drawing a line between late Baytown and early Coles Creek pottery assemblages throughout most of the area of Coles Creek dominance (Phillips 1970).

Brain (1978a:337), in his summary of Mississippian settlement patterns in the Lower Mississippi Valley, views Coles Creek as "a closely ordered and highly successful cultural adaptation . . . restricted to the rich bottomlands of the southern part of the valley." He describes the settlement organization as consisting of ceremonial sites, situated along watercourses near the main channel of the Mississippi River and of roughly equal size, having two to four rectangular substructural mounds arranged around a plaza. Such sites were essentially unoccupied, and the populations they served apparently lived in dispersed small settlements or farmsteads. Over its range, the material culture of Coles Creek was quite uniform, reflecting "the close interaction of well-developed but independent sociopolitical units" (Brain 1978a:337). Its pottery assemblage was distinctive and consistent in both technology and decoration for nearly five centuries (Brain n.d.).

No very clear picture of Coles Creek sociopolitical organization emerges, however. The mounds do indicate a corporate effort, and evidence of buildings on them exists (Williams and Brain 1983:307–9), but the purposes for which they were built are far from certain. Burials are found in some of the mounds, but they offer far fewer clues to social organization than had those of the Marksville period, since the Coles Creek people did not bury objects as offerings with their dead. That is not to say that they did not care for the dead; the evidence suggests charnel-house processing of bodies of both sexes and all ages (most burials are of bundles of disarticulated bones; Brain n.d.). Yet this "egalitarian" impression lent by the burials is not a universal trait: some few individuals were accompanied to their graves by the bodies of several children or young people (Williams and Brain 1983:38–56; especially Burial 49). Thus, although the lack of inorganic grave goods makes these burials seem simple, the suggestion that hereditary social ranking was absent among the Coles Creek people may be premature.

Brain (1971) and Webb (1982) have suggested that evidence of pottery style influences coming from the east along the Gulf coast during the preceding period may argue for an introduction of maize agriculture via the same route, together with some notions of ideology – for example, sun-worship. Yet, as has been said, Coles Creek sites contain no unequivocal evidence of corn, and the remains of corn from comparable Mississippian sites indicate that even cooking methods unlikely to preserve corn elements in a burned state (Belmont 1967) cannot possibly account for such a serious absence if Coles Creek peoples depended heavily upon corn agriculture. Recent analysis of skeletal remains has suggested that Coles Creek peoples made use of starchy seeds in a significant dietary shift but that maize was probably not the basis of their diet (Rose, Marks, and Tieszen 1991:10–15). If it was not – if corn was in fact grown only in a small way as a garden crop (as the Hopewellians had probably done) and the culture depended mostly upon the broad range of "wild" cultigens and gathered foods as during the preceding period – then the question remains of why the settlement pattern favored the rich bottomlands especially prized for agriculture. Coles Creek subsistence is thus not a solved problem.

Doubt also remains as to the significance of mound-building and its possible relationship to complex social organization. A common assumption is that Coles Creek peoples were organized as at least incipient chiefdoms having leaders and an elite who enjoyed hereditary status. Various evidence – most notably the "egalitarian" nature of the burials – suggests that this was not the case. Instead, a more reasonable hypothesis is that Coles Creek was characterized by modest agriculture; a continuation of segmentary tribal organization, with increasing emphasis on formalized kinship ties; and mounds constructed for refuge, storage, and burial purposes. The culture was vigorous and resistant to outside influence: it was only modified, not replaced, by the overwhelmingly successful Mississippian cultural adaptation.

While the Coles Creek culture was developing and entrenching itself in the southern end of the Mississippi Valley, the Baytown phases simply continued in the upper Yazoo Basin and across the river in what is now Arkansas. Out of these late Baytown phases, through population increase, agricultural intensification, and technological innovation, developed the early "Emergent Mississippian" phases contiguous to and doubtless having contact with the developments of the Cairo Lowlands and American Bottom (see Marshall 1988; B. Smith 1990). This process has been somewhat confused and obscured by Phillips's (1970) placement of late Baytown/early Mississippian phases of the northern Yazoo Basin in a "Coles Creek Period" – hence the "Coles Creek" Walnut Bend and Peabody phases appear to be replaced sequentially by the "Mississippian" Walls and Parchman/Quitman phases when in fact, as Starr (1984) has shown for at least the Parchman phase sites, pottery from many of these latter sites has a significantly "southern," Coles Creek look.

Another difficulty, which Phillips recognized (1970:923), is that his final distribution map for the Mississippian period plotted sites and phases of eight hundred years on a single map, thus obscuring the patchwork development over time. His reason for this lack of time differentiation unfortunately still exists: for many sites in the northern Yazoo Basin, researchers have virtually no criteria for dating beyond the crude identification of a Mississippian-period occupation on the basis of a few potsherds collected from the surface more than forty years ago (Phillips 1970:246). In most cases these same sites, due to intensive agribusiness development of the area, are today either damaged or completely destroyed. Because of how the original survey was carried out, most of the sites in question had at least one mound; very few smaller sites are known at all.

In spite of all these problems, it is possible to assert the existence of some fairly large-scale trends. First, just as Coles Creek developed without significant external influence, so the same may be said of the Mississippian developments out of late Baytown in the northern Yazoo Basin. Although the data to show *in situ* development on any single site are lacking, the balance of the evidence is firmly on the side of an evolutionary Baytown-to-Mississippian succession in most areas. A second trend is population increase, as the multiplication of sites indicates, and their concentration along the natural levees of watercourses suggests that the inhabitants were interested in rich, arable land. Since nearly all known sites had at least one substructural mound, there may well have been sufficient social organization to command a local community effort; only somewhat later do larger sites with multiple mounds and a plaza arrangement appear.

The very fact that distinctive pottery assemblages can be isolated and called phases indicates that the northern Yazoo Basin was "growing its own" Mississippian. Phillips's characterization of the relevant Mississippian phases depended not only upon the occurrence of pottery types but upon the *relative frequencies* of pottery types – in fact, the phases in question have mostly the *same* pottery types, present in different proportions. Since some of these variations in proportion may well be temporal variation, Phillips suggested that the Parkin phase west of the river in Arkansas preceded Walls just south of Memphis on the east side, which in its turn preceded the Kent phase, again west of the river. As for the Parchman phase, excavation at Walls suggests an earlier phase there to which Parchman may be comparable. Citing this very complexity, Phillips (1970:940) cautioned against "the too easy assumption that Mississippian culture . . . marched down the River in so regular a procession that individual phases can be dated by reference to degrees of latitude."

All the "Mississippian" phases, from north of Greenville, Mississippi, to the Ohio River junction, are largely based on two pottery wares, Mississippi Plain, *variety Neeley's Ferry* (the coarse ware), and Bell Plain, *variety Bell* (the fine ware), both containing the revolutionary burnt and crushed shell temper that characterizes Mississippian pottery. The proportions of these two wares do vary from one phase to another, but I suspect that this variance is more a factor of the dominant type of site represented in the phase (Walls, with larger ceremonial sites, has "ceremonial" fine ware dominant; Parchman, with mostly smaller sites, has coarse ware and fine ware roughly equal, coarse ware sometimes dominant) and secondarily of the dominant date represented by sites of the phase (if social organization increases in complexity over time, then late phases are likely to have more complex civic-ceremonial sites). Much might change if more farmstead and hamlet sites were known (cf. Morse and Morse 1983:237).

Still, even given the poor temporal control and the skewed nature of the sample, the distinctive, more localized pottery types, which appear in smaller numbers but become "marker types" for the named phases, suggest that the northern Yazoo Basin participated in cultural developments stemming from the lower St. Francis Basin west, north, and south of Memphis, and from the extreme north of the Yazoo Basin itself. As the Central Mississippi Valley Mississippian populations seemed to look to the north, where the more complex sites were located "closest to the major important outside resources" (Morse and Morse 1983:238), so the peoples of the upper Yazoo Basin may have looked to their north for sources that could supply Mill Creek chert hoes and the like. For the present, the lack of temporal control prevents any secure characterization of sites and phases as Early (700–1000) or Middle (1000–1350) Mississippian, as has been done for the Central Valley. Failing such characterization, I must generalize: in the northern Yazoo Basin the full adoption of maize agriculture was accompanied by a growth in population and an apparent centralization of some sociopolitical functions at nonresidential civic-ceremonial centers. Despite some evidence of influences from the north in exotic artifacts and "ceremonial" pottery pieces, the northern Yazoo Basin was not directly influenced by the culture of the Cahokia "superchiefdom"; instead, the influences came from directly neighboring chiefdoms.

We may also assume a similar source for the initial Mississippian influences on the areas of Coles Creek "hegemony" further south. Although evidence from the lower Yazoo Basin reveals some sort of brief direct contact with the great Cahokia site around A.D. 1050–1150, this contact was clearly not sustained, nor is it reflected elsewhere in the Lower Valley (Williams and Brain 1983:410–12; Marshall 1988). Yet indirect contact must have occurred, transmitting subtler influences; the Coles Creek culture that had persisted so conservatively for so long was ultimately transformed by that contact into the "Mississippianized" Plaquemine culture.

Hypotheses of conquest or migration are not necessary to account for this change (see B. Smith 1984). Instead, a model suggesting some degree of acculturation is probably more appropriate; Brain (1989) prefers the idea of "transculturation," since Plaquemine is just as distinctively local a development as Coles Creek, implying a voluntary and selective adoption of cultural characteristics. Existing studies have not attempted to focus on Mississippian–Coles Creek interaction from this viewpoint because of a lack of data, so at present only a sketch of an outline of the process can be offered.

Williams and Brain (1983:409–19) see the Mississippian–Coles Creek interaction as a sequence of two broad events: initial contact (A.D. 1000–1200) and "ecumene" (A.D. 1200–1400). Initial contact apparently began between the Mississippian cultures of the upper Mississippi and the "terminal" Crippen Point phase of Coles Creek about A.D. 1000. By the time the two cultures had accomplished formal contact, about A.D. 1200, the Mississippian culture had reached a fair approximation of its canonical form; Brain (n.d.) has provided an outline of the two cultural systems at "the critical time of the Cahokia contact," shown here as table 2.1. Although several points presented in the table are questionable, a cursory examination quickly shows that the differences between the two cultures were primarily structural. As they met, the initial contact was marked in the archaeological record as "cultural modes that were casually transmitted through unknown processes of secondary diffusion" (Williams and Brain 1983:409). In other words, we cannot point confidently at evidence that defines either the contact situation or the relations between the cultures. On the other hand, the cultural processes set in motion by the contact are fairly clear.

The first things transmitted seem to have been technological innovations: shell temper for pottery and probably the crucial Northern Flint maize. This category contains numerous items, including the hooded bottle form for seed storage and Mill Creek chert hoes, both found only north of the Coles Creek area. It is probably significant that utilitarian objects are *not* found further south. Braun and Plog (1982) have suggested that only as intercommunity bonds become strong do plain, utilitarian objects appear as items of exchange. The presence of such items in the northern Yazoo thus implies that this area was part of the Mississippian sphere. The technological innovations that do appear in late Coles Creek are not objects but rather ideas and practices, implying influence at a high, "foreign diplomacy" level.

Of course, the most important transmission may have been the Northern Flint maize strain. It is hard to imagine why a society that had it would want to share it, since the strain conferred so much productive advantage. Two possible explanations present themselves. First, Cahokia and its dependencies were not in direct competition with Coles Creek: at this point of contact each floodplain basin was sufficient unto its own chiefdom, apparently. Second, help from Cahokia may not have been necessary; the strain was developed in Mexico or the Southwest, and the Coles Creek peoples could have obtained it for themselves through Caddoan peoples to the west, whose pottery is sometimes found on Coles Creek sites (Neuman 1984).

Still-sparse data from the Big Black River valley, between the southern Yazoo Basin and the Natchez Bluffs, seem to reflect some of these changes. New studies of old excavation data (Shaffer and Steponaitis 1983) and recent fieldwork (Lorenz 1990) are revealing a sequence that clearly demonstrates Coles Creek origins as early as A.D. 1000, increasingly overlaid by Mississippian influences. The patterns are particularly interesting because they show lesser centralization at any period than obtained to north and south and *increasing* egalitarianism over time, expressed in a decrease in both the quantity and the quality of grave goods. In fact, Shaffer and Steponaitis have suggested that the Big Black region, cut off from significant participation in regional trade networks by the influences of larger centers in neighboring regions, may have

Table 2.1 Coles Creek and Mississippian Culture Traits (after Brain n.d.).

	Coles Creek	Mississippian
Subsistence	Corn-based swidden agriculture	Corn-bean-squash intensive agriculture
Settlement Pattern	Dispersed around many subregional small and vacant ceremonial centers approximately equal in size	Nucleated around large mound sites, one of which is larger than the others, located at the most strategic point within the region and clearly dominant
Site Plan	Several small mounds around plaza	One focal mound emphasized over all the rest, sometimes multiple plazas
Religion	Ancestor worship (?) focused on charnel house	Sun worship (?) focused on temple
Mortuary Practices	Charnel house processing of all ages/sexes and disposed of equally with no grave goods in common feature	Individual interment with grave goods of selected portion of population in various features according to ranking or other social criteria
Social System	Little apparent ranking although probably socio-religious leaders	Definite social hierarchy evident in burials and symbolized by the great focal mounds at the dominant sites
Economics	Internal exchange	Broad interregional trade and interaction
Material Culture	Few artifact classes; pottery displays highly formalized decorative intent with simple repetitive designs and limited range of shapes and sizes with only modal distinctions between fine and utilitarian wares	Great diversity of artifacts, exotic trade goods; pottery exhibits a wide range of designs, shapes, and sizes with strong typological dichotomy between utilitarian and fine wares

progressed steadily into backwater status as neighbors increased their political complexity. Certainly both this evidence from older excavations and Lorenz's recent fieldwork suggest that such centralized organization as existed along the Big Black was modest at best.

The contact that produced the thoroughgoing change in Coles Creek that resulted in the distinctive Plaquemine culture took place well after the initial contact, during the period of "ecumene" when the Mississippian adaptation was becoming naturalized across the Southeast. In the Natchez Bluffs region the Anna phase and site are the classic reflection of this influence. Coles Creek pottery, which had been characterized by a fairly sober decorative tradition, was quickly transformed to the eclectic and exuberant decoration of Plaquemine types – yet the underlying ceramic technology, tempering with grog (crushed pottery), remained essentially unchanged and partook very little of the Mississippian shell-temper revolution (Steponaitis 1974:196–97, 1981). The most striking changes, as Brain (n.d.) has noted, seem to have been born in a contact context in which the medium of exchange was *ideas*. Thus the complex of changes reflected in the archaeological evidence – marked increase in the size of one mound over others at a center, growth in the size and complexity (though not population) of mound centers, orientation of those centers to the main channel of the Mississippi, nucleation of settlement pattern, and development of site hierarchies – suggest rather drastic sociopolitical change.

The Plaquemine peoples were obviously the same as those of Coles Creek, and the transition was clearly evolutionary, if rapid, but no one has offered an explanation beyond the old ones of invasion or conversion. The process of "peer polity interaction" – supposed to foster a degree of competition and thus a leveling of complexity (Renfrew and Cherry 1986) – might be a useful model, however, especially given the existing centralization of Coles Creek culture. Perhaps it is more to the point to wonder why the Coles Creek people waited to participate fully in the Mississippian ecumene, as their concentration on the main channel of the Mississippi suggests they chose to do as Plaqueminians. Full commitment to agriculture means commitment to hard work in a demanding cycle. Perhaps the Coles Creek people did not turn to it until demographic pressures forced them to, and those same demographic pressures would argue strongly for the same sociopolitical mechanisms that the Mississippian culture probably developed for the same reason.

The picture will not stay so unified as more archaeological evidence emerges to decrease the impression of uniformity during the Coles Creek period (cf. Belmont and Gibson 1988). The large-scale impression of social change will doubtless remain stable, but researchers may be able to say something about the timing and locus of the first changes, and hence come closer to the causes. There may be some justification for invoking Mary Helms's (1979) model, developed for modest Panamanian chiefdoms in long-distance contact with more complex political entities to the south through their elites' quest for esoteric knowledge. This model views the recipient elites as benefiting locally from a cognitive "good," much as Braun and Plog (1982) see big-men as benefiting from their ability to call upon material goods from long-distance allies. Perhaps elites learned to manage large agricultural populations under the guise of the study of other esoteric knowledge.

However the Mississippian influence was transmitted, it seems to have affected sociopolitical organization and then to have exerted additional influence only gradually. Plaquemine culture, like Coles Creek before it, developed in its own way. In the southern Yazoo Basin it was displaced by full Mississippian development of the populations, and this development led to further interaction between Plaqueminians to the south and Mississippianized neighbors and also to the adoption, during the Foster phase, of additional Mississippian practices such as burial with grave goods. At the same time, the contracting sphere of Plaquemine influence led to a change in the orientation of construction toward sites located away from the Mississippi, looking to inland routes such as the Natchez Trace and the eastern trail to the Mobile delta. By the Emerald phase, the centers on the river were altogether abandoned, and political and religious activity had a regional focus (Steponaitis 1974; Brain 1978a).

Other areas of Plaquemine tradition apparently lie to the east, most as yet little known. A major multiple-mound site is situated due east of Natchez on the Pearl River, with possible subsidiary single-mound sites in its vicinity. This site has strong Late Archaic and Woodland components beneath its unbroken Coles Creek–Plaquemine sequence, but it shows no evidence of historic-period occupation (Mann 1988; T. Mooney, pers. comm. 1993). Survey further east, on the upper western tributaries of the Leaf River, has shown possible Plaquemine farmsteads, probably connected with the major Pearl River site. The often-mentioned but not yet located Pascagoula delta mound center may have connections to the Plaquemine region as well, though its primary link will probably be to the traditions of Mobile Bay (Knight 1984). Evidence of Coles Creek and Plaquemine ceramics on probable shellfish-collection sites east of Pascagoula Bay (Marshall 1982) suggests that far-reaching linkages along the Gulf coast were possible.

The question of what would have happened had Mississippian culture expanded its influence further south remains moot (although Jenkins and Krause [1986], for example, think it had run out of steam in any case). The Plaquemine culture maintained its independence and participated only marginally if at all in the Southeastern Ceremonial Complex – a late prehistoric assemblage of decorative motifs, artifacts, and practices found in mature Mississippian contexts across the Southeast (Waring 1968; Galloway 1989c). Although European disease and European influence caused changes that disrupted existing developments totally, Plaquemine chiefdoms, though reduced in size, survived into the protohistoric period at least – even later in the case of the Natchez. Ironically, the Natchez heirs of the Plaquemine culture survived to become the most well-documented southeastern chiefdom and thus retrospectively (and probably erroneously) the most frequently used window through which Mississippian societies are seen.

Unfortunately, the evidence for what happened along the Gulf coast during the Late Woodland through Late Mississippian periods is both slight and relatively unsynthesized. The region was clearly exploited for its marine foodstuffs from an early date, but settlement on the littoral may never have been as significant as it apparently became along the rivers that emptied into Mississippi Sound. The traditions of the lower Mississippi Valley also evidently mingled with those of west Florida and the Mobile Bay region along this same coast, but survey coverage is not yet adequate to provide any precise idea of where each tradition left off, though preliminary suggestions have been made (Weinstein 1987).

Knight (1984) has argued that the Moundville-related late prehistoric Pensacola complex, centered on Mobile Bay, stretched in several variants from Pensacola Bay in the east to the Louisiana delta region in the west. Discussions of this complex date back more than eighty years, but good definitions of the variants and their developmental sequences are still lacking, although the work of Stowe and Fuller on the Mobile Bay sequence is beginning to clarify the Pensacola variant proper. But for the coast to the west of Mobile Bay, very few sites are known other than some shell midden accumulations on the barrier islands and the shore; Davis (1984a:223) has suggested that the Pensacola complex is in fact confined to estuarine and deltaic environments within twenty to thirty miles of the coast. Nor do we know the extent to which horticulture and sedentary settlement characterized these cultures through the Mississippian period, but early historic contact narratives suggest that shore sites were mostly devoted to gathering activities, with more permanent sites at the heads of the Pearl and Pascagoula river deltas and on the back of Biloxi Bay. The population thus supported was less dense than in the major river floodplains, and its social organization was probably more fluid.

ORIGIN OF MOUNDVILLIANS

The Tombigbee Valley was not rich enough to attract or support populations as large as that of its neighbor to the west, but its populations were not necessarily less influenced by generalized cultural developments in the region. In this valley there is also evidence of the influence of a Hopewell "interaction sphere," although, apart from the "Copena" culture of the Tennessee Valley to the north with its funerary copper and galena, this influence was far less spectacular than it had been in the Mississippi Valley, and toward the end of the Woodland period it was replaced by that of the vigorous Weeden Island culture of northern Florida.

Again, regional variations were localized to different watersheds. These cultural boundaries remained fairly clear-cut throughout the period of interest, defining the following regions: the upper Tombigbee River valley, from the confluence with the Black Warrior River northward, including connections with the upper end of the Natchez Trace overland route; the Black Warrior and Cahaba Valleys, although for some purposes these two were separated also; the Alabama River valley from the Coosa-Tallapoosa confluence to its confluence with the Tombigbee; and the lower Tombigbee Valley, including the Mobile Bay and delta. Each region had advantages and disadvantages that shaped its human settlement.

The upper Tombigbee region in the Woodland period was the home of the Miller culture, characterized by grog-tempered pottery, mound burials, and a rapidly growing population. Early development of the culture apparently took place near the Natchez Trace and was characterized by a use of copper and galena, imported pottery, and specially prepared burial pits beneath mounds, that suggest connections with Hopewell and with the Marksville traditions of the Mississippi. The settlement pattern is bimodal, showing large "base camps" or villages and smaller transitory camps, possibly reflected in the two Gainesville and Cofferdam phases as originally defined by Jenkins (1981). As the Miller culture developed over time, however, it acquired its own peculiarities. Blessed by an exploding population, Miller III peoples apparently ceased construction of burial mounds to practice cremation and the use of charnel houses (Walthall 1980:154–55). Variations in burial practice may indicate some differentiation in status among certain mature males. Apart from this mortuary differentiation, general similarities in pattern to the Lower Mississippi Valley Baytown-period phases are striking.

In the Black Warrior–Cahaba region there was apparently little occupation before the late Woodland West Jefferson phase. Welch (1980, 1990) has argued convincingly that West Jefferson peoples were following a seasonal schedule that included floodplain villages for the late spring–early fall period at least in the Black Warrior Valley, with smaller hunting camps for the winter season; population was thinner year-round in the Cahaba region. Gardening was carried on in the vicinity of the near-permanent floodplain villages. Circular structures surrounded by storage pits made up these villages, but, notwithstanding some evidence for corn, collected foods were dominant (Jenkins 1976). The lack of evidence for any sort of distinction in rank suggests wholly egalitarian tribal organization.

Woodland populations along the Alabama River seem to have been affected by tides of influence from the east and south; the later Woodland-period peoples were clearly in communication with the Weeden Island culture through the peoples of the Chattahoochee region to the south and east, but influence also came from Mobile Bay and even the upper Tombigbee. Yet the Alabama River region would become depopulated at the end of the Woodland period and remain so until late Mississippian or protohistoric times (Jenkins and Paglione 1982).

The Mobile Bay region saw a mixture of cultures from north, east, and west during the Woodland period. The early Woodland Porter phase showed participation in the Hopewell complex through copper panpipes and ear spools found in burial mounds, but the region was as much a crossroads for trade in exotic goods – shell and mineral resources – as it was the terminus for consumption of Hopewell objects. Porter groups processed the bodies of their dead before burial and sometimes buried them within their villages, which could be more sedentary than those of other hunters because they had the advantage of aquatic resources year-round. The Mobile Bay region also felt the powerful influence of the Weeden Island culture of Florida, however, resulting in the McLeod and Tate's Hammock phases, with even more varied burial practices and the addition of stamped decoration to the sandy Porter ceramic wares (Trickey 1958; Trickey and Holmes 1971).

The "Emergent Mississippian" transition from these Woodland cultures was not uniform over the region, nor did it lead to a uniform "Mississippianized" cultural tradition. As in the Mississippi Valley, the question of agriculture or increasing complexity of social organization as a triggering force has long lain moot. Jenkins (1976) and Walthall (1980) first suggested that in the Late Woodland period McKelvey peoples abandoned the Pickwick Basin of the Tennessee River and moved south into the Warrior and Cahaba Basins, where they became the West Jefferson peoples, carrying Mississippian influences with them. Since then, however, increased survey in the Tombigbee Valley and particularly Jenkins's more recent work has suggested a continuity of ceramic tradition in the Black Warrior Valley, with the late Miller culture of the Tombigbee resulting from a probable in-migration of Miller peoples (Jenkins 1981; Jenkins and Krause 1986). Even more recently, Atkinson (1986) has recognized a West Jefferson–like phase in the northern Tombigbee Valley, implying that at least in some areas the transition to West Jefferson was made before movement onto the Warrior.

But this answer to the source of the West Jefferson population of the Warrior-Cahaba does not answer the question of how their culture metamorphosed into Moundville I. Welch (1990) has shown that this problem hinges on the assumed priority of agriculture or political organization in the "chiefdomization" of a culture. Drawing on the work of Margaret Scarry, he argued that, in the Warrior and Cahaba Valleys, West Jefferson culture had managed to develop a strong horticultural settlement basis *before* the social stratification of the early Bessemer and Moundville I chiefdoms appeared on the scene, so there is no question of "proto-Mississippians" migrating in. Scarry's (1980a, 1986) study of plant remains from West Jefferson and Moundville I phases had demonstrated that the transition to maize agriculture preceded the change to chiefdom social organization. She maintained that under population pressure the already diversified West Jefferson procurement strategies could only be intensified, and that the only strategy that could be profitably intensified was agriculture. As in the Mississippi Valley, this change had to be permanent, since the clearing of the floodplains and the occupation of the people with agriculture altered both the ecological setting and the seasonal schedule of food procurement activities in an irreversible way (see Cronon 1983).

The Emergent Mississippian transition was gradual in all cases, but the resultant more intensively agricultural cultures, maintaining continuity with the underlying Woodland traditions, varied through the region. The lower Alabama River region, where the river passes through the Central Hills physiographic zone – a crossroads of influences during the Woodland period – was apparently abandoned; we know of no sites for the early Mississippian period. Apparently Larson's (1980) argument – that the floodplains of rivers crossing the greater Gulf Coastal Plain were in general not broad enough or rich enough to support intensive agriculture – applies here, with the further qualification that this portion of the Alabama was isolated from both the rich resources of the Mobile delta and the ecotone resources of regions further to the north. At any rate, modern surveys have demonstrated that the lack of sites is real (Jeter 1977; Jenkins and Paglione 1982; Chase 1982). The westward extension of the same zone in modern-day Mississippi was also virtually empty of significant permanent settlement during the period.

Two developments occurred in the more northerly regions where floodplain resources combined with the ecotone resources of neighboring upland forests. Welch's (1990) analysis of the transition in the Warrior/Cahaba and upper Tombigbee drainages uses settlement pattern, subsistence, and mortuary evidence to show that the elements involved in the transition were ordered differently in the two regions. In the Warrior/Cahaba region, the intensification of agriculture preceded sociopolitical changes by enough of a margin to be noticeable. The first flourishing was probably on the Warrior, where the loci of perhaps five large West Jefferson floodplain villages apparently evolved *in situ* into the single-mound centers of the Moundville I phase. At Moundville itself this first single mound may have been constructed where the West Jefferson village had been located (Steponaitis 1980). A similar process took place on the Cahaba, where West Jefferson evolved into the manifestation seen at the Bessemer site, a multiple-mound site that seems contemporary with the Moundville I phase (DeJarnette and Wimberly 1941; Walthall 1980:209–10). In both cases the population concentrations, which had occurred at least seasonally, reversed themselves and evolved into the dispersed ceremonial center–farmstead–hamlet arrangement characteristic of Mississippian agriculture. In both cases also, Welch argues, the social formation of these initial simple chiefdoms was characterized by the addition, under external political pressures, of political functions and prerogatives to the activities of a priestly figure. Mortuary evidence from both Moundville and other sites confirms that at least one elite level was distinguished from the rest of the population during the Moundville I phase (Peebles 1979a).

A contrasting process eventuated in the emergence of the Summerville phase from the Miller tradition on the upper Tombigbee. Evidence of some social differentiation on the big-man model exists as early as the late Miller phases. According to Welch (1990), the serious subsistence stress evident in the changes in subsistence patterns on Miller III archaeological sites of the Gainesville/Cofferdam phases may well have sanctified as chiefs those political leaders who were able to take advantage of horticultural innovations being introduced by their neighbors. In any case, it seems that social differentiation did precede adoption of maize agriculture on a large scale. The Summerville I phase, which in many locations developed on or near Miller III sites, represents a clear-cut and substantial shift to maize agriculture, resulting in improved health in its populations. Early Summerville sites show single mounds, suggesting the corporate labor characteristic of nonegalitarian social organization; in at least one case (Blitz 1983) the mound was built atop the site of a domestic complex, suggesting the sanctification of a secular leader.

Excavations at the Lyon's Bluff site in the early 1970s revealed a sequence that began with the early Mississippian Tibbee Creek phase, dated to ca. 1100–1150, leaving the precedent cultural factors unknown (Marshall 1977, 1986). Apart from the pottery evidence little is known of this phase at Lyon's Bluff, but early development here was probably very similar to the Summerville I phase developments, since the later phases (Sorrells and Summerville III) are so similar. Certainly the mound at Lyon's Bluff was built in more than one stage (Galloway n.d.c), but as yet the overall development of the site is unclear.

We do not know how early the "Mississippianization" of the Mobile delta region began, probably because there was little subsistence stress to induce its residents to intensify agricultural activity. The complex broad Tombigbee/Alabama delta and the estuarine resources of Mobile Bay are richer in natural food sources than many parts of the Mississippi Valley, in spite of the lack of migratory bird routes, and the delta region supported large populations in the Woodland and Mississippian periods. Curren (1976) has examined the issue of subsistence for this area, highlighting the Woodland and Mississippian periods. He detected a single general pattern of increasing emphasis on agriculture and a corresponding concentration of population toward the delta region over time. The pattern also included a considerable emphasis on the collection of marine resources, both shellfish and vertebrates, throughout the Mississippian period. This argument implies that factors other than subsistence stress were responsible for the evolution of a chiefdom in the region. Knight's (1984) recent amendments to Curren's scheme do not alter this conclusion.

Stowe and Fuller argue that the Bottle Creek chiefdom, centered on an elaborate multiple-mound site in the Mobile delta, was a late development, beginning after 1200 (Stowe 1985; Fuller 1985; Fuller and Stowe 1982). No earlier significant Late Woodland or Emergent Mississippian occupation has been discovered, although more evidence may yet appear for these periods as research proceeds at the site (Brown and Fuller 1992:58). Stowe cites evidence of associations of Moundville I ceramic types with Late Woodland types from these phases at saline sites to suggest that the development of an agricultural chiefdom was delayed in the region until the middle of the Mississippian period. The area was emphatically not depopulated, however; rather, the peoples of the Mobile Bay and delta simply elaborated their collecting strategies – perhaps even providing salt, shell, or dried foodstuffs to the inland chiefdoms. The very presence of such chiefdoms may have provided a spur to the development of chiefly power in the delta through control of such trade (see Frankenstein and Rowlands 1978; Renfrew and Cherry 1986).

Once the transition to agriculture as a primary ingredient in the subsistence base and to chiefdom organization as a social mode had been completed, developments in the Tombigbee Valley continued in the direction of "more of the same": the development of a mature Mississippian culture complete with field agriculture and a multi-level chiefdom on the Black Warrior and, later, in the Mobile delta. On the upper Tombigbee, with its slightly less rich resources, apparently independent and more modest two-level chiefdoms developed.

The emergent Mississippian Summerville and Lyon's Bluff sequence communities of the upper Tombigbee probably developed fully into small simple chiefdoms. The Lyon's Bluff site, located near the juncture of two Tombigbee tributaries, is a mound site for which Marshall (1977) has defined three Mississippian phases ranging from A.D. 1100 to the protohistoric period; the mature Mississippian Lyon's Bluff phase is characterized by pottery very similar to Moundville types but apparently locally made. The site is very large at its greatest extent and includes a village situated across a plaza from the mound as well as a number of outlying hamlets and farmsteads, such as the Tibbee Creek site's latest component (O'Hear et al. 1981) and the Mississippian occupation at the Kellogg site (Atkinson, Phillips, and Walling 1980; see also Solis and Walling 1982). O'Hear (pers. comm. 1986) feels that the political as well as the cultural connections with Moundville may have been quite strong.

The Lubbub Creek Archaeological Locality, or simply the Lubbub site, is perhaps the most extensively excavated single-mound site in the Southeast. The site has a long history, and its mound precinct began as a domestic compound toward the end of the tenth century, probably built by Late Woodland Miller III people (Blitz 1983, 1993). With the transition to agriculture, the Woodland village at Lubbub developed into a single-mound ceremonial center of the Moundville-related Summerville I phase. Fortified early in its development, later the site expanded and fortification was no longer needed; Peebles (1983a) has surmised that this may have been because it fell under the Moundville sphere of influence and stability – its "ecumene" in Mississippi Valley terms. At any rate, the Summerville II and III phases at Lubbub reflect strong Moundville ceramic influence. An elite that enjoyed preferential treatment with regard to food supply and burial honors was associated with the mounds at the Lubbub site, and the health of the general population was good (Peebles 1983a).

The development of the Mississippian community at the Moundville site itself is certainly among the best understood in the Southeast. Through careful study of the site's ceramics and their distribution, Steponaitis (1980, 1983) has established the sequence of development at Moundville itself, while Peebles (1978), Bozeman (1980), and Steponaitis (1978) have studied the expanded context of the Moundville chiefdom on the Black Warrior River.

During the Moundville II–III phases the development of the site proceeded apace.

Although at first the resident population declined, those settled in the hinterland grew in number (Steponaitis 1991). Increasing numbers of burials at Moundville point to its growing ritual importance, and patterns of artifact distribution on the site suggest a development of craft specializations over time. Massive public works projects were undertaken, of course, as mounds were built throughout the periods. Already in Moundville II the site was a major political and ceremonial center, and its importance increased during Moundville III, when the total number of mounds was brought to twenty. Regionally, the development of an apparent Moundville hegemony was carried to completion. Survey in the Black Warrior Valley has shown that Moundville phase sites appeared earlier in the north than in the south of the valley (Bozeman 1980), and at first the Moundville site was but one of several early single-mound centers. It must have enjoyed significant advantage, however, for by about A.D. 1100 it had begun to show more elaborate development than the other centers, and by 1200 the other centers were clearly subordinate to Moundville.

Steponaitis's application of locational analysis to the Moundville chiefdom has pointed out some aspects of Mississippian settlement patterns crucial to a general understanding of complex chiefdoms. His analysis is of particular importance for the region because of the relative richness of the Moundville data. "Complex chiefdoms are usually organized according to a principle wherein a higher-ranking chief has control over a number of lower-ranking chiefs, each of whom, in turn, directly controls a certain territorial district or social unit. . . . What is important . . . is that different nodes in the political hierarchy are usually associated with spatially discrete (and archaeologically recognizable) central settlements" (Steponaitis 1978:420–21). Once a near-complete survey of the Black Warrior Valley had been carried out (Bozeman 1980), researchers could draw several conclusions from such an analysis.

An important principle of spatial patterning is based on the relation of centers to one another. Lower-order centers, because their authority is based on division of land and the makeup of the community of their hinterlands, do not compete with one another and therefore do not need any particular spatial relationship to one another. More important is their relation to the paramount center, since tribute flows from them to the paramount and information and prestige goods to them from the paramount (Welch 1991). Steponaitis has argued effectively that these flows of tribute and prestige goods offered considerable incentive to locate lower-order centers efficiently with relation to the paramount center: lower-order centers were located not at the demographic center of their districts but relatively near the paramount center while remaining within their districts. Similarly, the paramount center was near the "center of gravity" of the cluster of minor centers. Although data on the hamlets and farmsteads that were actually the productive units of the chiefdom are limited, the relation of these smaller units to their centers may have been governed by another kind of locational efficiency: one that favored a reduction of the labor required to reach farmland (Peebles 1978).

In the case of Moundville, this settlement system model for the Moundville III phase suggests the structure of the chiefdom. The single paramount center, Moundville, was located roughly in the center of the agriculturally favorable part of the valley (Peebles 1978). Six other centers, each having a single mound, were clustered near Moundville or were strung out along the river (Peebles 1987:9). The former sites, Steponaitis (1978) argued, were linked to the capital by land, while the latter probably communicated by river. Most of the population, however, lived in dispersed hamlets and farmsteads.

The ranking of the citizens of Moundville's chiefdom, as demonstrated by burial goods, confirms what the spatial pattern suggests. Two offices are indicated at Moundville by the presence of copper "symbol badges" of nonlocal origin and of paraphernalia connected with body paint. Burials of persons so accompanied took place in or near the mounds themselves, and the patterns of accompaniment respected neither sex nor age, implying that these people held their rank by virtue of birth. Other dwellers at Moundville, buried primarily in cemetery areas, were variously accompanied according to age and sex, suggesting that their relative importance was based upon their achievements. At the minor centers, no burials included copper "symbol badges." Burials in the mound at these sites apparently reflected a single lineage of secondary chiefs, one whose accompaniment by mineral paints and stone palettes implies that these secondary-level leaders bore some ceremonial task connected with their office.

If Fuller and Stowe (1982) are correct, the gradual intensification of agriculture in the Mobile Bay and delta region eventuated in a chiefdom organization around A.D. 1200 at Bottle Creek, the largest Mississippian mound site known along the Gulf coast. Clearly, however, the culture represented by the Bottle Creek phase of the Pensacola culture still depended strongly upon marine vertebrates and shellfish for subsistence, as attested by the large number of shell and fish-bone middens with Bottle Creek style artifacts along the Gulf coast and Mobile Bay (Holmes 1963:26). Curren's (1976) suggestion that such collection activities may have been seasonal – amplified by Knight's (1984:214) assertion that they may have been more limited during the preceding period – is quite likely to be correct, since the majority of mound centers belonging to the phase are located further inland, in river floodplain agricultural areas (Stowe 1985).

The Bottle Creek phase certainly has some links to Moundville, but it is also a distinct cultural entity. The characteristic Pensacola pottery series shares some features with the Moundville series, but many of these, particularly the curvilinear incised decorative motifs, mark a broad temporal and spatial horizon that includes the pottery of the Plaquemine phase of the Lower Mississippi Valley (Fuller and Stowe 1982). This "horizon style" of motifs may be significant in interpreting the history of interaction between the regions.

The Bottle Creek chiefdom was in a geographical position to dominate the salines of the lower Tombigbee, and pottery found at these salines suggests that it did so (Curren 1982a). There has been much discussion of salt as a dietary resource in prehistoric agricultural communities (Brown 1980), and it was clearly in great demand at least protohistorically, so these salines were likely an advantage to the people who dominated them. We do not know whether Bottle Creek was the arbiter of the Tombigbee-Alabama salt trade (Brown and Fuller 1992:38), but seasonal gatherings of people to manufacture salt may have been the kind of occasion for asserting solidarity that led to the formation of a ceremonial center in the region.

The Tombigbee region thus boasted at least two important chiefdoms during the Mississippian period, and the evidence of interaction at both Moundville and Bottle Creek implies that cooperation between them could have given each one access to the other's relationships over a wider area. A sort of Moundville–Bottle Creek axis of peaceful interaction apparently existed, to which the "domestic" and "foreign" relationships of the two chiefdoms contributed.

The connections between Moundville and the Summerville and Lyon's Bluff peoples of the upper Tombigbee led to an extended network of communication westward to the Mississippi. The reasons for the attraction of western contacts are now not so obvious as they seemed when Mississippian missionaries or conquerors were thought to be the source and fount of all Mississippian development. Clearly, however, there had been contact westward to the Mississippi before the Mississippian period. Pottery vessels such as the indigenous wares of the Walls and Nodena sites on the Mississippi, found at Lyon's Bluff and Moundville, are evidence that such contact continued through the Mississippian period; Peebles (1978:411) has pointed out the convenience of the Alabama-Chickasaw trail to Moundville-phase sites (see figure 2.3). Sites certainly traded in high-status goods, but the precise patterns remain to be defined. Indispensable to these western contacts were the relatively autonomous simple chiefdoms located west of Moundville on the Tombigbee and its tributaries; perhaps not only distance but also usefulness allowed the western groups to maintain their independence.

That the relationship between Moundville and Bottle Creek was long-term suggests that it was advantageous for both groups. One of the most famous ceramic artifacts from Moundville is in fact a specimen of the Pensacola Incised pottery characteristic of the Bottle Creek phase; the black-filmed Moundville ceramics are frequently found on Bottle Creek phase sites. The attractions of intercourse with the Bottle Creek chiefdom for Moundville are obvious in one respect, in that marine resources were at the command of the southern neighbor. Perhaps more significant, however, was Bottle Creek's access to coastal cultural traditions. To the east, communication with the Fort Walton culture of the West Florida coast may have had some ceremonial significance, but it more certainly offered connections with other coastal chiefdoms to the east and their trade in exotic shell.

Stowe and Fuller (1993) have noted similarities to Plaquemine pottery in the Pensacola types that characterize the Bottle Creek phase, but they have attributed these more to a Middle Mississippian horizon style than to any cultural connection. I would suggest, on the contrary, that a connection is possible. Though Knight (1984) and Stowe (1985) argue that the Pensacola culture extends along the coast westward from Mobile Bay to the mouth of the Mississippi, and some sites along the coast certainly yield ample coarse shell-tempered pottery bearing some Pensacola motifs (Galloway n.d.a), this cultural adaptation is limited to the immediate coast. As discussed in the previous section, the inland Pascagoula forks–Leaf River region just west of Mobile Bay is Plaquemine country, and the probable Pascagoula River chiefdom would have been the first link in a westward connection with the Plaquemine chiefdoms of the Lower Mississippi Valley via the ancient inland trail paralleling the Gulf coast (Meyer 1928; Mann 1988; see figure 2.3).

Although the ascendancy and hegemony of the Moundville chiefdom dominated the Tombigbee Valley for nearly five hundred years, it ended in an unspectacular manner by simply ceasing to exist. The collapse was apparently not due to a failure of resources to support the population; in Peebles's (1983a:10) phrase, "It was the nonsubsistence sectors of the economy which went into a recession." The evidence of change in this sector is a drastically curtailed frequency of imported objects in burials. What followed was a large shift in population – from Moundville III farmsteads, hamlets, and ceremonial centers showing clear hierarchical arrangement to large villages bearing a culture labeled Alabama River and distributed equidistantly across the landscape.

The development at least began *in situ*. Not only Moundville but also several other Moundville-phase sites in the Warrior Valley have Alabama River components. Within the Warrior Valley, however, the cumulative Alabama River occupations are much smaller than those of Moundville III, and the evidence is strong for an outmigration into the Alabama River valley. Other evidence suggests that a parallel "decline" also overtook the Moundville-related small chiefdoms on the upper Tombigbee and Bottle Creek to the south, resulting respectively in the Sorrells, Summerville IV, and Bear Point phases, which exhibit many parallels to Alabama River and share some of its pottery styles (Marshall 1977; Solis and Walling 1982; Peebles 1983a; Stowe 1985).

These phases are largely those of the "Burial Urn Culture," a cultural manifestation noted as early as 1899 and studied in detail by Sheldon (1974), who clearly defined these spatially distinct but culturally related groups on the basis of analysis of pottery types and settlement patterns. What is remarkable about this particular manifestation of the "Mississippian Decline" is that these people did not alter in any way their mode of subsistence (Sheldon 1974:74); what they did alter was nearly everything else in their manner of living.

None of the Burial Urn peoples built substructural mounds, and most did not use existing ones. They accorded extra burial ceremony to few. They did not accumulate exotic durable goods, nor did they support specialists who made them. Remaining as agriculturists, they distributed themselves differently over the land and entered for the first time some more modest river valleys. In short, they abandoned the complexity and cost of chiefdom-level social organization and returned to a tribal system. In the process they developed, probably before the first out-migration from Moundville, the distinctive urn burial of infants or disarticulated adults from the Moundville practice of burial with inverted vessel (see Sheldon 1974:54).

Sheldon (1974:43–49) has demonstrated the overwhelming evidence for the development of Alabama River phase ceramics from those of Moundville, particularly the "domestic or non-ceremonial" ceramic assemblage. Although he postulated a distinct if brief decline period between the final Moundville phase and Alabama River, subsequent research has ignored such a distinction (e.g., Peebles 1986), and Sheldon (1974:79) himself emphasized the complexity of the process: "the Moundville-Proto-historic transition cannot be characterized as a simple declining or reducing cultural tradition, but rather as a series of interrelated processes in which some traits and practices disappear altogether while others are retained with essentially little modification." This process needs examination in more detail for the Burial Urn cultures because of their immediate relevance to the topic at hand; these, it seems, were Western Muskogeans, among whom would be found the largest number of the proto-Choctaws.

Attribution of historic tribal identifications to the Burial Urn peoples has been popular since the beginning: Brannon (1935:234) thought the Alabamas were the best candidates; Cottier (1970:7–8) identified his Alabama River phase with the Alabamas and Mobilians; Sheldon (1974:120) equated the Burial Urn culture with "certain historic Muskogean speakers (i.e., Alabama, Mobile, Tohomé, etc.)." At this point in my argument I have little reason to designate the successor cultures to the Moundville-Pensacola axis by anything other than archaeological phase names. What they called themselves during this era is unknown, and the upheavals caused by

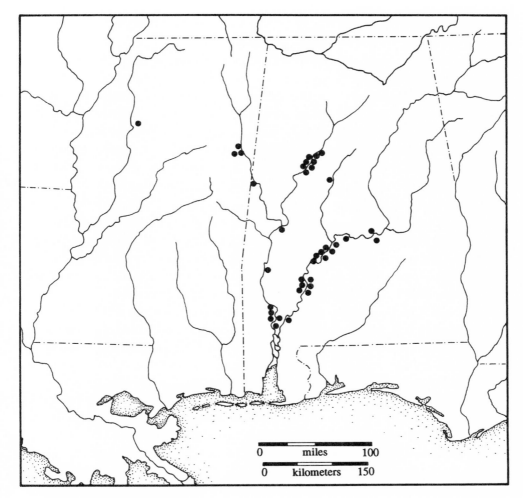

2.5. Sites with burial urn evidence.

European contact, which took place before the emergence of names known to history, have to be taken into account as the second major ingredient in historic tribe formation in this region.

Instead, we should examine briefly the alterations that have been made in Sheldon's site distributions by the archaeological work of the intervening time (figure 2.5). The main clusters of Burial Urn evidence have remained as Sheldon defined them, although Curren and his colleagues have amplified the site inventory for these areas (Curren 1984b): on the Alabama River between its Tallapoosa and Tombigbee junctions, on the lower Tombigbee above its junction with the Alabama, and on the Black Warrior.

Nevertheless, scattered additional evidence on the upper Tombigbee has suggested the presence of a related development on late Sorrells/Mhoon phase and

Summerville IV phase sites (Marshall 1977, 1986; Atkinson 1979; Solis and Walling 1982; Albright 1983), which seem in some cases to demonstrate fairly undisturbed evolution from the phases that preceded them. At former mound sites (Lyon's Bluff, Lubbub), however, the Burial Urn phase was the terminal one. Johnson and Sparks (1986) have argued effectively that the phases equivalent to Alabama River on the upper Tombigbee represented a significant shift in settlement pattern (to upland prairie and smaller sites) and perhaps in subsistence strategies also (increased emphasis on hunting), and that this shift took place well before the Hernando de Soto expedition in 1540. Furthermore, additional evidence discovered by several other researchers is beginning to suggest that such a pattern may mark a good deal of the Black Prairie region in Mississippi and Alabama, linking the predecessor cultures to historic Chakchiuma, Chickasaw, and Alabama in a single continuum (Johnson, pers. comm. 1989). This argument is persuasive and fits well with the model advanced here for the Alabama region. As additional support, new evidence presented by Sheldon and Jenkins (1986) shows that the characteristic elements of the Alabama River phase pottery decoration were introduced from the central Mississippi Valley into the western Summerville III and Sorrells phase assemblages by 1450–1500. These elements are "rare or virtually nonexistent at the site of Moundville itself" (Sheldon and Jenkins 1986:100), which suggests to these researchers that the development of the Alabama River phase took place *after* the collapse of Moundville.

Despite theoretical differences, Curren's work makes an important contribution to the current study by elucidating the details of cultural alteration from Moundville III to Alabama River. He shows that the variety of burial practices of Moundville III was replaced by extended processing of remains to arrive at defleshed bundles of bones, which were frequently, in the case of children, placed in ceramic containers; elaborate grave goods were rarely used (Curren 1984a). Skeletal evidence suggests a higher level of nutritional stress than for the Mississippian period. In addition, settlement patterns favored large villages without mounds. These conclusions, coming from newly excavated sites on the Black Warrior and elsewhere, confirm most of Sheldon's ideas about process.

Further details have also been forthcoming about the transition the Pensacola culture made on the Mobile Bay and delta from the Bottle Creek to the Bear Point phase, thanks to the work of Stowe and Fuller. Fuller's (1985) characterization of the most recent work to establish more securely the chronology of the Bear Point phase points to a newly defined "Ginhouse Mortuary Complex" of several Burial Urn sites in the Mobile delta, with a possible geographical spread to Biloxi and Choctawhatchee Bay on the Gulf coast and northward into the lower Tombigbee and Alabama Valleys. Defined on the basis of a site (Pine Log Creek) with sixteenth-century

European trade goods, the Bear Point phase still awaits description of a clear sequence of development from the Bottle Creek phase.

TRIBE-CHIEFDOM CYCLES AND THE CORE CHOCTAW POPULATION

The Mississippi and Tombigbee/Mobile drainages obviously had entirely different scales of resource availability; the preceding outlines of prehistoric social evolution in the two regions demonstrate that such variation in resources could lead to differing paces of development and even to differing cultural textures. Theories of social evolution from tribe to chiefdom and the presumed material correlates of that process through the Mississippian period have been examined in both regions. Now it is time to delve into theories of sociopolitical *devolution* in order to understand the processes that underlay the release of populations from chiefdom hegemony.

Friedman (1975:186) defines devolution as "the structural transformation that occurs when a social formation reproduces itself in continually deteriorating conditions of production." Conventional evolutionary theory has long held that the chiefdom as a form of sociopolitical organization is inherently unstable. Whether it is viewed as the most integrated end of the tribal continuum (Sahlins 1968) or a developmental stage in its own right (Service 1971b), the chiefdom is seen as more or less transitional, the culmination of kin-based political systems, between tribal and state societies. Because special circumstances – namely, sufficient resources to support intensification of production – seem to be required to cross the threshold into state organization, chiefdoms often fail to so develop. The Mississippian cultures, for which in many cases even the "natural energy subsidy" of their meander-belt environment (Smith 1978a:481) was not sufficient in the long term under the stress of agricultural production, apparently did not fulfill the requirements for further development. When resources fail, the pressures pushing chiefdoms toward greater complexity are equally likely to cause them to disintegrate, as Fried (1967:225) has pointed out for stratified societies.

Friedman (1975) has proposed that a cyclic progression from tribe to chiefdom and back to tribe is a function of population density and ecological options and constraints impinging on the long-term evolution along this tribal continuum, and that the cycle is normative under certain conditions. His arguments have not yet been transferred in detail to the Southeast, although Peebles (1978, 1986) has cited the applicability of Friedman's model, and John Scarry (1990) and Anderson (1990) have begun to examine archaeological evidence for such cycles in the region. If applied to the Mississippian case, this model would suggest that the symptoms of the "Mississippian Decline" would have appeared in most of the Mississippian chiefdoms sooner or later had the European intrusion not taken place, and that the cycle would have continued to operate until population and ecological parameters had drastically changed. To apply this model in the Southeast, however, we must first reconsider the likely result of the devolution of a southeastern chiefdom.

Several forms of tribal organization may have represented a developmental cycle. We should bear in mind, however, that a perfect developmental sequence may not exist in the real world; much depends upon the authority (Sahlins, Service) one chooses to follow. For the purposes of this discussion, I will follow Sahlins (1968) in viewing the social forms from segmentary tribe to chiefdom as a continuum with the single label "tribe," and will assume that this continuum can be viewed as either descriptive or developmental.

According to Sahlins (1968:29–32), one ideal type of the segmentary tribe can be found in what he terms "forest agriculturists": forest-dwelling peoples who practice slash-and-burn agriculture and seasonally scheduled gathering. They remain divided into hamlet or village segments because dispersed settlement is necessary to reserve sufficient land for fallowing while permitting the village to remain stationary. "Big-man" entrepreneurs organize production beyond household needs, persuading their supporters to produce a surplus in order to achieve political power through conspic-uous consumption. Although agriculturists of this kind survive today only in areas of tropical forest, many of the post-Mississippian peoples of the Southeast seem to fit this mold quite well, especially since it accounts for their dispersed settlement pattern.

At the other end of the tribal continuum is the chiefdom, characterized by a hierarchical system of ranking and authority capable of organizing large populations as political and productive subdivisions of a single integrative organization. Sahlins (1968:42–44) considers "intensive agriculture" to be one ecotype especially favoring chiefdom development through the need to organize people and resources. As Bruce Smith (1978a) has pointed out, Mississippian societies coalesced in the Southeast where agriculturists could benefit from the natural renewal of fertility through flood-ing. In this environment the Mississippian chiefdoms did apparently develop ranked societies and mechanisms of social control that permitted them to manage agricul-tural production, attain comfortable surpluses, and even support craft specialists.

An intermediate form could also exist between these two extremes. This modestly integrated form of society would have formalized kinship links from one settlement to another, and the heads of kinship groups might begin to gather to themselves and to their authority positions on a permanent basis the right to accumulate surplus not just for conspicuous consumption but for the long-term benefit of the lineage. Be-cause these lineage links extended beyond the individual village, leaders could orga-nize production regionally, so that each settlement would not have to maintain so much fallow land. This intermediate form would thus begin to look something like a "simple chiefdom" as discussed by Steponaitis (1978, 1983), with one modest center for the functions of lineage authority.

Thus I list three crude divisions of the tribal continuum suitable for agriculturists:

Segmentary tribe: organized on a local level by the activities of a big-man; loose supralocal integration through shared cultural features and infrequent pan-tribal ceremonialism;

Partial integration: beginning of integration beyond the local level through strengthened lineages, culminating in a "simple chiefdom";

Chiefdom: full hierarchical integration, depending upon ranked lineages; integration is centralized and frequently renewed through ceremonialism.

How might chiefdoms collapse or otherwise dissolve and what would happen to their institutions when they did? One obvious difference between Sahlins's two extreme examples of forest or swidden agriculturists and floodplain or intensive agriculturists is the carrying capacity of the lands they exploit. Peebles and Kus (1977) have pointed out that an increase in carrying capacity can result from social integration where such integration – for example, from loosely organized tribes toward hierarchical rank societies or chiefdoms – increases the efficiency of information processing within the society. Such an increase in efficiency permits a greater concentration of population in a region by increasing the efficiency of agricultural production. But what of the inverse?

Friedman (1975) has described in detail the process of intensification through which a tribe evolves to chiefdom organization and has created a dynamic model that takes into account the elements of population, available territory, and the technology of cultivation. The main features of this model are shown in figure 2.6. The reader will recognize in this model the very ecological constraints that Bruce Smith has described as the defining elements of the Mississippian adaptation. In addition, the principal crop supporting the development of chiefdoms in the Southeast, maize, is the staple crop that most quickly depletes the fertility of the land. Thus Mississippian chiefdoms in the Southeast could exhaust their options in several ways. Despite the benefits of annual flooding on soil fertility, and despite possible fertilization as posited by Dobyns (1983:214-44), exhaustion of the narrowly circumscribed soils most suitable for maize cultivation with stone technology would have been a major problem in many places, probably only partially solved by the late introduction of beans as a companion planting. And even if the soil were not exhausted, the depletion of forest resources – both wood and game – in the vicinity of settlements would likely become a serious problem in a few generations. With population growth inevitable under successful sedentary adaptation, these pressures could only become more severe.

All these problems could make a mature chiefdom unmanageable. Population

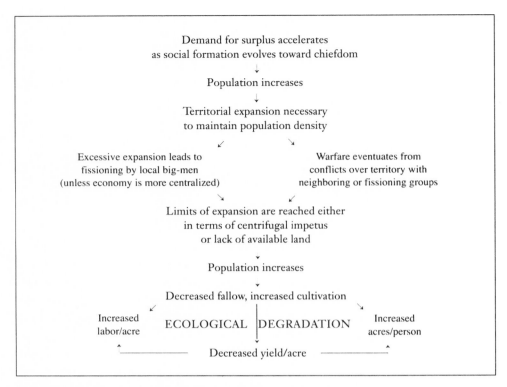

Demand for surplus accelerates
as social formation evolves toward chiefdom

↓

Population increases

↓

Territorial expansion necessary
to maintain population density

Excessive expansion leads to
fissioning by local big-men
(unless economy is more centralized)

Warfare eventuates from
conflicts over territory with
neighboring or fissioning groups

Limits of expansion are reached either
in terms of centrifugal impetus
or lack of available land

↓

Population increases

↓

Decreased fallow, increased cultivation

Increased
labor/acre

ECOLOGICAL DEGRADATION

Increased
acres/person

Decreased yield/acre

2.6. Chiefdom intensification (adapted from Friedman 1975:figure 9).

pressures would lead inevitably to environmental stress, which at some point would be more than a chiefdom with limited technology and without coercive powers could handle. When this vicious circle had intensified to the extent that food production failed to meet the requirements of the labor force, the system would collapse completely. First, however, with the decrease of the absolute surplus available to the chief to support his rank's privileges – and to support dealings with external trading partners and maintenance of internal ideological hegemony (cf. Parker-Pearson 1984) – the very system of ranking had to collapse. This would happen when the chief's demands on the surplus accelerated as the absolute surplus began to decelerate. Strain would accordingly enter into established relations of obligation, so that sub-chiefs would be motivated to revolt and repudiate the political hierarchy and its access to surplus. Such social fission would lead to population dispersal, easing the pressure on resources and beginning the cycle again.

Friedman's (1975) theory holds that this cycle could repeat itself many times, serving as a feedback system to restore ecological equilibrium. If the structure were held stable long enough at an excessive level of population density, however, or if it returned to this level often enough over time (for example, if long-term territorial expansion were halted, as was the Mississippian case given the limited areas of suitable environment), ecological degradation would become serious enough that changes in social structure and environment would be irreversible and would settle at the "devolved" end of the continuum.

In the face of such environmental stress and incipient collapse, Friedman has suggested, leaders of junior lineages might choose to form new loci of power on the fringe of an existing chiefdom. Such a process need not have been limited to junior lineages. Where central organization was failing, another political force might also prove effective: a pulling-away of groups already on the fringe – perhaps "foreign" groups that had been adopted – through the formation of factions by the functional equivalent of local big-men, to start the cycle again at the segmentary level (see Nairne 1988:62–63, which describes just such a process).

If devolution along one or more of the lines described above is to be considered as the cause of the collapse of many chiefdoms in the Southeast, including Moundville, I have to specify what kind of archaeological evidence would justify such attribution for the Moundville–Alabama River transition. As usual, available archaeological evidence comes mainly from burials and settlement systems. Burials and their accompaniments help to distinguish individuals, and the deprivation of surplus to an elite in a failing chiefdom would be manifested in the disappearance from burials of the exotic craft objects obtained by elites through long-distance trade. Instead, burials should begin to display a uniformity of treatment. If adequate skeletal remains survive, they may manifest the symptoms of worsened nutrition that are among the few direct effects of subsistence stress that can be observed archaeologically.

The second class of evidence comes from the way the archaeological remains are disposed in the ground. On the smallest scale, craft specialization, as indicated by specific precincts on large sites in which waste materials of manufacture are found concentrated, should disappear from the archaeological record. The central sites would be abandoned as the services they provided became a luxury the society could not afford. The organization of the settlement system itself, with its hierarchy of site importance and size, would disappear, to be replaced by autonomous sites lacking public constructions or other features to distinguish them from one another.

All these kinds of evidence mark the Moundville–Alabama River transition. The exact details of the process are as yet unclear, but the evidence strongly suggests that the Moundville chiefdom had dissolved before the beginning of the sixteenth century (Peebles, pers. comm. 1989). Peebles (1986) has enumerated a number of proximate causes for this collapse, which he acknowledges are so far not testable: (1) population pressure withdrawing surplus from its function in supporting the elite; (2) decline in production due to Little Ice Age onset, ca. 1450; (3) usurpation of

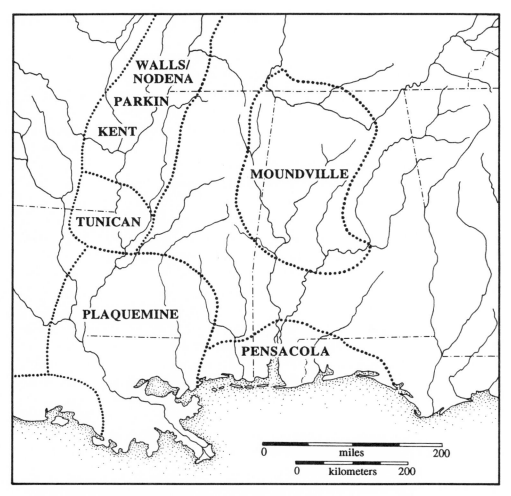

2.7. Late Mississippian phases in the Mississippi-Alabama region (data from Jeter et al. 1989:figure 22; Jenkins and Krause 1986; Knight 1984; Weinstein 1987).

access to foreign exchange; and (4) collapse of external trade partners. Any or all of these factors could have played a part in triggering the disintegration phase of the tribe-chiefdom-tribe cycle.

The work of Sheldon (1974) and Peebles (1986) has clearly established where and in what social form Moundville's peoples went after this dissolution. Some remained in the Black Warrior Valley, living in autonomous villages; others went where as a complex chiefdom they could not have gone: into river valleys to the southwest and southeast where the concentrations of soil and faunal resources were less favorable than a chiefdom-level population concentration would demand. And they went as tribal segments, culturally linked with other post-Moundville groups but politically autonomous.

The people of Bottle Creek, on the other hand, made no significant population shift, since the richness of their environment could stand a far more lengthy and sustained stress. Yet the Bear Point phase population left evidence strongly suggesting that the settlement hierarchy and social differentiation of a chiefdom had gone. If Moundville had indeed been Bottle Creek's most important external trading partner, the cause of this devolution may be neatly explained. Frankenstein and Rowlands (1978) have outlined a model of the "prestige goods economy" of chiefdoms that depend upon external sources for the objects and materials needed to validate and perpetuate the chiefly hierarchy. Clearly the long-distance trade in durable craft objects throughout the Southeast during the Mississippian period reflects a comparable situation, but the direction of trade and the timing of devolutionary episodes is likely to have made decline in one place more significant than in another. The late development of the Bottle Creek chiefdom implies that it was affected and probably stimulated by the development of its northern neighbor. That it declined at the same time merely confirms the closeness of the link attested by so much other evidence.

Sheldon (1974:117) has claimed that the devolution eventuating in the Burial Urn culture was a localized phenomenon. I would argue, however, that it was more likely a localized *cycle* whose period happened to be shorter than that of other chiefdoms in the wider region. The Cahokia chiefdom, perhaps the earliest to develop, had begun to decline around 1350 (Milner et al. 1984). Also of importance are the repercussions on the simple chiefdoms that were apparently part of Moundville's sphere of influence. Lyon's Bluff and Lubbub continued to function in some limited way through the early stage of the Alabama River transition (Marshall 1986; Peebles 1983a), which they may indeed have led in some cultural respects (Sheldon and Jenkins 1986). By then these smaller centers were free of direct allegiance to the paramount center, and may eventually have received some of its population. But deprived of their role in Moundville's prestige goods economy, and located in an ecological setting that could not support local evolution to a complex chiefdom, these groups devolved as soon as the failure of external subsidy had its full effect. The same is probably true of some of the single-mound sites in the southern part of the Warrior Valley (Peebles, pers. comm. 1986).

The chiefdoms of Plaqueminian extraction had not suffered the same fate by the end of the prehistoric period. Most were located in the richer environments of the lower Mississippi Valley, and although they had contracted somewhat in size they had not undergone sociopolitical devolution. Their chiefs, like many of those in the rest of the Mississippi Valley, were still in control when the Soto expedition saw them in 1541–43. The chiefdom represented by the impressive Pearl Mounds site (Mann 1988), though more limited in its access to subsistence resources, seems to have been able to maintain itself for so long on the relatively narrow Pearl floodplain because it commanded the river crossing of the important trail between the chiefdoms of the Natchez region and those of the Mobile delta (cf. Rowlands 1979). But this additional commerce in information could not sustain the Pearl Mounds chiefdom when cultural devolution hit its eastern connection, and like Bottle Creek it too dissolved in late prehistory.

CHAPTER THREE

Evidence from the Early Sixteenth Century

Of the patriotism and undaunted bravery of Tushka Lusa, and his ability as a commander of his warriors, DeSoto had satisfactory proof at the battle of Mombinah. But so little of the history of those ancient Choctaws has escaped oblivion that in sketching a line of their history at such a distance of time we necessarily pass through unknown fields. – Horatio B. Cushman, *History of the Choctaw, Chickasaw and Natchez Indians*

[T]he study of method and sources is the epistemology of the discipline, without which we could as well accept chroniclers' accounts as the pure, complete truth, and have done. – James M. Lockhart, *The Men of Cajamarca*

EVALUATING THE EVIDENCE

In the last chapter I attempted to reconstruct cultural process on the basis of material remains. Hundreds of years of fascinating events were condensed into a few pages through the hieratic dance of theoretical reconstruction; no one spoke. After 1500, however, the European entry into the North American continent gave history a voice, though it is the voice of biased observers. Like the physicist attempting to describe subatomic particles observed with instruments that alter their conditions of existence, explorers and colonists were describing cultures that, as a result of their very presence, were undergoing massive changes. The conditions of contact and the "Columbian Exchange" (Crosby 1972) of cultigens, people, animals, and especially microbes changed the native cultures irrevocably.

For this reason we must be especially critical of the documentary evidence left by Europeans, just because they did not mean to leave it; it was part of their own dialogue with themselves about what they were doing in what they were pleased to call the New World, and its very categories expressed their understanding of a world in which they were the dominant residents. In the introductory chapter of this book I discussed the necessity for careful textual analysis of every document used. The most abundant narrative genre for the period of interest in the present chapter requires this kind of analysis particularly because of its deep differences with modern notions of fact in narrative history, combined with its strong superficial resemblance to that modern genre. Part of my task is to place these texts at arm's length and try to discover such useful data as may be beneath their convincing surfaces.

My chief interest in the exploration narratives of the sixteenth century is their snapshot portrayals of sociopolitical groupings in different stages of social change. I think it possible to confirm the theoretical reconstruction of the last chapter by showing that groups were differently organized from one place to the next and that the Southeast did not constitute a solid paving of chiefdoms. With luck, suggestions as to the cause of change – indigenous devolution processes or European contact – may also be possible.

Disentangling the Spanish evidence for locations, however, particularly that provided by the Soto expedition, has created an industry in itself. Aside from textual difficulties, other problems present themselves. One arises from the lack of consistency in reported landforms and directions: discerning where the Spaniards were when they observed different native groups is not at all straightforward. A second is that the exploration narratives differ among themselves in recording times and distances, even for the same expedition. Another is that the Spanish explorers called many of the groups by names different from those the French and English later applied. Finally, the native population movements that resulted from rapid demographic change confused contemporary observers no more than 20 years apart, so at 450 years' distance reconstructing what they saw should be all the more difficult, particularly since much of the potentially relevant archaeological evidence is still unknown or has been irretrievably lost.

To trace early exploration routes more effectively, archaeological researchers have tried to correlate cultural variations found in artifact assemblages with the apparent chiefdom boundaries ("provinces") suggested by the Spanish narratives (cf. Phillips, Ford, and Griffin 1951; Brain, Toth, and Rodriguez-Buckingham 1974; and the Hudson et al. group [summary in Hudson 1990]). Of course, problems exist with both the dating of cultural patterns and the identification of cultural boundaries from the Spanish evidence, but ignoring archaeological evidence while evaluating the routes is no longer acceptable; historical assertions must at least correlate with the archaeological pattern, if they do not always elucidate it. Here I do not attempt to identify specific sites but rather attempt what seems more feasible – to identify such observations as may be gleaned reliably from the narratives with the archaeological cultures discussed in the last chapter.

In pursuit of the important variation in social structure that I believe existed as a result of devolutionary cycles and the initial impact of European contact, I try first to

76

recover as much of what the Spaniards actually saw as is now available through the surviving authentic narratives. Using that evidence, I attempt to identify the organizational complexity of each polity, derived from the presence or absence of certain features anthropologists have identified as signaling a certain stage of organization. The documents produced by European observers are particularly helpful in providing direct – if poorly understood – behavioral evidence of the degree of political sway wielded by the representatives of polities that they met. Political authority ranged from absolute power over all other members of the polity, through moral coercion, to no centralization of authority at all. This variation is evident if one reads the narratives without presuming uniformity, and if one looks for what the observers saw rather than what they thought about it.

Settlement pattern is a particularly telling factor for degree of social hierarchization, as the discussion in the last chapter of the Moundville pattern for a complex chiefdom suggests. Although lack of soil replenishment technology dictated somewhat dispersed settlement at all stages of social organization for groups in the Southeast that made use of agriculture, the ranking of the sites should vary between the two extremes of tribal development. The autonomous settlements – segments – of a segmented tribe should not differ significantly in size or internal organization, as each is equal to every other and equally capable of providing most of its domestic needs. Chiefdom settlements, on the other hand, though they may be no less dispersed and most may even be of similar size to tribal segments, should be spatially nucleated around primary and secondary civic-ceremonial centers.

Site structure is one of the more blatant desiderata of social organization, since segmentary tribes do not build or functionally occupy civic-ceremonial centers, even if they are their cultural inheritors. Differential mortuary practices could theoretically be equally elaborate for big-man and chief, but in the Southeast the chief was likely to be buried in a substructural mound whose generations-long construction attested to his genealogical links with power, whereas the big-man was not. Segmentary tribes should also lack identifiably communal structures such as centrally located sites, which alone have plazas and communal granaries.

One feature of site structure that has been discussed at length is fortification (Larson 1972; Gibson 1974; Peebles 1983a). Warfare or at least contention is reflected to some degree in the documents of the sixteenth-century Southeast, and archaeologists maintain that it is also reflected in the presence of site fortifications. The evidence has been confused because nobody has yet been able to make a case for a "fortification horizon" in the interior Southeast (but see Bass n.d.). Clearly the Spaniards observed fortified towns in some areas at mid-century, but, except for a limited number of sites, we do not know how long they had been a feature of the southeastern landscape. Fortification is obviously more likely to appear at towns near borders between sedentary groups, but except that it is used by sedentary peoples, we can make no reliable assertion about its correlation with organizational complexity.

Though the Spaniards were far from welcome guests as they crossed the Southeast, and were hurried more or less bluntly on their way, they did leave a scattering of artifacts behind to serve as a nearly invisible harbinger of Indian entry into the world economic system (Wallerstein 1980). Such evidence is also powerfully suggestive in nailing down exploration routes (M. Smith 1977, 1984; Smith and Good 1982; Weinstein 1985), although of course the portability that made the objects useful trade goods also keeps them from providing direct evidence of the Spaniards' path. The presence of Spanish artifacts in Indian cultural contexts, if they can be dated reliably, can be of more help in the evaluation of changes that took place during the more than one hundred years between the last Spanish visit and the first penetration by the French and English into the hinterlands of the Southeast.

THE SPANISH ENTRADA INTO THE CENTRAL SOUTHEAST, 1519–43

Spanish efforts to explore and colonize the Southeast met with limited success in the sense that ultimately the Spanish were only able to hold the Florida peninsula and its environs with any security. Perhaps the most significant achievement of the various expeditions that set forth during the sixteenth century was their revelation of the earliest glimpses of cultural groupings in the southeastern interior.

Alvarez de Pineda, 1519

Historians have long assumed that the first Spanish expedition that would have had a chance to encounter Choctaw-related peoples was the exploratory voyage of Alvarez de Pineda from the west coast of Florida to the eastern Mexican coast in 1519 (*Cédula* 1883). Backtracking north from the region of Veracruz, following the coast, the four ships of the expedition landed at a large *pueblo* at the mouth of a large river, where they stayed for more than forty days to repair their ships. They were well received by the people they met, who willingly provided them with food and other supplies. During the stopover the expedition explored for six leagues up this river, finding forty *pueblos* along the two sides of the river. They reported inhabitants of extremely tall and extremely short stature, all bedecked with gold jewelry.

Carl Sauer (1971), convinced that this could not have been the Mississippi, considered the Mobile bay and river to be the most likely identification. The fanciful touches to the description of the people Sauer simply discounted as wrong, since the account also reported gold-bearing streams emptying into the large river. Certainly, the observers of the Soto expedition twenty years later did not report Indians wearing lavish metal ornaments in the vicinity of Mabila, which Sauer assumed was the closest they came to this postulated location, and no such ornaments are known from this period archaeologically. Nor does the source of the account offer a strong guarantee of fact: it is the royal *cédula* granting the discovery to Francisco de Garay, governor of Jamaica, who had outfitted the expedition at his own expense. A very brief document summarizing the discoveries in order to grant them to Garay, and presumably based on an account that had been filtered through Garay, it constitutes a stereotyped, formulaic description of lands with sufficiently praiseworthy qualities to be worth such a claim, and no Spaniard of the age could have been unaware of the favor with which the Spanish Crown viewed sources of precious metals.

Can we accept Sauer's identification of the Mobile bay and river with confidence? Robert Weddle's (1985:94–108,130–46) more recent examination of accounts of Gulf coast exploration agrees with Sauer in rejecting the Mississippi but offers a contrary view that is very persuasive, since it depends not upon the slender evidence of the single brief document so distant from direct observation, but upon the whole context of Garay's enterprise in sending Pineda and the steps he took to follow it up. According to Weddle, Alvarez de Pineda, dispatched to search the Gulf coast for a strait passage to the Pacific Ocean, had sailed along the coast from Florida to Villa Rica (near Veracruz) without making a significant stop until thirty leagues north of Nautla on the Pánuco River, where he had begun a settlement before sailing on to establish the claim. Sending representatives ashore at Villa Rica to meet with Cortés, who considered the expedition unwarranted competition, Alvarez de Pineda lost them when he refused to come ashore himself. With that he returned north to the alleged settlement.

There, on the Pánuco River (and not the Mississippi or Mobile Bay, according to Weddle), he rested with his ships for forty days to clean and repair them for the return trip to Garay in Jamaica. Alvarez de Pineda may have stayed behind to establish the settlement that was joined early in 1520 by another expedition sent by Garay and led by Diego de Camargo. Shortly after the arrival of the second expedition, however, the Indians (Huastecs) attacked the settlement and drove the decimated Spaniards away on two damaged ships, aboard which they straggled southward to Villa Rica (Weddle 1985:95–108). According to Cortés, the reason for the massacre, reported to him through Pánuco chiefs he had won to loyalty earlier, was cruel treatment (Weddle 1985:134).

The Alvarez de Pineda expedition undoubtedly sailed along the Gulf coast. Along with the report of the voyage supplied to the king was a map sketch showing the entire coast and the extent of Garay's claims. The sketch has been important for its identification of the Río del Espíritu Santo (Delanglez 1945), but it does not indicate that Alvarez de Pineda made anything more than coastal observations along the northern Gulf (figure 3.1). Thus the best that can be said about the expedition's observations of the region's native population is that they may have seen some people from the ship while they "observed very well the land, ports and rivers, and people of it, and all the rest that ought to be observed" (*Cédula* 1883:515; translation mine) before reaching Cortés's base at Villa Rica – and even this phrase is a formula repeated elsewhere in the document. Others, more surreptitious than the Pineda expedition and therefore leaving behind no document, may well have spent time with the people of the central Gulf coast before or around this time, but it now seems quite clear that Pineda and his men did not.

Panfilo de Narváez, 1528

More can be learned from the experiences of the survivors of the Narváez expedition. The expedition had exploration as its purpose; Panfilo de Narváez, with a commission succeeding Garay as *adelantado* of the lands bordering the Gulf coast to Pánuco, intended to take stock of the lands he had acquired. The two accounts of this expedition are based mainly upon the observations of one of the three Spanish survivors, Alvar Núñez Cabeza de Vaca. The *Relación* is his account written for publication after his return to Spain (Núñez 1542, 1972); a previous account, a version of which Fernández de Oviedo y Valdés included in his *Historia general* (1924, bk.35, chaps.1–6), was apparently written as a "joint report" by Cabeza de Vaca and fellow survivors Andrés Dorantes de Carranza and Alonso del Castillo Maldonado somewhat earlier, shortly after their return to Mexico. Both accounts were shaped by the circumstances of their creation.

The so-called Joint Report, like many of Oviedo's contemporary sources, does not survive in its original form. It was prepared as an exercise in self-justification and presented by Cabeza de Vaca during the hearing held by the Audiencia of Santo Domingo on the fate of the Narváez expedition in 1537, and like many accounts so presented it was apparently handed over by some official means to Fernández de Oviedo y Valdés, military commander of Santo Domingo and appointed royal historiographer, for incorporation in his *Historia general y natural de las Indias*. Received opinion holds that the Oviedo version is superior in detail to Cabeza de Vaca's own *Relación*, "due, perhaps, to the fact that it was the work of three memories pooled" (Bannon 1972:xiv). Yet historians have not subjected Oviedo's work to the detailed textual critique that would justify that claim, and since several sixteenth-century accounts of exploration in the Southeast have been transmitted through Oviedo, we must pay some attention to his use of sources here. The case of Cabeza de Vaca is the ideal ground for such examination, since the man's own separate published account exists for comparison.

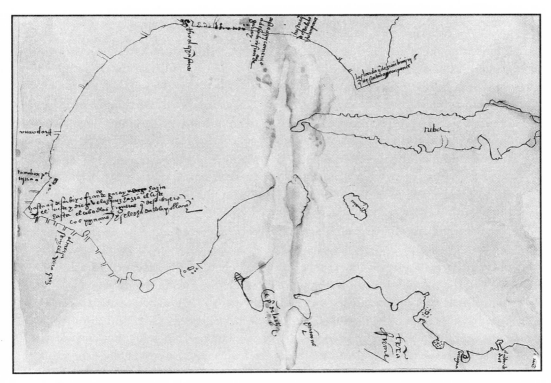

3.1. The Pineda map, ca. 1519 (original in Archivo General de Indias, Seville; tracing from the J. P. Bryan Map Collection). Courtesy of the Center for American History, University of Texas at Austin.

One would expect the two accounts to be near duplicates, since one would assume that Núñez retained a copy of the Joint Report when he returned to Spain, if only as insurance against some later proceeding or as evidence favoring his own preferment at court. A careful reading of the Spanish originals confirms, by the frequent repetition of lengthy passages with identical phrasing, that they must have been derived from essentially identical written originals, in spite of the received opinion that implies their independent creation; one suspects that such received opinion owes much to the fact that the two versions have never had the same translator. Most scholarly attention to these issues has focused on the overland segments of Cabeza de Vaca's journey, after he left the Gulf coast (see Adorno 1991:166 and notes); little comparative analysis has been done for the rest. For the region of interest, as it happens, there is indeed negligible variation in the substance of the two narratives, so the following analysis is based on Cabeza de Vaca's own published version.

When the Narváez expedition set out it consisted of five ships and some four hundred men, but when he failed to find treasure at first landing, Narváez decided to send the ships on westward along the coast while taking most of his party along an inland route in search of treasure at the rumored rich town of Apalachen, probably around Tallahassee. This town was rich in food but not in treasure, and here the Spaniards began to encounter scorched-earth resistance: the inhabitants deserted their town and burned it to thwart the Spanish advance. The same thing happened as the expedition passed southwestward to the town of Aute. By this time, having been three months on the road and with a good number of his men ill from poor food, Narváez decided that his best hope to save the lives of the party was to build small boats and coast westward to Pánuco. They set out from the region of Apalachee Bay on 20 September, having lost forty men to Indian attack and illness while building the boats.

Proceeding on and in ever more dire want of everything, the expedition was trapped by a storm among islands probably near the mouth of Pensacola Bay (Weddle 1985:193) or Mobile Bay (Sauer 1971:44), where in the absence of fresh water some of the party drank salt water and died suddenly. Taking the direction of some canoes that had appeared to scout the Spaniards the night before the storm, the expedition found on the mainland a village of mat-covered houses and ample provisions of smoked fish and water in jars. Invited to partake of these by the "chief of that land," Narváez was taken into his house and exchanged some of the expedition's meager store of corn for the fish offered by the chief, who wore a "marten" fur cloak. Narváez gave some trinkets in exchange, but after dark he and all his party, including several men lying ill upon the beach, were attacked suddenly by the inhabitants. Narváez himself was wounded "by a stone" and packed off on a barge by his men, most of whom followed to the boats while a few staved off furious attacks in which all were wounded. They finally drove off the attackers, and the next morning the Spaniards destroyed more than thirty Indian canoes to thwart pursuit, after which they stood offshore for two days to wait out a storm and then continued on their way.

Three or four days later, after their flotilla had entered a bay or lagoon (Weddle [1985:193] says Mobile Bay; Sauer [1971:44] says Pascagoula Bay/Mississippi Sound), Indians approached and offered to bring water. Accompanied by a Greek man and a black man from the expedition, the Indians went to get it, but though they returned to try to free two hostages they had left behind, they brought back neither the promised water nor the two members of the Spanish expedition. The Indian hostages were therefore not returned, and the next day a crowd of canoes appeared, including three to six "chiefs" with long hair and "marten" fur robes, who attempted to negotiate for the return of the Indians in exchange for the return of the Christians. No agreement for a safe exchange could be made, however, and ultimately the Indians began hurling stones and arrows until the wind changed and the Spaniards were able to get away. Their next landfall was at the mouth of a torrential river (the Mississippi) whose current was so strong that it eventually drove the rafts apart, so that finally the one containing Cabeza de Vaca was left with only one other to fetch up on the Texas coast.

The main interest of the Narváez expedition here is the strikingly belligerent attitude of the people they met along the Gulf coast. One may speculate that unreported early contacts with Europeans along the coast had perhaps been followed by horrifying and inexplicable contagion – which might be supported by the attack on sick men near the coastal village – or that the obviously desperate plight of the Narváez expedition lessened the native people's fear of the unknown, and they simply followed their inclinations in attacking it. All that can be observed, however, is that on an island at the mouth of Mobile Bay (Sauer 1971:44) or on Santa Rosa Island at the mouth of Pensacola Bay (Weddle 1985:193), the expedition was attacked by the inhabitants of what looked to Cabeza de Vaca like a permanent settlement with houses covered with matting, where a great deal of fishing had been going on; the date was sometime in October. The man recognized by the Europeans as a chief, who invited Narváez to share food, was dressed in a fur robe identified as marten. Weapons used in the attack, which was directed against the sick as well as the other Spaniards, were stones and stone-tipped arrows, though these latter were not used in great numbers. The number of canoes being used by the village population exceeded thirty.

The next group Narváez encountered dwelt, Sauer (1971:44) thinks, around the mouth of the Pascagoula, although travel times and the fact that reports of the two men left behind were received by Soto on the Alabama or the Mobile River suggest the mouth of Mobile Bay to Weddle (1985:193). Again there were a great many canoes, chiefs dressed in "marten" skins – this time worked with other furs in particolored patterns – and stones and arrows used as weapons. The only difference here was that two members of the expedition were left behind: the Greek, Doroteo Teodoro, and an unnamed black man remained with the inhabitants as hostages. Also in this case the Indians seem to have had prior warning of the coming of the expedition, as they had sent out a canoe to scout it before it was able to reach their lands. The settlements of this group (the presence of three to six "chiefs" would seem to imply multiple settlements) were not seen at all by the Spaniards. The archaeological evidence suggests that the main population centers were to be found at the northern end of both the Mobile Bay and the Pascagoula delta, so either location would be in accord with the account.

Can we identify these people? Sauer (1971) assumed that because these chiefs wore their hair long they may have been culturally related, at least, to the Choctaw, since Swanton (1931:57, 1946:504) cited Adair and Romans to the effect that this was a Choctaw trait two hundred years later. The tie-in that Swanton used to strengthen the argument across such a span of time was the Choctaw word for "long-hairs," as

Adair says they were called: *pansfalaya*. Since Soto's expedition met a group of people who may have been known by the name *pafalaya*, Swanton concluded that both Narváez and Soto must have met Choctaws. This link is far more tenuous even than Swanton made it seem. Adair (1775:195ff.) had read Elvas's account of the Soto expedition, which uses the name *pafalaya*, and the conception of Soto's route in Adair's time would have taken him straight through east-central Mississippi, which was by then Choctaw country (see Delisle's 1718 map of the region, *Carte de la Louisiane et du Cours du Mississipi*, printed in Cumming 1958: plate 47); modern research, however, has suggested that this was nowhere near the actual route, nor was the region even populated in the sixteenth century. In addition, by Romans's testimony around 1770, the hairstyles of some Choctaws at least had changed within living memory in his time (Romans [1772] 1961), and the narratives of the Narváez expedition singled out only the "chiefs" as wearing long hair, not the whole populace. This ground for identification thus seems far-fetched to me.

The only other distinctive feature of the people met by the Narváez expedition was the "marten" fur cloaks worn by the "chiefs." Whether they were in fact marten is moot; Cabeza de Vaca observed their strong musky odor and the skillful way the furs were worked in patterns. In later literature mentioning native dress, only buffalo and feather cloaks were described for the region, and no distinctive skill in the working of furs was indicated. Yet Cabeza de Vaca cannot have been wrong about the cloaks' having been made of fur, at least, since in the first fracas the cloak was literally snatched from the chief's back by the Spaniards as they attempted to hold him. Whatever it was made of, it does seem to indicate sumptuary distinction of some kind and could also indicate long-distance prestige-goods trade. The issue of the cloak should also be considered with reference to the season, October, and to the fact that the Spaniard frequently remarked upon the cold weather.

The season is also a material consideration in trying to identify the kind of village the Spaniards saw. If it was in fact a kind of fishing base camp, which Sauer surmises based on the water stored in large earthenware containers and the smoked fish arrayed in front of the lodges, then we may be able to refer to similar sites known to archaeology: coastal villages characterized by evidence for fishing technology and large pottery jars. The fact that the season was well into autumn, at the end of the season for some species, supports to some extent the base-camp idea, and certainly plenty of people were exploiting the coastal region in this way in the sixteenth century (Curren 1976; Milanich and Fairbanks 1980; Walthall 1980; Knight 1984; Davis 1985a; Stowe 1985; Fuller 1985).

The observations of Cabeza de Vaca give little information regarding the cultural affiliations of the two groups encountered, but neither do they contradict the continuities and contrasts offered by the archaeological evidence. The Pensacola culture's influence stretched from Pensacola Bay to the Mississippi Gulf coast (Fuller and Stowe 1982; Stowe 1985; Knight 1984; Lauro 1986; Galloway n.d.a), but the influence of Plaquemine decorative motifs became progressively dominant as one moved westward. Cabeza de Vaca says that the more easterly group was taller (Núñez 1972:39), so he at least thought he could tell the difference between the two. Both groups included proficient seafarers, however, and both seem to have distinguished their leaders.

The Narváez expedition did not have enough contact with settlements for their observations to be of much use for judging the effects of social devolution or disease, but Cabeza de Vaca mentions a few suggestive facts. No women were observed in these two groups. For the first group, seen in its village, this may tell as much about the attitude of the Indians as about the composition of the group, since they may have hidden the women in anticipation of trouble, as was common throughout the later Soto expedition.

Observations about the men the Spaniards recognized as chiefs may have implications for native leadership. Certainly the men seem to have been set off from the other members of the groups by sumptuary distinction, at least while performing "chiefly" duties. In the first case, the "leader" took upon himself the danger of hosting the foreigners while his people prepared an attack that would put him in danger; in the second case, the three to six "leaders" seem to have been proficient in negotiation. These facts argue for something more complex than egalitarian organization, though the degree of institutionalized leadership cannot be specified. Likewise, we cannot determine whether the variation in behavior between the leaders of the two groups was merely contextual or reflected possible different levels of organization (a single paramount in the first case and a confederation of autonomous villages in the second). For that matter, no one can guarantee that any of these men were authentic leaders at all and not other persons taking the place of real leaders in the dangerous proximity of the strangers; even the Spaniards with Soto eventually discerned examples of such a practice. We should, however, keep in mind the apparent selflessness of the single "chief" when considering Soto's meeting with Tascaluça.

Hernando de Soto, 1540–43

The first Spanish expedition that passed through the interior of the Southeast was that of Hernando de Soto and his men. Most authorities agree that its effects upon the native inhabitants of the interior were probably greater than those of any other Spanish expedition, but this is about the extent of the agreement regarding this expedition, since over the years local boosterism has claimed so many stopping places that it is hard to imagine how it was supposed to have made any progress at all. In spite of these conflicting claims, most scholarly opinion has until recently accepted in broad outline the conclusions of the U.S. De Soto Expedition Commission as reported by John Swanton in 1939. With the accumulation of much additional archaeological evidence, however, and increased awareness of the importance the expedition's reports have for the history of Indian tribes, the need has been felt for a reexamination of the Commission's conclusions, although its abstracted assembly of much of the documentary evidence remains useful as a starting point. Several studies have brought a new view of various portions of the route (Brain, Toth, and Rodriguez-Buckingham 1974; Lankford 1977; Brain 1984, 1985, 1988; Hudson et al. 1985; DePratter, Hudson, and Smith 1985; Weinstein 1985; Curren 1986; Hudson 1987; Hudson, Smith, and DePratter 1990). Efforts to attain a more complete knowledge of the route continue, and with the reprinting of the De Soto Commission report in 1985 and the commemoration of the 450th anniversary of the expedition, a second regional commission from the southeastern states was convened to pay particular attention to the archaeological evidence in marking a commemorative highway route through the region (National Park Service 1990); its work was not conclusive. The current discussion uses these new studies as far as they are helpful, although for much of the Mississippi region the route still awaits thorough reexamination and the outcome of recent and proposed archaeological projects. The route itself, however, is not my primary concern here. Instead, I hope that the Spaniards' observations can tell something of the state of social organization and the progress of European disease in the interior.

The sources for the Soto expedition are five texts allegedly reflecting the testimony of seven eyewitnesses. Only one of these, the account of expedition factor Luis Hernández de Biedma, is a primary source, a complete report of the journey Biedma had written down by the time of his report to the Crown in 1544 (Smith 1857:47–64). A written diary plus oral testimony were allegedly the basis for Oviedo's presentation of the account of Roderigo Ranjel, Soto's private secretary; both were apparently gathered and the account substantially written by 1546 (Oviedo y Valdés [1851] 1959:153–81; see Galloway n.d.b). The Ranjel account may also have been consulted by the anonymous Portuguese writer who incorporated the memories of a Portuguese expedition participant in a romanticized narrative published in 1577 and attributed to "a gentleman of Elvas" (Elvas [1557] 1932; see Elbl and Elbl n.d. and Galloway n.d.b). The Inca mestizo author Garcilaso de la Vega may in turn have used the Elvas account, together with the oral account of participant Gonzalo Silvestre and – allegedly – two manuscripts by Juan Coles and Alonso de Carmona, to create the epic *La Florida*, published in 1605, that is so beloved of students of Latin American literature (Garcilaso de la Vega [1605] 1982; see Henige n.d. and Dowling n.d.). Finally, a brief abstract drafted by a notary of Puerto Rico in 1565 does little more than hint at the contents of an additional account by the priest Cañete, now lost (Lyon 1993).

The detailed evaluation of these sources and their relationships to one another is lengthy, and the interested reader is directed to other studies (Galloway n.d.d). Here my chief concern is to avoid the trap of drawing indiscriminately on these sources to create a single narrative; my intention is not to create a narrative history at yet another remove but to isolate genuine observations from literary constructions. This task is far more easily announced than carried out, for not only are these sources of different value, but they offer different kinds of evidence and hence must be consulted carefully and consistently.

The details of the expedition can be laid aside for a moment to trace an overview of the journey and the issues it raises. The accounts all affirm that the expedition landed on the western coast of the Florida peninsula in May of 1539. In accordance with exploration practices of the period, their ships were left behind to be summoned later, while the main exploration party proceeded north and then west to spend October through March in the lands of Apalachee, where Indians told of the prior activities of Narváez's party on the coast. During that time groups were sent to find a harbor at the coast and then to summon the boats from the peninsula to the newly discovered harbor, Apalachee Bay. From there boats departed to scout the coast at least as far west as Pensacola Bay. This much is relatively certain and anchored by reasonably well identified archaeological sites (Milanich and Hudson 1993). Thenceforward the reconstruction is more at the mercy of recent research – or lack of it. In March the party proceeded in a dogleg path tending northeast, reaching the extensive lands of Cofitachequi in northeast Georgia or western South Carolina by the end of April. Through the next two months they continued in a northwestward arc to cross the Appalachians, stopping in the region of the Tennessee-Georgia-Alabama border (Hudson, Smith, and DePratter 1984).

Before the journey through Alabama and Mississippi that is of particular interest here is traced and discussed in greater detail, we should review some generalities about what the expedition had already encountered in order to understand the reactions of the Spaniards to what they were seeing. One factor to be considered is the behavior of the Indians, which was influenced by prior contact with Europeans, the social organization of the particular group, and the behavior of the Spaniards.

Prior contact seems to have led uniformly to hostility. Some groups reacted by flight from their villages, with or without scorched-earth tactics depending upon the lead time they had but nearly always accompanied by guerrilla harassment. In the few cases where they did not resort to flight, the group in question either was taken by surprise or, according to the Spaniards, saw a possibility of rising above more powerful neighbors through alliance with the Spaniards. Other groups fled initially but launched more massive attacks later. In the case of the pacific Cofitachequi, the slender evidence of one account has been taken to imply that the hospitable reception and cooperation accorded to the expedition could be attributed to a more subtle effect of prior contact: European disease passed along from the Ayllón settlement on the Atlantic coast in 1526 could have broken the organization of the province (Smith 1987:55; but see Henige 1986c). All groups took advantage of one aspect of Spanish behavior, greed, by retailing rumors of richer provinces further on so as to get rid of the intruders.

The Spaniards' behavior is recounted differently in the various narratives, but it is now accepted that Garcilaso's glorified descriptions of Spanish chivalry fall considerably short of the truth, and that the party tended to demand food and slaves and then to take these by force if they were not immediately forthcoming. Hundreds of native bearers were taken away in chains, their good behavior guaranteed by the imprisonment of their chief. When the Spaniards judged that they had reached the next "province," surviving burdeners were sometimes released to return to their homes. The demands of the Spaniards were not limited to sustenance and labor; in their search for riches, guided by the experience of Peru, the Spaniards looted charnel houses as well as granaries.

The Spaniards, like the Indians, also exhibited bellicosity. Although Garcilaso makes much of gentlemanly challenges to single combat, the rule was merciless attack by both sides with no quarter offered, with the advantage always going to the Spaniards when a clear field permitted the use of cavalry. Some historians have implied that the Indians may have feared Spanish horses because they thought the beasts were supernatural; a simpler explanation acknowledges that the Indians would have been foolhardy to ignore the advantages of mobility and brute force that horses provided. In addition, a war-horse of the age, trained to fight as part of a unit with its rider, had fearsome capabilities (note that horsemen earned a double share of the proceeds of Spanish conquest). Such horses would intentionally charge and trample a man on the ground if directed to do so, would rear, leap into the air, and apparently pounce on command (Cunninghame-Graham 1949). Small wonder that the Indians made a point of killing such formidable warriors, or that the Spaniards bewailed their shrinking numbers.

What Soto and his men observed, then, was not the full complexity of southeastern Indian cultures but the faces of those groups turned outward toward the stranger – in this instance a particularly exotic and dangerous stranger – in a structural pose for war or diplomacy (Gearing 1962). This fact dictates a fundamental circumscription of the evidence that must be kept in mind when consulting the Soto narratives for information about social organization. To examine that evidence as dispassionately as possible, I enumerate explicitly the features described for each town by each author. These include infrastructural features, such as mounds, plazas, public architecture, and fortifications; and superstructural features, such as sumptuary differentiation of the elite, storehouses of tributary food contributions, ability of the chief to organize labor, long-distance contacts used by the chief to maintain elite status, and the chief's role in the redistribution of both subsistence and wealth-object goods.

Further evidence from archaeology cannot be added until a good candidate route has been put forward, but, unfortunately, the actual route can never be definitively identified. It seems simple enough to specify that the route must be based upon a reasonably congruent distribution of sites of the proper period with gross topological features (such as mountain ranges and major rivers) and population distributions as described by the Spaniards, factoring out rhetorical features that might distort such descriptions. These requirements present problems, however, since few sites have survived undamaged and the narratives can never be completely understood. The presence of sixteenth-century Spanish artifacts on native sites is of dubious assistance; because such artifacts were highly portable, their presence can support very different reconstructions.

A more generalized approach to the problem can be fruitful, even though less appealing to the popular imagination. In the last chapter I demonstrated that the archaeology of the region shows complex hierarchical organization persisting on the Mississippi, while in the Tombigbee region it either had not developed in the first place (on the western tributaries) or had devolved to simpler arrangements (on the Black Warrior). The Soto narratives should confirm this and, more important, may suggest why.

I am concerned here with only the Alabama-Mississippi region and its borderlands, the trail from Chiaha or Coça to Quizquiz and later the flight of the failed expedition down the Mississippi, with some minor overlap where necessary for coherence. This region is wide enough to bracket the archaeological cultures discussed in the last chapter. For the eastern part of this area, the Alabama and Tombigbee Valleys, I discuss the work of the team led by Charles Hudson, which has proposed a radical reworking of the route. For the western part of the region, approaching the Mississippi, I refer to evidence from the long-sustained research of the Lower Mississippi Survey and its friends, who have concerned themselves especially with the region where Soto crossed the Mississippi and where the expedition set out down the Mississippi after Soto's death. No unified program of research exists for the middle of the region, but such information as has appeared in the work of regional institutions suggests that the accounts are correct in portraying it as empty of settlement.

Figure 3.2 represents a proposed composite corridor based on the reviews of Brain (1985) and Hudson, Smith, and DePratter (1990) to help situate the narrative accounts. Most current researchers would agree with much of this configuration.

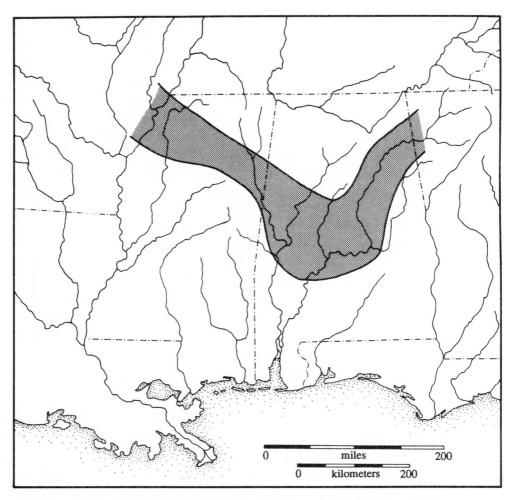

3.2. General path of the Hernando de Soto expedition across the Mississippi-Alabama region (data from Brain 1985:figure 5-3; Hudson et al. 1990).

The Soto expedition passed through the Alabama-Mississippi region from roughly June or July of 1540 to June of 1541. Students of the route generally agree that it passed down the Coosa Valley from northwest Georgia to the Alabama River, and from the Alabama River region northwest to cross the Tombigbee River in the region of modern Columbus, Mississippi, proceeding eventually across the upper third of the state to encounter the Mississippi River somewhere between Clarksdale and Memphis. A narrative summary of the sequence of events of that journey, drawn from Oviedo's account, provides a context for the later discussion of the expedition's observations.

The party entered the lands of Chiaha in early June of 1540; their first contact with Chiaha Indians was when the latter brought them corn the day before their arrival at the island town of Chiaha, in the middle of a broad river. The Spaniards and their horses were tired, so they decided to rest there, and the Indians provided food. After two weeks of peace the Indians ran away when Soto requested women, and the Spaniards had to consent to leave off collars and chains before the leader granted five hundred carriers.

They departed Chiaha on 28 June, passing five or six villages; that night they camped near one of them. They crossed a strongly flowing river with the aid of a line of horsemen breaking its flow. On 29 June they passed through a town, obtained corn, and set up camp. The next day they crossed another river and passed through another village, then crossed the river again, camping out at the end of the day.

On 1 July they met with the leader of Coste, who bivouacked them in a village; but the Spaniards stole corn from the granaries, and the next day the leader slipped away to the island town of Coste, where the Spaniards shortly arrived. The Spaniards crossed the river and had begun to plunder the town's storehouses when the Indians took up their weapons. Soto chided his men and persuaded the leader to accompany him to an open area where his men would camp; there he put the leader and ten or twelve important men into chains. Soto sent two men to investigate the province of Chisca, alleged to be a source of gold, while the rest of the expedition rested for a week.

On 9 July the Spaniards left Coste and camped on the riverbank. The following day the Indians of the town of Tali on the opposite bank attempted to escape in canoes but were captured by the Spaniards; the leader of Tali then offered to ferry the Spaniards across to the town, where they spent the night and obtained carriers. The next day they traveled without incident and camped for the night. They crossed a river on each of the following two days, and during this traverse from Tali they were brought food from neighboring villages but did not stay in any of them. On the third day they crossed another river and slept in the village of Tasqi. The following day they passed one small village, then others.

On 17 July Soto and his men reached Coça, where they were met by the leader ceremoniously borne on a litter. The Spaniards stayed there for more than a month, during which they held leaders and principal men; the people fled. The Spaniards rode out to capture bearers and put them in chains, and on 20 August they finally left, leaving the Levantine Christian Feryada behind but taking the Coça leader to ensure their safety. That night they camped beyond Talimachusy. The next day they bought women at the large village of Itaba in exchange for mirrors and knives; they apparently stayed in Itaba for more than a week.

They left Itaba on 30 August, camping in an oak forest. At the village of Ulibihali the Indians were under arms to attempt a rescue of the leader and captives, but the Coça leader warned them off, and they lay down their arms. There Soto obtained carriers and twenty women but lost "a gentleman of Salamanca" named Mancano and a Spanish-speaking black slave, Johan Biscayan. The party left Ulibihali on 2 September, spending the night at a small village. Continuing by the river they came to Piachi, where they stayed a day. The following day, 4 September, was without incident and ended in an open-air camp, and the next day the party reached Tuasi, where they spent a week and obtained carriers and thirty-two women, leaving on 13 September and camping that night. The fourteenth also entailed a long march and outdoor camp, but on the fifteenth they came to an old village with walled and towered fortification, presumably empty. The next day they reached a "new village" beside a river, where they rested for another day.

On the seventeenth the Spaniards reached Talisi and found it evacuated, with rich food supplies left behind. At Talisi a messenger came from the feared leader Tascaluça, followed by a man assumed to be one of his sons. Soto sent them back with two Spaniards instructed to gather information. The Spaniards meanwhile stayed in Talisi for a week, until on 25 September its leader finally appeared and supplied food, carriers, and women. Here the leader of Coça was released, angry because Soto kept his sister and released him "so far from his country."

On 5 October the Spaniards finally left Talisi to spend the night in the small village of Casiste. On the sixth they slept at the "wretched" village of Caxa, but they slept on the riverbank opposite Humati on the seventh. The next day saw them in the new settlement of Uxapita, while the following day they came within a league of Tascaluça's village and camped in the open, sending a message to this leader that they had arrived.

On 10 October Soto and his men entered the "recent" village of Athahachi and encountered Tascaluça in splendor arrayed on a mound surrounded by servants. Soto joined him and then withdrew to eat, taking Tascaluça into custody for the night after having been entertained by dancing. Tascaluça sent his counselors away, and the next day he granted the Spaniards four hundred carriers, promising more carriers and women at Mabila. On 12 October the Spaniards departed with Tascaluça in custody, mounted on a horse and surrounded by a group of important men and servants. That night the army camped in the open, but the following day the leader of Piachi (apparently a second town of that name) offered resistance and killed two Spaniards and Tascaluça's men as the party crossed the river. They stayed a day in Piachi, where they learned that two of Narváez's party had been killed, and the following day they met on the road the Spaniards who had been sent to investigate Mabila; they reported a gathering of men and arms there. The next day Tascaluça was brought chestnut bread from Mabila at a "fenced village" on the way.

On 18 October the Spaniards and their prisoner passed several villages in a "populous' region before reaching Mabila. The army spread out among the villages to forage, and forty mounted men accompanied Soto and Tascaluça into the fortified town. At first entertaining the Spaniards with a dance, the Indians waited until Tascaluça was able to move to safety inside a building before they blocked the entrances to the town and began to attack the few Spaniards inside it. Most of the Spaniards escaped alive and began to fight from horseback before the gates. When the rest of the army arrived they attacked the walls, cutting them down with axes and setting fire to the houses within; the whole town burned. In the fighting 22 Spaniards were killed and 148 wounded, while around 3,000 Indians, including the "son" of Tascaluça, were apparently killed. In the fire most of the army's baggage was lost. The expedition remained in the vicinity of Mabila, looting and burning the countryside and nursing wounded men and horses, until 14 November, when they departed.

Nothing of note is mentioned on the journey until 17 November, when the army came to a river called Apafalaya. After forging through swamps, the army found corn in the village of Talicpacana on the eighteenth and saw another village from a distance across the river. Apparently the army rested in Talicpacana for a few days; on the twenty-first they entered the village of Moculixa a half league away and saw that the inhabitants had crossed the river with their corn and intended to defend it. Perhaps operating out of Talicpacana, the Spaniards built a barge, which they moved to Moculixa on the twenty-ninth and launched manned with sixty soldiers, who drove off the Indians and appropriated the corn.

On the thirtieth this lead party reached a village called Zabusta. Apparently the main army had not yet crossed the river, for they brought up the barge and used it to cross to Zabusta, spending the night in yet another village on the opposite side, whose leader, Apafalaya, they seized as guide and interpreter. They remained in Apafalaya's town until 9 December, when they set off for Chicaça.

After five days of travel through swamps and rivers, the Spaniards reached the river of Chicaça on 14 December. The army apparently suffered from cold (after the loss of their clothes at Mabila) and hunger on this journey, and when they found the river it was in flood and armed Indians lined the opposite bank. On the sixteenth the army crossed on another barge constructed on the spot, and Soto led the way to a deserted village where they spent the night and remained through a Christmas snowstorm. On 3 January the leader of Chicaça came offering peace, guides, and interpreters for the famous land of Caluca, described as more than ninety villages in a fertile region. The Spaniards instead settled for the winter in the empty village – *chicasa* in the language of the Apalachee (e.g., Hann 1988:401; see Kimball 1994:5 for a similar description/placename confusion).

The next passage is rather confusing in Oviedo's Ranjel and not even mentioned in Biedma's account: Soto ordered half his men to attack Sacchuma (no narrative gives details of this foray), and their leader Miculasa sued for peace, followed by messengers from Talapatica possibly sent for the same reason. The Spaniards decided to leave even as this apparent native war continued, and the Indians reluctantly agreed to provide carriers on 4 March. On the evening before, in spite of a warning from Soto, expedition members failed to take precautions, and at dawn the Indians attacked and burned the camp, killing twelve Spaniards and taking fifty-nine horses.

The Spaniards moved their camp to an open plain a league distant, where they repaired their equipment. On 15 March the Indians attacked again, but the Spaniards were able to drive them off. Finally on 26 April the army departed from Chicaça. That night they arrived at the deserted village of Limamu, which they searched for corn. The following day they encountered a barricade in another plain they were crossing, defended by Indians; the Spaniards fought through it. They rested there for two days, and on 30 April they left to march for nine days through deserted, swampy country.

On 8 May they successfully assaulted and subdued the town of Quizqui by taking large numbers of hostages, then proceeded to two more towns, both well provided with corn, before reaching the Mississippi. Apparently they returned and dwelt in one of the villages for two weeks, for it was not until 21 May that the army proceeded to a flat space between the river and perhaps yet another village, where they camped to build barges to cross the river.

I am not concerned here with most of the expedition's activities on the western side of the river, where they wandered for more than a year before Soto's death and a failed attempt to reach Mexico overland made the new leader Maldonado decide to descend the Mississippi as the most certain means of reaching their goal. What is of interest is a powerful polity called Quigualtam, apparently located on the eastern side of the Mississippi, that had threatened all through the Spaniards' last winter camp and that sent out flotillas of boats filled with archers to intercept them as they passed.

The account of the expedition's "return to the river" appears in Elvas but not in Oviedo's Ranjel, which ends before this point is reached. Because Elvas agrees so well with Ranjel elsewhere, I am inclined to believe that this segment's bare facts from Elvas are reliable, especially as they tally reasonably well with Biedma. Two episodes are relevant to the discussion here. The first was when the expedition arrived at Guachoya on the banks of the Mississippi in April of 1542 intending to go to the sea to meet with resupply; in Guachoya Soto died, and Maldonado chose to leave the region to seek Mexico by striking westward overland. When that effort failed, the expedition returned to the same neighborhood of the Mississippi at Aminoya to winter and to build boats; they left the town and started down the Mississippi early in July of 1543, arriving in the Gulf of Mexico toward the end of the month. Since they must have encountered Plaquemine peoples on their journey down the river, it is necessary to be concerned with what is said of the region east of the Mississippi on both occasions.

The first episode is simple enough. Having stripped the town of Anilco of its leader and of provisions, Soto was visited by a leader of the town of Guachoya, located further down a major tributary of the Mississippi, who had intended to attack Anilco. Soto took his party to Guachoya by both water and land in mid-April. Although the leader had abandoned his town and crossed the Mississippi to the eastern side, he returned with gifts of provisions after Soto's men began stripping neighboring towns. This man told Soto that little could be found to the south on the western side of the Mississippi but that the province of Quigualtam lay three leagues south on the eastern side of the Mississippi. Soto sent a party down the western side that confirmed what the leader had said; he also sent an arrogant message to the leader of Quigualtam that was apparently returned in kind. Fearing the collusion of Guachoya and Quigualtam, Soto sent another party to butcher the people of what was probably another Anilco town, while Indians of Guachoya plundered it. Soto died shortly afterwards, and when it seemed that an ordinary burial could not be concealed from the Indians, his body was cast into the Mississippi. After this the expedition made its futile westward journey.

Returning to the Mississippi once more, the Spaniards followed the same path as on their westward course; they found Anilco in December destitute of supplies because their own prior forays had prevented planting. The people directed them to another polity on the Mississippi, Aminoya, which they reached overland through rain and cold. Many expedition members died of exposure, while the Indians apparently abandoned their towns. Seven brigantines were built while the Indians brought supplies. Suspicion of the Indians led to the torture of a captive who claimed to know of a plot by some twenty polities, among them Guachoya and Anilco, to attack the Spaniards. After maiming thirty Guachoya messengers, the Spaniards coopted the Guachoya leader, who apparently colluded in the chastisement of his erstwhile allies.

The expedition departed down the Mississippi in early July, leaving the people of Aminoya and most of the surviving Indian slaves starving behind them. As they passed Guachoya, its leader urged them to take a distributary of the river to attack Quigualtam, but they declined to do so. The second day out they plundered a town of Quigualtam, Huhasene; while there they were observed by Indians on the river, and when they took to the water again they were followed. After the Spaniards burned a bluff-top town, an armada approached numbered in the Elvas account at a hundred canoes, each bearing sixty to seventy men, by which the leader of Quigualtam made overtures of peace. When Juan de Guzmán was sent with a detachment of canoes to drive them off, the Indians mobbed the detachment and killed all but four men.

The Quigualtam Indians continued to harry the expedition until it passed beyond their lands, after which fifty more canoes took up the chase, less well organized but so determined that the Spaniards, seeking to lighten their boats' burdens, were forced to put to shore to butcher most of the horses they had brought along and to release

Table 3.1 Towns Mentioned in the Hernando de Soto Narratives
in Order Encountered.

Oviedo/Ranjel	Burgos/Elvas	Biedma	Garcilaso
Chiaha	Chiaha	Chiha	Ychiaha
5–6 villages		towns	
village			
village			
village [of Coste]			
Coste	Acoste	Costehe	Acoste
Tali	Tali		numerous towns
Tasqui			
village?			
villages?			
Coça	Coça	Coça	Coza
Talimachusy	Tallimuchase	towns	
Itaba	Ytava		
Ulibahali	Ullibahali		
village	village		
Piachi			
Tuasi	Toasi		
village	villages		
village			
Talisi	Tallise	Italisi	Talise
Casiste		towns	town
Caxa			
Humati			
Uxapita			
[Athahachi]	Tastaluça	Taszaluza	Tascaluza
Piachi	Piache		
village			
villages			

the rest. Shortly thereafter the fifty canoes left off and seven more from a small riverside town took up the pursuit for a short time, after which the expedition traveled downriver without molestation until it was attacked by seven more canoes and some Indians on shore. The Spaniards succeeded in driving the Indians away and shortly took to the Gulf of Mexico.

The information conveyed by the accounts from Chiaha to Quizquiz contains the evidence needed to sketch the Spaniards' view of the sociopolitical environment to the north and east of the later Choctaw homeland; the account of the descent of the river provides information for the west. Absolute locations are less important than the system of intervillage, intertribal, and perhaps interchiefdom relationships the Spaniards saw. The differences in the accounts of the expedition's travels through this region are not substantial, but the testimonies of independent witnesses embodied in the Elvas and Garcilaso accounts do occasionally introduce variants. There-

Table 3.1 *Continued*

Oviedo/Ranjel	Burgos/Elvas	Biedma	Garcilaso
Mabila	Mavilla	Mavila	Mauvila
Talicpacana	Taliepatava		
Moçulixa			
Zabusta	Cabusto		
[Apafalaya]			
village			
Chicaça	Chicaça	Chicaza	Chicaza
			Chicacilla
Niculasa	Saquechuma		
Talapatica			
Sacchuma	Miculasa		
Limamu	Alimamu	village	Alibamo fort
Quizqui	Quizquiz	Quizquiz	Chisca
village	village		town
village			
village			
. . . .			
	Nilco	Anicoyanque	Anilco
	Guachoya	Guachoyanque	Guachoya
	[Quigualtam]		[Quigualtanqui]
	Guachoya		Guachoya
. . . .			
	Nilco	town	Aminoya towns
	Aminoya	town	[Anilco]
	Guachoya		[Guachoya]
	[Quigualtam]	[attackers]	[Quigualtanqui]
	Huhasene		town
			[dark attackers]

fore, I have constructed in table 3.1 a parallel itinerary demonstrating gross differences in listed towns, to be used for reference in the following discussion.

Analysis of the social environment described through this chain of events has been so influenced by Spanish prejudgment of what they saw that the Spanish "provinces" have been taken as sociopolitical reality without hesitation and subsequently mapped as chiefdoms when that became a popular construct for interpreting southeastern prehistory. When descriptions seemed to confirm patterns from modern ethnographic parallel or comparable sixteenth-century sources, they have been deemed "reasonable" and "likely" without regard to the internal evidence of the texts or the external evidence of intertextual influence. Nor has much allowance been made for the preinterpretation that is manifest in the narratives – the fact that the Spaniards were trying to make sense of what they were seeing, to fit it into previously established cognitive models. I want to correct that lapse here, to get around the Spanish preconceptions and focus on what they said they saw.

As Clive Orton (1980:23) has so cogently observed, "there are rarely such things as 'objective' facts: more often the data are a record of the relationship between the recorder and the recorded." With these materials, problems of source identification and possible borrowing between them make their interpretation as a cumulative, corroborative body of data erroneous to begin with (see essays in Galloway n.d.d). With the goal of taking the best advantage of all the information, here I use the native towns and the features ascribed to them as a grid to foreground the relationship Orton mentions by exposing descriptive patterns in the sources, unpacking the elements of the Spanish picture and displaying them with attribution in a synoptic table (table 3.2 below).

The four lists of towns, given comparatively in table 3.1, are taken as a single sequence in table 3.2. Against this list the table tallies the features ascribed by each author – Biedma, Oviedo, Elvas, Garcilaso – to these towns and their inhabitants, grouped under "material" and "behavioral" headings. "Framing conditions," consisting of values that could not be tallied for simple presence or absence, are given in table 3.3. I have not attempted to disentangle "real" from "rhetorical" descriptions in tallying these features, nor have I tried to indicate where data may have been borrowed or copied.

The features enumerated in table 3.2 are intended to be exhaustive of features of native culture or behavior actually mentioned, but all features were obviously not enumerated by each author for all towns: towns did not have all the features, observers did not report the same details, and historians who wrote the observers' stories were not similarly motivated. Nearly all the features enumerated are "nominal" or "qualitative" observations, but they are scored on presence alone, indicated by the initial of the reporting author; in most cases a score on absence would require inference. Where no observation was recorded by any author, the relevant space is left blank in the table. Where all four authors agree, the space is solidly shaded. Definitions of these features follow.

Material Features

Environmental setting: The focus of these observations is to establish correlations with subsistence adaptations.

> Broad floodplain: So scored if the Spanish observations note a wide river or extensive fields of crops.
> Narrow floodplain: So scored if the Spanish observations note only a narrow river and few or no standing crops.
> Other: A few towns are specifically described as lacking a floodplain locus.

Evidence from the Early Sixteenth Century

Physical features and settlement layout: Derived from descriptions of the towns and the implications of the activities carried on in them.

Dispersed: Houses are spread out among gardens.

Clustered: A more "urban" concentration with surrounding fields.

Small: In Spanish judgment.

Large: In Spanish judgment.

Old: May also indicate "abandoned."

New: May also imply newly cleared fields.

Plaza: The Spanish word is used to indicate a public open space.

Mound: Any mentioned substructural elevation.

Large and/or unusual buildings: Public buildings, not dwellings.

Dwelling houses: What the Spaniards called "cabins" or "huts."

Fortifications: In some cases inferred from blanket statements.

Food in evidence: Simply records the foodstuffs the Spaniards saw or obtained, and the relative quantity when they estimated it.

Abundant: Abundance relative to observed population.

Meager: Meagerness relative to observed population.

Corn: Corn in any form – stored, prepared, etc.

Beans: Beans in any form.

Gathered foods: Fruit, nuts, and prepared foods made from them.

Game: All meat is included under this rubric.

Communal food store: Implied by "barbacoas."

Individual food store: Implied by Spanish ransacking of dwellings to find food.

Behavioral Features

Leadership: These features are strongly colored by Spanish preconception, hence the neutral statement of the feature names.

Single leader: Spanish "cacique."

Sumptuary distinction: Unusual clothing or ornament.

Litter: The carrying of a single individual.

Service retinue: People performing tasks for the leader's safety or comfort.

Principal men: Men distinguished in some way but clearly not so distinguished as the leader.

Visiting leaders: Men of equal distinction to the leader but not observed in their own towns.

Huhasene	Aminoya	[Quigualtam]	Guachoya	Nilco	..	..	village	village	village	Quizquiz/Chisca	Limamu	Chicacilla	Chicaça	village	[Apatalaya]	Zabusta	Moçulixa	Talicpacana	Mabila	villages	village	Piachi	[Athahachi]/Tastaluça	Uxapita	Humati	Caxa	Casiste	Talisi	village	village
EG	B EG	EG	EG	B					O	O EG	O ▓	O	B G	▓	O G	O	E O	E O	▓ E O B EG	O		E O B EG	▓ G	O	O	O	E O	▓ EG	O	
EG	B EG	EG	EG	EG				O	O	O EG	▓		G		G			E			E		G					O EG		
											G			G																
											O	G	G O	O						O										
			E										EG						E B									E		
	G	G	G							B									B											
G		G	G					O			E		E						B G	O	O	O				O	O	E		
	EG	G	G	EG									G			O							O				E		O	
																								O	O				O	
		G	G										E						EG O				E O							
		G	G							G													EG O							
			G																G				G							
G	G	G	G	G						EG			EG						▓				G							
	B EG		E B										E								O									
E	B EG	G	G	EG				O	E O	B		G	B EG			E	O		E									G E O		
											E	E						E	B											
EG	EG	EG	EG					O	O	B E	E	G	EG			E	O	O	E									E O		
																		E												
G	G	EG	EG							B		G	G B			E			O											
G		EG	G										EG B			E														
		G											E																	
										G																				
E		EG	EG	G					G		G EG		BO E						B EG									▓		
			G	G									B			O			G											
		EG	G							G			E B										E BO							
		G	EG	G						G			E						E				EG O							
		G											BO E						EG B											
																							B							
																							E B							
		EG	EG										B						B G				BO E					B		
		G	EG	EG									EG B						G				O							
				EG															EG B				O							
		G	G										G			G		O				E	G					G		
	G	EG	EG						G		B		G	G		G	O	O												
G E	G	G	EG					G		B EG	G	G	▓	G		G	O O					O						BO E		
E	G	G	EG	EG						G	G	G	G B G O			E	O												
													EG B																	

village	Ulibahali	Itaba	Talimachusy	Coça	villages?	village?	Tasqui	Tali	Coste	village [of Coste]	village	village	5-6 villages	Chiaha	List of Towns
m o	m o	m o	m o	▓	G o	o	o	m o	▓	o	o	o	BO	▓	mentioned
	o	m o		EG			o	o						B EG	broad floodplain
	m									o	o	o			narrow floodplain
															other topography
				EG										m	dispersed settlement pattern
															clustered settlement pattern
o				G o	o	o		o	o		o	o	o		small town
	o	o	m	G o				o	o				BO		large town
															old town
															new town
									o						plaza
															mound
															large/unusual buildings
				G	G			m						EG	dwelling houses
	m												B	BO	fortifications
								m	m					m BO	abundant food
															meager food
				m				o	EG	o		o		m o	corn
				m					o						beans
m o				m BO										m BO	gathered foods
														m	game
				m				m	m o	o				m	communal food store
															individual food store
	m			▓				m o	EG o					EG o	single leader
				EG o											sumptuary distinction
				m BO											litter
				G											service retinue
	m			EG o					EG o					m	principal men
														m	visiting leaders
				B				o	m						hostage value, own town
				m BO				o							hostage value, beyond town
	m			m B				m	m					EG o	hospitality
				G	G			m o						m o	food gifts
				B										G	entertainment
				o				o						m o	women protected
	m							o	EG					EG	water transport
	m o								EG o						offensive weapons
			m	m o				o						m o	flight
															scorched earth

Table 3.2. Synoptic Table of Classificatory Features of Selected Interior Southeastern Polities, 1540–43, according to Biedma, Oviedo's Ranjel, Elvas, and Garcilaso.

Hostage value of leader in own town: If held hostage while Soto party was in his town.

Hostage value of leader beyond town: If taken along as hostage outside his own town.

Interaction with Spaniards: Where observed, these features seem to be pretty clearly observed, since they pertained directly to Spanish self-interest.

Hospitality offered: Apparently uncoerced, unhostile welcome.

Food gifts offered: Apparently uncoerced.

Entertainment offered: Music, dance, etc.

Women protected: By evacuation, threats, etc.

Water transportation in evidence: Boats and rafts and skill with them.

Offensive weapons used: For attack or defense.

Flight: Used as defense.

"Scorched earth": Including carrying food away.

Framing Conditions

Length of Spanish sojourn in days.

Time of year reported as month.

Number of bearers obtained.

Number of women obtained.

Many of these features, of course, have been explicitly labeled as markers of chiefdoms, often on the strength of their appearance in these narratives. The distribution of these features in the different narratives is, therefore, particularly interesting. Do all the narratives agree on the enumeration of such features for so-called province centers? If not, is there any reason why? And if so, which features are enumerated and by whom? Because these narratives have been used to create paradigmatic descriptions of southeastern chiefdoms, particular care should be exercised in understanding how their authors arrived at such descriptions.

Royal factor Luis Hernández de Biedma left the only account written by an eye-witness; it is an official report and has no literary pretensions (Altman n.d.). Much to the chagrin of past researchers, it is also very laconic, sometimes in the extreme – a glance at table 3.1 shows that Biedma did not even mention very many specific locations. Its lack of rhetorical baggage, its character as almost a simple chronicle stating a chain of events, should add to its value. Given its rather sparse detail about the Indians, however, it turns out to have greater value for chronicling what the Spaniards did than for informing us what the Indians did in response.

List of Towns	mentioned	length of stay in days				time of year (month(s))				bearers obtained				women obtained			
		B	O	E	G	B	O	E	G	B	O	E	G	B	O	E	G
Chiaha	▓	27		28	10		6	6			500	some					
5-6 villages	BO	some															
village	O																
village	O																
village [of Coste]	O																
Coste	▓			7	1			7				?					
Tali	O/E			2				7			?	2					4
Tasqui	O																
village?	O																
villages?	O/G				24												
Coça	▓			25	12			7-8		?	many	some	?				
Talimachusy	O/E																
Itaba	O/E	6?		6				8							some		
Ulibahali	O/E										?	?				20	30
village	O/E			1				9									
Piachi	O																
Tuasi	O/E			1				9			?	?				32	30
village	O							9									
village	O							9									
Talisi	▓			20	10			9			?	40	?	27	?		?
Casiste	O/E			1													
Caxa	O			1													
Humati	O																
Uxapita	O																
[Athahachi]/Tastaluça	▓			3				10									
Piachi	O/E							10									
village	O																
villages	O																
Mabila	▓	29		28	24	11		10-11									
Talicpacana	O/E							11									
Moçulixa	O																
Zabusta	O/E							11									
[Apafalaya]	O																
village	O/G				1												
Chicaça	▓			120	60			12-4									
Chicacilla	B/G	28			30												
Limamu	O/EG				4												
Quizquiz/Chisca	▓				6												
village	O/EG				20												
village	O																
village	O																
:																	
:																	
Nilco	B/EG				4	3						?					
Guachoya	B/EG																
[Quigualtam]	EG																
Aminoya	B/EG																
Huhasene	EG																

Table 3.3. Summary Table of Polity Statistics, 1540–43, According to Biedma, Oviedo's Ranjel, Elvas, and Garcilaso.

Biedma names only a few towns, and those he names are by and large those viewed as "province" centers; for that reason it is notable that Biedma apparently did not recall a "Pafalaya" province at all. At Chiaha, Mabila, and Quizquiz he was clearly concerned with the food supply, understandably since the expedition spent more time in these places than in others, yet his report contains little detail about food at

Chicaça, even though the party stayed there a whole winter. Matters of social organization were evidently of interest to him only at Coça, Tastaluça, to a lesser degree at Chicaça, and to little avail at Mabila. Biedma mentions chiefs at Coça, Talisi, Tastaluça, and Chicaça, but of these clearly the Coça and Tastaluça chiefs were more impressive to him and engaged his observation of their behavior. In other instances, as especially at Quizquiz and for the sites west of the Mississippi River listed here, Biedma either did not observe political matters or did not choose to record them. Because archaeological evidence attests to the size and prosperity of the chiefdoms of the Mississippi Valley, Biedma seems to have been as selective in his own way as the other authors.

The version of the Soto story told by Gonzalo Fernández de Oviedo in the name of Roderigo Ranjel is a much more artistic production than that of Biedma, even though Oviedo ostensibly intruded his own commentary only in a limited and overt manner. Ranjel clearly provided a lot of data, however; table 3.1 suggests that his enumeration of even unnamed towns was close to exhaustive, and that Oviedo must have chosen to use most of what he found in his source.

It is not possible to know whose preferences, Ranjel's or Oviedo's, are reflected in the clear partiality for specific kinds of information apparent in table 3.2. The very frequent observations of town size are fairly consistent, but matters of social organization are recorded for a much more restricted set of towns: Chiaha, Coste, Tali, Coça, Talisi, Athahachi, Apafalaya, and Chicaça. Of that set only Tali, Coça, and Athahachi seem to have powerful chiefs, and only Coste, Athahachi, and nonmember Mabila are recorded as having elements of communal architecture. In terms of observed features presumed to be correlated with paramount chiefdoms, Oviedo clearly thought Ranjel believed Athahachi to be the most impressive polity observed in the region, while almost nothing at all was observed of Chicaça.

If there was a gentleman of Elvas, his identity is not yet known, but recent research has shown that although the story in the narrative is authentic, it is very much an "as told to" effort, with an active author of literary pretensions at the helm (Elbl and Elbl n.d.). Some access to Oviedo's account may well be implied in the Elvas narrative: table 3.1 shows, for example, that the small segment of the expedition it records contains references to eight towns that only Ranjel and Elvas mention by name; six of these are not mentioned at all in the other narratives.

Yet the themes explored in the two narratives differ very interestingly in their observations about Indians, as an examination of table 3.2 will show. The Elvas narrative is much concerned with the details of food provisions, more consistently so than any of the other narratives. Many more chiefs are cited as well, although the information on social organization here almost directly mirrors that in Oviedo, and the simple citation of numerous chiefs seems to be connected with the well-known penchant of the Elvas narrator for the introduction of manufactured chiefly speeches. This account does, however, tend to record more observations of towns where more time was spent, thus offering more details, for example, about Chicaça than any other narrative. These additional details are also partially a product of increased rhetorical emphasis on these towns.

The Inca mestizo Garcilaso de la Vega has presented researchers with a seeming feast of information, but the seductively artistic quality of the narrative has complicated the difficulty of disentangling the authentic from the invented. Thus, although the listing of towns in table 3.1 suggests that his narrative might be as laconic as that of Biedma, such is emphatically not the case; the sparseness of the set of towns mentioned by Garcilaso stems from his artistic motivation to write focused set pieces centering on a few towns in order to tell his story in terms of a few memorable images (see Dowling n.d.).

Although Garcilaso's account compresses the number of places where features are enumerated, his interests in the food supply tally closely with those of the Elvas narrator; similar parallels occur in the enumeration of dwelling houses. Garcilaso, with his interest in demonstrating the knightly fighting qualities of the Indians, chose to elaborate on features connected with that topic, but for the region under discussion east of the Mississippi, he noted very little evidence of significant chiefly grandeur compared to the other historians Oviedo and "Elvas," and his account does not even report a distinct single leader for Chicaça.

The tabulation of this evidence in tables 3.2 and 3.3 immediately exhibits one major problem with gathering details from such narratives: the observations are selective, chosen by the eyewitnesses and by the authors of the texts (only Biedma is both). More detail generally correlates with lengthy sojourns or with dangerous events, both of which would have served to anchor memories (cf. Lankford 1993). Furthermore, at least in the case of the Oviedo, Elvas, and Garcilaso accounts, the amount of detail depends, to a degree that is no longer precisely recoverable, on the artistic aims of the historian who composed the narratives. Finally, we cannot entirely rule out interdependence – even if only that fostered by the mythmaking activity of "campfire tales" (Lankford 1993) – and literary borrowing is possible as well (Galloway n.d.b; Elbl and Elbl n.d.; Henige n.d.).

In other words, agreement in testimony cannot be taken simply to reflect corroboration of the same observation; although these four sources ostensibly represent six testimonies, only one testimony is directly available, and even that one is not a consistent and literal recitation of facts. This caveat should be borne in mind in the discussion that follows.

The synoptic presentation of the Iberians' observations in tables 3.2 and 3.3 shows clearly why researchers taking them at face value and cumulatively have been tempted

Table 3.4 Groupwise Authorial Agreement on
Observations in Table 3.2.

Author(s)	Number of Observations	Percent of Total
B	13	3.5
O	83	22.8
E	48	13.3
G	78	21.4
BO	3	0.8
BE	6	1.6
BG	4	1.0
OE	25	6.8
OG	6	1.6
EG	40	10.9
BOE	10	2.7
BOG	0	0.0
BEG	16	4.3
OEG	14	3.8
BOEG	18	4.9
Total	364	

Key: B = Biedma, O = Oviedo's Ranjel, E = Elvas, G = Garcilaso

to assume a uniformly complex degree of social organization in the groups they purport to describe: additively, the accounts provide a satisfyingly "thick" description. But these tables and derivative ones that tabulate authorial agreements and singularities (tables 3.4 and 3.5) also show that no single author provides all the evidence (fully 61 percent of all observations were cited by only one author, but no author was responsible for more than 37 percent of these unique observations). Furthermore, not only is consensus the exception rather than the rule, but the strongest consensus over this segment of the route is between the least authoritative of the authors, Elvas and Garcilaso de la Vega.

Certain of the more thoroughly described towns where the Spaniards passed more time were obviously larger and more populous than others in their vicinity, and they account for the bulk of the agreements among the accounts. Two factors, however, disallow the uncritical acceptance of their identification as paramount chiefdom centers. The first is their location: all students of the Soto route have agreed with the overt evidence of the narratives that he and his men followed major rivers, and to the extent that the Mississippian adaptation selected for broad floodplains, this would mean that the expedition encountered the most important of such settlements *on the rivers they followed.* They did not explore all major rivers in the region, however, and not all major sites were located on large rivers; after more than five hundred years of floodplain use – even allowing for annual renewal of soil through flooding (Smith

Table 3.5 Pairwise Authorial Agreement on
Observations in Table 3.2.

Author Pair	Number of Observations	Percent of Total
BO	31	10
BE	50	11
BG	38	8
OE	67	15
OG	38	8
EG	88	21
Total	312	

Total number of observations by author, including those made alone and those agreeing with other authors.

Author	Number of Observations	Percent of Total
B	70	4
O	159	9
E	177	10
G	176	10
Total	582	

Key: B = Biedma, O = Oviedo's Ranjel, E = Elvas, G = Garcilaso

1978a) and other means of fertilization (Dobyns 1983:235–36) – one might expect to find some settlement in other locations. Some villages seen at a distance or passed through quickly were evidently quite large, and the Spaniards likely did not see all the villages of a given region, so the towns they considered significant were not necessarily the chiefdom centers.

The second reason for caution in using the Spanish evidence to reconstruct a mosaic of southeastern polities is that the Spaniards were so certain of their moral and material superiority that they made many unwarranted assumptions about social organization. These sources unanimously hold the general view that Indian leaders were so naive and their planning abilities so poor that they could be counted upon to react with a knee-jerk regularity to Spanish tactics that had been effective in Mexico and Peru, in very different sociopolitical contexts after very different histories of contagion. Tribes and even chiefdoms are not so strongly affected by the loss of their leaders as are incipient states, so in fact the kidnapping of chiefs was relatively ineffective in the Southeast. Nor did disease precede this set of Spaniards so devastatingly into the heart of the Deep South; by the time Soto and his men reached Chiaha they had been more than a year on the road and could have transmitted very few acute diseases (Ramenofsky and Galloway n.d.), and the only alleged evidence in any of the sources for serious population depletion by disease that preceded them does not concern the Alabama-Mississippi region.

The Spaniards assumed that, beyond a few simple military ruses, the Indians were incapable of deception and other actions that would direct the Spaniards to go where the Indians wanted, and that in any case the Spaniards would not have been susceptible to such manipulation. Yet the evidence of the Oviedo/Ranjel narrative shows consistently that the Spaniards bypassed many villages or passed through quickly, and none of the accounts mention food supply in those villages. A reasonable conclusion is that the people had vacated the villages, taking their food supply with them. Nor were such vacated villages merely small ones. Such actions could even have lured or directed the Spaniards away from some polity centers. The expedition also camped frequently and uncomfortably in the open while within easy reach of Indian habitation – without further explanation from the narratives.

An Indian view of the expedition's progress, quite different from the one the sources present, is possible, though more difficult given the handicaps associated with the sources. Patterns of occurrence of fancy native trade goods as well as of pottery design influences, amply attested in the archaeological literature, can argue strongly for the view that the Indians of the Southeast did not huddle in embattled agglomerations but were acquainted with neighbors and indeed frequently allied with them, so that an interlocking network of trade and communications covered the entire Southeast. Some groups were doubtless more active participants in this network than others, and enmities between neighbors could create local discontinuities, but its existence would have made it impossible for the Soto expedition to wander very far unremarked across the Southeast, or for its purpose and methods to remain unknown. Brown (1989) has suggested that the absence of formal greeting ceremonies offered to the expedition argues that the calumet ceremony was a late introduction in the Southeast, fostered by the French in the late seventeenth century. To my mind this absence suggests much more eloquently the Indian attitude toward the Soto expedition – that southeastern Indians had no intention of offering formal welcome and a ceremony for making guests "not-foreign" to these particular people, who advanced demanding welcome and dragging their neighbors in chains.

The Indians must have realized early on that the Spaniards were offering little in the way of prestige-goods trade; only seldom do the accounts mention gifts to the Indians, and the range of these gifts was limited (see Swanton 1939:55; Smith 1987: 23–53). The Spaniards' only consistent actions, by their own testimony, were demands for obedience to their king, questions about gold and other stones, abuse of hospitality through seizing and chaining bearers and raping women, and capture and imprisonment of chiefs or people they perceived as chiefs. These strange white barbarians were, however, too many, too well mounted and armed, and too well rehearsed in combat to be attacked and killed outright, at least in their full strength at the beginning of the journey. Two other strategies were available – getting rid of them with the least possible loss of life and freedom, and attacking by ruse and entrapment – and both strategies were used. The less confrontational tactic of guerrilla-style harassment was also available and also used. I do not mean to suggest a unified scheme of expedition containment in operation across the Southeast (although this point could be argued for some regions), but the Indians in most cases were likely aware of what had transpired among their nearest neighbors and often had even more forewarning. I would like to suggest that variation in reaction to the Spaniards may correlate with variation in social organization. Where chiefdoms were still in operation an organized strategy was in evidence; indeed, evidence of concerted action is a far better indication of the central place of a chiefdom than is the Spanish perception as reflected in what chief to grab. Where autonomous towns were led by big-men or the leaders of simple chiefdoms, alliance with peers among their neighbors was reflected in a "pass-along" effect.

The patterning of the data in tables 3.2 and 3.3 can be more informative than the content. The greatest amount of detail ought to be reported of the places where the Spaniards stayed the longest, but this is not true except on average. Certainly we have a large amount of detail about Chiaha, Coça, and Mabila, where the Spaniards spent twenty-three, thirty-six, and twenty-six days respectively. More impressive detail, and perhaps a larger amount of detail, is available for Tascaluça's town, Athahachi, although the expedition passed only two days there. The longest stopover, ninety-nine days at Chicaça, yielded hardly any description of either social organization or lifeways. A justified conclusion from these simple facts is that Athahachi was the most impressive town they visited in the Georgia-Alabama-Mississippi region, while what they saw of the Chicaça region was the least impressive. In organizational terms, Athahachi was a nucleated town with a familiar-looking hierarchical social organization, while Chicaça was a dispersed settlement of autonomous towns whose organization the Spaniards did not comprehend.

Several other facts are striking. To begin with, only two Indian leaders in the region were taken and held prisoner beyond what the Spaniards considered the leader's main town. This practice contrasts strongly with the usual assertions regarding both Soto's methods and social organization in the region: that a tightly dovetailed series of chiefdoms would supposedly be controlled by the sequential captivity of their chiefs. Indeed, recent studies of the Soto expedition have laid great stress on the existence of hierarchically organized chiefdoms across the Southeast in the sixteenth century (see DePratter 1983). Nevertheless, the data for the region of interest show that Soto looked in vain for such men at frequent intervals, and in the instance of Coça this pursuit led him to drag one chief "far from his own country." This fact has led one group of researchers to claim that Coça was one of the more extensive of these chiefdoms, lying two hundred miles long on two major watersheds and taking in at least two and possibly three cultural traditions, including all the towns from Chiaha to Talisi (Hudson et al. 1985). This proposal has been criticized, however, for failing to offer a credible chiefdom model that would account for the central place being as modest a site as the one claimed for it, Little Egypt (Boyd and Schroedl 1987).

More important in my view, the documentary evidence simply does not support such a picture. The narratives give no hint whatsoever – beyond the assumptions of the Spaniards and Garcilaso's assertion that the "province" of Coça stretched for a hundred leagues – that Chiaha, Coste, or Tali were in any way subordinate to Coça or to anyone else. Even the supposedly powerful chief Tascaluça was not all-powerful: inhabitants of the Piachi town between Athahachi and Mabila attacked the expedition and killed some of Tascaluça's own retinue. The Spaniards speak of "provinces" and "subject towns," but what evidence do they offer of such phenomena? How much of it was real, how much what they expected to see?

I have suggested that a good deal of the Spanish representation of native "provinces" and their power structures could be attributed to what the Spaniards wished to see and how they understood human society. It is worth pausing for a moment to consider how Spanish society itself was structured and how that structure was deployed across the landscape. In sixteenth-century Europe in general, the cities and their "satellite" towns formed "planetary systems" (Braudel 1972, 1:327). Lockhart and Schwartz (1983:3–4) have summarized modern research in outlining the importance of the city-state as the fundamental unit of social and political organization in the Iberian Peninsula:

> The province, the city, and the neighborhood were crucial reference points in helping individuals to define themselves in relation to others. Nothing but family had as strong a hold on the emotions of Iberians or was as essential to their sense of identity as regionalism. . . . The city proper was indissolubly integrated with . . . its territory, where many of its citizens had their holdings; people domiciled in surrounding hamlets were as much citizens of the city-province as the true urban dwellers. The percentage of the populace living within the city walls was not necessarily high, but nearly everyone with any position was located there. All organizations . . . had their directorship and headquarters in the city. . . . [T]he nobility too, both the high nobles and those only locally prominent, were urban based. . . . The Iberian city . . . was a theater of action for the entire society.

Indeed, Ferdinand and Isabella made their most important contribution to Spain's history when they brought the cities of Aragon and Castile under the control of a unified territorial state government in 1521 (Haring 1963:2–3).

Not surprisingly, this description of the Iberian city-state coincides closely with the picture of native "provinces" from the narratives, and the Spanish habit of assuming that a province or town bore the same name as its chief matches the European practice of referring to a nobleman by the name of his estate. Three of the four narratives – those with the most descriptive detail – were written by literary men for a continental European audience, so by replicating a familiar model the writer could communicate more readily. A few examples can show, however, that the systemic behavior of the entities bearing the Spaniards' interpretive labels – towns, chiefs, councilors, vassals, and so forth – often contradicted those labels; the labels were thus an act of wishful thinking or artistic license. Spaniards in the Americas, after all, had come to extract labor and profit from the Indians through an institution known as the *encomienda*, whereby an individual conquistador was granted rights to the production of a native political unit, which might range from a single Arawak village on Santo Domingo to an entire province of the Aztec or Inca empire. Chiefs and people remained in place, and the tribute and corvée labor formerly the prerogative of the chief was instead channeled by him in large part to the Spanish grantee in good feudal fashion (Simpson 1966; Lockhart and Schwartz 1983:69). If southeastern native polities could be parceled out in that way, then the region was worth Spanish effort.

Soto and his men were clearly seeking the kind of population concentrations and chiefly governing apparatus that would have made *La Florida* a candidate for the *encomienda* system, as can be seen from Oviedo's constant asides asking why, once a prosperous region such as Apalachee or Cofitachequi or Coça was found, Soto did not at once take action to found a settlement and establish communications with his line of supply; indeed, these same questions were apparently raised among his men, particularly once the expedition reached the rich Mississippi Valley. Equally clearly, the area did not fulfill one requirement: precious metals or gemstones that could be extracted with *encomienda* labor; the pearls of Cofitachequi were the sole real possibility the expedition encountered. I would suggest, however, that whatever image the narratives now seem to paint, Soto himself could see very well that adequate chiefly apparatus, and more particularly the kind of centralized state and multilevel province that enriched the *encomenderos* of Mexico and Peru, simply were not present in southeastern North America; and so he did not stop until he died.

In my opinion, the behavioral evidence from the narratives argues for at most a handful of paramount chiefdoms from Coça to the Mississippi, numerous "simple" chiefdoms, and, particularly in the Tombigbee region, tribal confederations. Part of this evidence relates to settlement patterns: the Spaniards saw several sizes of permanent settlement and several arrangements of such settlements across the landscape. Some towns, including Chiaha, Coste, Coça, Athahachi, and Mabila, were large and specially sited. Others, many of them unnamed, were small villages or hamlets. The narrators say that at Coça and Mabila numerous small hamlets were spread across the landscape among cultivated fields. But at Chicaça, settlement was so dispersed that the explorers could barely distinguish a central town at all.

Athahachi, Quizquiz, and probably Quigualtam are the only three reasonable candidates for paramount chiefdoms in the area of interest. For when the narrative says that the chief of Tali had food brought to the Spaniards from his villages as they passed, it is a Spaniard who has decided why the food was brought – a Spaniard who hopes to see subject towns performing at the command of a province leader. Athahachi stands out because Tascaluça's messengers met Soto in another leader's town (Talisi), and although there is no proof that Tascaluça alone orchestrated the attack at Mabila, he was a vital part of the charade that brought the Spaniards to the spot. The explorers coerced the leader of Quizquiz by capturing people not from his own town, although the chief himself was never seen. Finally, the leader of Quigualtam, also not seen, was able to frighten his neighbors from the relatively impressive Guachoya and Aminoya polities west of the river and to set a significant armada of canoes on the Mississippi.

The arguments Hudson and his colleagues have made for the massive hegemony of Coça over three watersheds and two hundred miles of country (Hudson et al. 1985), based upon the cumulative descriptions of the Spanish accounts, seem to be yielding to a model of ad hoc alliance on closer examination of the archaeological evidence. The archaeology of the Tennessee-Georgia-Alabama border region is revealing only very modest chiefdom settlement patterns and no evidence of the kind of intrapolity exchanges characteristic of dynamic paramount chiefdoms (Hally, Smith, and Langford 1990). Hally and his colleagues cannot explain why the Spaniards saw a paramount chiefdom, since no physical evidence for one exists; they conclude that the Coça paramountcy's having been "unstable and short-lived" (Hally, Smith, and Langford 1990:134) might account for such a state of affairs. The simpler answer is that the multileveled Coça polity was an artifact of Spanish wishful thinking and overinterpretation of the evidence, perhaps even that some of Coça's connections with its neighbors were alliances called into being by the Spanish presence. Coça may have been important, but either it did not hold such expanded sway as the narratives claim or the archaeologists are all wrong in their construction of how chiefdoms were held together.

These observations are important for two reasons. First, if Coça was more figment than fact, then the identification of paramountcies elsewhere based on these narratives must be called into question or at least examined with some care. Second, since the records make no mention of contagion in this region, we must assume that the variety of social organization seen here was a product of the native natural and political environment.

The far larger class of "simple" chiefdoms is made up mostly of what the Spaniards observed as less important "provinces" from Chiaha to Mabila, including Chiaha, Coste, Tali, Tasqui, and probably Itaba, Talisi, and Piachi. Itaba and Piachi seem to represent independent pockets in regions allied with Coça and Athahachi and may be more closely related in organization to the autonomous towns of the "Apafalaya" confederation and the scattered "Chicaça" towns that may have included Alimamu, Sacchuma, Miculasa, and Talipatica. Across the Mississippi, the Anilco, Guachoya, and Aminoya "provinces" were described in detail only by Garcilaso, who presented them in confused order and was so obsessed with his theme of "good Indian versus bad Indian" that he also obscured their social organization, but they too probably represented simple chiefdoms that may or may not have stood in some tributary position relative to Quigualtam.

Other evidence that would support the argument for multilevel chiefdoms is more concrete: communal food stores (*barbacoas*) under the control of the leader and "civic" architecture. As seen in table 3.2, the Spaniards broached chiefly *barbacoas* only in Coste and another unnamed town near it. Where food was supplied elsewhere, the narratives did not mention a communal food store. "Civic" architecture is likewise scarce in the reliable narratives. Only at Athahachi was a substructural mound portrayed in use for ceremonial purposes. Fortifications seem to have been too widespread to be a reliable sign of chiefdom boundaries: Biedma's statement that from Chiaha onward the towns were fenced implies that fortified towns were not limited to those on "province" borders (cf. DePratter 1983:38–39). Fortifications were specifically noted at Chiaha, Ulibihali, an unnamed village after Tuasi, another after Piachi, and of course Mabila; several of these could not be province boundaries by any argument. Mabila, finally, exhibited what seems to have been an unusual form of public building: large structures much like longhouses. Given any view of Mabila – inhabited town or empty ceremonial center – they are unusual for the region. But the sum of all this evidence represents almost nothing conclusive as an argument for a multilevel chiefdom.

The picture of the chiefs may provide more direct evidence. Table 3.2 includes several items said to be characteristic of chiefly status: sumptuary distinction, litter bearing, and the presence of a clearly menial service retinue. These features are all present in only one case, that of Coça, and then only if one can supply the service retinue from Garcilaso alone. At Athahachi, whose leader waited for Soto to come to him, only the litter is missing according to Biedma, Ranjel, and Elvas, but there was clearly no occasion for it to be recorded. And although Quigualtam was a threat never seen, the refusal of the chief to come to Soto echoes the behavior of Tascaluça. Two other features, however, may be more revealing because they are more often noted: categories of individuals the Spaniards perceived as "principal men" and visiting leaders. Principal men were observed at Chiaha, Coste, Coça, Ulibihali, Athahachi, Chicaça, and Guachoya, but they may have been anything from relatives to a village council to the elites one would expect to surround a chief. The visiting leaders are more interesting: present at Chiaha (Elvas), Mabila (Biedma?, Elvas?, Garcilaso), Chicaça (Biedma?, Ranjel, Elvas), and Quigualtam (Garcilaso), they must have appeared to be chiefs in order to be so noted. Their presence, however, could imply an alliance of equals just as well as the subordination of a multilevel structure.

A more extended examination of the powers of the region's chiefs shows an even more complex pattern. Biedma, Ranjel, and Elvas all refer to the "chiefly" leaders as *caciques*, the title used by the Arawaks of the Caribbean Islands to designate their big-man leaders and picked up by the Spaniards from that context. By the time of Soto's exploration, the term had been applied to such a wide range of native offices that it had lost all precision. Only Garcilaso, drawing on his own Peruvian background, refers to the chiefly leaders as *curacas*, the term applied to the rulers of Inca city-states. In other words, only the fabulist used the term that should apply specifically to the leader of a complex chiefdom or state.

So much is claimed for the ability of chiefs to organize corvée labor that a closer look at the chiefs' actions is worthwhile. Through this portion of the journey the Spaniards obtained bearers at Chiaha, Tali, Coça, Ulibihali, Tuasi, and Athahachi. At Chiaha, imprisonment of the leader coerced his people to return to the town to serve as bearers; at Tali, Soto held women and children captive to force the leader to grant bearers. At Coça, though Ranjel says its *cacique* ruled *mucha tierra*, he apparently did not rule his people; Soto's men had to round up and chain the bearers even though they had already captured the leader. His rule may have been more effective at Ulibihali, where no resident leader appeared and danger to the Coça leader caused the people to give Soto bearers and women. At Tuasi there is likewise mention of no leader, but bearers and women were given here too. The people of Talisi first abandoned their town; its leader provided carriers and women when the Spaniards did not leave. Finally, at Athahachi, Tascaluça provided some bearers, with promise of more – and women – at Mabila. This last promise was never kept, nor did the Spaniards obtain any other bearers until after they crossed the Mississippi.

Apparently, then, leaders along the Chiaha to Mabila section of the route had some limited ability to command corvée labor, although the capture of a chief or people may have altered the corvée labor condition; personal threat to a popular local leader might well have persuaded a number of his neighbors to step forward as bearers when normally he might never have had the power – or the desire – to demand such labor of them. The case of Coça is especially confusing: the leader could not command labor in the town the Spaniards took to be his, but apparently danger to him elicited bearers in two other towns, Ulibihali and Tuasi, whose leaders were absent. And although Tascaluça could grant bearers in Athahachi, his professed power to grant bearers in Mabila was not demonstrated.

Conspicuously, the Spaniards did *not* spend the night in every village they encountered at the end of a day's march. Certainly they crossed some country that was barren of settlement, but for the Chiaha-to-Quizquiz segment of the route they camped out-of-doors but within easy reach of one or more villages no fewer than ten times. The Spaniards obviously preferred the comforts to be had in a permanent settlement – witness the pattern of lengthy sojourns in single towns separated by relatively steady travel. Of course, Soto may have preferred to keep his army uncomfortable when they were on the march in order to move them along, but this practice would seem dangerous in the long term. I suggest that the expedition did not pause in certain towns for two reasons: because the towns had been emptied of people and provisions, and because Soto was afraid to stop in those towns.

Many of the avoided towns, as table 3.2 shows, were not even named – quite possibly because there was no local leader or indeed anyone else to greet the Spaniards. Half of the ten instances noted occurred while the Spaniards had in their custody a supposed sovereign chief who, by the chiefdom argument, should have held sway over the avoided towns and thus assured a welcome if kept in captivity and under threat. I would conclude that the Spaniards more likely held leaders to assure the good conduct of the *bearers* they had provided, holding the leaders as long as the bearers lasted. Even in chains, the bearers were in such great numbers and were so resentful of their captivity that they could be dangerous until worn down somewhat, as the Spaniards had learned to their cost at Iviahica. The expedition thus avoided settled environs until it had broken in a large new batch of bearers, depending on the presence of the chief, when they held him, to keep the bearers in line. This pattern is quite clear after Coça and Athahachi, where they received "many" and four hundred bearers respectively.

Another apparent pattern may account for some of the cooperation accorded the Spaniards: the necessity to safeguard food crops. I infer this possibility because of the correlation between cooperation and time of year. Soto passed through the eastern part of the region, meeting with some degree of cooperation, in summer and early autumn, when the promise of ripening crops and the need to protect them made giving away year-old food stores practicable; but in October and thereafter, at Mabila and in the "Pafalaya" region, the expedition met with hostility and resistance – and found no food worth mentioning.

Thus a closer consideration of the behavior and observations portrayed in the narratives obviously does not support an elaborate framework of unbroken chiefdoms. What the evidence does support is a patchwork of variation in social organization (see Smith 1986:58). If we consider the actual behavior of the Indians rather than European interpretations, the evidence also suggests that, at least for the purpose of coping with the crisis created by the expedition's presence, cooperation rather than intergroup warfare was the rule in the Alabama-Mississippi region. I can perhaps present this interpretation more directly through a reconstruction of the chain of events presented earlier, this time attempting to take account of Indian motivations.

Having heard of the power and number of the Spanish group from his neighbors of Guaxale, the leader of the simple chiefdom of Chiaha decided with his council to provide the Spaniards with whatever food they might need, since the year's harvest promised to be a good one and any depleted stores would be replaced. This policy of appeasement seemed to be working until the Spaniards demanded women, causing the population of the town to flee to their neighbors. The chief was taken into custody and threatened, but the people would not return until the Spaniards consented to take bearers instead of women and to leave off collars and chains. By this means the people rid themselves of the Spaniards and kept their chief. During the several days that this wrangling went on, the Chiaha people warned neighboring villages of the Spaniards' perfidy so that most of them were able to take the precaution of evacuating people and frequently also food supplies; Soto and his men consequently had to pass through or near five or six villages before they came to one with any corn left in it.

The Coste chief thus had plenty of prior warning to make his plans, but he traveled to meet Soto in a vacated town in the open while his own people made ready to attack the expedition in their fortified island town. The Spaniards behaved as expected, helping themselves without invitation to the communal food supply the people had left behind to occupy them, and the Coste chief was able to slip away to complete preparations in his town. When the Spaniards arrived and began their plunder, the people of Coste were ready for them and sprang to arms, placing the Spaniards in such an awkward position that Soto had to resort to cudgeling his own men to gain the upper hand. Convinced of his sincerity, the chief and his council showed him where to camp in order to reduce tensions, at which time Soto had chief and council seized and held prisoner for the remainder of the week the Spaniards spent in Coste. The people provided the Spaniards with food and remained peaceful for the sake of their leaders, secure in the knowledge that the difficulties of the crossing off the island would make demands for bearers too dangerous.

Fearing any nearby village, the Spaniards camped in the open until they reached Tali. Although this town was located on another island, the Spaniards thwarted the chief's efforts to evacuate his people, capturing a number of women and children and forcing the Tali chief to admit the expedition to the town. Hoping to rid himself of the Spaniards quickly, the chief supplied them immediately with food and carriers. Faced with managing a new group of carriers, the Spaniards departed the next day. Villages near their path sent out food in the hope of being avoided, since the Spaniards already had all the carriers they needed. The expedition stopped to camp in only one village, Tasqui, where the people had managed to evacuate before the arrival of the Spaniards.

The chief of Coça thought to meet with Soto on equal terms and so met him in state carried on his litter. After the Coste experience, however, Soto simply threw him and his council in chains and moved into the town as the people fled. There the Spaniards made themselves at home for more than a month, and when it was time to leave they scoured the countryside for captives to put in chains. They took the Coça chief and his sister with them, but they avoided the next neighboring town of Talimachusy and camped out. The people of Itaba accepted the extraordinary prestige items that the Spaniards were suddenly offering for the access to women that they had been unable to obtain by force at Coça. The expedition camped there for a week.

Departing Itaba, they avoided the next neighboring villages, a procedure shown to be justified when they were confronted at Ulibihali by the town in arms. By then harvest time was near, and villagers could not leave their towns or crops to the mercy of the Spaniards if any other possibility offered itself. So when the Coça chief suggested that they offer a few carriers and some women, they acceded but did not fail to take their revenge on two incautious members of the expedition, who were "lost."

The Spaniards then traveled onward, staying in a small vacated village but otherwise avoiding Indian contact until they reached Tuasi, where again the goal of protecting their crops induced the people to provide carriers and women. After Tuasi they encountered several evacuated villages, one of which seemed to be abandoned. At Talisi, which had been evacuated, the Spaniards encamped so long, in spite of a message from Tascaluça and although the people had left rich food supplies to speed the explorers on their way, that the chief acceded to fate and returned with the inevitable carriers and women. By that time nearly all the Coça carriers had been exhausted or killed, so the Coça chief was released; his sister, however, was kept in custody and indeed may have survived the journey all the way to Mexico.

Departing for Tascaluça's town, the Spaniards took no chances and camped only in small deserted villages or in the open. From such a camp outside Athahachi they sent messages to Tascaluça, who spurned meeting them and instead completed preparations to destroy the Spaniards with the help of his allies. Thus the Spaniards entering the town were greeted with the spectacle of Tascaluça arrayed with the signs of his rank in his ceremonial center. Dances were provided to entertain and perhaps distract the Spaniards, and when Soto predictably took Tascaluça into custody, the chief sent his council away to act for him in making further arrangements. The next day four hundred carriers were granted to Soto, and women were promised in another town to increase the expedition's incentive for departing.

This ploy was successful. As arrangements went forward among Tascaluça's allies, he proceeded in Spanish custody toward the ambush being laid at Mabila. On the way some enemies of his in the small village of Piachi took the opportunity to attempt to assassinate him; they succeeded in killing some of Tascaluça's service retinue but not the chief himself. After Piachi, and in spite of passing through an agriculturally rich region of numerous dispersed villages, the expedition camped in the open constantly, a report of a gathering of arms and men at Mabila making them cautious. The Spaniards met no resistance along the way, but from the safety of fortified villages the Indians sent out provisions to urge them along.

At Mabila preparations had been proceeding, perhaps masterminded by Tascaluça but carried out by the leaders of several autonomous groups acting under his temporary leadership. In the ceremonial center of Mabila warriors had gathered, storing weapons and secreting themselves in the large clan houses of the vacant center for days. When the mounted Spaniards entered the circle of fortifications, the feint of women dancers was offered to support the false promises of women and to lull the Spaniards into a sense of security. Tascaluça watched for his chance, and as soon as he was able to slip from the custody of the Spaniards the attack began – ironically, much the same kind of trap as Soto had sprung on the Inca Atahualpa at Cajamarca (Lockhart 1972:10–11). Because of their horses and steel weapons, the Spaniards were able to escape from the ambush with heavy wounds but few mortal casualties, and they then proceeded to take advantage of the open countryside around Mabila that favored their cavalry. The infantry contingent reduced the walls of Mabila and burned the town, unintentionally also burning the entire contents of Soto's baggage train. The Indians sustained heavy casualties, as they knew they would and as they had sworn to do if necessary, but Tascaluça escaped and the Spanish expedition was crippled.

When Soto and his men finally moved northward and westward, they entered a region that was both sparsely settled and forewarned. Along a minor floodplain they encountered several autonomous villages – Talicpacana, Moculixa, Zabusta, and Apafalaya – that had been essentially emptied of both their population and their recent corn harvest, only a part of which the Spaniards were able to recover. Yet no bearers were evident, although the Spaniards had taken an important man prisoner at the Apafalaya village.

The expedition next moved into a much more sparsely settled region of even smaller floodplains, with autonomous villages loosely connected by marriage alliances. Again they found villages abandoned and emptied of their provisions, and the weather was growing bitter. The Spaniards were thus forced to settle in one of the deserted villages, and when it became obvious that they had no intention of leaving until the weather was better for traveling, the chiefs of the region gathered to decide what to do. One of their number made contact with the expedition and attempted to get rid of them by speaking of a fabulous land known as Caluca to which he would supply guides. When that tactic failed, he claimed a need for military aid against the "rebellious" Sacchuma in an attempt to split the Spaniards' force, but this effort also was unsuccessful, as the poorly equipped Spaniards were doubly on their guard. Finally the allied chiefs, unable to agree on any action, decided that the best plan was to keep the Spaniards in one place for the winter while taking the chance to observe them, so the chiefs of Sacchuma and Talapatica came to feign obedience. To keep the Spaniards away from their villages and people, the allied chiefs provided them with food through the winter, hoping to learn enough about them to make an effective attack should the expedition try to make demands before leaving.

When the inevitable demand for carriers came, the Indians attacked the camp with some success, particularly in capturing and killing horses. With the village burned, the Spaniards were forced to move their camp to an open plain, where the Indians attacked them again two weeks later. The Spaniards had to spend another week in the region, but they were forced to depart without carriers or women when they began to run low on food, which the Indians had cut off with the first hostilities. They moved on to search the deserted town of Limamu for provisions, without success, but the men of Limamu drew them westward by making a stand behind a fortification, escaping as the Spaniards broke through. Left without provisions and with unremitting hostility behind them, the Spaniards began a desperate search westward for food.

Entering another major floodplain at last, they had unknowingly passed out of a region whose language and culture were sufficiently related to enable cooperation over long distance, into another whose communication with the first was more limited. Thus they were able to surprise some of the citizens of the prosperous chiefdom of Quizquiz, although they did not happen to enter the main town first. Ample provisions were maintained, even at the end of winter, in the communal stores administered by the chief, permitting the Spaniards to regain their strength for the next great leap of their journey: the crossing of the Mississippi. They then passed beyond the region of interest for some time.

Having heard rumors of the strange intruders who had passed north of his country, the chief of Quigualtam was alert to scattered reports of their wanderings west of the Mississippi, but aside from meddling inconclusively in several interpolity squabbles, the strangers did nothing of note but survive, in spite of various wiles exercised to make them lose their way and in spite of a serious run-in with the Tula people far to the west. The Quigualtam chief was thus surprised and offended to be summoned into the presence of the leader of the ragtag homeless band, and he returned an insulting message instead. Delighted when his mere message and the messenger's report of his grandeur caused the death of the alien leader and confusion of his band, the Quigualtam chief was nonetheless vexed when he heard that the group had returned to the river to prepare to depart. Knowing that the sea to the south was far too dangerous for anyone to navigate successfully, he determined to chase the strangers into it as quickly as he could, so he summoned all the boatmen of his polity to assemble in time for spring high water, when they would be unable to work in the fields anyway. Thus Quigualtam once more demonstrated his dominance of the river as his impressive navy amused itself in chasing the hairy-faced strangers and their strange animals down the river, passing them along to the tender mercies of reinforcements to the south who would see them to the mouth of the river.

Although the authentic narratives clearly support this picture, it is not the interpretation now being argued by archaeological researchers. Table 3.6 is based upon the several narratives of the Soto expedition still accepted as useful, as analyzed by the De Soto Expedition Commission (Swanton 1939) and modified by M. Smith (1984) in accordance with the results of the research of Hudson and his coworkers. Archaeological researchers admit that several of the presumed polities in the area confused the Iberian observers, who seem by this reconstruction to have viewed the statuses of the Talisi, Tascaluça, Pafalaya, and Chicaça "provinces" variously.

Yet recently these researchers, perhaps eager simply to find chiefdoms in North America that can be identified through site identification and European description, have tended to describe most if not all of these groups as chiefdoms. They propose that such entities still existed in the interior because disease had not yet reached them, and that they met their decline in the first waves of serious disease that supposedly followed the *entrada* of Soto (Curren 1984a; Hudson, Smith, and DePratter 1990). This argument, however, is based not upon detailed demographic studies that profile burial populations – the data are simply lacking for such studies (Ramenofsky 1985, 1987; Smith 1987) – but rather upon a few radiocarbon dates from a period for which radiocarbon dates are notoriously unreliable.

Some of the most important arguments for chiefdom organization in the region of interest for the Choctaws – west of Mabila and east of the Mississippi River – have been advanced by Hudson, Smith, and DePratter (1990); they address two named groups of particular importance here. They conceive of the Apafalaya "province" as the Moundville chiefdom in decline, with its center shifted to the Snow's Bend site, and they argue that because the Spaniards encountered a chiefdom, the Moundville III phase must have continued until 1540, in spite of evidence presented elsewhere that the Moundville chiefdom must have been in a state of devolution by this time (Peebles 1986). Yet Hudson and his colleagues do not give any reason, apart from the circular one of the expedition's having been on the Black Warrior River during the time of Moundville III, for concluding that the Spaniards *did* encounter a paramount chiefdom, and in fact there is no evidence for such a claim. Biedma did not so much as

Table 3.6 Southeastern Polities as Observed by Hernando de Soto Expedition in Mississippi/Alabama Region (after Smith 1987:table 2.2, reconstructed from Soto and Luna narratives, Coosa to Tascaluça; remainder of table from analysis in Hudson, Smith, and DePratter 1990).

Province, Chiefdom, or Head Town	Known or Probable Subject Towns or Provinces	Known or Probable Subject Villages
		→ six days' travel through towns subject to Coosa (E)
	Tasqui (R)	
	→ Napochies (L)	
Coosa (E,R)	Numerous towns of Coosa (E)	
	Talimachusy (E,R)	
	→ Itaba/Ytaua (R/E)	
	Ulibihali (R)	small villages subject to Ulibihali (E)
	Tuasi/Toasi (R/E)	old village with palisade (R)
	Onachiqui	
	Casiste (E,R)	
Talisi/Italisi (E,R/B)	——————————————→ towns subject to Talisi (E)	
	→ Caxiti (L)	
		Caxa (R)
Tascaluça (B,E,R)	Athahachi (head town; B,E,R)	Humati (R)
		Uxapita (R)
	Piachi (R)	
	→ Mabila (B,E,R)	
	Talicpacana (R,E)	
Pafalaya (E)	Moçulixa (R)	
	Zabusta (R,E)	
	Apafalaya (R)	
		scattered villages (E)
Chicaza (R,E,B,G)	Chief's town/Chicaçilla (E/G)	dispersed dwellings (E)
	Alimamu (R,E,G)	
	Talapatica (R)	
	Sacchuma/Miculasa (E,R)	
Quizquiz (R,E,B,G)	Chief's town (B,E,G,R)	
	second town (E)	
	third town	

Key: B = Biedma, E = Elvas, G = Garcilaso, L = Luna, R = Oviedo's Ranjel.
Note: Arrows denote political relationships documented in narratives (e.g., tribute paid); other relationships are probable.

mention such a polity, nor did Garcilaso (he attributed the only towns between Mabila and Chicaça to Chicaça), and neither Oviedo/Ranjel nor Elvas portrayed any features – service retinue, sumptuary distinction, litter carrying, principal men, or hostage value – identified elsewhere as marking the honor and ceremony accorded to a paramount chief. Only Ranjel even mentions encountering a chief, at "Apafalaya" village, and there is no evidence that the man even was a chief; he certainly did not deliver any bearers or food. I think it fair to say that *the actual evidence* of the Spanish narratives does not controvert the argument in favor of autonomous villages instead of a chiefdom at "Pafalaya."

The same arguments hold for Chicaça. Hudson and his colleagues have apparently considered the Chicaça "chief" a paramount because he was borne on a litter, since little other evidence is found in any of the narratives, and indeed only Biedma mentions the litter. Furthermore, although chiefs could be carried on litters, the Spaniards would only observe such a thing if the chiefs chose to come to them – and the most impressive of the chiefs Soto met, like Tascaluça and the leader of Quigualtam, disdainfully refused to do so, perhaps making the use of a litter almost a sign of less rather than greater power. Finally, the notion of the Chicaça leader as a paramount flies in the face of archaeological evidence from the Chicaça region identified by Hudson and accepted by most other researchers: the area around Columbus, Mississippi. Even if the region's few extremely modest simple chiefdoms had not already devolved by the time of Soto (although Johnson and Lehmann [1990] offer compelling evidence that they had), they were certainly not ever centers of paramount power on any interpretation of the archaeology of the region.

It seems to me that ranking all these social groupings as chiefdoms because of an assumption that they must coincide in some way with Mississippian groups is not only unjustified in terms of the evidence, as I have shown, but it begs a multitude of questions. Such a ranking ignores the many gradations of the tribe-chiefdom continuum discussed in chapter 2, thereby implicitly reasserting the old chestnut that "progress" is unidirectional. It also commits the same interpretive errors as the Spanish observers: it ignores what they *saw*. I think a more appropriate reconstruction, in greater agreement with both historical and archaeological evidence, can be offered, as in table 3.7.

How well does the proposed model fit with the protohistoric archaeological site distribution in the area? The Soto observations of the interior Southeast should be compared with the archaeological evidence both for indisputably contemporary intact chiefdoms and for the decentralized Burial Urn groups in the region suggested by figure 3.3. The sources for the relevant data are the dissertation of Craig Sheldon (1974) for the Burial Urn evidence and the work of Marvin Smith (1984, 1987), who has reviewed the archaeological evidence for the eastern part of the interior, supple-

Table 3.7 Southeastern Polities as Observed by
Hernando de Soto Expedition in Mississippi-Alabama
Region (new reconstruction).

Autonomous Towns (May Be Chiefdom Centers)	Subordinate Towns	Subordinate Villages
Chiaha	5–6 villages	
Coste	2(?) villages	
Tali	villages	
Coça	Tasqui Talimachusy Itaba Ulibahali Tuasi	10–12 chiefs?
Talisi	Casiste?	
Tascaluça/Athahachi	Caxa Humati Uxapita Piachi	
Mabila?		
Talicpacana Moçulixa Zabusta Apafalaya?		
Chicaça Limamu Talapatica Sacchuma Niculasa?		
Quizqui	3(?) towns	
Anilco		
Guachoya		
Aminoya		
Quigualtam		Huhasene

Note: Subordination linkages are not indicated here because of interpretation problems as indicated in the text; divisions between "polities" are indicated by vertical spacing where enmity or geographical barrier was indicated.

mented by data from the Lower Mississippi Survey (e.g., Brain 1978a) and other sources, including the surveys done for the Tennessee-Tombigbee Waterway Project (see Jenkins and Krause 1986), a research project to locate the 1541 winter camp (Johnson et al. 1991; Johnson n.d.), and a mapping project undertaken to provide evidence for Soto research (Knight 1988; Morgan n.d.). Although survey coverage is in many places very poor to nonexistent, and although little is known of the secondary and tertiary sites that made up the bulk of Mississippian settlement, most likely few if any of the major sites have been missed. Unfortunately, the same is less likely to be true for contemporary sites representing segmentary groups. Returning to the model I have suggested, which argues for Soto's having encountered complex chiefdom organization only in the Chiaha-Coosa-Tascaluça area to the east of the region of most interest and in the Quizquiz and Quigualtam areas to the west, it is evident that a good deal of this region has seen very little archaeological attention. Nevertheless, the paucity of significant large mound sites of the right date is real, and the region is clearly characterized by smaller and apparently more autonomous sites, probably no paramount chiefdom, and only a few "simple chiefdoms."

Readers may have noticed that no significant Mississippian population has been mentioned or indicated in the Pearl-Pascagoula-Tombigbee region. This is not merely an accident of survey coverage, as was discussed in chapter 2, or of the Soto route. Several modern surveys in different parts of that area (Penman 1977; Padgett and Heisler 1979; Blitz 1985) have demonstrated that Larson (1980) was correct in predicting that large Mississippian populations would not settle in the piney woods sector of the Gulf Coastal Plain. Larson did suggest that where good-sized meandering rivers crossed the plain, providing sufficient arable soils, populations limited to the floodplain areas could settle, and such seems to be the case with a limited number of sites that may have been the centers for "simple" chiefdoms: Nanih Waiya, the "mother mound" of Choctaw myth at the headwaters of the Pearl; Pearl Mounds, on the central Pearl near the Natchez–Mobile Delta trail; an unnamed site at the head of the Pascagoula delta; and a major site on Deer Island in Mississippi Sound. The first two were probably deserted by 1500, but we know too little of the others to supply a terminal date. New evidence, however, suggests that the Pearl Mounds' hinterland populations may have ended up in small dispersed farmsteads and hamlets in the Leaf River drainage by the historic period, thus providing an important source of Plaquemine-tradition population to make up protohistoric groups (C. B. Mann, pers. comm. 1985; T. Mooney, pers. comm. 1994). The data for all these generalizations are presented in figure 3.3.

The crux of this sort of analysis has always been seen as identifying historical polities with the archaeological cultures. Yet in spite of intensive studies lasting many years, eventuating in tentative identifications of sites with named polities, definitive identifications remain to be made, and I will not attempt any startling revelations here. The good consensus for localizing Chicaça to the Columbus, Mississippi, area is helpful, since it in turn binds Chicaça and "Pafalaya" to the two sides of the Tombigbee Valley and connects them with the Summerville IV and Alabama River phase

3.3. Known archaeological sites in the Mississippi-Alabama region, ca. 1540, after Knight 1988 and Morgan n.d. Southeastern counties of Mississippi excluded from both studies.

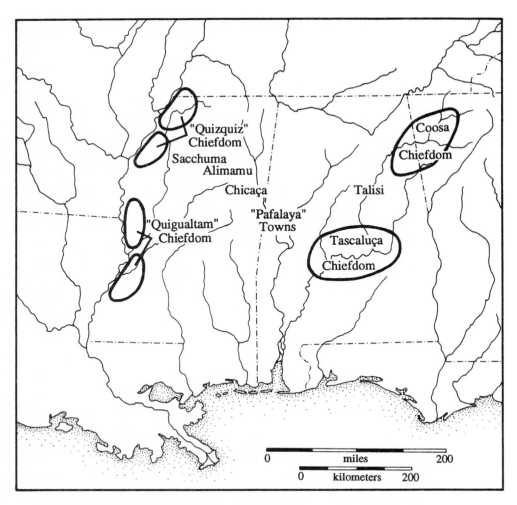

3.4. Geographical reconstruction of interior southeastern groups at European contact, 1540–41, with alternative locations for the Quizquiz and Quigualtam chiefdoms.

traditions respectively. Tascaluça and its neighbors are then placed on the Alabama River and tributaries and Coça and its neighbors on the upper Coosa River system. Although scholars have made much of their differences with regard to the locations of Quizquiz and Quigualtam, as the alternative locations on the map show, these differences are not terribly significant for my purpose of delineating the native political context of the Choctaw homeland region, particularly since the Spaniards never actually saw Quigualtam – so whether it was Natchezan or Tunican remains moot – while Quizquiz's links to the southern Tombigbee region were remote at best.

Figure 3.4, then, establishes these general regional identifications in order to localize the discussions that have preceded and will follow. Identifying Pafalaya, Chicaça, Alimamu, and Sacchuma with tribes or at most simple chiefdoms fits both the archaeological and documentary evidence. Further studies may succeed in pinpointing specific sites – such as Soto's winter camp near Chicaça – and permit a more coherent social history of the groups involved, but for my purposes this demonstration of variability in social organization from the Coosa/Alabama region to the Tombigbee to the Yazoo Basin is sufficient.

Thus at the time of the Soto expedition, Moundville, the primary chiefdom at the center of the region of interest, had dispersed. Smaller derivative populations had spread out in the Black Warrior Valley and had also moved south and east into areas too poor in resources for a full-scale multilevel chiefdom (Sheldon 1974; Larson 1980), while modest simple chiefdoms on its western periphery had either devolved in turn, once deprived of connections with the larger entity, or had remained in place. Around the periphery of the region, on the Mississippi and on the Coosa and Alabama Rivers, other chiefdoms were still functioning. European explorations would soon change the situation completely.

CHAPTER FOUR

Evidence from the Late Sixteenth Century

It is a wonder to see how, when a man greatly desires something and strongly attaches himself to it in his imagination, he has the impression at every moment that whatever he hears and sees argues in favor of that thing. – Bartolomé de Las Casas, *Historia de las Indias*

Our tribe unraveled like a coarse rope, frayed at either end as the old and new among us were taken. – Louise Erdrich, *Tracks*

THE LEGACY OF SOTO

As suggested in the last chapter, the damage wreaked by Soto on the peoples of the Southeast was minimized to some degree by their management of the contact situation. Clearly some direct and immediate demographic effects occurred, however. Although the statistical details available now are limited, an estimation of this effect is possible. Immediate population damage to the polities encountered by Soto resulted from two causes: the taking of slaves for bearers, and deaths incurred through direct aggression.

The sources are rather silent about the ultimate fates of the hundreds of Indians taken from their homelands in chains to bear the baggage of the expedition. What happened to these people as time went on is not clear. I have discussed the likelihood that captive chiefs were held more to guarantee the good behavior of slaves than to pacify the region through which the expedition was passing. Sometimes indeed the accounts report that slaves were released to return home, but this was seldom; yet the expedition continued to demand and obtain slaves. If the previous slaves were not released, we must assume that something happened to them. The narratives mention only a few escape attempts, either foiled or successful. One would not, however, expect the Spaniards to be very forthcoming either about large numbers of escapes or about many cases of the Indians' expiring under harsh treatment. If the latter happened rather than the former, then on the basis of numbers mentioned an estimated

Table 4.1 Indian Slaves Taken in the Mississippi-Alabama Region According to the Hernando de Soto Narratives.

Town	Biedma	Ranjel	Elvas	Garcilaso
Chiaha		500	some	
Acoste			some	
Tali		some	6	
Coça	some	many	some	some
Itaba		some		
Ulibahali		20+	30+	
Tuasi		32+	30+	
Talisi	26–27	some	40	some
Athahachi		400		
Nilco				some

Table 4.2 Spanish and Indian Deaths in Battles According to the Hernando de Soto Narratives, Mississippi-Alabama Region.

Battles		Biedma	Ranjel	Elvas	Garcilaso
Mabila	Spaniards	20+	22	18	82
18 Oct. 1640	Indians	5,000	3,000	2,500	11,000
Chicaça	Spaniards	13–14	12	11	40
4 Mar. 1641	Indians		some	1	100
Alibamo	Spaniards	7–8	a few	15	3
28 Apr. 1641	Indians	some	many	3	2,000+

maximum of two thousand Indians from the Alabama-Mississippi region were lost to their homelands through slave-taking, most of them in the Alabama region (see table 4.1).

The toll of direct aggression is even harder to estimate, since the sources, though far from reticent, do not agree and tend toward large numbers in order to glorify the heroism of the expedition members (see table 4.2). There is no reason to assume that these men were any less varied in their backgrounds than the band that conquered Peru, and Lockhart (1972) has shown how few real military men participated in that expedition. The list found in the Spanish archives that names survivors of the Soto expedition suggests a similar makeup for this group: tailors, carpenters, shoemakers, notaries, and seamen are as well represented as professional soldiers, while those who are actually identified as military men are mostly officers (Avellaneda 1990).

By the time it reached Mabila the Spanish force consisted of 490 to 520 men (Swanton 1939:87). The carnage claimed for Mabila ranges from 2,500 (Elvas) to 7,500 (Garcilaso's 11,000 includes 3,500 killed by fire) in a battle that lasted from midmorning until nightfall, or about seven hours. These figures would suggest that in that time every expedition member killed 5 to 15 Indians, if we assume that all expedition members were active in the battle; yet the rear guard did not even arrive until well after the battle had started. This assumption is further unlikely in view of the necessity of controlling the bearers and in view of the sources' testimony that most of the killing was done by men on horseback. If the killing is restricted to horsemen, the number of Spaniards fighting is reduced to at most 200 (Ranjel's figures [Swanton 1939:89]), which would seem a generous estimate, assuming that all the horses were fit for battle. With this number of men in action, each would have had to kill just over 12 Indians in seven hours to make Ranjel's estimate, 37 – one every eleven minutes – to reach Garcilaso's figure. Clearly the latter figure passes the bounds of belief, although it does include 2,000 who were wounded but able to flee the town before dying.

The preferred Spanish method of fighting with sword and especially lance from horseback could not have been countered effectively by native weaponry, to be sure, but neither did it lend itself to mass slaughter; this is credible only if musketry and crossbows had been brought massively into play, which neither the narratives nor the topography credit. The lower figure for Mabila of 3,000 (Ranjel) or 2,500 (Elvas) is believable in these terms, adding the caveat that this was the number the Spaniards *thought* they had killed and not necessarily the number that actually died of wounds (Ranjel believed that additional numbers died of wounds). A few Indians were said to have been killed in the course of the attacks at the Chicaça winter camp and at the Alibamu fort, but the total here was fewer than 10, since the Indians had the advantage of surprise and control of the terrain. Thus the number of Indians lost through direct aggression in the Alabama-Mississippi region would have been around 3,000 to 5,000 at most, making generous allowance for fire deaths and wounds, with this loss concentrated in the densely populated Mabila region. Adding the estimated number of captives, the total number lost from the Alabama-Mississippi region is about 7,000 maximum, concentrated on the Alabama side of the line.

This is a large number of people to have lost, but probably no one town bore the bulk of the loss. The Indians who died at Mabila were not necessarily residents of the town; in fact, they may not even have been residents of the immediate region but rather contingents of warriors sent by Tascaluça's allies. In other words, what I mean to suggest here is that most likely the 2,000 lost to slavery were fairly evenly distributed among the major population concentrations west of the Appalachians and east of the Tombigbee River, while the 3,000–5,000 lost to direct aggression would have come from a more restricted area roughly central to this region.

Such a loss of population calls for some sort of compensation. Although Soto persistently sought female slaves, by far the majority of slaves were men, and most of the people lost at Mabila were also men. Henry Dobyns (1983:303) has pointed out that every society has a good idea of what constitutes the proper minimum size for a population unit. There is nothing mystical about this; in Marxist terms, there is a minimum size below which a population cannot reproduce its social structure. In whatever terms, loss of population calls for remedy of some kind, and in the context of a tribe-chiefdom continuum two kinds of remedy may be applied. Population units may amalgamate with others; southeastern groups under contact stress definitely used this solution (Dobyns 1983; Smith 1987). The second solution is intensified warfare – not for land but for slaves to be adopted into the group to make up for its population loss.

Population losses sustained by native groups in the central southeastern region seem to have been selective as to organizational level. More centrally organized groups, which could call for slave labor as corvée, tribute, or alliance reciprocity, lost bearers to Soto's demands or confronted him militarily with organized resistance. Alliances of autonomous towns not only delivered no slaves, but because of their dispersed authority structure and dispersed settlement, the Spaniards could not control them militarily. Hence, the groups that suffered most from demographic loss in this episode were also those that were best organized. The evidence from later sixteenth-century expeditions demonstrates that some degree of population amalgamation may have taken place only in the case of the Tascaluça polity, which possibly sustained serious leadership losses at Mabila.

Another aspect of the Soto expedition's contact with the Indians of the Southeast was cultural exposure. Clearly this brief contact and the small quantity of trade goods distributed by the expedition would do little to foster the usual kinds of acculturative effects: there were far too few iron axes to go round. The more important exposure must have been to *possibilities*. Coastal peoples had been encountering whites and their works in the Caribbean and Gulf of Mexico for fifty years by the time of Soto, and news of their coming had doubtless reached the interior through trade contacts in fairly short order. What southeastern Indians did not know was what the Europeans wanted and how they would behave in order to get it, and Soto's expedition provided an indelible lesson in both. Clearly, too, Indians had not only to devise a behavioral posture to assume toward Europeans, but in order to fit Europeans into their established system of interaction, they had to change other aspects of that system. As I see it, the southeastern Indian world-view was "preconditioned" for systemic change by Soto's incursion, making these groups better able to cope with the disastrous change of European disease mortality when it came.

But disease did not come with Soto, or at least not the kind of wildfire pandemics that would later affect the region. Active acute illness that led to death was rare among Soto's men, and for the region in question it was almost entirely accountable to nutritional problems. The expedition had been on the road for a year by the time it reached the deep interior, and any acute disease had had more than enough time to work its way through the expeditionary group.

The recorded incidents of disease among the Europeans during their sojourn from Chiaha to Quizquiz can be quickly examined. Before arriving in the region of interest the party passed through Xuala, where food was scarce; the contingent under Baltasar de Gallegos, which had been left behind in Cofitachequi, joined the main party there, arriving with many men ill. No specific word is used to describe their illness, and Swanton (1939) has attributed it to food shortages they suffered due to following the advance guard, which had used up provisions – hence their illness was hunger and weakness. Making their departure from Xuala, a horseman called Alaminos, suffering from a fever, became lost and later joined the expedition in Chiaha, apparently recovered. All accounts agree that the stay in Chiaha was long due to the general hunger and fatigue of the men – the only indispositions mentioned. Two members of the expedition, Feryada and Johan Biscayan, were left behind in Coça and Ulibihali, only the latter because of unspecific illness. Also at Ulibihali another man, Mancano, was lost in the woods and never reappeared. Spanish lives were lost in the battles at Mabila and in the Chickasaw country, but not from illness, and the narratives contain no further such notes for the region being considered. Every one of these cases could be ascribed to poor nutrition or digestive upsets, except perhaps for Alaminos's fever. This latter indisposition, even if due to a chronic condition such as malaria, could not have affected the Indian population in the absence of a suitable vector to spread it.

The only serious opportunities for the expedition to spread disease, then, would have been offered not by the temporary contacts between healthy Indian and healthy Spaniard that were the norm for this expedition but by two types of more prolonged contacts: those between Spaniards and slaves (including women acquired for sexual purposes) who survived their enslavement, and those between indigenous groups and expedition members who stayed behind. The difficulties in estimating the number of bearers returned to their homes are enormous. In the narratives the Spaniards commonly promise to return their bearers, but they are rarely portrayed as doing so; more often – and this is striking in view of the likelihood of a strong bias against portraying abuse – bearers are said to die of cold or hardship; but most often the narratives say nothing at all. The natives are merely replaced with a fresh lot. If few returned home after service, perhaps others escaped; the accounts contain some examples. Still, most escapees would not have had long-term exposure to the Spaniards, so again, in all likelihood the numbers of surviving, disease-exposed Indians were small.

These small numbers would have had the opportunity to be exposed to several endemic diseases carried by the Spaniards, such as tuberculosis and the common cold. Although endemic among their captors, those diseases not already experienced in a related variety by southeastern natives (who apparently already represented a reservoir of endemic tuberculosis and a nonvenereal treponemal syndrome akin to syphilis [Ross-Stallings 1989]) would likely have been highly dangerous to the Indians. Their deaths from these diseases may explain the constant replacement of bearers. And this very replacement, constantly providing new populations for the infections to colonize, could explain how such an infection as the common cold might remain virulent in such a small population as the expedition personnel. It might have killed its new hosts, but not before they reinfected the more resistant Spaniards.

A remote possibility exists that Soto's expedition or those that preceded it may have carried with them smallpox in its dormant dried form. There is no indication that any expedition members actually suffered from it, but they gathered supplies in Cuba, where it had been virulent, and may have taken the virus, capable of survival in dried form for years (Ramenofsky 1987:146), unwittingly with them.

No researchers have discussed a further possibility – Soto's pigs as a disease vector – although the lack of domestic animals has been cited as one reason that the Indian population was relatively disease-free (Thornton 1987:41). The popular notion that the progeny of pigs escaped, stolen, or given as gifts were the ancestors of wild pigs in the Southeast, which apparently had no native peccary, is much too sweeping a claim. Nevertheless, the expedition certainly left some pigs behind, and the natives discovered in short order that pork was very good to eat: Elvas claimed that Soto had one Chicaça Indian's hands severed for helping himself to this new source of food. The frequent fertility of healthy sows and the difficulty of controlling boars on the long overland trek must also have contributed to the occasional release or abandonment of pigs, since expedition members would have had to abandon, eat, or carry newly farrowed litters when they moved on. If the pigs did become a new part of the native environment in one way or another, then the diseases they may have carried must be considered.

Modern pigs are capable of carrying a large number of diseases, in addition to the well-known trichinosis, that are transmissible to humans without causing the death of the infected animal (see table 4.3), as McNeill (1977:45) has observed. Many of these diseases are of concern today because they pose a danger to workers exposed routinely to live animals or the flesh of slaughtered animals, and although the history of some is known well enough to place their presence among domestic pigs only in recent times, others could be much older. The numbers of these diseases suggest that even if the specific modern range of swine diseases transmissible to other animals is not ancient, it is likely representative of a possible range of disease in the past. Sixteenth-century manuals of animal husbandry and estate management mention several causes of illness or mortality in swine, their usual advice being to slaughter the animals to cure their meat before they died (Tusser 1878). Presumably the processing of the meat eliminated infection or European constitutions had adapted to it. Clearly the possibility of infection spread by pigs is at least worth consideration, particularly in view of the unexplained and none too well diagnosed illnesses that struck southeastern natives during the first century of contact. Modern swine diseases can be carried to humans through contact with a live pig, its wastes, or its flesh; ingestion of its flesh; and even the bite of an insect that has bitten an infected animal. Perhaps even more significant, in view of the importance of turkey and deer in the southeastern native's diet, is the potential for other species to carry several of these diseases. The range of symptoms these diseases cause in humans is wide and notably nonspecific and, in "virgin-soil" populations – never before exposed – would be deadly. As protohistoric and early historic sites provide zoological samples, they should be analyzed with attention to the possibility that pigs could have represented a serious disease vector.

VIRGIN-SOIL EPIDEMICS

As shown in chapter 2, even if the presence of Europeans had brought no changes, the cultural landscape of the Southeast that the earliest European explorers encountered would have been varied in both complexity and texture. They would have come upon chiefdoms, certainly, but also populations in other stages of the tribe-chiefdom cycle. Some areas would have been empty of settlement for environmental and cultural reasons. And spheres of influence and routes of communication would have constituted an unbroken web across the region. If observations of such a situation unchanged by the Europeans were available, giving faces and color to the Mississippian bones would be reasonably simple, allowing for the usual observational bias.

The situation is not so uncomplicated as that, however. Europeans did not observe Indian populations in a pristine state. Although Frederick Jackson Turner ([1894] 1961:39) was referring to metaphorical ideological contagion when he said that "our early history is the study of European germs developing in an American environment," modern researchers have shown the assertion to have been all too literally true. By the time even the earliest of European explorers penetrated the interior Southeast, European disease could have preceded them in some areas. Argument still rages on the extent of the effects at this early date (cf. Dobyns 1983 and Henige 1986b, 1986c), but archaeological evidence demonstrates that either immediately before or at the time of the Soto expedition, populations near the Atlantic coast were experiencing serious social disruption as a result of European disease (see Smith 1987). The goal here is to find out when it affected the populations in the Alabama-Mississippi region. Thus the evidence for the sixteenth and seventeenth centuries should be examined for the presence of virgin-soil epidemics.

Table 4.3 Swine Diseases with Zoonotic Potential. Compiled by Dr. Roderick C. Tubbs, Mississippi State University College of Veterinary Medicine. Source: Leman et al. 1986.

Name	Type	Course and Symptoms in Swine	Symptoms in Humans	Transmission	First Identified	Other Carriers
Streptococcus suis Type 2	bacterial	can kill in hours or lie dormant in lymph nodes	septicemia, meningitis	pig handling	1950	one case known from a dog
Brucella suis	bacterial (Brucellosis)	venereal disease; most recover spontaneously but remain infected	recurring fevers, arthritis		1914	dogs
Erysipelothrix rhusiopathiae	bacterial (Swine Erysipelas)	acute or chronic; skin lesions and arthritic joints	skin lesions and (rarely) septicemia	contact with flesh or bodily fluids	mice, 1878; pigs, 1882	sheep, turkeys; mammals, reptiles, fish
Salmonellosis	bacterial		severe diarrhea, possible septicemia	contamination of pork by sick or carrier pigs	1886	
Swine influenza	viral, type A influenza	onset rapid in whole herd; rapid recovery after six days	acute respiratory disease	pig handling	1918 (first in human)	avian species (turkeys, waterfowl)
Swine vesicular disease	viral	onset in 2–4 days, recovery in 3 weeks with loss of hoofs	Coxsackie enteroviruses, carried in all tissues	lab work	1966	
Vesicular Stomatitis	viral	lesions; onset 2–3 days, recovery 1–2 weeks	influenza-like disease	lab work and pig caretaking	horses, Civil War; cattle, 1925; swine, 1943	cattle, horses, raccoon, deer
Vesicular Exanthema	viral	lesions; onset 1–3 days, recovery 1–2 weeks		ingestion of infected meat, possibly lab work	1932	fish, sea mammals, sheep, buffalo, donkeys, zoo primates
Japanese Encephalitis virus		affects reproductive and central nervous systems	affects reproductive and central nervous systems	mosquito	1933	birds, mammals; Asian epidemics in humans
Trichinella spiralis	parasite nematode		painful intramuscular cysts	ingestion of improperly cooked infected pork		
Balantium coli	protozoan		severe colitis: ulcers, sloughing of mucosa, watery diarrhea	fecal contamination of food or water		
Taenia solium (*Cysticercus cellulosae*)	tapeworms			ingestion of improperly cooked meat containing larvae		human is primary host, swine intermediary

Students of early European-Indian contacts in the Southeast have postulated a series of significant pandemic episodes for which documentary evidence exists, either for the specific area in question or for areas from which disease could reasonably have spread, with important disagreements over the seriousness of the resultant population depletion. The evidence presently being developed through archaeological research is as yet inadequate to serve as the decisive factor (Smith 1987; Ramenofsky 1987). The high estimates of up to 90 percent population loss advanced by Dobyns (1983) and others have been called into serious question, not least because they are based upon a less than critical reading of the available historical sources. David Henige's (1986c) critique of thirteen of the disease episodes discussed by Dobyns in *Their Number Become Thinned*, which shows that the language of the original documents does not support Dobyns's conclusions, would remove several of the earliest southeastern episodes from table 4.4.

Henige's arguments fall with greatest force on the earliest posited epidemics, not because it is impossible to imagine circumstances in which they might have taken place but because the existing evidence as adduced by Dobyns simply cannot support such claims and sometimes directly contradicts them. Henige's argument from verbatim citations of the sources in the original languages is persuasive, with one exception that has important implications for the interior Southeast.

Henige complains that Dobyns's argument for disease spread in the circum-Caribbean region via "a possibly still very large aboriginal-style trade in religious goods" (Dobyns 1983:260) is unsupported by adequate evidence for such trade, since "as far as we know, neither the Panfilo de Narváez expedition nor Cabeza de Vaca's party encountered any of these traders during the several years that one or the other was in the area" (Henige 1986b:711–12 n.18). This complaint ignores both the ample evidence that exists for such traders within Mesoamerica (the *pochteca*) and the fact that from Texas onward Cabeza de Vaca was able to masquerade as such a person. Similarly, it does not take account of the unquestionable appearance of Mesoamerican decorative motifs and mythical characters in the plastic arts of the Southeastern Ceremonial Complex of late prehistory (Waring 1968; Galloway 1989c). Even if the appearance of these motifs is more likely to reflect imitation than direct trade, analyses of the "Hopewell Interaction Sphere" of the Woodland period, along with studies of the sources of minerals used in the manufacture of Southeastern Ceremonial Complex ornaments (Brown, Kerber, and Winters 1990), leave no doubt that eastern North America was crossed and recrossed by many "contact routes." In other words, influence could be passed, whether by means of a few long-distance trajectories or, more likely, by a multitude of face-to-face contacts (see Webb 1989). The real task in constructing a believable argument for early contagion is establishing how the infections spread and whether such a model fits the archaeological evidence for routes of contact.

Postulating early disease epidemics for the "deep interior" is difficult because so few explorers penetrated it, either early or late. The deepest penetration before the coming of the English and French at the end of the seventeenth century was made by the Soto party, and since that same party may have spread disease to many peoples as yet relatively untouched by it, the party could only report preexisting disease, not the

Table 4.4 Probable Disease Epidemics in Florida, 1512–1672. From
Smith 1987:57, after Dobyns 1983.

Date	Disease	Probability	Mortality
1513–1514	malaria?**	likely	unknown
1519–1524	smallpox**	nearly certain	50–75%
1528	measles/typhoid**	nearly certain	about 50%
1535–1539	unidentified*	documented	high
1545–1548	bubonic plague*	nearly certain	about 12.5%
1549	typhus	very probable	perhaps 10%
1550	mumps	possible	unknown
1559	influenza**	nearly certain	about 20%
1564–1570	syphilis**	documented	severe
1585–1586	unidentified	documented	severe
1586	vectored fever	probable	15–20%
1596	measles*	documented	about 25%
1613–1617	bubonic plague*	documented	50%
1649	yellow fever	documented	about 33%
1653–?	smallpox	documented	unknown
1659	measles	documented	unknown
1672	influenza?	documented	unknown

*probable source in Mesoamerica
**evidence inadequate (see Henige 1986b, 1986c)

effects of its own passage. A list of disease episodes for the deep interior thus depends upon inference. Marvin Smith's (1987) reasoning seems sound: the epidemics that Dobyns mentions as arising in Mesoamerica or the Southwest (marked on table 4.4 with single asterisks) are even more likely to have reached the area between the Mississippi and Tombigbee/Mobile through *native* contacts than they were to have reached Florida by that means, although it should be noted that Dobyns does not attribute any of the very early episodes to such a source. Brief contacts through coastwise journeys such as that of Pineda in 1519 were also likely to spread disease if transmissible disease was present in the ships' crews and if contacts were made with Indians on the shore. Finally, where other evidence is lacking, archaeological evidence of population diminution and movement may indicate the depredation of disease, particularly if multiple coeval burials of unusual demographic composition are found on affected sites (Smith 1987:54–85).

Given the variety of ecological adaptations and cultural systems in the Southeast at the time of European contact, it would be unreasonable to assume that the spread of European disease was uniform (see Milner 1980). The diseases came in epidemics echoing infectious episodes among the Europeans, and demographic changes followed each epidemic. The specific histories of all southeastern groups through this turmoil may never be traceable, but some useful generalizations have so far survived criticism.

Dobyns (1983) has maintained that the primary impact of disease in the Southeast was felt in areas easily accessible via major waterways. This assumption seems reasonable at first glance, but it disregards the real importance of overland communication routes and the existence of mobile disease vectors that could penetrate inland using those routes (see figure 2.3; also Tanner 1989). In addition, since southeastern chiefdoms selected for important river floodplains, Dobyns's theory as stated amounts merely to a correlation of disease with major population concentrations. Clearly the arguments for and against various pathways of transmission need additional examination. For the present it is enough that most researchers agree that pandemics did spread and did seriously affect the population aggregates of the interior Southeast.

A further argument made by Dobyns (1983:303) is more defensible: that Indians under stress of depopulation migrated to amalgamate with other groups in pursuit of "a cultural model of a proper settlement." This "proper settlement" was a matter of numbers, but only as numbers reflected the population size required to accommodate accustomed marriage rules and hence to allow the society to continue to reproduce itself. Taking among others the example of the Natchez, Dobyns argues that under sufficient stress even ethnic amalgamation could occur, leading to novel rationalizations such as the apparent rank exogamy of Natchez marriage rules (cf. Brain 1971). These facts are not only relevant to the model I am constructing for the origin of the Choctaws, but they can also to some extent be verified archaeologically (cf. Brown 1985).

So far, however, archaeological evidence for devastating epidemics in the Southeast is sparse, not because none exists (that remains to be demonstrated) but because by and large no one has looked for it. Marvin Smith (1987) has examined the evidence for the eastern half of the area with great care and has determined that the available evidence does confirm in general terms both depopulation and displacement of tribal groups. In addition, where the evidence can be pinned down chronologically it does not contradict substantially the disease chronology established by Dobyns, though it is not adequately fine-grained to judge the presence of very early disease episodes. For the western half of the area of interest, Ramenofsky's work (1985, 1987) evaluates the even sparser evidence for the lower Mississippi Valley to conclude that a sharp population drop occurred in the early contact period. And Brain's (1978a) work on settlement patterns suggests the outlines of protohistoric population movements under demographic stress in the Mississippi Valley.

Depopulation, as Smith has pointed out, is manifest archaeologically as smaller and fewer sites. With fine enough chronological control, it may be possible to observe unusual mortality in larger sites for the time period coincident with the postulated depopulation. Then, if areal samples are sufficient, we may be able to determine whether depopulation was accompanied by the movement of remnant populations.

For the northern Yazoo Basin, a drastic falloff in the number of sites over time clearly indicates that depopulation occurred, but the sampling of sites in the area has been essentially haphazard, not permitting a more specific conclusion. Some depopulation seems to have taken place prior to 1540, but this impression cannot be asserted with assurance. Brain's investigations of the Tunicas have shown that the upheavals of disease and disruption following Soto's passage almost completely emptied the southern Yazoo Basin (Williams and Brain 1983); Brain (1978a) has described a clear overall pattern of population displacement in the late prehistoric and protohistoric periods in the lower Mississippi Valley. According to these researches, populations retained a semblance of Mississippian organization but moved their major centers away from the main channel of the Mississippi River and turned to focus upon tributaries or even overland routes such as the Natchez Trace. In addition, populations of these periods apparently moved to congregate toward the mouth of the Yazoo River and the area around Coles Creek and St. Catherine Creek, thus creating a serious shrinkage in the spheres of influence of the lower Yazoo Mississippian and Natchez Bluffs Plaquemine cultures.

The Natchez Bluffs region, too, obviously contains many fewer sites, and the sites are smaller, but although it has been argued that serious population decline began in the late sixteenth century, not long after the Soto expedition's presence (Ramenofsky 1987:69–71), the archaeological evidence may equally well support the kind of population shifts Brain has described, as well as a degree of dispersal. The intermediary Big Black basin seems to have supported simple chiefdoms at best in the late prehistoric period, but from about 1500 on no settlement occurred and most sites were abandoned (see pottery in Ford 1936:115–25; Shaffer and Steponaitis 1983; Steponaitis 1991; radiocarbon dates in Lorenz 1990).

In the Black Warrior Valley, where Moundville and its accompanying towns and hamlets represented a complex chiefdom, the Moundville polity had probably collapsed and most of its people dispersed well before direct European contact and perhaps even before the European discovery of the Americas (see chapter 3). According to Sheldon (1974), the middle Tombigbee and the lower Alabama received a good deal of the Moundville population; thus the Burial Urn populations in these locations are incomers. In the burials of these successor peoples some of the ravages of European disease may be discernible; however, because this culture evolved *in situ* into some of the peoples of the eighteenth century and because few of its sites have been excavated, isolating episodes with certainty may be impossible. Still, the number of multiple burials, and particularly the special urn interment of infants (the culture's eponymous feature), may indicate a response to the new epidemics (Smith 1987:65–66).

Displacement of populations was equally dramatic in the Tombigbee area. The

Moundville population did not just disappear; as manifested by its successor culture, the Alabama River phase, this population apparently spread out down the Tombigbee perhaps as far as the Mobile River delta, and up the Alabama as far as modern Montgomery (Sheldon 1974). In this case disease clearly did not precipitate the initial, gradual displacement away from the center in the Black Warrior Valley (Peebles 1987), but disease probably did push the populations more deeply into the coastal plain region, which had not been capable of supporting chiefdom population concentrations (Larson 1980).

And what of the area between the Pearl and the Tombigbee that had been virtually uninhabited during the Mississippian period? Existing archaeological evidence offers little relevant information; chronological control is not yet adequate to suggest precisely when proto-Choctaw populations arrived. Tracing a population through a geographical displacement is difficult, especially where the population in question moves through an area of ethnically homogeneous populations or where many populations are in movement at once. Migration is obvious only if a population chooses to move into just such an uninhabited area. Some of the historical evidence reviewed in the next chapter suggests that the particular population movement that pushed one segment of the Choctaws into the area did not occur until the late seventeenth century. It may turn out that this particular "empty quarter" did not fill until worse stress than epidemic disease compelled the movement of peoples.

Disease mortality of a magnitude to cause major population upheavals must inevitably have serious effects on social organization in any society, but it is particularly hard-hitting in a nonliterate society structured by noncoercive institutions. The people who die in greatest numbers in pandemics are the very old and often the very young, and secondary effects of disease – including emotional distress and famine – may limit the future fertility of reproductive-age females, making the replenishment of the population difficult (Le Roy Ladurie 1982:255–71). When the pandemics are multiple and strike repeatedly at a virgin population, their result must be pronounced demographic decline.

The deaths of a majority of the older members of a traditional society can lead to the death of that society's past. Where skills, traditions, and esoteric knowledge are passed on by the old to the young, much knowledge may be completely lost when its bearers die off quickly without the chance to pass on instruction that may require years. But this effect is, in a sense, indirect, only setting the society up for cultural change; deaths of the old can have more direct effects in a society that depends upon the deliberations of its older members to provide guidance.

The collapse of tradition occurs more or less instantaneously according to the complexity of the society it serves. In a segmentary tribe, where each social group has to provide for its own needs in this as in other matters, tradition – including everything from household remedies to rules for conduct toward the gods – is a distributed commodity without specialists (Sahlins 1972:41–99). In a chiefdom, at the opposite extreme, specialists control such realms of traditional lore as medicine, planting, and the sacred (Knight 1986) – that is, an esoteric "great tradition" has been separated from the "little tradition" of everyday life (Redfield 1956). Because this kind of knowledge is hard won, it follows that its practitioners are most frequently of mature or advanced age and members of a specialist elite. Because this elite has few members and these people are involved in maintaining external contacts with other polities, the likelihood that they will die in a pandemic and that their knowledge will die with them is accordingly high.

Yet even a society without a past might survive if it were led by people of vision and wisdom. Again, however, vision and wisdom tend to die with the old and to take years to develop in the young. Differences related to level of social organization are important here too. In a chiefdom the hereditary leader gains a good part of his legitimacy from the support of the senior members of clans, who function both as advisors and as barometers to the sentiments of their kin (Gearing 1962). In the more egalitarian segmentary tribe, on the other hand, more people have a say in how things should be done for the benefit of all, and thus more people have experience in considering actions. Thus, in the loss of their elder members, chiefdoms will clearly suffer more than segmentary tribes in terms of organizational capabilities. In other words, when a chiefdom loses its elders, it can collapse precipitously, with all the demoralizing effects thus implied; when the same fate befalls a segmentary tribe, it merely shrinks and loses a measure of cultural richness.

As the death of the old is the death of the past, so the death of the young is the death of the future. Massive mortality among a society's young can lead to serious demoralization among those who remain. In addition, in an economy whose productive units are households, in which the young have significant roles, loss of these young learning producers can deplete the ability of the household to meet subsistence requirements and to provide for the requisites of social interaction (Sahlins 1972).

When young and old are the principal victims in pandemics, the system of kinship itself may be altered. An immediate difficulty arises in the loss of genealogical lore, traditionally in the keeping of the old in nonliterate societies. The conical clans said to be the building blocks of chiefdoms (Sahlins 1968:24–25,49–50) required a good deal of management of marriage arrangements. One might expect that when much of the traditional lore of ancestry was lost, the society might move toward a more simplified pattern. Indeed, Eggan (1937, 1966:15–44) and Spoehr (1947) have argued that the nineteenth-century Choctaw pattern was a distortion of a Crow kinship system under acculturative pressure; might the Crow pattern itself have been a distorted one produced by the processes postulated here? Beyond guessing that disease forced simplification of kinship systems, little can be said without more data, but the question deserves further study (cf. Galloway and Kidwell 1990).

I suggest that chiefdoms and segmented tribes would suffer differential numerical losses in epidemics. The diseases brought to the New World were primarily diseases of urbanism, most deadly in large population agglomerations. Chiefdoms would be particularly ill-served by their exchange and communication institutions, since external exchange would bring in disease and obligatory internal interactions would hasten its spread. So although all peoples in the Southeast were equally susceptible to European disease, fewer would have been infected where populations were dispersed in smaller autonomous groups.

Finally, the effects of demographic disaster on native ideology must have been many and varied. Some loss of faith or at least substantial confusion is likely, as native gods appeared powerless to avert epidemics. This may have led, as elsewhere, to innovation and even intensification in ceremonialism and other religious practices (Trigger 1981:21–32); recent scholarly opinion has tended to contradict Martin's (1978) thesis that complete apostasy would have been a common outcome (Krech 1981). At the same time, as religious elites probably depended upon esoteric lore, that lore was presumably lost to some degree. More crucially, the information exchange that permitted chiefdom organization (Peebles and Kus 1977) – and that probably depended upon religio-political channels – quite likely ceased or was drastically curtailed.

This loss or curtailment of an information network may prove to be the decisive effect of demographic catastrophe on chiefdoms, removing the element without which the chiefdoms could neither survive nor reconstitute themselves. It has long been obvious that a chiefdom cannot begin to be constituted below some threshold of population density, and certainly pandemics could cause population to drop below this threshold. If the communicative and organizational apparatus survived more or less intact, however, and if the administrative overhead were not too great for the surviving population to bear, the chiefdom could simply cut its losses, contract territorially, and rebuild its population. If, on the other hand, the infrastructure dissolved, the chiefdom would have no mechanism through which to reorganize, and the survivors would fission into the locally viable groups that remained.

The implications of a differential effect of epidemic disease on groups at different stages of tribal organization are important for my argument about the genesis of the Choctaw tribe. I propose that the bulk of the Choctaw population came from among the "prairie" peoples of the upper Pearl and western tributaries of the Tombigbee and the "Burial Urn" peoples emerging from the devolved Moundville chiefdom.

Because these peoples were more dispersed and autonomous than multilevel chiefdoms such as Tascaluça or Natchez, they suffered far less from epidemic disease. These functioning chiefdoms, and probably also the ones centered on the lower Pearl and the Pascagoula delta, were left, after the first waves of disease, with a suddenly and forcibly decentralized population. I think that at this point outlying population groups formerly attached to chiefdoms joined the neighboring, ethnically related tribe that, because of its established decentralization and local autonomy, was already functioning better than the smashed chiefdoms surrounding it. When chiefdom groups joined this tribe, their genealogical lore and esoteric knowledge would have been largely lost, facilitating their adoption of classificatory kinship principles and a simpler social organization.

THE SPANISH ENTRADA, 1559–66
Tristán de Luna y Arellano, 1559–61

Virgin-soil epidemics, however they were transmitted, would have had rapid and drastic effects, and later observers should have remarked upon them. Whether or not Soto witnessed the results of contagion brought by Ayllón or other coastwise travelers, his successors must have witnessed the result of his passage if the hypothesis of early drastic population loss is to be sustained for the interior. The first of these successors, sent in 1559 to the Florida coast to establish a haven for the treasure fleets at the height of Spain's "corsair war" against French pirates, was Tristán de Luna y Arellano; evidence that the Luna expedition did indeed witness the effects of dramatic depopulation is, however, equivocal at best.

Clearly the expedition was eager to draw what profit it could from Soto's failure. Part of its original impetus may have come from a letter written in 1557 to the king by the canon Pedro Hernández Canillas and Roderigo Ranjel, by then *alcalde mayor* of Pánuco in northeast Mexico, suggesting that a settlement be established at Ochuse (Pensacola Bay) to provide shelter for ships in distress and a base for the settlement of Florida. Ranjel cited his knowledge of the port as a Soto expedition participant and recommended a major settlement inland at Coça (Arnold and Weddle 1978:172–73).

A second letter of the same year, addressed to the king from the inspector Dr. Pedro de Santander as he was on his way to examine the treasury records in New Spain, also urged the settlement of Florida. He specified that the first settlement should be made in that "most fertile" province of Chuse, where a new town called Filipina would soon become a center for trade with and conversion of the natives. Further, he suggested that a second such town, Cesarea, be established in the Tascaluza province on the fertile banks of the Despiche River; it would serve to attach "all the nearest bordering towns to your royal service" as large numbers of Spaniards settled there. In the same way settlements could be made further inland, first at Talesi and then at Coza, which Santander portrayed as rich in fruits, nuts, berries, grapes, and fish. Finally, he recommended that the settlements be pushed on to the pearl-rich "Gulf of Bermuda" to protect shipping along the Atlantic coast (Santander 1557; Hoffman 1990:149–52). This list of interior polities offered by Santander is of special interest for two reasons: it shows that the sequence of large polities in the interior seen by Soto was common knowledge at the Spanish court by 1557, and it also suggests that the name of Tascaluça was connected in the popular imagination with political influence over numerous dependent towns, whereas Coça was known for its fertility and abundance of food.

Information about Soto's expedition was thus clearly available, doubtless because of its more than 250 survivors. Many had settled in Mexico and might have been willing to return to Florida (Avellaneda 1990:73). Weddle (1985:266) has observed that Luna's expedition included one man, Alvaro Nieto, who had certainly survived Soto's march, and at least two others, Roderigo Vázquez and Juan de Vargas, whose names had appeared on the list of survivors or in accounts of the expedition; many other survivors with more common names may also have joined Luna. Luna's mission was to establish a base on the Gulf of Mexico and then to find an overland route through the rich lands of Coça to set up another base at Santa Elena on the Atlantic. Luna himself had had exploration experience with Coronado and was a favored friend of the Mexican viceroy Velasco. Although Luna was as well informed as possible, and although an advance coastwise exploration by Guido de Lavazares had established where Luna would land, clearly both he and the viceroy were still confused about the interior – more specifically, they did not know which rivers debouching on the Gulf coast led to which Indians inland, and an important part of the expedition lay in finding out. Since that is my interest here as well, it is fortunate that for this expedition there is very little question about which rivers the Spaniards saw.

The careful reconnaissance by Lavazares, carried out on the orders of the viceroy of Mexico, had as its pilot Bernaldo Peloso, survivor of the Soto expedition (listed as a caulker [Swanton 1939:351]). The report of the journey indicates that the party sailed northward and eastward along the Gulf coast to Pánuco, Matagorda Bay, Breton Sound, the Chandeleur Islands or Mississippi Sound, and Mobile Bay (Arnold and Weddle 1978:173–75), which Lavazares named Bahia Filipina and reported to be the largest and most excellent bay he had seen. He noted a large population of natives growing corn, beans, and pumpkins lining its shores as well as an abundance of game, fish, fruit, and nuts; he lauded the easy availability of materials for naval stores, the excellence of the open woodland for grazing (and military maneuvers), and the presence of red clay for brick on the east side and gray clay for pottery on the west. Even the climate seemed healthful. Lavazares attempted to sail on further east but was thwarted from making the port of Ochuse by bad weather (Priestley 1928, 2:332–39). Weddle (1985:259–60) notes that an obscure service record of 1564 suggests that in early 1559, after Lavazares's return, a second reconnaissance ship commanded by Juan de Rentería did manage to explore "Polonza" (Pensacola Bay) as well as the Bahia Filipina; it may have been this expedition that decided Velasco to direct Luna to land in the bay of Ochuse rather than Filipina.

The quality of the data for Luna's expedition is fairly good, although most of the documents do not describe the Indian polities directly. Two accessible printed sources exist. One is a narrative account composed from the thirty-year-old reminiscences of one of the expedition's clergymen, Fray Domingo de la Anunciación, and included in Fray Agustín Dávila Padilla's 1625 *Historia de la fundación y discurso de la provincia de Santiago de México* (Dávila Padilla [1625] 1955). The other source is a dossier of letters and legal papers assembled in the course of the lawsuit issuing from the expedition's failure, translated and edited by Herbert I. Priestley as *The Luna Papers* (1928). The Spanish and Mexican archives certainly contain other relevant materials, but Priestley's work has seemed so definitive that it has tended to discourage further research.

The Dávila Padilla history of the expedition, part of a general account of Dominican activities in New Spain, has much the character of the individual narratives previously discussed in connection with Soto, and it has been criticized on several grounds. Weddle (1985:250) mentions Dávila Padilla's "lack of reportorial skills and geographical knowledge"; Priestley (1928, 1:ix) remarks that the work's status as oral history thirty years after the fact causes it to fall "into the class of memoirs or reminiscences rather than that of contemporary narratives," and although he drew from it to craft a narrative introduction to *The Luna Papers*, he admitted elsewhere that "it is a matter of more than ordinary interest that none of the contemporary documents collected and preserved by Luna himself mention any of the exciting incidents which the garrulous Dominican historian obtained thirty years later from his coreligionist Father Anunciación" (Priestley 1936:129). In evaluating its worth as a history of the Mexican missions, Robert Ricard (1966:317) remarked that it "would be even more valuable if the author . . . being excessively concerned with singing the personal virtues of his confreres . . . had not too often put the main task in the background" – and Ricard, a friar himself, was a sympathetic reader of the work.

To the critical secular eye Dávila Padilla has written a mass hagiography in praise of his Dominican brethren, so full of miraculous events that separating the real from the supernatural becomes difficult, and only the lack of an English translation of the entire history has kept this fact from being blatantly obvious to English-speaking researchers. No one has evaluated Dávila Padilla's narrative of the Luna expedition for its historical value since Swanton (1922:230–39 and *passim*) gave it his imprimatur by drawing on it verbatim for evidence about Creek towns. It has been popular with ethnographers and anthropologists ever since because it is the only Luna document that discusses or describes social organization at any length, and researchers have been particularly tempted to use its extended account of a Spanish–Coça Indian expedition against the "Napochies" Indians (see Hudson 1988). Since Swanton identified the Napochies with Choctaws, I have to discuss the general value of the Dávila Padilla account here.

Dávila Padilla undertook the task of compiling an account of the Mexican Dominicans' activities by order of the General Chapter of Mexico in 1589. At that time he was given a manuscript and papers from a project started in the mid-1550s by Andrés de Moguer, added to by Vicente de las Casas and Domingo de la Anunciación, and translated into Latin by Tomás Castellán (Millares Carlo 1986:189). By the time Dávila Padilla began to work on the history, Domingo de la Anunciación had been martyred in Mexico, and indeed the history contains an account of his saintly life. Dávila Padilla allegedly worked from manuscripts and from oral interviews with his confreres, and he explicitly mentions having heard the Luna conversion story from Anunciación's own lips, but clearly what he and his predecessors were writing was providential history, and Dávila Padilla did not merely transcribe the words of informants. That he changed the materials that came to him is plain in the Luna expedition account: his biography of Anunciación argues for the friar's saintliness and speaks particularly of his modesty, so it is unlikely that Anunciación gave a central place to his own actions in his account of the expedition, yet Dávila Padilla's story does just that. According to Dávila Padilla, Anunciación was the only religious present at the "Napochies" excursion that only this source relates, having left his confrere Domingo de Salazar behind in Coça.

Dávila Padilla tells this tale of Luna's expedition to magnify Dominican holiness as he does with all the stories in his book, and that intention strongly shapes the story of the Luna expedition, with the theme of Dominican steadfastness against evil reiterated in nearly every chapter. One need only enumerate the miracles performed by Domingo de la Anunciación to get the supernatural flavor of the whole: Anunciación and Domingo de Salazar pray chestnuts into ripeness on the way to Olibahali, and God causes a poisonous caterpillar crawling on the chalice of the mass to drop dead at Anunciación's request; observing the Coça chief make a pact with the devil for his people to defeat the Napochies, and failing to persuade them to eschew killing, Anunciación prays – and God tells the Napochies to flee and escape the Coça surprise attack; Anunciación finally breaks Luna's stubborn resistance to advice after five months of praying, when God speaks through him to chastise Luna, and Anunciación then correctly predicts the day relief ships will arrive; for the last five months of the colony's ordeal, God multiplies a tiny quantity of flour to enable Anunciación to prepare the Host for the mass and make gruel for the sick. Does all this, cheek by jowl with supposedly accurate ethnographic observation, foster confidence? Clearly Swanton thought not, for he eliminated most of the supernatural apparatus from the segment he quoted (1922:231–39). Clearly Hudson agrees, for he mentions only the caterpillar story in his retelling of the raid on the Napochies (Hudson 1988:612–22), so that the reader of his article sees only the detailed description of the Indian army leader's actions (including a rousing rally from atop a mound that even Dávila Padilla does not mention), being unaware that these events form the central episode of the story so the teller can focus on how Anunciación, to thwart the Coça pact with the devil, is able to call on God to deliver the Napochies and thus save the Coças from the sin of killing them. As neatly told a story as it is, I do not make central use of Dávila Padilla's history here because of these serious doubts about its authenticity.

With the materials presented in *The Luna Papers* the self-conscious narrative history is left behind for the first time. Priestley says that the main body of the papers he edited and translated came from one Spanish archival dossier, which related to the complaints brought against Luna by his subordinates. The collection is composed of "gleanings from numerous bundles in the Archivo de Indias," researched by one Irene Wright and said to include "all available materials" (Priestley 1928, 1:x–xi). The largest coherent group is that of the lawsuit of Luna's captains, but apart from odd bits of information and the general framework provided, most of this material is of little interest to the purpose at hand except as the lawsuit itself and the veiled revolt it implies underline the terrible straits in which the expedition found itself. The most useful documents fall into two categories: reports from religious and military men of the discoveries of the detachment sent to Coça, and depositions from three soldiers regarding the whole expedition.

This group of documents is very different in its evidentiary status from the narratives of Narváez or Soto: in one way or another, each of these documents reports evidence on the Indians to a superior who, as far as the writer knew, might well eventually have the opportunity to check its truthfulness. In addition, these documents do not have the same communicative purpose as the overtly historical narratives written after the fact; they intend not so much to tell the story of events that have passed but rather to contribute to the ongoing discourse of events still in flux. They display the character of the chronicle, which represents reality "as if real events appeared to human consciousness in the form of unfinished stories" (White 1987:5). And precisely because they do not achieve the narrative closure of a history by the imposition of an interpretive structure, they are more immediate and reliable as sources. To be sure, each of these documents also "emplots" the events it portrays as they impinge upon the progress of the author's own private story, but the authors do not interpret those events apart from selecting which events to mention and in what sequence.

The first step toward exploiting these data is reconstructing the explorers' route

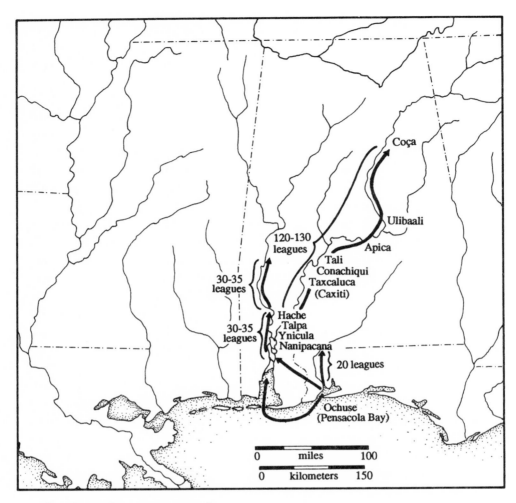

4.1. Luna's *entradas*, new reconstruction.

(figure 4.1). Other researchers have done so numerous times, but in my opinion without paying adequate attention to the nonnarrative texts. A more than adequate picture is possible without the work of the friar Dávila Padilla. Interestingly, this picture offers no certain evidence of serious population depletion. It also suggests that Luna's men saw evidence of populations *not* seen by Soto.

The expedition initially made its landfall at Mobile Bay, at the recommendation of Lavazares, but returned eastward to establish its base at what was said to be the better anchorage of Ochuse, thought to be Pensacola Bay (Priestley 1928, 1:xxiv; Swanton 1939:164; Weddle 1985:267), on 14 August 1559. Early on, a hurricane struck, destroying their ships and much of their supplies. With the delays and vicissitudes of the long supply line from Mexico, expedition members soon had to rely upon the resources of the countryside, which meant that, like Soto, they had to find Indians to find food. The motivation discussed earlier for Soto was explicitly stated this time: Velasco asked the king to allow the *encomienda* tribute to begin immediately after the land was laid under conquest and settlements were established.

Shortly after landing, Luna had sent a party of men to explore the river emptying into the bay of Ochuse. One of the two captains leading the exploration was Alvaro Nieto, a Soto veteran. In the face of Velasco's manifest concern with the Soto evidence, we must conclude that the purpose of this detachment was to find the same key to the interior that Soto had provided, and that the party of one hundred infantry probably followed the bay's largest tributary river, the Escambia, in a northerly direction. According to the report of the *arquebusier* Cristóbal Velázquez, the party pursued its route inland for twenty leagues, finding nothing but a small town at half that distance, and, having captured a woman named Lacsohe to serve as an interpreter, returned to the coast (Priestley 1928, 2:302–3). It seems fair to conclude that the party had determined to its own and the expedition's satisfaction that Ochuse was not where Soto thought it was and that the Luna expedition had chosen the wrong river. All the men had to do was point upriver and say "Mabila"; all the Indian woman had to communicate was "no."

Lavazares's report of the rich and populous shores of Mobile Bay, together with intelligence supplied by Lacsohe and the Coça Indian women who had been brought from Mexico (perhaps including the Coça chief's sister taken by Soto) probably lay behind the direction taken for the next sortie, which set out overland by 24 September, ranging westward to the Mobile-Tensaw delta to seek Indian settlements and food (cf. Priestley 1928, 2:286–87). Led by Mateo del Sauz, it consisted of some two hundred men, and it succeeded in finding "towns, a moderate number of people, and some provisions" (Priestley 1928, 1:93). Although the Indian reaction to their presence was less than enthusiastic, Sauz and his men behaved with restraint, made friends of the natives, and sent word to Luna to join them in the town of Nanipacana.

Hudson has argued that this detachment went north instead to seek Mabila. "From the De Soto documents and from the soldiers who had been on the De Soto expedition, Luna would have learned that Mabila and Piachi were 40 leagues to the north of the coast," he asserts (Hudson et al. 1989:34). In fact, Biedma wrote that Mabila might be "*as much as* 40 leagues from the sea"; Oviedo/Ranjel offered no estimate; the Elvas narrative estimated a traveling time of six days from Mabila to Ochuse (which, by Hudson's usual estimate of 4 to 5 leagues per day, would amount to only 30 to 35 leagues); and Garcilaso quotes someone (Gonzalo Silvestre?) as quoting Indian captives after the battle of Mavila (Mabila) as saying that they had seen Maldonado's ships on the coast and that the province of Achusi (Ochuse) and the seacoast were "a little less than thirty leagues" away. Clearly 40 leagues is thus an outside estimate on the strength of the narrative accounts; in addition, the only accurate distance would have to be the one in days, since a Mabila Indian captive would not be likely to quote a distance in leagues. Whether the distance was thought to be 30 leagues or 40, in view of Hudson's insistence that these land leagues were the *legua común* of 3.5 miles/5.6 km (while the distance of 20 leagues from Mobile Bay to Pensacola Bay would have been in nautical leagues of 3.2 miles/5.1 km), it seems especially odd that when the expedition was so desperate for food, explorers would travel 103 or 138 miles on a *possibility* when Luna already knew that the populated Mobile Bay region lay only 64 miles to the west (a full two to four days closer) and the expedition had already spent a month there. What had happened during that stay is not known, but the Spaniards would certainly have learned of the rich and populous lands of the Mobile-Tensaw delta.

The location of the Nanipacana town found by the exploration party in the delta is not immediately obvious. What is obvious, however, is that Luna was convinced that this party would find what he sought, for he outfitted it more seriously than he had the previous one: the leaders of this expedition were the *sargento mayor* Mateo del Sauz and Luna's two nephews Cristóbal de Arellano and Carlos de Zuniga; the personnel consisted of 150 men, cavalry and infantry; and the two friars Domingo de la Anunciación and Domingo de Salazar were sent along, probably to attend to legal requirements for the good treatment of Indians at the time Spanish assertions of sovereignty were made. The *Luna Papers* contain no participant's report of this detachment's activities, but once Luna decided, six months later, to transfer his forces to Nanipacana, the move provided a multitude of observers – nearly 1,500 people – making the region the best reported of all. The first news indicated that large quantities of corn were available in Nanipacana, plenty to support the entire camp (Priestley 1928, 2:304–5,314–15). The residents, it seems, were at first friendly.

By the time Luna overcame an illness enough to take the decision to go inland, however, the situation had changed. The exploratory party had reported on conditions at the end of the fall harvest, but by February the Indians, aware that the Spaniards had no plans to be temporary guests, had gathered their corn and women and simply absented themselves (Priestley 1928, 2:288–9,304–5,314–15). A broad cross-section of expedition members described the Indians as "in revolt," but because the Sauz detachment's six months' residence is unreported, we cannot know if the Spaniards had treated them badly or if they simply feared the influx of the main force. When Luna sent an expedition up the river from Nanipacana – led by *maestro de campo* Jorge Ceron, Alvaro Nieto, the expedition accountant, and a cavalry captain and consisting of a hundred men in four boats – the news that the Indians had abandoned a heavily populated area extending upriver some thirty to thirty-five leagues (Priestley 1928, 2:290–91) came as no surprise. Foraging parties in the environs of Nanipacana had already reported similar conditions for twelve to fifteen leagues' circumference (Priestley 1928, 1:156–57). This "revolt" amounted to a thorough scorched-earth tactic: destruction and burning of all crops not harvested, burning of villages, and disappearance of population and food supplies. It also apparently involved some sniping at stragglers and undefended foragers (cf. Priestley 1928, 1:154–55,162–63).

Thanks to the measures taken to scour the countryside, however, a good picture of the Nanipacana region emerges from the frustration of the searchers. It was a complex and populous delta floodplain, thickly settled and cultivated from Nanipacana upstream some thirty leagues and downstream apparently twelve to fifteen leagues (Priestley 1928, 1:162–63, 2:290–91). It included a Nanipacana town and river, a "Tome" River, and towns called Ynicula, Talpa, Upiache, and Utchile. The lower Tombigbee and the complex Mobile-Tensaw delta with its distribution of protohistoric sites fits this description very well and certainly offers many toponymic links with the Tohome and Naniaba peoples later found settled there. Hudson has unaccountably conflated this northward trip with the subsequent first half of the later Coça journey (cf. Hudson et al. 1989:36–37 and Priestley 1928, 2:291), maintaining that this expedition went up the Alabama halfway to Coça, but the account of cavalryman Alonso de Montalván, who was a member of the Coça expedition but not a member of the previous one, makes it clear that there were separate expeditions on two different rivers.

A second expedition sent up the rivers of Nanipacana and Tome was led by B. de Sotelo, Diego Tellez, and Juan de Porras after Porras had returned from partial participation in the Coça trip, and this may be the source of Hudson's confusion. This excursion, described in the testimony of camp master Jorge Ceron, clearly explored "the River of nanipacna and that of tome" and revealed that the natives had burned over their fields and pulled up their corn (Priestley 1928, 1:154–55).

Further clarification of the details of the Nanipacana region comes from the expedition meant to reach the Coça lands, the Spaniards' greatest hope. Led once again by Mateo del Sauz, it included many of the same personnel who had been entrusted with the expedition to Nanipacana: Soto veterans Alvaro Nieto and Roderigo Vázquez, Luna's nephew Cristóbal de Arellano, three other captains (two of infantry and one of cavalry), and the Dominican friars Domingo de la Anunciación and Domingo de Salazar, together with some fifty horsemen and one hundred infantry. This is the best reported of all the detached explorations, described by four letters written from the Coça region (two to Luna, one to Velasco, one to a friar), two transcribed oral testimonies, and additional oral information from participants incorporated into the lawsuit against Luna, as well as the narrative of Agustín Dávila Padilla.

The four letters were dispatched from Coça, though not all were written there.

The expedition departed on 15 April from the Talpa, Ynicula, and Atache area north of Nanipacana, which expedition personnel unanimously recommended as equal or superior to Coça because its grasslands were suitable for cattle (Priestley 1928, 1: 220–21). They had some forty days of hard going until they reached a town named Caxiti (according to the detachment leaders) in the province of Taxcaluça (according to Alonso de Montalván), where they sent food (either thirty-five to forty or eighty *fanegas* of corn) downstream on rafts with Juan de Porras and nine men (Priestley 1928, 1:224–25, 234–35, 2:290–91), thus indicating that the expedition had been following a river from the Atache area. Beyond Caxiti some ten days was Onachiqui (or Talis), which they believed to be the first Coça town (Priestley 1928, 1:224–25, 236–37, 2:290–91). From this point on they found the Indians at least nominally in residence (women and clothing had been taken away), food for the asking, and crops ripening in the fields. Rations were short, since the first crop was not yet ready, but especially in Coça the natives willingly sold provisions to the Spaniards. The expedition passed through two further named towns, Apica and Ulibahali, before reaching the main Coça town on 1 August, where three of the letters were completed and carried to Luna by his nephew, Cristobal de Arellano, and twelve horsemen.

Although the expedition depended on forest resources until reaching the Taxcaluça town where the corn was found, it apparently did not pass through completely unoccupied lands: the dearth of food was due to the time of year, not the lack of towns, which had been found deserted and empty of food (Priestley 1928, 1:220–21, 236–37). Among the things they did eat were "oak acorns which, if not prepared as the Indians know how to do, are too bitter to eat" (Priestley 1928, 1:235–36). A message from their friends at Nanipacana was passed to them via "some friendly Indians" (Priestley 1928, 1:235–36); the people of Coça were said to have trading interests as far as Atache (Priestley 1928, 1:218–19, 228–29). Nevertheless, the accounts do suggest that although communication and trade passed along roads between the Nanipacana-Atache-Upiache region and the Coça towns, settlement was scattered and cleared fields few. It would be hard to match such a pattern with anything in the region other than the sparsely populated lower Alabama River area linking the Mobile-Tensaw delta and the Coosa-Tallapoosa forks region.

The Spaniards' characterization of what they found in the two populated areas was conditioned by what they were looking for: places to plan Spanish towns where they could be supported by *encomienda* labor, clearly stated several times as being most desirably based upon field agriculture and broad pasturage for cattle (Priestley 1928, 1:200–201, 206–7, 214–17, 220–21, 226–27, 240–41). To the Spaniards the Indian fields looked meager and poor, and the depth and impenetrability of the forests enabled the Indians to escape Spanish observation – and thus also domination – at will. The marginal superiority of the Coça region and the apparent exploitability of its population was offset by its large population's full utilization of its resources: if Spaniards settled, Indians would have to be ejected, for the area could not support both populations (Priestley 1928, 1:240–41).

The Nanipacana-Atache-Upiache-Talpa region was seen in two states: as originally encountered by the small exploration party and as seen by the already disillusioned full company when it went there to escape hunger. The first explorers, arriving just after fall harvest, encountered an abundance of food and thick settlement, consisting of small floodplain villages scattered through the delta. By the time the whole camp was transferred, the Indians had managed to steal away with the bulk of their crops. According to the Spaniards, the whole delta's fields and gardens had been willfully destroyed, sometimes burned over; even some towns had been burned – to deny the Spaniards shelter, as they thought. Yet this state need not have been particularly unusual for the Indians of the Mobile delta region; fields would have been burned over after harvest in any case, and if their subsistence pattern included a winter hunt (cf. Curren 1976), they may merely have gone, with all the food, to their hunting camps in the rolling hills to the west. In any case, the Indians would have needed to evacuate fully only Nanipacana itself; spies could easily monitor the movements of exploration and foraging parties and give warnings for temporary evacuation as needed. The Spaniards complained of snipers, so clearly the empty villages they entered were watched from the forest's edge. The whole camp of Spaniards remained in the Nanipacana village from February to the end of June, 1560. If the people returned to their towns after the Spaniards' departure, they would simply have missed making the early crop and still would have had time to plant and harvest at least once.

Although the initial party spent five months in Nanipacana, after which the main body spent an additional six months there, they wrote no description at all of social organization, no hint even of the Spaniards' having met with leaders. This silence would seem to suggest that the towns of the region, though some of the most populous seen by the Spaniards, were organized autonomously, an assemblage of coequal towns with possibly the largest, Nanipacana, at an old chiefdom center.

At some point between Nanipacana and Coça the detachment crossed a linguistic boundary, apparently that between Western and Eastern Muskogean language families. From Coça Domingo de Salazar wrote to a friend in Nanipacana that "the language [of Coça] is another one [than at Nanipacana], very different and more difficult, although they have some words from there" (Priestley 1928, 2:244–45; cf. Hudson et al. 1989:39). Where that happened is not precisely clear, however, nor is the organization of the population in the intervening region obvious, either from the first-person documents or from Dávila Padilla's history.

Hudson and his colleagues have suggested that the Luna documents imply a much-reduced Tascaluça agglomeration whose fall may be accountable to the Soto expedition, but they base their argument upon the conflation of two explorations, up the Tombigbee and up the Alabama, and thus spend a great deal of time attempting to prove that the Hatache village of the Nanipacana group is Soto's Athahachi, Tascaluça's town; that the Tascaluça chiefdom consisted of three simple chiefdoms ruled by a paramount from Piachi; and that because Athahachi seems Eastern Muskogean and Nanipacana and Tascaluça Western Muskogean, then the Tascaluça chiefdom must have been as bloated in size as the Coça chiefdom (Hudson et al. 1985; cf. Boyd and Schroedl 1987) and multiethnic to boot (Hudson et al. 1989:36–39). It is not clear to me that the Coça detachment saw all or even much of what would have been such a chiefdom; the only town identified as belonging to a Tascaluça "province" is Caxiti, for which Hudson et al. (1989) seem to have substituted "Atache," leaving Caxiti to belong to another grouping.

Information about the lower Alabama River area could be scarce simply because the sparse villages along the river were abandoned and watched just as those around the Nanipacana river had been, since the Spaniards remarked upon the change when the Coça people remained in their villages and willingly bartered food supplies for Spanish trade goods. It may have been the strength of their polity that made the Coça Indians observe the normal customs of hospitality; it may have been the confidence of distance from the main group of Spaniards; it may have been, as it was in Soto's case, a matter of time of year. The Coça people's trade reached to Atache, so they must have known about the movements of the Luna parties and thus known that a small party could be followed months later by a larger group. The exploration party arrived among them at the end of July, however, when crops were nearly ready for harvest. Had the Coça leaders lost their nerve and counseled evacuation, their subsistence for the winter would have been imperiled, just as had been the case with Soto, and the Coça people had rid themselves of Spaniards before by behaving calmly. The region was populous, so much so that the detachment's leaders several times remarked on the danger they were in and the advisability of going along with such friendly overtures as were offered, taking special care not to abuse hospitality by seizing food or allowing horses to trample gardens.

It is interesting to note that Coça was one of the expedition's ultimate goals from the beginning. As Santander's letter summarized above indicates, this polity had been remembered and described by the survivors of Soto's expedition as the richest they had seen: Velasco's letters repeatedly refer to "the good country where Soto was" (Priestley 1928, 1:181) and identify it with Coça, urging Luna to find and exploit the riches there. Velasco himself was familiar with available information about the Soto expedition; he mentioned sending Luna "the memoir given me by Alvaro de la Torre, the cleric who was with Soto in those provinces" (Priestley 1928, 1:75) and referred to a "painting and description" of the region he possessed. Certainly Soto survivors Nieto and Vázquez would have recognized a place where they had spent more than a month (Weddle 1985:266). This concentration on Coça to the exclusion of even a mention of other polities in the region is of particular interest in view of the arguments presented in the last chapter for variable levels of social organization as seen by Soto, since it suggests confirmation of the hypothesis that his expedition found no chiefdoms of significance (apart perhaps from that of Tascaluça) west of Coça until the party reached the Mississippi Valley.

In the Coça region the detachment found a large population in small towns of forty to fifty houses clustered along floodplains. All the towns had a public space (*placa*) outside the town containing a sort of post set up in the middle of it, and some had walls for defense and temples for worship (Priestley 1928, 1:338–41). The Spaniards observed both winter and summer houses. They remarked that the very limited cleared lands in the floodplains barely sufficed to feed the Indians themselves, but in default of corn the Spaniards had been able to subsist on nuts, berries, and acorns.

As for the main Coça town and its leader, the Luna papers imply and infer a great deal about his power. Upon entering the Coça "province," the detachment was sent a *prencipal* to serve as guide and messenger, and burden-bearers served willingly for payment in trade goods. Sauz worried that after the harvest the Indians might be less obliging, but he grimly soldiered on to Coça town to carry out his mission. Reaching Coça and settling their camp on cleared land outside the town, the detachment learned what it reasoned must be the cause of the cordial reception they had received. The chief of Coça willingly placed his people and lands under the protection of the Spanish king in order to obtain relief from "certain Indians" who had encroached upon Coça lands and cut off trade and communication routes (Priestley 1928, 1:230–33). Interestingly, the source that gives this information is the first joint letter from all the expedition leaders, including Anunciación, to Luna; these same people wrote a second letter on the same day to Viceroy Velasco that repeats much detail from the first but only says that the Coça chief "submitted himself to the protection of the king" (Priestley 1928, 1:238–39). Depositions made in Hispaniola by two soldiers after the expedition's failure do not mention the encroaching Indians or any Spanish efforts to eject them (Weddle 1985:284). Furthermore, the expedition's military leaders reported no follow-up by the Spaniards. The only source that elaborates on the incident is Dávila Padilla, reporting the story of the raid on the Napochies ostensibly told by Anunciación.

Even if the Napochies excursion is authentic, it is not of much help here, for several reasons. First, it deals with events that say more about the "just war" doctrine, which permitted Spaniards to conquer people who were at war with one another to save them from themselves, than about social organization in the interior Southeast.

It suggests that one polity might use the Spaniards as a tool against another, but there is conflicting evidence as to what the Spaniards saw. Dávila Padilla portrayed a clear-cut case of a feudal subordinate, the Napochies polity, being returned to its tributary status. The letters sent from Coça by the detachment leaders, on the other hand, indicated that the Coça chief was complaining of another who had "usurped" and "made demands" upon his people; who had cut off communication "with his own people," occupied roads, and stopped trade; he requested that the Spaniards aid him in restoring communication and trade with "his own natural lord" (Priestley 1928, 1:230–33). This picture is a very different one, suggesting that the Coça people had fallen into tributary status to some other group and that the "Napochies" were possibly incomers to the area. Finally, the identification of the Napochies with some Choctaw- or Chickasaw-related group dates to Swanton's (1946:218) desire to torture the name from *napissa* (Choctaw for "those who see" – cf. Acolapissa) after having decided that a Nanipacana (or even a Tascaluça) guide would not have given a river the name "Oquechiton" (Choctaw *oka*, "water," *chitto*, "big"); in fact, a guide would quite likely give them such a generic name. Southeastern Indians seem to have had specific, usually topographic or destination-related names for familiar watercourses (see Waselkov 1989). The letters may reflect an ill-understood political situation, but the detachment certainly did have a Coça interpreter with them. In the end, this evidence really gives no more than was already available from the information about Coça alone: that Coça apparently still operated as a chiefdom, but its power was not great.

Having found Coça, the party summoned Luna to examine the land for himself, reluctant to report that it was not all they had hoped. The communication arrived in Nanipacana too late to be of use: the starving thousand there, already seriously dissatisfied, formally refused to follow Luna deeper into the wilderness in search of food. After weeks of charges and countercharges, the main camp in Nanipacana broke up on 24 June, and the people returned to Mobile Bay to subsist on the area's seafood.

Some meager supplies had arrived at the port of Ochuse from Mexico, but with them were included royal orders to found a post at Santa Elena on the Atlantic coast without further delay. Luna sent a party by sea, but it was thwarted by storm and shipwreck; when reports at last arrived from the party at Coça he decided to return inland to Coça to establish a settlement, thence to proceed to the Atlantic coast. This proposal precipitated a massive lawsuit against Luna, in which everyone from soldier to captain to clergyman maintained that the men were unfit for such an expedition and the commander unfit to lead them. In the end a small contingent was sent to Coça to recall the detachment to the port of Ochuse, and Luna was replaced by

Villafañe. Again, they accomplished little save the gathering of intelligence about the interior.

What did the Luna expedition see that may be of use to this inquiry? First, surprisingly, they did *not* see any overt evidence of massive mortality from disease. It is true that they saw few edifices that they recognized as temples, but they found both the Mobile–Tensaw–lower Tombigbee delta and the Coosa-Tallapoosa forks regions well populated, and their evidence suggests that the agricultural potential of the two regions was right at carrying capacity, necessitating supplementing the diet with gathered foods. They remarked upon the healthy appearance of the natives, so they saw no evidence of deprivation. The settlement pattern they observed was one of dispersed villages of 250–300 people in at least the Coça region, with a very few large towns (Nanipacana and perhaps Coça). Only a handful of these towns are mentioned by name, and several of the names match those found in the Soto accounts – which does not guarantee that they were the same places that Soto visited or that the towns contained the same people. Hudson and his associates have argued that they were (Hudson et al. 1985; Hudson et al. 1989), but I would like to suggest that perhaps changes had already begun to take place, changes that may have included the movement of the Coça chiefdom that Marvin Smith (1984:108) postulated as occurring after 1540.

The first argument for this position is that Priestley's identification of Nanipacana with the Mobile delta (which, interestingly, Hudson has ignored) seems correct. Luna had been told to land first in Mobile Bay, and so he did. The pattern of explorations carried out by his men north of Pensacola Bay indicates that he next tested the hypothesis that Mabila was on a river debouching into the Bay of Ochuse, and the party's failure to batten down the camp at Ochuse and unload the boats, which had tragic effects when the hurricane hit, implies that Luna did not expect to stay there long. When they had found neither Mabila nor any food and their supplies were destroyed, he moved to test whether the bay of Ochuse was indeed Mobile Bay, which he had already seen. Once settled above Mobile Bay, he initiated a search up the delta and onto the western tributary, probably still seeking Mabila but also in need of supply from Soto's corn-rich Pafalaya towns, which, as Luna would have known, should have been in that direction. When that effort failed, he sent his men on the longer northeasterly journey that might leave the main body starving but that would surely reveal one of Soto's towns.

I see no convincing reasons, apart from a superficial similarity in some town names (Nanipacana/Talicpacana, Hatache/Athahachi, Upiache/Piachi), to argue that Luna and his main party were not in the Mobile delta. In fact, two of these names could, on linguistic grounds, call for a westerly location. Hudson himself (Hudson et al. 1989:39) suggests a Western Muskogean derivation for Nanipacana (Choctaw *nani*, "hill," *pakñli*, "bloom"), but he fails to consider an alternative (pakna, "top") for the second element that would plausibly suggest the bluffs to be found west of the Mobile-Tensaw Valley. The Talicpacana (Choctaw *tali*, "stone") reported by Ranjel after Mabila or Taliepatava reported by Elvas (Choctaw *patafa*, "split, cleft") suggests a different sort of topographic feature. Hudson depends very strongly on identifying one of the Nanipacana towns as the central town of the Tascaluça chiefdom seen by Soto, so he argues at length (Hudson et al. 1989:37) that the town name "Atache" (also "Hatache"; see Priestley 1928, 1:218,220,226) is to be equated with "Athahachi," which allegedly contains the Eastern Muskogean Creek *hahci* element meaning "river," and that it is a contraction of this word. But there is a perfectly good Western Muskogean Choctaw word – *hatachi*, "white" – that, in the political symbolism of colors in the Southeast, would have been an eminently suitable name for a town, particularly the town of an important chief with the Western Muskogean Choctaw name of Tascaluça.

Lavazares had clearly told Luna what to expect at Mobile Bay, and his report highlighted the availability of Indian crops. Certainly the distance of 120–130 leagues (414–448 miles or 666–721 km) that Hudson and his colleagues claim from Nanipacana to Coça (they use Dávila Padilla's distances only when convenient; in this instance the Dominican historian asserts that it was 200 leagues from Nanipacana to Coça!) fits much better the actual distance from the Mobile delta to Hudson's location for Soto-period Coça in northern Georgia. Since Hudson often seems comfortable with estimated distances in the documents, it amazes me that he rationalizes this particular estimate by claiming that the party traveled very slowly and thus believed it had gone further than it actually had; thus he can account for the shorter distance from the location he identifies as Nanipacana (near modern Selma). If this distance is an illusion – and I have already mentioned the problems with distances in all of these sources – then there may be some reason to look for the Luna-period Coça in northeast Alabama (cf. Boyd and Schroedl 1987), particularly if the main justification for its location further north and east is the dubious "Napochies" jaunt related by Dávila Padilla.

Again, however, I am less concerned with the precise location of these polities than with what can be learned of their structure and history. I do think that Soto never saw the Mobile delta, in spite of Curren's claims (1986, 1987), which I think are being made on the basis of large deposits of Luna artifacts. Luna's expedition saw and told precious little about the populous delta considering how long it remained there. A few hints suggest that the conglomeration of Nanipacana, Talpa, Atache, Ynicula,

Upiache, and Utchile (which contains more named locations than the Coça "province," as it should with so many more witnesses) may have incorporated some people from the Tascaluça group that had been involved at Mabila, and their cautious behavior fits such prior experience very well.

The Coça grouping looks to have been even less centralized when Luna saw it than when Soto passed through. Alvaro Nieto and Roderigo Vázquez may have drawn its boundary where the Indians began to get friendly, but in the last chapter I argued that even in Soto's time its dominance was not as far flung as some have maintained. Here, a chief who is able to send messengers demonstrates no other powers: the burden-bearers work for wages, and, as before, the people take a diplomatic course for the sake of their crops, not their chief. Clearly the deserted Taxcaluça-Caxiti town where hidden grain was found was thought to be one of Soto's Tascaluça towns, but if so its grandeur seems much diminished. The possible disappearance of the Tascaluça polity as such is therefore one possible important change, but only if Luna's men were in fact following Soto's route; with no mention of Mabila, I wonder if that was the case.

None of these possible changes supports an argument for truly massive disease mortality and population depletion by 1560. If the settlements were at carrying capacity, natural devolution as a consequence of environmental stress may have set in, and the few "savannas" that were greeted by the Spaniards with such enthusiasm as possible pasture for cattle were likely the remnants of exhausted old fields. The area Luna's men explored contained two major population agglomerations separated by a thinly populated buffer zone but joined by formal trading ties. Both were seemingly dominated by the autonomous villages characteristic of tribal segments (and in this case the Alabama River phase), but the northern end of the "Coça province," the area proximal to Coça itself, seems still to have had some degree of central organization. Apparently, the only clear candidate for serious depopulation is the Escambia River region north of Ochuse Bay, which had played host to the ships waiting in vain for Soto as well as probably to many other undocumented Spanish ships. One village in twenty leagues and no population at the bay certainly contradicts what the Narváez expedition saw.

It would be very helpful to know what Mateo del Sauz and the other leaders of the Coça expedition had to say about the region; as it is, only the brief letters survive to contrast with Fray de la Anunciación's possible flights of fancy. Surely these officers' service records are not impossible to find, and a later *probanza* may yet contain at least a word or two about what they did at Coça to corroborate or finally disprove the Dávila Padilla/Anunciación account.

Finally, if members of the Luna expedition did not witness any particular evidence of epidemic disease, they had ample opportunity to transmit it, since various parties spent months in Nanipacana and Coça, months during which the normal wastes of living had every opportunity to pollute and infect.

Juan Pardo, 1565–67

The failure of Luna and Villafañe might have meant at least the temporary end of Spanish efforts in Spain's Florida borderlands had Philip II not been increasingly disturbed by French pressure on the Spanish monopoly of the temperate Americas, this time manifested in Laudonnière's Huguenot settlement (Hoffman 1990; Lyon 1974). The next Spanish expedition to found a settlement on the Atlantic coast was based in Spain, and it was led by the influential privateer and merchant Pedro Menéndez de Avilés, who proceeded to massacre the French colony and to establish a settlement in 1565. Part of the basis for permanent settlement would have to be good Indian relations, and Menéndez was also eager to establish a reliable overland route to New Spain, so when reinforcements arrived from Spain in 1566 he sent Juan Pardo inland to undertake explorations and to establish forts, seeking and securing the route by fortifying the Coça town Soto had discovered and Luna's men had seen (Lyon 1974:126–27; Hudson 1990).

Unfortunately, Pardo never saw Coça, and the only report of it came to him via an unidentified soldier whose testimony – available only at second hand – is impossible to judge in terms of reliability. Four accounts remain of the second Pardo expedition of 1567–68 when he made this push westward: a very terse soldierly chronicle by Pardo; two accounts, one brief and the other very elaborate, by the notary Juan de la Bandera; and another, not yet fully studied, account by Domingo de León (Ketcham 1954; Hamilton 1910:520–27; Hudson 1990; Worth 1994). Pardo tells nothing of Coça except that west of Chiaha they were warned that the Indians beyond were inimical and that to advance would endanger their lives. This attitude was not surprising, since Moyano, the sergeant Pardo left in the interior, had spent his time by leading attacks on fortified towns in the region. The second Pardo expedition thus turned back to Chiaha, where they left a small detachment. Bandera's first account is nearly as bare as Pardo's, but it reports information Bandera says he obtained from Indians and from a soldier of the company who had allegedly been to Coça and returned.

According (presumably) to the soldier's account, from "Satapo" (where Pardo turned back) to Coça there were four small villages (Tasqui, Tasquiqui, and two unnamed ones) and a destroyed town named Olitifar. Coça was said to be a large town assumed by its size to have 150 residents (though most commentators assume that *vecinos* here is a slip and households is meant [DePratter, Hudson, and Smith

1983:150]) and surrounded by many small villages. Beyond Coça seven days was Trascaluza, with two or three villages intervening, and nine days beyond that, with only one small hamlet intervening, was Mexico.

The soldier could have seen Coça, but the mention of "Trascaluza" and two or three villages beyond Coça sounds like information secured from Indians of an alliance that included nothing beyond Trascaluza and accordingly little knowledge either. Beyond the implication of communication from Tasqui through Coça to Trascaluza, this account offers so little that it is impossible to tell if depopulation or movement had occurred since the Luna party's visit. The lengthier Bandera account of 1569, which amounts to the confirmation of fealty obligations (*requerimiento*) elicited on behalf of the Spanish king and recorded officially by the notary Bandera (see Hudson 1990:208,256), does not amplify this information. In fact, Pardo's journey generated good evidence only for what lay north and east of Coça in the late 1560s, and far less for the region of interest here than did Luna's expedition. This paucity of evidence is doubly unfortunate because the Pardo accounts are more objective than those for any other Spanish expedition in the region.

SIXTEENTH-CENTURY SUMMARY

In Chapter 3 I advanced a view of the Alabama-Mississippi region at the time of the Soto expedition that proposed much less complex social organization in parts of the region than others have argued for the Mississippian adaptation, and this simplification was seen as a consequence of a natural devolutionary cycle rather than of European contact. In this chapter I discussed the theoretical effects of epidemic disease in the region and then turned to two later accounts of the interior in an attempt to discern any early effects of disease that might have been introduced by Soto or other contacts – with very ambiguous results. Neither the Luna nor the Pardo expedition provided evidence that would establish whether disease had yet become a serious problem in the interior, but the Luna testimony did demonstrate a degree of simplification in social organization if not a clear-cut reduction in population. The Soto expedition's actions could have been responsible for some portion of such change by means of immediate population loss, particularly if the Mabila losses hit the Tascaluça polity most severely.

The sixteenth-century evidence does show a continued Indian use of traditional techniques for dealing with European intruders. The Luna evidence makes the natives' concern for their crops obvious, where it was merely suggested by the "seasonal scheduling" of Indian behavior toward Soto. While crops ripened, the Indians Luna met were cautiously friendly and willing to trade for food supplies. Once the crop was harvested, it would be carried off and the villages abandoned, sometimes even burned (though in the Nanipacana region this may have been accidental rather than intentional). Having seen how Nanipacana behaved, Sauz expected the same behavior from the Coça people, but when the full camp did not transfer there the Indians apparently decided to support the smaller troop without evacuation. Spanish behavior may have made it safe for the peoples of the Mobile-Tensaw delta simply to adjourn to their winter hunting grounds west of the delta, with which they were doubtless thoroughly familiar. During this occupation by the Luna camp, which lasted into the spring planting period of 1560, these proto-Choctaw peoples may have taken advantage of the agricultural potential of the Sucarnoochee and Noxubee floodplains, since they did not return while the Spaniards remained.

The Pardo accounts amount to a litany enumerating the ordered submission of eastern groups to Christianity and Philip II, a sort of sequential Mirandizing that legalized enslavement and the appropriation of land. This process came to a halt before it reached Coça when the expeditionaries were told that massacre awaited them ahead; Indian reprisals for Moyano's anachronistic conquistadorial behavior were clearly more feared than French revenge for the shoreline massacre. Yet a few years before, the Luna expeditionaries had found the Coça chief delighted to see them and anxious to enjoy the benefits of Spanish protection against enemies who were cutting off their communications with friends. Soto had heard this same story from the Chicaça chief regarding the supposedly rebellious Sacchuma, and he found that it was an ambush plan; it is hard to believe that Alvaro Nieto's memory was so short that he would have advised Mateo del Sauz to risk the same possibility with his much smaller troop. Since it is still not certain that Sauz countenanced such an expedition – and no good evidence is offered that the Coça chief was sincere – we can suspect that this solicitation of military assistance was another tactic of the Indians, or at least that the Spaniards may have misunderstood.

Finally, Pardo's lieutenant Moyano found out the hard way what happened when he attempted violence against his hosts: he ended besieged and cut off, rescued in the nick of time by Pardo's second expedition. Pardo's expeditions were both characterized by very cavalier and arrogant treatment of the Indians quite reminiscent of Soto, and I suggest that at least one reason for the eastern tribes' tame submission was their having already experienced the serious effects of European disease. Thus, when Moyano and Pardo ran up against resistance to the west, perhaps they were crossing a sort of "disease front." The peoples on the other side of such a front may already have begun to defend themselves against the encroachments of refugees. Whatever the reason, the final outcome was the denial of passage to Coça.

Pardo's penetration of the interior marked, for all practical purposes, the last visit these tribes and chiefdoms would see for nearly a century. These last two visits did not tell anything of the Mississippi River groups, but I think their records permit the conclusion that those on the Tombigbee watershed had not yet been seriously affected by European disease. They must, however, have become aware that Soto was not a fluke, and that their world was being touched on all sides by aliens whose purposes were becoming all too plain. If this breathing space did exist, if knowledge of the intruders' purpose preceded the calamity of disease, we must consider the possibility that such knowledge had as profound an effect on Native American thought as the discovery of alien people in a New World had upon European thought. Thus, while the elders still lived, perhaps they were able to begin assimilating a modification of the very concept of novelty into their teaching about human conduct in the world. The evidence suggests that this assimilation did not entail scrapping diplomatic tools, such as hospitality, but instead consisted of modifying those tools to include behaviors – such as demand for payment – to adopt when hospitality was abused.

CHAPTER FIVE

Seventeenth-Century Overtures to Contact

I inquired of the Indians of the southern part of the Mississippi whether there were no Englishmen at all in their quarters. They assured me that they knew only Spaniards. – Jean-Baptiste Le Moyne de Bienville, 6 September 1704 letter to Jérome Phélypeaux de Pontchartrain, in Dunbar Rowland and Albert G. Sanders, *Mississippi Provincial Archives*, vol. 3

The past is, by definition, a datum which nothing in the future will change. But the knowledge of the past is something progressive which is constantly transforming and perfecting itself. – Marc Bloch, *The Historian's Craft*

For the Indians of the deep southeastern interior the seventeenth century passed largely out of the sight of Europeans, but it was a time of change and consolidation from which even Soto's genuine chiefdoms emerged nearly unrecognizable as the historic southeastern tribes and confederacies. Inroads from the most disruptive product of contact, disease, were already being seen around the region's fringes by the few explorers who followed Soto in the sixteenth century, but the effects of the full demographic disaster are directly available only in reports dating nearly a century later. The reports of the earliest European settlers along the coasts and rivers show considerable confusion and contradiction, reflecting inchoate southeastern Indian settlement distributions and ethnic alliances in the wake of demographic disruption. Population movements had occurred and were continuing; ethnic combinations to compensate for population loss were in progress. Except for the missionized Indians of the Florida peninsula, however, southeastern groups had not yet been affected directly by the acculturative forces of sustained contact, although during the seventeenth century they were drawn inexorably into the developing European-dominated world economic system. The evidence of those same Florida missions permits a glimpse of the interconnectedness of southeastern groups and the recency of their reorganization.

THE EUROPEAN COMPETITORS
Marquette and Jolliet on the Mississippi, 1673–74

French colonization of North America began with the sixteenth-century penetration of the Canadian forests, and French entry into the interior Southeast probably began without record in the seventeenth century when fur-trading *coureurs de bois* illegally made their way southward from the forests of the Ohio region and the trans-Mississippi. Officially sanctioned explorations did not begin until Louis Jolliet and Father Jacques Marquette, with five *voyageurs*, descended the Mississippi as far as the Arkansas River and its Quapaw settlements in 1673. Father Marquette's report of their journey includes a map he drew of the lands they passed through. Jolliet's testimony is imperfectly represented by a copy of a map he probably drew; his journal of the expedition was lost in a canoe wreck. Both anticipated that their information would be used by explorers and missionaries.

What they learned of the tribes of the lower Mississippi was distorted at best, but one very clear feature was the efficiency of the communication system across the Southeast, which gave Marquette news of Europeans to the east and south with whom the Indians of the lower river traded. This information would not have surprised him; the *Jesuit Relations* of the 1670s contain several notices of southern contacts between Indians and Europeans, doubtless reported by *coureurs de bois*, and Marquette and Jolliet had informed themselves fully about the lands they would be approaching and the people they would be meeting. The news merely confirmed what they had learned previously. A group of Indians they encountered on the eastern side of the river, south of the Ohio and north of the Arkansas, told Father Marquette "that they bought cloth and other things" – which included guns, axes, hoes, knives, beads, and glass bottles that Marquette saw – "from Europeans on the eastern side; that these Europeans had rosaries and pictures; that they played on instruments; that some, who received them well, were like me" – that is, priests (Shea 1853:44).

Proceeding further south, the French party arrived first at a Michigamea village and then among the Quapaws at the Arkansas River. The Quapaws warned them against advancing further, indicating that the Indians possessing firearms met earlier "were their enemies who cut off their passage to the sea, and prevented their making the acquaintance of the Europeans, or having any commerce with them" (Shea 1853: 47). The European goods the Frenchmen observed among the Quapaws were, they said, sold to them through tribes to the east and the Illinois Indians to the north. Marquette remarked that they served watermelons, so hard goods were clearly not the only things they traded. This evidence of European presence near the sea was enough to cause the expedition members to return to Canada, since their mission – to find out where the Mississippi emptied – had been accomplished and they were able to conclude that it indeed debouched into the Gulf of Mexico rather than the Atlantic or Pacific. Marquette remarked that it would have been counterproductive for them to have gained this intelligence only to end up in a Spanish prison.

The records of this expedition of course supply no information on the Choctaws, but they do indicate that the Quapaws believed the whole of the lower river to be dominated by European-allied Indians. This was not true, and shortly La Salle would prove it; but the belief itself is an indication of the dread that Indians outfitted with firearms caused among their brethren who had none. Which Indians caused the Quapaws such apprehension is unclear: Iroquois raiding south along the Tennessee or Lower Creeks of the Chattahoochee newly acquainted with the English settlers of South Carolina. The Spanish policy – though not always their practice, particularly somewhat later on (Bushnell 1989) – was precisely *not* to arm their Indian converts, so the arms traders and friars they reported may have been representatives of two groups of Europeans, not one.

Bishop Calderón and the Spanish Missions, 1674–75

Spanish efforts in founding missions to the Florida Indians had begun to succeed when Menéndez de Avilés undertook the task in the 1560s after Luna's failure. The missions thus founded were concentrated along the Atlantic coast and on the peninsula of Florida. The Spanish missions of Apalachee that reached farthest west had only been founded in the 1630s and had made only limited and indirect contact with the region of interest by the fourth quarter of the century.

One abortive expedition to visit the "Chata" west of the Apalachicolas was made in the early 1660s by the officer Pedro de Ortes and some soldiers, but it amounted only to a brief meeting with four "caciques," their towns not named, in the Apalachicola village of Casista (Hann 1988:183). The chiefs turned Ortes away, pleading shortage of food. The reference is very intriguing, particularly as the name of the meeting place mirrors Oviedo/Ranjel's Casiste, most eastward of the Tascaluça towns, and perhaps the Caxiti that Luna's explorers thought was connected with Taxcaluça. If it is not simply a chance similarity, then these "Chata" were indeed some of the proto-Choctaws, the successors or neighbors of Tascaluça; this would then be the first known reference to the Choctaws by name.

Indian pressures had forced the withdrawal of the missions along the South Carolina coast in the 1660s, and permanent English settlers arrived in South Carolina in 1670. At the time of Bishop Calderón's visit in 1674, the Spanish missions were on the verge of their greatest threat from the new British element, and although the request for Apalachicola missions (which Calderón had come to answer) would be briefly met, abandonment and massacre at the hands of the British would be the eventual fate of the westward missions as the two imperial forces squared off to face one another in the "debatable land" (Bolton and Ross 1925).

Calderón's visit to Florida was an official inspection by the bishop in authority – and no such visit had been made to the Florida missions, Calderón told the queen regent Mariana, for sixty years. The purpose germane to this study was "to investigate the state in which the priests of San Francisco have the work of converting the Indians" and also "to lend encouragement to the converting of the Indians of the province of Apalachocoli" (Wenhold 1936:2), and that entailed a visit of ten months that apparently included all the existing Indian missions. The bishop's report describes the Florida settlements and missions, listing villages, missions, population and distance figures, and descriptions of the coasts and of the Indians themselves and their culture. This account is not a unique document; a large governmental and mission correspondence and the records of the missions themselves contain many passing references to contacts in the interior that still await detailed investigation (cf. Hann 1988). Undocumented penetration of the interior had certainly occurred as well, from the beginning of the seventeenth century (Geiger 1937:145).

Thus Calderón's report represents a summation of the information about the area west of modern Georgia that had begun to accumulate with the beginning of the Apalachee missions, which over time had become an important conduit for products of the interior destined for Havana and St. Augustine (Bolton and Ross 1925:26). Which tribes were bringing in the dried meat and other foodstuffs that figured in this trade is not yet clear, but it seems that groups the Spaniards knew through the missions may have served as brokers for the produce of tribes further west, since the Pensacolas were found ten years later to be rich in European trade goods (Dunn 1917; Hann 1988:142). The trade also consisted of more than edibles: complaints of English piracy in a 1678 raid on a Spanish storehouse at San Marcos, the Apalachee port, listed doeskins and amber among the lost goods (Pearson 1968:238–39). The relevant point here is that this established market could have begun to foster commercial hunting in the interior by the middle of the seventeenth century, along with all the associated implications for economic change. This trade with the Apalachee missions must have been the source of the tales Marquette and Jolliet heard from the Indians they met east of the Mississippi, so the network could have reached indirectly to the Mississippi and beyond.

Calderón's report focused upon the matters he had come to Florida to address, and it is of most use here because the Apalachicola mission was Calderón's own foundation. After listing the eleven Christian Indian settlements of the Timucua "province" and the thirteen of Apalachee, Calderón described his work in creating the newly established province of Apalachocoli, including his plans for a new church in the village of Sabacola located just below the falls of the Chattahoochee and his hopes for thirteen other villages along the Chattahoochee River that had agreed to be converted likewise. Under the heading of the Apalachocoli province he also listed the new mission to the Chatot Indians and the names of additional heathen tribes the bishop had presumably targeted for conversion in the future. The Apalachocoli province contained the autonomous groups comprising what would later be seen as the Lower Creeks: village names such as Oconi (Oconee), Ocmulgui (Ocmulgee), Cazithto (Kasihta), and Cabita (Coweta) are immediately recognizable; they were said to be located some thirty leagues up the Apalachocoli (Chattahoochee) River.

The Chatots, found nearer the new Santa Cruz de Sabacola mission, are also familiar. They should not be confused with the Choctaws, although both may have lost their tribal names in Spanish nomenclature. The adjective *chato* is Spanish for "flat" or "roman-nosed" and was probably a generic term applied to this people because they practiced cranial deformation (G. Keyes, pers. comm. 1992). The feminine form is *chata*, which would be the appropriate modifier for *cabeza*, so it may be that the emergent Choctaws, who also practiced cranial deformation and indeed were known to the English later as Flat Heads, had been described to Pedro de Ortes rather than named. The two forms are phonetically distinct, however, and the two tribal names were distinguished throughout the eighteenth century.

Calderón next mentioned the heathen nomadic "Chiscas," identified by Swanton as the Yuchi (Wenhold 1936:5), living near the Chatot, and then turned to a brief description of the Toassa "province" of heathens located "between the northeast and west, about 30 leagues distant, on the bank of a large river" (Wenhold 1936:10).

Swanton's notes on this material, included in the Wenhold article, identified the Toassa province as the Upper Creek towns but noted that the list is "very incomplete" (Wenhold 1936:5); I have already expatiated on Swanton's failure to recognize culture change over time in the Southeast, and later work (especially Smith 1987) has shown how strongly population movements affected the Creeks during the seventeenth and early eighteenth centuries. Hence Calderón's list may not be incomplete at all; it may merely describe a single synchronic state. The information probably came from native informants, for there is no indication that Calderón visited these groups. The towns he lists are fourteen: Toassa, Imoclasa, Atayache, Pacani, Oslibati, Afaschi, Escatana, Atassi, Tubassi, Tiquipachi, Achichepa, Hilapi, Ilantalui, and Ichoposi.

Labeling this collection of names of disparate linguistic origin the members of a "province of Toassa" is obviously mistaken, but certainly this state of affairs is very different from what Luna observed. Presumably the reason it so irritated Swanton was that if it was complete, his desire to draw continuity from 1540 to the nineteenth

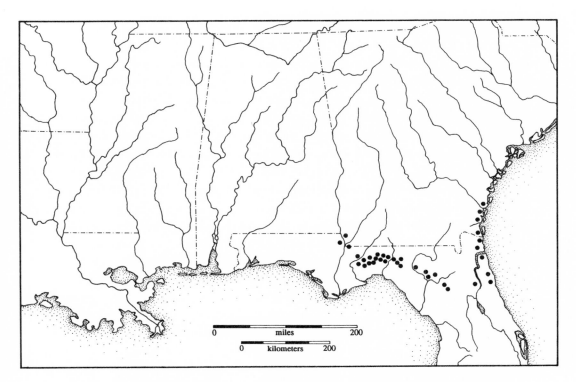

5.1. Spanish missions of north Florida in 1675 (data from Boyd, Smith and Griffin 1951; Gannon 1965).

century would have to be thwarted. The assumption that it was complete, even for its time, would be unjustified, however, since we have no way of knowing how a native informant might interpret a request for information. A contemporary document enumerating villages of Apalachee and Timucua, written on 15 July 1675 at the behest of the governor by Spanish captain Juan Fernando de Florencia, commander of the Apalachee province, clarifies the reason for this confusion: "although there are other provinces such as that of Apalachecole which have given submission to Your Majesty, and of that of Toasa, of these I cannot give information because they have not given [information] that is reliable, and only could have some error in the number of inhabitants of the villages, since I have not taken a census and they die daily" (Boyd 1948:187–88). As contact with the interior increased, so did mortality. When Governor Hita Salazar sent Domingo de Leturiondo to perform a *visita* of the Apalachee province just two years after Calderón founded the Apalachicola mission, his report made no mention of the mission's existence (Pearson 1968). In fact the first mission, in the village of Sabacola, was expelled by order of the cacique of the Caveta in 1679; a second attempt failed in 1681, and the mission finally found its permanent home in a new town of converts built at the Chattahoochee-Flint confluence in that year (Bolton 1925:119).

Calderón was even more obviously dealing with vague thirdhand information when he wrote of the tribes beyond the Toassa: the powerful Chacta of 107 villages at seventy leagues' distance and the Mobile on an island near Espíritu Santo harbor. This evidence does suggest that the "no man's land" between the Nanipacana and Coça areas observed a hundred years before had not only persisted but had grown larger. The apparent lack of communication between Spaniards and western Indians that may have led to this vague picture of the Choctaws and Mobilians was remedied by the Apalachocoli mission that Calderón established, as will be seen in the discussion of the Delgado journey ten years later.

But where had the powerful Choctaws originated? As Swanton noticed (Wenhold 1936:5), this is the earliest extant European document mentioning a Choctaw people by that name (the 1660 Pedro de Ortes encounter was documented by a 1687 letter only [Hann 1988:183]), yet Calderón's informants characterized them in terms of great numbers and power. Luna's expedition, which by any reckoning had much more nearly approached the region to which Calderón refers, reported nothing of such people, although they likely saw a very populous Mobile delta. Thus these "Chacta" are either new people or known people under a new name, and they must have acquired their reputation between the 1560s and the 1660s or 1670s. In my opinion this evidence establishes the time of origin for the Choctaws as a unified people known to history, but to bring them more fully into focus we must examine the reports of Spain's rivals in the region.

Dr. Henry Woodward's Back-Country Adventures, 1666–85

Calderón's visit and his aim of founding the Apalachocoli mission were not only a matter of routine; the activities of Englishmen beginning to breach the Appalachian barrier and push south from the new Charles Towne settlement were clearly influential in prompting this Spanish response, as doubtless was the Anglo-Spanish treaty of 1670 that established lands held as lands owned (Wright 1964; Alvord and Bidgood 1912). The larger part of this interior indeed became a "debatable land" as Spain and England sought to pursue their goals of empire. The man who moved between the two sides, Dr. Henry Woodward, also came to know the Indians of the interior most thoroughly, and would eventually place that knowledge at the disposal of Carolina.

Woodward must have possessed great linguistic and diplomatic gifts, for he was able to master Indian languages and to learn a great deal about interior tribes from Indian informants. He began his adventures in 1666 when he was left behind by an exploration ship near Port Royal (Spanish Santa Elena) to learn the language of the Indians. Captured by the Spaniards of St. Augustine, he escaped in 1668 and served as a surgeon on a privateer until chance provided the opportunity to return to the infant colony of Carolina in 1670. His skills were soon useful to the settlers when food ran low and he made the first of his famous inland treks to the northwest to establish alliance with the "Chufytachygs" (McCrady 1901:137).

This alliance did not affect the displeasure of the fierce Westos, who threatened to help the Spaniards run the newcomers off until the British made a determined attack on Santa Elena. To ensure that such an alliance should not arise again – and also apparently to tap into the lucrative skin trade with Virginia – the Earl of Shaftesbury had contracted with Woodward to explore the Westo and Cussatoe country. He was able to begin that task in the company of some Westos who had appeared at his plantation near Charles Towne seeking trade. Woodward's report of his journey indicates that he reached the main Westo town on the Savannah River and found the Westos "well provided with arms, ammunition, tradeing cloath and other trade from the northward for which at set times of the year they truck drest deare skins furrs and young Indian Slaves" (Salley 1911:133).

Woodward observed something of the intertribal turmoil of the hinterland of which this slave trade was an intimate part: during his stay a party of "Savana" (Shawnee) Indians from west of the Apalachicola came requesting alliance against the "Cussetaws, Checsaws and Chiokees," who were supposedly about to attack the Westos. These Shawnees also possessed Spanish beads and other trade goods they had obtained from "white people like unto mee" (Salley 1911:134). Woodward confidently assured his employer that the Westos would appear in short order with the deerskins, furs, and young slaves that they had formerly traded to the older colonies of the north, and for his trouble the Proprietors designated him as official manager of the Indian trade and beneficiary of 20 percent of its profit (McCrady 1901:177). Crane (1956:17) has speculated that Woodward may have penetrated the interior again as early as 1675 to treat with the Kasihtas, causing alarm in Apalachee, for by 1677 the Proprietors were ready to declare for themselves a monopoly on the trade with the Westos and Kasihtas established by Woodward. The 1677 *visita* to Apalachee ordered by Governor Hita Salazar was incited by rumors of British traders among the Indians of the interior threatening the province (Wright 1964:472).

Favoring the Proprietary monopoly, Woodward opposed the Westo war that was prosecuted to benefit private Indian traders and slave dealers, but the Carolinians effectively wiped out the Westos and set the immigrant Shawnees Woodward had met in their place as brokers to the interior. After having left Carolina briefly as a result of the persecution of Governor West, he was commissioned by the Proprietors in 1682 to make further explorations for a passage over the Appalachians (McCrady 1901:347). Some of these explorations must have led him to the Chattahoochee River, for in 1685, in spite of opposition from the Scottish colony that had set itself up at Port Royal, he was leading English trading parties to the influential Apalachicola (Lower Creek) towns of Coweta and Kasihta there (Bolton and Ross 1925:46–48). Unsuccessfully pursued by the lieutenant of Apalachee, Antonio Matheos, he returned in a few months and again escaped, as Matheos, after first confiscating deerskins and trade goods from a blockhouse Woodward had built, burned villages for sheltering him. Yet these actions did not prevent Woodward from taking out 150 loads of skins and pelts shortly thereafter, though he was so ill he had to be carried himself (Bolton 1925:120–23; Serrano y Sanz 1912:193–98; Hann 1988:188–89).

According to Thomas Nairne, writing in 1708, Woodward traveled into the interior again in around 1688, this time further to the north, when he laid the groundwork for alliances with the "Ochesees and Tallapoosies" and sent two men westward to establish trade with the Chickasaws (Nairne 1988:50). "Ochesees" is an anachronism introduced by Nairne: the Kasihtas and Kawitas inhabited the Chattahoochee when Woodward met them and moved eastward to the Ochesee several years later. As in later times they were allied with the Tallapoosas, and the Tallapoosas, in turn, with the Chickasaws.

Woodward ceased his involvement in the Indian trade and his explorations, but his activity to the west of Carolina had opened up various native groups to direct exploitation by European traders as the Spanish presence had not done. Crane (1956:22) observed that the Indian trade was the "chief instrument of Carolinian expansion" and noticed further that Indian slavery, encouraged by the Europeans' fomentation of intertribal warfare, was concomitant to the trade. It is therefore not surprising to observe that although Woodward must have obtained a good knowledge of the Lower Creeks and their intertribal relationships – good enough to permit the kind of manipulation that led to their wholesale migration to the Ocmulgee River by 1690 to be closer to the English trade – the trading advantage such knowledge conferred made Woodward and his colleagues keep to themselves the detailed observations that would allow us the better view of the interior they had doubtless accumulated. The Spaniards stung by his efforts among the Lower Creeks were the ones who left an explanation of events.

Lieutenant Matheos, who had pursued Woodward in vain, reported on the result of the Englishman's efforts in a letter dated 19 May 1686 (Serrano y Sanz 1912:193–98). The letter was based on the observations of his Indian spies in the towns of the Apalachicola province; it clearly reflects a reasonably sustained acquaintance with the Indians in question and their disposition toward the Spaniards. In the letter Matheos and the Lower Creeks are portrayed interacting in ways that became much more common under the French regime: the Spanish gave or withheld gifts depending upon Indian behavior; the Indians shifted the blame for trade with the British to a single chief; exaggerated rumors of British trading parties circulated; the Spanish tried to manipulate Indian groups against one another; and frontiers in the interior, past which information could not flow, were maintained by warfare.

Specific relevant facts include limited dealings with the Tawasas of the Upper Creeks and their clearly longstanding acquaintance with the Chickasaws, who reportedly intended to visit the Apalachee presidio. The governor had requested better data from Matheos about the famous Espíritu Santo bay, but Matheos said that in spite of his best efforts, what data he gathered made little sense, and he would need orders to make a coastwise journey west in order to obtain the needed information. What he did report was that the Mobilas, settled on an eponymous river beyond the Pensacolas by twelve leagues, had constant wars with the latter and therefore never traveled to San Marcos to be questioned. The rumors he had heard (and that he doubted on the basis of available sea charts) described an important river and province of Estanani four days beyond Mobila; its first town, seven days upriver from the sea, was said to be Ducascaxi. A party of privateers cast away on the Gulf coast in 1685 had been pursued by "Ystamanes" Indians from the Mobile River until they reached the safety of the Pensacolas (Weddle 1973:34–45), so if the Estanani was a separate river to the west (Pascagoula? Pearl?), its people were allied with the Mobilas.

The focus of this letter is Matheos's efforts against the British drive to gain the allegiance of the Lower Creeks; the efforts of the British led those Indians to move their villages eastward to be close to their trading partners. For that reason – and doubtless also because of the information blockade of which Matheos complained – his report says less of conditions to the west, although Matheos knew or soon learned more, as will be seen in the discussion of Marcos Delgado's mission. The Chickasaws were shown as allies of the Tawasas, but apart from the Mobila and the obscure "Estanani" nothing was known of the region directly westward. From Matheos's information, we may conjecture that the clearly important presence of the Mobila stands as a synecdoche for the whole of the forming Choctaw confederacy and that its bellicose boundary maintenance activities are symptomatic of a confederacy in process of formation. If this is true, its subsequent power may be partly due to the presence of its Pensacola, Upper Creek, and Chickasaw neighbors, who screened the confederacy from direct contact with the Spanish and English. The extent to which the Choctaws deliberately exploited this state of affairs will have to be explored through other sources.

La Salle and Tonti on the Mississippi, 1682–86

The narratives of Robert Cavelier de La Salle's famous voyage are important for the ethnohistory of the interior Southeast because of their descriptions of representatives of Quimby's (1942) "Natchezan" culture, especially the Taensas. Observations by various members of the expedition give information about intertribal relations, demographics and disease, and the political organization of several tribes. The evidentiary value of the various accounts has been recently evaluated (Galloway 1982d), and the reliability of the major accounts from Nicolas de la Salle ([1682?] 1898), Tonti (1684), and Minet (1684–85) is assured.

La Salle first established that no other Europeans had yet seized control of the lower Mississippi, as Marquette and Jolliet had feared, but effects of European contact were seen everywhere. The ravages of European disease were reported among the Quapaws, indicating a drastic decline since the time of Jolliet and Marquette. Settlement pattern is difficult to deduce from passing observations, but the descriptions of the Natchezan groups – Taensa, Coroa, Chitimacha – suggest that in no case had more than a simple chiefdom survived the stresses of population collapse. The confederation of the Natchez, Tioux, Grigra, and Coroa, representing both Natchezan and probably Tunican language groups and probably eventuating in the "Natchezan" kinship arrangement observed later by the French, shows that this situation had forced disparate groups to band together in order to secure claim to favored areas (Brain 1982). Pressure from the armed tribes to the east that had been reported to Marquette and Jolliet may have contributed to this amalgamation as well, and groups east of the Pearl River, formerly within the sphere of influence of Natchezan peoples west of the Pearl, could have tried to avoid the diseases plaguing their relatives to the west by severing those ties and turning toward the east.

La Salle's men learned little of the tribes of the Yazoo Basin, partly because of the Quapaws' enmity for its residents, partly because its population seemed too thin to warrant an effort to contact its natives. The one significant contact, made before the expedition arrived among the Quapaws, was with Chickasaw hunters ranging to the Mississippi River at the Chickasaw Bluffs; the abortive effort to reach them by traveling to the east may not have revealed Chickasaw settlements but certainly established that they dominated a large area of western Tennessee and northern Mississippi and were probably allied with the Natchez confederation dominating the lower Mississippi (Stubbs 1982a). Linking this evidence with Spanish rumors to the east produces a picture of an extraordinarily well traveled people – perhaps the southeastern equivalent to the Shawnees of the Ohio Valley.

The 1682 exploration was meant only as a prelude. La Salle's plans included establishing a chain of forts down the Mississippi to its mouth in order to exploit the Indian trade west of the river, and he left his lieutenant Henri de Tonti behind in Illinois while he returned to France to obtain the necessary royal backing for a return via the Gulf of Mexico. His efforts were successful, and in 1685 he embarked with a colonizing party to find the mouth of the Mississippi. Missing it by sailing too far west, he attempted to found his colony on Matagorda Bay and then to travel overland to find his river once more; in this effort he failed, as intransigent members of the expedition killed him and deserted (Weddle, Morkovsky, and Galloway 1987).

Meanwhile, Henri de Tonti had the task of holding together what he and La Salle had already won. Hearing of La Salle's success in France, he descended the Mississippi to link up with the colony in 1686 but failed to find it. The fruit of this second journey is some additional information confirming the observations made four years before: that the tribes of the lower Mississippi were under actual or potential threat from enemies to the east, many of them armed by Europeans. The discrepancies between Tonti's first account of the Indians and his later account show that the entire lower valley was in ferment, with shifting populations and alliances. The whole vexed question of the Quinipissas is a case in point. La Salle's first expedition reported seeing them; later expeditions searched for them in vain until Bienville found a letter that Tonti had left with them in 1686 for La Salle; this letter was in the custody of the Mongoulachas, who had merged with and apparently submerged the Quinipissas before being absorbed in turn by the Bayougoulas (Iberville 1981:89).

To bolster his and La Salle's claim to the Indian trade of the Mississippi Valley, Henri de Tonti built a trade house among the Quapaws as he returned back up the Mississippi in 1686, settling there a number of voyageurs led by Jean Couture. Tonti used this trade house as the base for another foray into the lower valley, in 1690–91. This particular journey is significant for the ethnohistory of the tribes west of the river, but Tonti made only scant contact with the Natchez and reported little of interest. More important was the apparent defection around this time of Couture, who left the trade house on the Arkansas, carrying with him all the knowledge of the lower river and its tribes that his sojourn had given him, to travel eastward to Virginia to guide Englishmen to the Mississippi (Galloway 1991b).

Yet still the French made no mention of the Choctaws. Beginning with La Salle in 1682 the Chickasaws were in evidence, and smaller tribes of the lower Mississippi increasingly complained to the French of pressure from the Chickasaws via the Yazoo and perhaps the Pearl, but no word surfaced of the great inland tribe. Its fame was, however, growing greater in the Spanish borderlands to the east.

Barroto's Reexploration of the Coast, 1686–87

Spanish response to the French penetration of their formerly Spanish sea, with its implied threat to the Spanish treasure fleet, was swift and strong. The major Spanish concern was to locate La Salle's landfall on the coast and the mouth of the great river on which the French claim was built, and to that end they sent several expeditions overland from the east and along the Gulf's northern coast from the west (Weddle 1991). The first Spanish search by sea for La Salle, led by Enríquez Barroto and Antonio Romero, is reported in a log kept by a volunteer from Havana, Jordán de Reina. According to Reina, the expedition sailed first to the Spanish mission settlement at Apalachee, where they obtained Indian pilots and heard – from Lieutenant Matheos – of troubles with English traders among the Apalachicola mission Indians, and on 30 January 1686 they began their coastwise journey to the west.

On 6 February the expedition arrived at Pensacola Bay and was led by its Indian pilot to the Panzacola Indian village on the following day. There the Spaniards were well received, presumably because of beneficial contact with the missions, as the Indians had a crucifix in their possession. They reported hardships inflicted upon them by "three strong villages of bold and warlike Indians" on a great bay of Mobile, which they warned the Spaniards to approach cautiously (Leonard 1936:554). The expedition must have taken great care indeed, for although they sailed into Mobile Bay on 11 February and spent two weeks there, all Jordán reports of it is that they saw "many campfires at night" (Leonard 1936:555). Sailing westward, then, the expedition coasted along the barrier islands to the mouths of the Mississippi and then home to Veracruz without, apparently, seeing or hearing anything else of the Indians of the hinterland.

Meanwhile, two new ships, shallow-draft *piraguas*, were being built to accomplish a more detailed examination of the complex Gulf coast. They sailed on Christmas of 1686, under the command of Martín de Rivas and Pedro de Iriarte, with Barroto and Romero as pilots. This expedition, recorded in Barroto's log, would follow the Gulf coast eastward from Tampico beginning on 7 March, carrying two native interpreters from Tamaulipas and two Apalachinos from the previous voyage (Weddle, Morkovsky, and Galloway 1987:174; Weddle 1991:53). With the aid of the Indians and repeated contacts with natives seen on shore, they minutely examined the coast. After examining the mouths of the Mississippi, on 22 May the expedition arrived at Mobile Bay, which they explored for two days without managing to contact any Indians; the few they saw at a bonfire on Pine Grove Point fled. One of the Apalachinos showed them the mouth of the Mobile River at the head of the bay, which suggests both that the main population was concentrated in the delta and that the Apalachinos were more familiar with the region than the warlike reputation of its inhabitants might have led the Spaniards to believe. Sailing from Mobile Bay on 24 May, the expedition passed Pensacola because they judged relations with the Apalachees familiar enough that anything known to the Indians there would be known in Apalachee, where they landed at San Marcos on 26 May for provisions before coasting down to Cuba and then returning to Mexico.

Without what is known from the intervening exploration reports, these reports of coastwise reconnaissance tell little more than Pineda's account. Certainly Barroto's explorations did much to disambiguate the "Espíritu Santo" problem, since by 1687 it was no longer believed that the Mississippi might flow into Mobile Bay or that that bay was in fact the "Espíritu Santo" (Weddle 1973:103). In contrast to the Texas and western Louisiana coasts, few signs of Indian habitation along the Gulf were visible from the sea, but, as was already known from the reports of Indians, and as Delgado would soon prove definitively, that did not mean that the coast was unpopulated or the hinterland laid waste.

Delgado Enters the Back Country, 1686

The Spanish effort to discover La Salle's colony also included overland expeditions, for by then the Spaniards had *two* possible rivals in the east: English traders had been seen among the Apalachicolas. In 1686 Governor Cabrera of Florida ordered Marcos Delgado, a soldier and rancher of the Apalachee *presidio*, to carry a letter overland to the viceroy of Mexico. The real objective of the mission, however, was the bay and river of Espíritu Santo, which was believed to be the destination of the French party (Boyd 1937:5). As Bishop Calderón's report shows, the Spanish in Florida thought the Mobilians lived on that bay, and after Delgado had spoken with the Mobilian chiefs he returned satisfied to Apalachee. His reports are of interest here because he took an inland route and described what he saw.

Documents relevant to Delgado's journey have been translated by Boyd (1937). They include Delgado's orders; two letters from Lieutenant Antonio Matheos of Apalachee to the governor; two letters, dated 19 September and 16 October, from Delgado to the governor; and the formal report of the outward journey dated 30 October and sent by Cabrera to Spain. The orders issued by the governor enjoined Delgado to behave toward the Indians who were not subject to Spain with great circumspection "and in no manner to do injury to the goods or persons of any Indians of those provinces" (Boyd 1937:10) – and Delgado's subsequent actions indicate that here the spirit of Las Casas and the Spanish New Laws is fully in force, recalling Luna rather than Soto or Pardo. Delgado was instructed to take careful note of everything, including Indian political organization, but not to meddle with it.

The letters of the jealous lieutenant Matheos, dated in August, betray his wish for the assignment, which he had requested in May, and criticize Delgado's decisions as to route. They also supply information on Indian groups that was apparently well known to the inhabitants of this border *presidio* but otherwise unrecorded (figure 5.2). Matheos reports a meeting with a Pensacola Indian leader who had come to Apalachee to trade but was unwilling to invite Delgado's detachment of fifty people to eat up the food supplies of his village in a drought year. In the course of Matheos's ensuing threats against the Pensacola "principal man," the lieutenant reveals that the Pensacolas were familiar with the route to the Choctaws; that the Pensacolas were at war with the Mobilians and the Choctaws; that the Mobilians were acquainted with the Apalachee *presidio*; that another tribe at war with the Choctaws, the Estananis, lived west of Mobile; and that the Choctaws were located farther inland than the Mobilians. Matheos says the Indian reports implied that the Choctaw polity "must be a very large province"; he sends with Delgado a Choctaw speaker captured as a boy by the "Chisca" (Yuchi?) of Apalachee as an interpreter and remarks that entry into the Choctaw country will make a success of the journey (Boyd 1937:11–13). Matheos's second letter, commenting on Delgado's choice of an inland route, supplies additional facts: that Apalachee had some contact with the Indians of Tavasa (presumably Tawasa); that it was six days from Tavasa to the Choctaws, while the Chickasaws lived at forty leagues' distance; and that the Chickasaws had the reputation of familiarity with the Espíritu Santo river and bay, and in Matheos's opinion would be Delgado's best guides (Boyd 1937:16–17) – an irony we can appreciate more than the governor could, knowing that the Chickasaws in alliance with the English had already become the scourge of most of the tribes around them.

Delgado's own letters and report give a great deal more information about the interior and its inhabitants but are highly elliptical in places and require careful analysis. The two letters offer an informal, impressionistic account of the sequence of events on the outward journey, while the report presents a more formal litany of observations, but the three must be taken together for a complete picture to emerge, and even at that it is hard to reconcile the contradictions without making some rather bold assumptions.

The first Delgado letter begins with the departure from San Carlos de Sabacola, the Apalachicola mission. It recounts two meetings with Indian leaders deep in the interior, the first at an unnamed village of the province of Tabasa (Tawasa) with six chiefs from unnamed "different places," the second at a town called Culasa with at least the chiefs of Miculasa, Yaimamu, Pagna, and Cusachet, all of whom accepted the friendship of Spain and one of whom sent messengers to the Mobilians to arrange a meeting. The second letter, a sequel to the first, states that, not finding sufficient provisions where he was, Delgado decided to go to Tiquipache province, "lands and villages which had not given obedience or seen either Spaniards or Christians in their life," in search of food until the messengers' return; this may well indicate a tour of villages terminating in a return to Culasa, but the account is vague. At the return of the messengers, who brought chiefs of the Mobiles and of the Thome, Ysachi, Ygsusta, Canuca, and Guassa, Delgado held a meeting at which he made peace between the warring provinces of Tiquipache and Mobile. He learned that there were no provisions to be had for a journey to the west and that the Choctaws, whose province took ten days to cross, would bar the way in any case, but that his message to the viceroy could be carried around the Choctaw province. Delgado thus decided to give up the journey and return home.

The formal report, which concentrates upon characteristics of the land and dis-

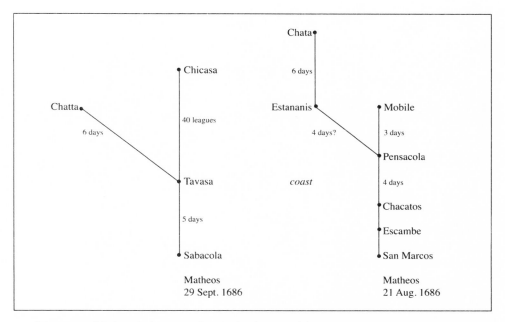

5.2. Lieutenant Matheos's data regarding Delgado's possible routes, configured as strip maps.

tances, presents a very different picture. It begins with a departure from San Luis de Apalache, never mentions San Carlos de Sabacola, and gives minute details of topography until the expedition reached "the first place in the province of Tiquipache" (Boyd 1937:25). It then gives the distances and directions from there to several villages: Ogchay, Quita, Qusate, Pagna, Qulasa, Aymamu, Tubani. Delgado indicates that these villages make up two groups: that of Pagna (Pagna, Qulasa, Aymamu), which had fled east from the Choctaws, and that of Qusate (Qusate, Tubani), which had been driven from the north by the English and the "Chalaque" (Cherokees?) and Chichimecas (Spanish usage for "wild Indians"). This description of village locations suddenly becomes the description of a meeting of "all of the chiefs and principal men of the provinces" of Mobila, Cortaje, and Tavasa, at which Delgado urged them to cease warring with one another and scolded the Mobilians for killing Chickasaw emissaries on their way to the meeting. The document closes with the assurance that this meeting had opened the way west for the Spaniards; it is dated from Tuave in the province of Cosate.

Some of the village names in the two accounts are the same, but the formal report seems to ignore or telescope the three meetings mentioned in the letters. The two accounts can be combined into a single one that seems to make sense of all the data at hand (figure 5.3) and to rationalize Delgado's formal report. Delgado probably did hold three meetings, as the two letters imply, but since he may have traveled among the villages whose chiefs he had met in the first two meetings, perhaps he assumed

179

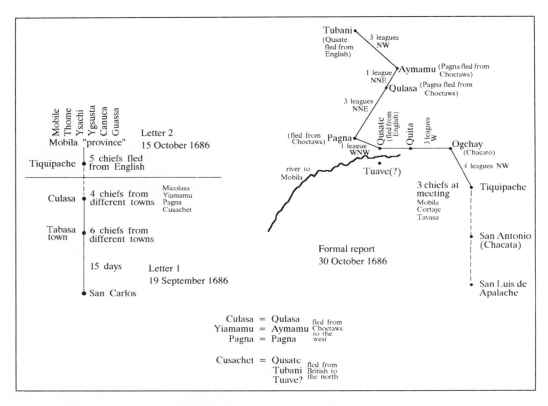

5.3. Reconstruction of Delgado's journey among the Creeks and Alabamas.

that the third meeting, which he says included both chiefs and principal men and the Mobile representatives, was the one that made the real contribution and thus the only one worth mentioning. Perhaps, indeed, the first two meetings were simply designed to secure invitations for village visits.

What is important here is that these reports provide some very specific information on population movements: the "Pagna" (Pacana?) people, including Miculasa/ Culasa and Aymamu/Yaimamu, had been driven eastward by the Choctaws, while the "Qusate"/Cusachet (Koasati?), including Qusate, Tubani, and Tuave, had been driven south by the English and their allies, perhaps including the Cherokees. The second Delgado letter implies that the region he visited contained only refugees (Boyd 1937:21), and the scenario would seem to account for the presence of some of the Upper Creek peoples (Smith 1987:137–39) and the Alabamas around the Coosa-Tallapoosa-Alabama confluence at the end of the seventeenth century. Although nominally at war with these refugee peoples on the Coosa and Tallapoosa Rivers, the Mobilians seemed also to serve them as a partial buffer from the Choctaws. If the Mobilians planned to become intermediaries for Spanish contacts to the west, that would explain why they killed the Chickasaw emissaries Matheos considered so potentially useful. Furthermore, throughout Delgado's accounts it is evident that none of the Indians he met were subordinated to a paramount chief: to speak with a tribe, he had to speak with all its chiefs.

The reports of the peoples of the Coosa/Tallapoosa region show that English trade had already begun to reach them where English aggression could not. Spanish trade and Spanish people had also reached them; the chiefs told Delgado that for twelve or thirteen years they had been aware of the activities of the Spanish at Apalachee, and that some forty-six Spaniards were living among them and married to Indian women (Boyd 1937:28). These Spaniards had likely been intermediaries for trade with the coast, and the Indians, who were offering to send them back to Apalachee, were now ready to trade directly. This picture of the region is not complete – nothing is said of the peoples on the Coosa that had been reported to Calderón, nor is there any detail to the west – but it does show how unsettled the population distribution was at the time. Perhaps most important, it clearly states that the coalescing Choctaw confederacy was involved in the aggressive boundary maintenance that was suggested earlier.

The English Push to the Mississippi, 1698–1700

The Spanish were not the only ones spurred by La Salle's expedition to consider more thoroughgoing exploitation of the hinterland. The third player in the European borderland triangle, England, had already established herself in the Indian trade but had barely passed the Appalachians at the time of La Salle's journey. News of the Frenchman's claims and of his second expedition led to a sudden support from the home country for the English traders' activities.

This is not to say that there had not been earlier efforts to penetrate the interior, apart from the southern efforts of the Carolina traders that sought profit from the Indian trade. Further to the north, Virginians had attempted to locate mines in the mountains and beyond and in the process had crossed the Appalachians. The journey of Batts and Fallam in 1671 led them across the divide to the headwaters of the Ohio tributaries, where they discovered that they were not the first Europeans in the region, since they found recognizable initials carved on the trees: the *coureurs de bois* had preceded them (Alvord and Bidgood 1912).

Probably the most famous, certainly the most significant, but paradoxically the least documented of the British efforts at the end of the seventeenth century was that of one Thomas Welch, who led a party from South Carolina to the Quapaw villages on the Mississippi River in 1698, establishing the Upper Trading Path as a trade route and himself as premier Chickasaw trader at the same time. Yet apart from the clear delineation of this path and its attribution to Welch on both British and French maps of the eighteenth century, there is very little other evidence of his journey. Other circumstantial evidence, including the testimony of the French regarding the situation as they found it when they made permanent settlement in 1699, suggests that the British effort among the western tribes had begun in the early 1690s and that Carolina traders were well established among the Upper Creeks by that time (Crane 1956:45). The immediate outcome of Welch's exploit seems to have been the establishment of a permanent trade house among the Chickasaws and a relatively unsuccessful attempt to establish a trade with the Quapaws for slaves from the trans-Mississippi. Establishing a slave trade with the Chickasaws was a much easier task, probably begun as soon as a secure footing was established among the Upper Creeks, building upon Woodward's early contacts.

Meanwhile, a very different route was being explored for what may have been very different reasons: the route from the Appalachians to the Mississippi via the Tennessee and the Ohio. Verner Crane's famous article (1916) on the Tennessee River as a route from Carolina to the Mississippi first explored the evidence that lay behind indications on the Delisles' maps that Frenchmen had indeed established this route. Discussion of this aspect of British penetration has dwelt upon the activities of Jean Couture, Tonti's "commandant" at the Arkansas trade house established in 1686, who apparently defected to the British of Virginia and Carolina at some time in the 1690s and who in 1700 conducted a party of British traders to the Mississippi via the Tennessee and the Ohio. Crane masterfully assembled the evidence, leaving the identity of the expedition's leader inarguable, but although none of the sources shows more than an incomplete external view of what happened (Galloway 1991b), this expedition can cast additional light upon the native context of the hinterland occupied by the Choctaws and their neighbors.

What the Couture affair shows is first that slave-raiding on the part of the Chickasaws had been occurring for some time by 1700, and that it had certainly been directed to the west, against the Quapaws – as the evidence of French missionaries arriving among them in 1698 also attests. A second observation is that around 1700 the Chakchiumas were seen as close allies of the Chickasaws, since the Quapaws, once provided with guns vital to defending themselves against their eastern tormentors, were prepared to make a slave raid upon them in revenge against the Chickasaws. Finally, it shows that European-Indian alliances at the time were far from fixed, since the Englishmen led by Couture were not disturbed by the notion of encouraging Quapaw attacks on the Chakchiumas or indeed on the Chickasaws, even though by that time the Chickasaws were trading partners with the British through Welch and Dodsworth. Again, however, much was said about the western borders of the Choctaw lands but not a word about the Choctaws.

As far as the story of the Choctaws is concerned, and indeed that of British penetration of the interior, Couture's exploit bore little sequel. The Tennessee–Ohio–Mississippi route did not become important to trade with the western Indians; instead, the British traders followed Welch's Upper Path. The importance of Couture's route was not as a usable route but as a threat: this drive to the heart of the Mississippi Valley showed the French quickly enough that they would have to occupy the whole river valley or ally themselves with those who did to meet this threat. To the extent that French presence in the area had different effects on native societies than a British presence would have had, the Couture journey may have altered the fates of these nations.

That Couture stayed among the British or at least in the area of their hegemony seems certain; a few years later several other Frenchmen, led by Soton and Bellefeuille, tried to make the eastward journey to trade their contraband furs, only to find Couture living under a kind of house arrest among the Shawnees of Carolina and their own business unwelcome (Galloway 1991b:81). Although this discovery brought the Frenchmen no comfort, their arrival in the tentative Louisiana colony with a report of their adventures underlined this possible danger and further strengthened French resolve to establish that colony securely.

THE BEGINNING OF THE FRENCH ALLIANCE, 1699–1702

In 1699 the French finally made good on La Salle's sacrifice and sent Pierre Le Moyne d'Iberville to the Gulf of Mexico to investigate the Mississippi as the potential hinge of a new colonial venture and as the obstacle that would hold the British in check (Giraud 1974:11). With this expedition, the picture of the aboriginal landscape of the Old Southwest began to come into sharper focus. At last Europeans met the Choctaws face to face and wrote about it. Because this delayed "first contact" was the true debut of the Choctaws on the stage of European maneuverings, the 1699–1702 period during which the French made contact and then became allied with them is treated in this chapter as the culmination of Choctaw emergence as a confederation.

This colonizing effort was very important to the French, and the sources providing knowledge of it are accordingly rich. They fall into the rough categories of journals and letters. The journals may be official in some sense, as are Iberville's ships' logs or Ensign Sauvole's journal of his months at Fort Maurepas, or unofficial, as are the journals of Father Paul du Ru or the carpenter Penicaut. Likewise, the letters sent by missionaries to their superiors in Canada and France are formal and those sent by Henri de Tonti to his friends in Canada informal. As this incomplete list of citations suggests, however, many such sources exist, so we may expect and require corroboration for the evidence they contain.

A third and more tangential category of sources, memoirs, contains the long essays and other expository communications that outline the plans and expectations of the various government officials and of the new colonizers themselves. From the outset, Iberville planned for Indian alliances, as had La Salle; Louisiana, like Canada, enjoyed from an early date the services of young Frenchmen sent into villages to learn Indian languages (Galloway 1987). It was evident from the start that France would not soon provide huge numbers of settlers – she never had the teeming excess population of Britain – and that Indians would provide a vital buffer between the infant French colony and the British to the east. Iberville did entertain grandiose plans of Indian relocation and population concentration, but it soon became obvious that such policies would work no better in Louisiana than they had in Canada. The Indians would be dealt with on their own terms rather than on those of the French (see Usner 1992:13–104).

Iberville and Colonization

The initial motives that sent the French to the Gulf coast, arising from conditions in France, largely dictated the mode of French and Indian interaction. The Crown's main aim was to thwart British efforts to take control of the Mississippi River. British aims, embodied in 1698 by the plans of Daniel Coxe to settle refugee French Huguenots on the Mississippi, were seen as a threat to France's ambitions in the valley, which had not been relinquished but were put on hold after La Salle's failure. In addition, French intellectuals, merchants, and members of religious orders were eager to exploit these lands to the south of New France (Giraud 1974:14–22; Usner 1992:15–16). Iberville was to investigate the feasibility of settlement and to return with recommendations on where and how to found a settlement, leaving a few men behind to defend the Mississippi from the British. If the minister Pontchartrain judged the effort worthwhile, a colony would be established.

The most important roles of the Indians in the French colonial plan would be political and economic. The British had already begun to prove that southeastern natives could help the colonial economy as producers: they were enlisted as hunters for the Carolina skin trade. The other face of that role was one of consumption; in producing raw materials and trading for European goods they would behave as the mercantilists felt they should. Indians could also protect the nascent colony against the growing population of Carolina. Finally, for the French Catholic church the Indians of the Mississippi represented a desirable extension of their missionary field in America.

The first French expedition of 1699 is described in the logbooks of Iberville's ships (Iberville 1981). Unfortunately for the Indians he met, these logs record that "plague" and an unspecified fever were active among the crews of his ships. He sought to land first at Pensacola, only to learn that the Spanish had fortified it just months before. So Iberville coasted westward, to explore the mouth of Mobile Bay and judge that it was not the Mississippi. At the entrance of the bay he christened the island later to become Dauphin as "Isle Massacre" because he found the incompletely decomposed bodies of some sixty adults who, according to Penicaut, were Mobilians who had died of disease; their bodies had been gathered together, he said, because "the manner of savages is to gather together all the bones of the dead" (Penicaut [1723] 1953:11). Around the entrance to the bay Iberville found no more than the evidence of vacated Indian houses; he met no people and saw no extensive settlement. Further west he found the best harbor on one of the Mississippi Sound's barrier islands, Ship Island. Leaving his ships moored there, he took to smaller coasting vessels to meet the inhabitants. First contacts, naturally, were with the tribes of the coast and of the lower Mississippi River; only gradually did the French come to know of the imposing presence of the Choctaws inland.

Clearly Iberville knew something of the conventions of Indian communication, since he scratched pictographs of himself with a calumet and three ships onto trees to explain himself to any natives who might have fled at his approach, and left behind trade goods such as edged tools and beads whenever he left an area where he had seen signs of Indian occupation or presence (Iberville 1981:39,43). Each time he managed to encounter a native, he attempted to communicate his pacific intentions through kindness and presents, even aiding a sick old man who had been unable to flee. This action was apparently his entrée; the next day members of the Biloxi and Moctobi tribes – Penicaut ([1723] 1953:5) adds Pascagoulas, Capinans, Chickasaws, and Pensacolas – came to perform the calumet ceremony and to offer a feast, which Iberville returned. Nevertheless, Iberville felt that these Indians were still suspicious of Europeans and remained prepared for flight, even though a smaller party accepted an invitation to go aboard the French ships.

The following day, having heard cannon shots Iberville had fired from his ships for the Indians' amazement, a hunting party of Bayougoulas and Mugulashas joined the Frenchmen to discover whether they were the same as the people who had come among them from the upper Mississippi or *Malbanchya*. These Indians behaved quite familiarly with Iberville and his party, subjecting them to greeting ceremonies that Iberville, at least, found rather uncomfortable, but that he was given to understand had secured him the alliances of several nations, with names he gave as Mougoulaschas, Ouaschas, Toutymaschas, and Yagueneschytos west of the Mississippi and the Bylocchys, Moctobys, Oumas, Pascoboulas, Thecloels, Bayacchytos, and Amylcous east of the Mississippi (Iberville 1981:48–49). All these names were clearly expressed in a Choctaw-like language, presumably that of the Bayougoulas.

Iberville made an appointment to meet with this hunting party in a few days' time to explore the route to the Mississippi's mouth, but when the Indians departed leaving only an inscrutable smoke signal to indicate that they had run out of food and were returning home, the French party prepared to advance up the river on its own, as Iberville was anxious to find the tribes mentioned by La Salle and Tonti and thus to verify that he had located the Mississippi from the sea. The party met an Annochy guide on the way, who explained to Iberville that his people had recently been attacked by the Chickasaws and Napyssas. The explorers proceeded up the river, meeting several parties of Indians along the way.

They arrived at the Bayougoula/Mongoulacha landing on 14 March, met at some distance away and escorted in by a Mongoulacha with a calumet. Two chiefs, one Bayougoula and one Mongoulacha, carried out the greeting ceremonies and offered a feast. Iberville, preoccupied with the mysterious Quinipissas whom the La Salle narratives had prepared him to find on the Mississippi, was told that the Quinipissas had had seven villages, one of them the Tangibao that La Salle had seen in ruins and the remainder at some distance overland; the Tangibaos, they said, had been forcibly annexed by the Oumas.

During the visit to the Bayougoula/Mongoulacha village Iberville observed the village temple ornamented with carvings of animals and judged that they worshiped the opossum. He was told that smallpox, still rife, had killed a quarter of the population. Because of its recency he was also able to observe the many scaffolds near the village on which bodies covered with matting were rotting.

Guided by the Bayougoula chief, Iberville proceeded toward the Oumas, passing the famous *baton rouge* marking the boundary between the two. At the Ouma landing they were met by an Ouma and a Quinipissa, and when they reached the village the Indians treated them to a dance entertainment and invited them to stay overnight. The Quinipissas in the village told Iberville their village was seven days away, and he resolved to go on upriver. At the landing he was able to take on as a guide a Taensa Indian.

This Taensa was a mine of information, making a map for Iberville and marking the locations of tribes and villages. He first named the Caddo groups to the west on the Red River, then the villages of the Theloel or Natchez: Pochougoula, Ousagoucoula, Cougoucoula, Yatanocha, Ymacacha, Thoucou, Tougoula, Achoucougoula (note that most of these village names contain the Choctaw *ougoula*, "people"). Further on the guide named the Taensa villages as Taensa, Ohytoucoula, Nyhougoula, Couthaougoula, Couchayon, Talaspa, and Chaoucoula. He said the Yachou and Coloa would be found settled together on the west bank of the Mississippi, while the Tonyca, Vyspe, Opocoula, Taposa, Chaquesauma, Outapa, and Thysia would be found on the "river of the Chickasaws" (the Yazoo). He claimed that the Chickasaws and Napyssas were settled near one another and united, and that "south of the Chycacha all the nations are at peace with one another" (Iberville 1981:74).

Disgusted with the apparent inaccuracy of the accounts he had read, Iberville decided to turn back southward and take leave of the Oumas. At this point he observed that a long list of tribes (some of which he had not met, so this information must have come from the Taensa guide) spoke the same language – or were capable of making themselves understood to one another: Ouma, Bayougoula, Theloel, Taensa, Coloa, Chycacha, Napyssa, Ouacha, Choutymacha, Yagenechyto, Bylocchy, Pascoboula. He observed also that some of the older Ouma men exhibited cranial deformation. Returning to the Gulf coast by way of the Manchac portage and through Lake Pontchartrain, he sent his brother, Jean-Baptiste Le Moyne de Bienville, via the Mississippi; Bienville finally recovered the letter left by Tonti for La Salle that confirmed the equivalence of Quinipissa and Mongoulacha and that they had found the Mississippi. With this major issue settled, Iberville had his men build a fort on Biloxi Bay and left a garrison stationed there, leaving for France on 4 May 1699.

Other efforts during the early days of the French presence also bore fruit in establishing peaceful Indian relations. While Iberville had been arranging to sail for the Mississippi, the Seminary of Foreign Missions had been preparing to take up the mission to the Indians of the Mississippi that it had been granted in 1698. A party of Recollect missionaries, de Montigny, Davion, La Source, and Saint-Cosme, descended the Mississippi accompanied by Henri de Tonti from the Illinois country in the winter of 1699, dropping off missionaries among likely-looking tribes as they traveled south (Shea 1861). When they stopped at Tonti's Arkansas post for a guide to escort them the rest of the way, they heard rumor of Iberville's arrival on the coast and hastened down to meet them before returning upriver to establish their missions. Their guide Delaunay, being one of Tonti's men, was able to inform Sauvole that the Quinipissas, nearly wiped out by disease, had ascended the Mississippi and been taken in as Mougoulachas by the Bayougoulas (Sauvole [1699–1701] 1969: 31,37).

From the few letters the missionaries wrote and their additional communications with the coast as reported by others, we can gather a great deal of information, particularly with reference to the inroads of European disease. Saint-Cosme observed that the Quapaws were "entirely destroyed by war and sickness. It is not a month since they got over the small pox which carried off the greatest part of them. There was nothing to be seen in the village but graves" (Shea 1861:72). Father La Source described a similar scene at the Tunicas: "sickness was among them . . . they were dying in great numbers" (Shea 1861:81). These reports are not surprising: the French themselves were carrying disease. In 1700 Father Gravier, on his way down the Mississippi to the coast, observed that the voyageurs escorting him were all afflicted with tertian fevers (malaria?); that he found Father Davion at the Tunicas sick with fever; and that the Bayougoulas near the coast, by then host to a French chapel, were decimated (Shea 1861:133).

The missionaries also observed the tribes of the Mississippi from their own unique perspective, showing special interest in the "temples" among the Tunicas (La Source), Taensas (de Montigny, Gravier), and Natchez (Gravier) and making particular observations on funerary practices, especially retainer sacrifice at the death of a chief among the Taensas and Natchez (de Montigny, La Source, Gravier). The Tunicas, Taensas, and Natchez were all still using mounds for ceremonial activities, had special public buildings connected with worship (and used as charnel houses for elites), and had at least two levels of ranking and possibly more, with elites accorded a significant degree of control over commoners' lives: thus these Mississippi River groups had managed to retain the trappings of simple chiefdoms at least.

Ensign Sauvole was Iberville's choice as leader of the small garrison of men he left behind at Biloxi Bay. He was charged to continue establishing contacts with the Indians and to explore the coast and hinterland; to fulfill those duties he gave presents to the Indians with whom friendship had been established and dispatched exploration parties. News of the presents must have traveled fast, for visits by Indians became more and more frequent. A visit to the small fort by the Bayougoula chief Antobiscania gave Sauvole the occasion to send two cabin boys with him to learn the Bayougoula and Ouma languages; this chief soon returned with a young man who was to learn French. Meanwhile, Bienville's reconnaissance up the Pearl River to the Acolapissas confirmed that they were not the same people as La Salle's Quinipissas. Sauvole also sent a party to examine the Pascagoula River. They discovered and visited villages of Pascagoulas, Biloxis, and Moctobis sixteen or twenty leagues up the river. The Pascagoulas soon returned the visit, bringing deerskins to the Biloxi fort as presents, and this visit was not their last; Sauvole ([1699–1701] 1969:21–33) was able to detect an existing trade with the Spanish when he noticed that the Pascagoula chief Chenoua possessed a Spanish musket.

Sauvole had specific news of the Choctaws from a Pascagoula who said he lived among them. This man said they had forty-five villages and had become embroiled with Englishmen who were established among the Chickasaws and were encouraging them to take slaves from their neighbors (Sauvole 1969:35–36). The English threat also made itself felt on the Mississippi, where Bienville, traveling downriver from the Manchac portage, encountered an English ship on the lower Mississippi and forced it to turn back.

Sauvole sent out another party led by Bienville to explore the coast west of Biloxi Bay, a route that took it along the Gulf coast to Lake Pontchartrain and then counterclockwise around the shore of the lake, exploring to the Mississippi via Bayou Saint Jean and then returning to complete the circuit. Penicaut's extended description of this trip ([1723] 1953:11–17), with its Indian place names and topographical feature names translated into French, indicates that the language their Pascagoula guide spoke must have been Choctaw or very like it.

The second voyage of Iberville in 1700 marked the widening of the colonization effort. Once again there was fever among his crew, from which he himself suffered and which afflicted many of the Frenchmen during the months Iberville was on the Gulf coast. Sauvole ([1699–1701] 1969:42n) referred to it as the "French disease," which some have interpreted as yellow fever. Iberville himself explored ever further inland, traveling up the Mississippi as far as the Natchez-related Taensas and visiting the Mobile River, while he sent Bienville westward on the Red River.

Iberville was determined to establish a fort to guard the Mississippi, to explore the Mississippi further, and to stabilize the Indians. News had come to him from Davion among the Tunicas that an English slave-catcher from the Chickasaws had visited Davion (Iberville 1981:110). Iberville commissioned Tonti, who had come down from the Illinois country to escort some potential settlers, to go with him as far as the Taensas and then to stop at the Tunicas on his way upriver and try to arrest the Englishman who was fomenting Chickasaw slave raids. Tonti was also instructed to attempt to persuade the Chickasaws to make peace and leave off slave raids on the Natchez, Acolapissas, and Choctaws, with the threat that otherwise the French would arm the Choctaws.

Iberville himself traveled up the river to put a stop to the Ouma-Bayougoula squabble, finding half the Oumas dead of a diarrheal affliction that had raged there for five months (Iberville 1981:122). The same disease had laid low the Natchez chief upriver. Iberville observed that the chief's house was atop an artificial mound and that the Natchez language was after all different from that of the Oumas. Continuing to the Taensas, Iberville found de Montigny ready to build a church. The fine native temple was struck by lightning and burned while Iberville was there. Five infants were thrown into the flames, perhaps to compensate for de Montigny's having prevented retainer sacrifice when the Taensa chief had died not long before. The destruction of the temple permitted the French party to observe the lengthy ceremonies involved in the consecration of a new one (Iberville 1981:125–31).

After seeing Bienville off to the west overland to the upper reaches of the Red River, Iberville headed downriver with de Montigny, who was to establish a mission with the Natchez. They found the Natchez chief moribund and in no condition to discuss his enmity with the Chickasaws, but de Montigny was well received, and when Iberville reached the new fort on the Mississippi he sent the Natchez a cabin boy to learn their language. Back at the coast, Iberville pursued further exploration. On the Pascagoula River he observed a deserted palisaded Biloxi village, whose state was attributed to disease two years before, and overgrown old fields on both sides of the river. Further upstream he met the Pascagoulas, likewise decimated (Iberville 1981:132–40).

During Iberville's absence Sauvole had received Mobilian and Pascagoula chiefs and two Choctaws and had taken them aboard one of the ships, after which they said they would go to inform the Choctaws about the presence of the French (Sauvole [1699–1701] 1969:40). Meanwhile Iberville was receiving information about the Choctaws: they had some fifty villages and more than six thousand warriors. The Mobilians and Tohomés on the Mobile River, in contrast, had only three hundred warriors apiece. Iberville promptly sent two men with the Pascagoula chief and the chief's brother to invite the three nations to visit him on the coast, whither he returned himself. This group apparently went no further than the Tohomés, where they met two Choctaws and brought them back. Iberville invited the Choctaws aboard his ship, learned that their nation was at war with all the nations to their north and east, and sent presents to the Choctaw chief (Iberville 1981:141–43).

Some days before this, Sauvole reported that Tohomé and Mobilian chiefs had come to ask the French for protection against Conchas and Piniscas while they were carrying out spring planting. Sauvole, with an eye to a long-term grain supply for his garrison, had sent a few men. He also hoped to offset the influence of the Spanish of Pensacola, who had given these delta villages some hogs (Sauvole [1699–1701] 1969: 45–46).

Bienville arrived to report his westward mission partly rained out (his struggles through swamps are reminiscent of the toils of Soto's men and of Tonti's 1690 expedition west of the Mississippi). On his way back he had found that the Bayougoulas had massacred the Mougoulachas and replaced them with Colapissas and Tious (Iberville 1981:143,146–56). De Montigny and Davion appeared with Natchez and Tunica chiefs to report news of the English excursion to the Mississippi led by Jean Couture. They also apparently delivered a letter from Tonti reporting the disappointing outcome of his planned meeting with the Chickasaw: the chief had been leading a raid against the Choctaws and could not meet with Tonti. Tonti had instead sent him a present and offer of alliance with conditions through his nephew (Iberville 1981:144–45). Iberville left for France again on 28 May.

Perhaps the most active member of Iberville's second expedition in terms of Indian diplomacy was its chaplain, the Jesuit du Ru. Father du Ru kept a remarkable journal of his participation in the expedition that is rich in detail about the Indians among whom he hoped to work (du Ru 1934). Accompanying Iberville's party up the Mississippi, du Ru made the acquaintance of an old Bayougoula man who was to be their guide, and immediately began recording words of that language, such as *ouga* to mean "chief." He noted that – like Choctaw – the language lacked *r* and *d* sounds and that it was spoken by eight or ten tribes (du Ru 1934:5–9). When, after completing the construction of the fort on the lower Mississippi, the party arrived at the Bayougoula village, du Ru recorded that it was more than six hundred years old and had two temples, one Bayougoula and one Mougoulacha, each decorated with bird carvings on the roofs; one had a portico decorated with carvings, and both contained bundles of dead chiefs' bones wrapped in mats. Du Ru also observed that the Bayougoulas' pottery was very thin and fine and contained pulverized shell, and he also witnessed games and dancing (du Ru 1934:19–20).

When the party reached the Ouma village, the many deaths gave du Ru occasion for remarks about mortuary practices. He observed the rotting body of the chief – in the chief's cabin – and said that the bones would be placed in the temple, accompanied by the chief's possessions, when the decomposition was complete, and his cabin would be burned. Du Ru was apparently told about retainer sacrifice among such other tribes as the Colapissas, Natchez, and Taensas, and he observed with disgust the ritual purification of the mourners (du Ru 1934:26–29).

At the Natchez village du Ru had much to say about the manners of the people and especially their deeply respectful treatment of their chief or *ouachilla*. He observed the arrangement of the chief's cabin and the temple, where the bone bundles were accommodated in special niches, and he tried to persuade the chief's first wife to leave off retainer sacrifice if the chief should die. He also remarked that the Natchez language differed from the Bayougoula (du Ru 1934:35–39).

Du Ru followed Iberville by three days in leaving Natchez, having stayed behind to secure provisions. Some of the first news he received on landing at the Taensa village was of the burning of the Taensa temple and the sacrifice of infants, who, according to de Montigny, had at least been baptized. At the village du Ru observed the consecration rites for the new temple and tried to persuade de Montigny to go to work with the Natchez, whose greater numbers and apparent receptivity would bring greater rewards. On his return downstream du Ru left his servant to build a chapel at the Oumas (later to be used by another priest, Father Limoges), and at the Bayougoulas' homeland he settled in to build another on a plot of land purchased from a native named Longamougoulache. The chief organized the people to build a large wattle-and-daub house for the god du Ru had described to them as the "Great *Nanhoulou*" (cf. Choctaw *na hollo*, "supernatural being"). A Chitimacha chief came to visit and was entertained by the Mougoulacha chief while the Bayougoula chief directed the final plastering. Du Ru left after erecting a cross and planting a garden (du Ru 1934:41–50).

Once on the coast, du Ru planned to go with Sauvole to establish another chapel among the Colapissas up the Pearl River. Having stopped in a small village on a tributary east of the Pearl, the party then traveled by canoe to the main village of fifteen to twenty houses, surrounded by a palisade constructed in defense against Chickasaw attacks. The Chickasaws, under the leadership of two Englishmen, had destroyed two villages and carried off fifty people. Du Ru replaced the phallic symbol in the middle of the village plaza with a cross, and the party then returned after many vicissitudes to see Iberville off to France (du Ru 1934:65–67). Although du Ru remained as chaplain to the garrison at Biloxi until his recall in 1702, he apparently produced no other such account.

Soon after Iberville's departure, in May of 1700, Charles Levasseur and four Canadians proceeded to explore the Mobile bay and delta under orders from Sauvole. The party traveled up the bay and entered the Mobile River. In his description of where the Alabama River branched off, Levasseur gave a list of thirty-six tribes living further along it, information derived from a Maugoulacho Indian living among the Mobilians; this native also said that all these groups traded regularly with the English and raided their neighbors the Mauvillas and Pensacolas for slaves to trade.

Knight (in Levasseur 1981) has analyzed the town list given by Levasseur in some detail and concludes that it was not intended to incorporate any geographical order but did indicate towns located on the Alabama-Coosa-Tallapoosa system. Of particular interest here is the Alabama group (Alebamons, Maugoulacho, Touachee, Tomapa, and Conchaque) and a single town, Napache, which may conceivably be identified with Dávila Padilla's elusive Napochies.

The first villages Levasseur visited were those of the Mauvilla, further up the Mobile. He mentioned five villages and many fields over some five leagues on both sides of the river, and he named Igame mico, Totechoco, and Mauvilla. He named one chief, Mananboullay, and said chiefs were referred to as *ougas*, having assistants called *oulactas*. The party also visited the Thomées, said to be darker-skinned than the Mauvilla people and to have command of a salt spring from which they traded salt widely, including to the Choctaws via a seven days' journey (which Levasseur declined to make because the weather was so dry). On his return downriver Levasseur visited a village of Pensacolas (Villiers du Terrage 1922).

Iberville's third and last voyage was the one that really established the colony and, by locating its chief outpost on the Mobile River, set its orientation directly toward alliance with the large inland tribes. Iberville arrived at Pensacola on 15 December 1701, taking advantage of the new cordiality between France and Spain to recuperate from a wound in his side. The reports he had made in France and the arguments he had offered contended that the greatest threat to a new colony, once the mouth of the Mississippi was secured, lay to the east; accordingly, the Crown's decision was that the main settlement would be made on Mobile Bay. After the death of Sauvole in August of 1700 Bienville had become acting commander, and now he was ordered to remove all supplies from Biloxi to Massacre Island for the construction of the settlement at the head of the bay.

With the fort construction started, Iberville sent Tonti, who had stayed in the new garrison since the spring of 1700, to the Choctaws and Chickasaws to invite them to a meeting on the coast (Galloway 1982b). He sent Bienville into the Mobile-Tensaw delta to investigate Indian settlements, abandoned due to war with the Alibamons and Conchaques, for their appropriateness for French settlement. Bienville saw these and also visited a sacred mound site where he found and fetched back five ceramic images: man, woman, child, bear, and owl. Iberville investigated the delta on Bienville's return, observing abandoned villages on both sides of the Mobile River as far up as the settlements of the Mobilians and Tohomés, who had a population of 350 warriors speaking the same language as the Bayougoulas. He noted that tidewater extended as high as the Tohomé villages and that the frequency of abandoned settlements suggested that the valley had been thickly populated (Iberville 1981:168–70).

It was Henri de Tonti, however, who became, to our knowledge, the first Frenchman to go among the Choctaw villages. Having returned to the coast to serve Iberville as diplomat to the Indians, Tonti traveled through the Choctaw nation, across a no-man's-land partly populated by Chakchiumas, and to the settlements of the Chickasaws, returning back through Choctaw country to Mobile escorting a party of Chickasaws and Choctaws to meet with Iberville. Because his is the first fully documented meeting with the Choctaws on their home ground, I will examine it at some length.

The first consideration is their actual location; the maps in figure 5.4 show my reconstruction of Tonti's route, Delisle's portrayal of it on his 1718 map of North America, and a recent reconstruction of the Choctaw trail system by Carleton (1989). The interesting things Tonti can tell about the locations of the Choctaws, Chakchiumas, and Chickasaws are that the Choctaws were where their "homeland" is now said to be, the Chakchiumas were living near the southern edge of Chickasaw country but had previously lived near the northern edge of Choctaw country, and the Chickasaws were located slightly farther south than they would be later in the eighteenth century.

Tonti did not just meet with the Choctaws in their villages; a Choctaw "chief" accompanied him – along with two Mobilians and two Tohomés – throughout the journey to provide safe conduct both for him and for the Chickasaw embassy for the return trip through Choctaw country to Mobile. During the northward journey Tonti spent the night in "the first settlements of the Chacta," in "the cabin of the chief of the free settlements" four leagues further north, and in "the house of the chief of the last settlements nearest to the Chicacha" another five leagues on (Galloway 1982b:167). The implication of this information, even taking into account that they visited Choctaw hunting cabins eight leagues south of the first villages and that a fortified border town lay ten leagues east-northeast of the final one visited, is that enemy raids were forcing the Choctaw towns to cluster in a relatively small area. It also suggests that Tonti's party only visited a central region, where the headwaters of the Pearl, Chickasawhay, and Sucarnoochee came together, while also implying that what they visited was the entire Choctaw country in 1702.

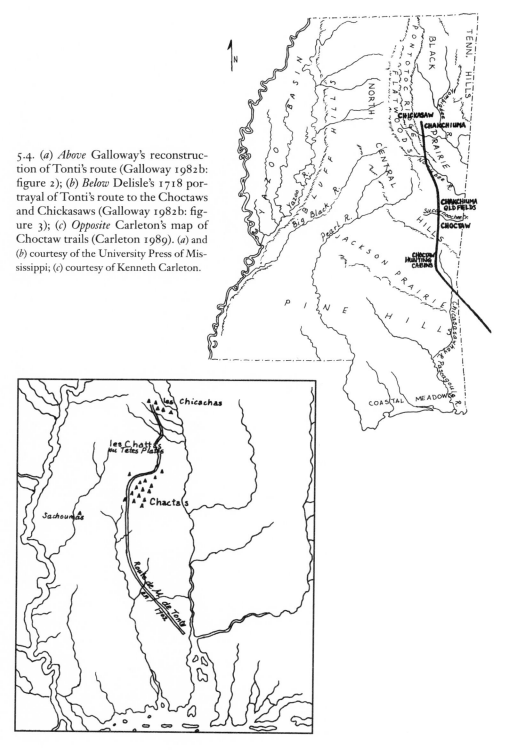

5.4. (*a*) *Above* Galloway's reconstruction of Tonti's route (Galloway 1982b: figure 2); (*b*) *Below* Delisle's 1718 portrayal of Tonti's route to the Choctaws and Chickasaws (Galloway 1982b: figure 3); (*c*) *Opposite* Carleton's map of Choctaw trails (Carleton 1989). (*a*) and (*b*) courtesy of the University Press of Mississippi; (*c*) courtesy of Kenneth Carleton.

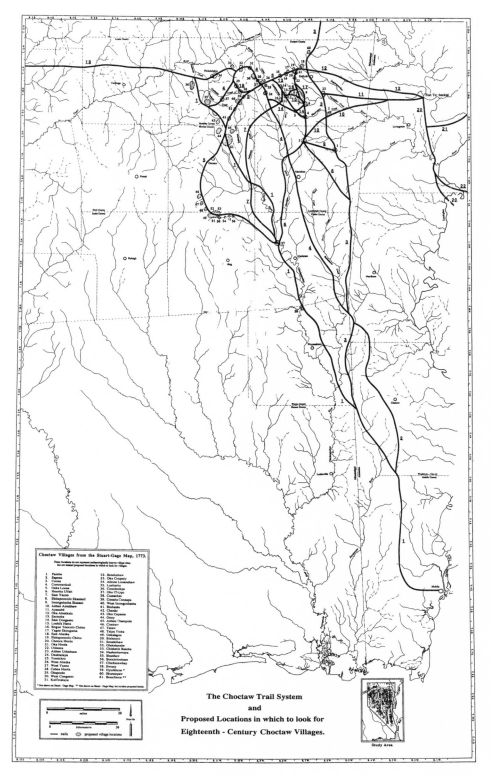

Choctaw Villages from the Stuart-Gage Map, 1773.

These locations do not represent archaeologically known village sites,
but are instead proposed locations in which to look for villages.

1. Panihe
2. Sapesa
3. Coosa
4. Commonkali
5. Oska Loosa
6. Haunka Ullah
7. East Yazoo
8. Ebitapoocolo Skatani
9. Imongoincha Skatani
10. Aithee Aimithaw
11. Ayanabé
12. Oka Altakkala
13. Escooba
14. East Congesto
15. Lookfa Hatta
16. Bogue Toocolo Chito
17. Yagne Skongama
18. East Abeika
19. Ebitapoocolo Chito
20. Choocs Hoola
21. Oka Hoola
22. Ubitassa
23. Aithee Uckahuca
24. Oeaktalaya
25. Tomickto
26. West Abeika
27. West Yazoo
28. Cahea Hoola
29. Okapoolo
30. West Congesto
31. Kolfitialaya
32. Senekahaw
33. Oka Coopoly
34. Allicon Loonashaw
35. Lushatta
36. Conchatikpe
37. Oka Chippo
38. Custachas
39. Concha Consapa
40. West Incongoolasha
41. Bishaska
42. Chanks
43. Oka Capassa
44. Omey
45. Aithee Champole
46. Coatraw
47. Talaw
48. Talpa Tioka
49. Oskalagna
50. Bishcoco
51. Senekithaw
52. Olukahaube
53. Chiskitik Baleka
54. Mashochawanya
55. Shanhaw
56. Boocziolookaoe
57. Chickasawhay
58. Bwany
59. Hyuikkone *
60. Skutampaw
61. Boochoca **

* Not shown on Stuart -Gage Map. ** Not shown on Stuart -Gage Map, but location proposed herein.

The Choctaw Trail System
and
Proposed Locations in which to look for
Eighteenth - Century Choctaw Villages.

—— trails   ⬡ proposed village locations

Study Area

0   miles   30
North

0   kilometers   30

195

Tonti, having failed in his mission to apprehend the British slaver among the Chickasaws who was behind the raids, had particular interest in witnessing their results. On his way through the Choctaw villages he was told that the outpost border town was unable to cultivate crops because of the attacks of Chickasaws, Conchaques, and Alabamas. Only the adroitness of Tonti's guides enabled the party to avoid two bands of Chickasaw slave raiders, one of ten men and one of four hundred, led by an Englishman. Soon, entering the first Chickasaw village, Tonti came face to face with the man's partner, dressed like a Chickasaw and trying to speak to him in Shawnee. The man's presence angered Tonti, particularly when he saw the Chickasaw chiefs hand over to him a large share of the French presents they received, and he was glad to be able to rescue a young Choctaw from his slave cords as earnest of Chickasaw goodwill. After some persuasion Tonti convinced five important Chickasaw men, three women, and two others (Iberville [1981:171] characterized this group as "three chiefs and four distinguished men"; he ignored the women) to accompany him back to Mobile. These had second thoughts when word came on their way south to the Choctaw villages that the Chickasaw raiding party had been successful and had killed three Choctaw men, but Tonti reassured them and sent the Choctaw chief ahead to prepare their reception, which was a good one. Tonti left the Choctaw nation with three Choctaw chiefs in his train, probably including the two chiefs in whose houses he had stayed, but this is not made explicit. Iberville (1981:171) mentions four Choctaw chiefs, so the group must have included the chief who had been part of the expedition as well. As always, of course, we should remember that these men might not have really been chiefs, in French or Choctaw terms.

The meeting at the new fort is reported in Iberville's log. He describes the presents allotted to each tribe: two hundred *livres* each of powder, bullets, and shot; 12 guns, 100 axes, and 150 knives; and kettles, beads, gunflints, awls, and other utensils. Each individual delegate was given in addition a gun, a cloak, a shirt, and other items. In Iberville's speech to the two groups he recited several facts that he must have learned from Tonti or other sources. He reminded the Chickasaws that the English had happily purchased Chickasaw slaves to ship to their Caribbean islands from others of their allies, and that although the English had given them 30 guns to take slaves from the Choctaws, the eighteen hundred Choctaws killed and five hundred Choctaws sold into slavery had cost them eight hundred of their own men. He told them that if they did not desist the French would arm Choctaws, Mobilians, Tohomés, Natchez, and Illinois to attack them; if they agreed to peace he would place a trading post in the no-man's-land between Choctaws and Chickasaws, where the French would purchase the slaves they preferred: the skins of animals.

The visiting Indians and the French apparently reached an agreement after working out the terms of trade. The Choctaws pledged not to attack the Chickasaws and to give safe conduct to their delegates, while the Chickasaws agreed to persuade the Conchaques and Alabamas to join them in ceasing to attack the Choctaws, Tohomés, and Mobilians, or they would themselves be attacked by the Apalachees. Iberville kept his word by sending five Canadians to accompany the Indians as far as the proposed post, three of them to go on to the Illinois with Chickasaw representatives to retrieve prisoners. One of the cabin boys who had been with the Oumas training as an interpreter was sent to stay with the Chickasaws. Iberville also wrote to Canada for missionaries for the Choctaws and Chickasaws and asked Davion, who was with the Tunicas, to tell the Chaquechoumas they could safely return (from their settlement on the Yazoo? cf. Galloway 1982c) to their location between Choctaws and Chickasaws.

Iberville also reported an informal census that the chiefs worked out on the spot. The Chickasaws had 580 houses and some two thousand seasoned warriors, seven to eight hundred of whom had guns; they also possessed two villages on the Tennessee River. The Choctaws, divided into three "villages," had a total of 1,090 houses, thirty-eight hundred to four thousand men, and no guns (Iberville 1981:174). But this was by no means all the information Iberville collected. The cartographer Delisle transcribed a list of thirty-eight Choctaw villages that Iberville gave him in 1702, apparently recorded at that meeting (Kernion 1925). This document is exciting for the many hints it offers of social organization, but it is also frustrating for all it excludes. It does not, for example, group the village names in any way, in spite of Iberville's suggested tripartite division of the tribe in the log.

The comparative table of town names gathered by Swanton (1931:59–75), though it unaccountably does not include all the names from Iberville's list, does allow the observation that some town names are missing, even given the change over time that Swanton did not recognize. As these data were supplied by the Choctaw representatives who met with Iberville, some towns could have been excluded because they had no representative. Given Tonti's route to the Choctaws, he would have missed the region of the Chickasawhays towns; on the other hand, if the Chickasawhays were late participants in the alliance, driven west by British slave raids after the foundation of Mobile in 1702, they would not have been visited or counted because they would not have been there yet (Galloway 1994). The Natchez-affiliated Sixtowns, who I have suggested were incomers, Natchez affiliates from the lower Pearl and western Leaf tributary region, are also quite notably absent. Thus western and eastern towns quite clearly dominate the list (Swanton's "Central" division has more to do with the eighteenth-century French view of the Choctaws than with any reality [Galloway 1981]), which is a good confirmation of the sequential process of tribe formation that will be suggested by the sum of the evidence. It does, however, contradict the neat idea that Iberville's four (or Tonti's three) chiefs represented the constituent peoples

Table 5.1 Iberville's List of Choctaw Town
Names, 1702 (from Kernion 1925).

Town Name	Number of Houses
Ayanabe augoula	30
Bauctoucoula	40
Coincha thoucoua logoule	33
Ougilousa	30
Boucfalaya	20
Yty thipouta	30
Pouscouiche tacase	40
Mogoulacha	50
Yachou	40
Cachetacha	40
Tohia sale	20
Cafeta saya	20
Abiska Thocologoule	40
Bitabogoula	20
Suabonloula	10
Thicacho oulasta	20
Bouctoucoulo	40
Ahipata bita Brugoula	60
Boulistache	40
Iscananba Thousena Togrula	30
Abiska	20
Touacha	20
Albamon	50
Itouichacou	30
Mogoulacha	10
Yacho	20
Calouche	10
Tabogoula	10
Thata tascanan gouchy	40
Touacha thoucoua togoule	30
Bita bogoula	60
Tolistache	30
Ocouhinan	23
Alibamon cheusare Lagoute	30
Onsacousba	30
Abisca	40
Choutoua togoule	30
Busca	10

making up the Choctaws (see Galloway 1982b) and once more foregrounds the uncertainty of European observations on this point without the extended acquaintanceship that would permit confirming behavioral observations. This is Indian testimony, the testimony of what were probably "Western" and "Eastern" Choctaw confederates, as to what villages counted as Choctaw in 1702.

It is of course possible that the Chickasawhay towns (Chickasawhay and Yowani) and the Sixtowns (Nashobawenya, Oskelagna, Tala, Siniasha, Boktoloksi, and Tousanna) all appear on this list under other names, but that seems simplistic. What is striking about the names here is the number of elements that differ from the later eighteenth-century situation. Not only are the Chickasawhays and the Sixtowns missing, but so is the leading eastern town, Concha (Coucha, Coosa). Yet there are strong Eastern-isms that are later lost: the two Alabama towns, for example, and the village Ahipata bita Brugoula, which may provide a strong link to the east (see chapter 6). These changes may indeed be name shifts.

Furthermore, two chiefs' names here stand for their villages, offering clues about the organization of the tribe: Thata tascanan gouchy (*tchata tashka nanukachi*, "Choctaw warrior who advises," the latter part a title for a war chief's assistant) and Thicacho oulasta (*tchicacha holahta*, "Chickasaw leading man," with the senior moiety name as the latter part, used as an honorific). The first name indicates a group office that includes "Choctaw" as a group designation, while the second, possibly implying a marriage alliance with the Chickasaws, happens to be the name of the man whom Bienville named as first "Great Chief" of the whole Choctaw nation in about 1707 (Rowland and Sanders 1927–32, 1:157–58). Clearly the Choctaws were functioning in 1702 as a corporate entity in some sense.

SEVENTEENTH-CENTURY SUMMARY
European Trade in the Interior

Although the Apalachee region had been missionized in the 1630s, the Spanish made the first real contacts with Indians in the hinterland to the north and west apparently only some thirty or more years later. The Spanish sought to meet several needs in the region. The Franciscans who ran the Apalachee missions needed to assure a source of food for themselves should the crops of the mission Indians fail, and to send food to St. Augustine, which remained in pretty constant want. The Caribbean islands had a demand for dried meat and hides, and ships calling at San Marcos bought Indian products from the interior. Profiting from these needs must have been a tempting proposition for the soldiers assigned to the Apalachee missions – they later established ranches to raise cattle, for St. Augustine and for external trade – and clearly some of them did simply desert to live among the Indians, perhaps to facilitate this trade.

Although Spanish policy, constantly reiterated, was not to give guns to the Indians for any reason, the policy must have been ignored on many occasions or Marquette and Jolliet would not have heard so much about armed Indians and Spaniards to the east. Also, once the British began to instigate native-led slave raids, the Spanish did not hesitate to arm their allies, as many sources testify. Still, guns were not the object of the trade, or at least not the entire object: Delgado's reports make it clear that the Indians desired such decorative items as ribbons and bells, as well as the more practical edged metal tools. The remaining question is why the Indians were interested in participating in the trade.

Before Europeans reached the North American continent, widespread trading connections characterized nearly every region of it. External trade for prestige items was important for maintaining chiefly status in ranked chiefdoms, where these items were redistributed to tributary chiefs or taken out of circulation (thus retaining their value) in mortuary ceremonialism; it was so important, in fact, that loss of external trade in particular items may have contributed to the collapse of chiefdoms. Where chiefdoms were still in operation, as on the Mississippi River and perhaps in a simplified sense elsewhere, European sumptuary goods could begin to function in precisely the same ways as had the exotic imported minerals for body paint, the elaborately engraved conch-shell dippers, and the repoussé copper plates associated with the Southeastern Ceremonial Complex.

On the other hand, where chiefdoms had dispersed, as the Soto narratives suggested was the case at least for the Tombigbee drainage, what would European trade have to offer the petty chief of an autonomous town, no longer claimant to hereditary divinity and more dependent upon the favor of his peers? Such a man accumulates power not by sinking productive capacity into monumental architecture or rare objects from afar but by giving away the accumulations that his power and popularity make possible. Further, he gives away those items that all require: food, clothing, and the tools to acquire such things. Even with the scanty evidence of the seventeenth century we can discern that the demand for subsistence-facilitating goods – edged metal tools and ready-made cloth could free remarkable quantities of time for other subsistence tasks – seems to have been higher than the demand for prestige goods. Furthermore, since neither the big-men nor even the surviving chiefs could monopolize access to the raw materials the Europeans wanted, once tribes began to participate in the trade they would remain tribes and would not reintegrate as chiefdoms using kin-based modes of production. In this way the new role of Indian tribes as peripheral suppliers of raw materials to the European core had the effect of *preventing* them from becoming chiefdoms or states again: the result of "underdevelopment" so familiar in modern times had its beginnings for Indians here.

The Spanish began this process with their requirement for food and skins. The Spaniards Delgado reported among the Indians of the interior had married Indian women, thus gaining access to their kin networks and probably facilitating a role as traders. The chiefs who spoke with Delgado may have been quite happy to establish a direct trade with San Marcos to cut out these middlemen, and the Shawnees and certain Upper Creek tribes were obviously beginning to jockey for the intermediary position themselves by the time Woodward came on the scene, just as the Iroquois were moving to dominate the northeastern fur trade. The British would take a cue from the resident Spaniards and marry into the tribes; they may even have set up their trade houses where the Spanish had already accustomed the Indians to bring their skins. Clearly the British traders were very efficient at their trade, for by the time Tonti encountered the Choctaws and Chickasaws in 1702 the Choctaws had already begun to hunt for the British trade, in spite of British slave-raids, and the Chickasaws were already enmeshed in a debt-and-credit system (Galloway 1982b).

This trade would have altered the political economy of the interior tribes, and it would have affected the domestic economy too, though not necessarily in a negative way. As the deerskin trade grew, it would not have impinged seriously on the agriculture practiced by the interior tribes, because the tasks of agriculture were seasonally scheduled in such a way as not to conflict with those of hunting. Furthermore, the motivation to hunt would have brought with it an unanticipated bonus in the shape of more meat for domestic consumption, at least after the Spanish demand for dried meat, apparently an ephemeral one in any case, had passed.

European Slaving in the Interior

The underlying theme of much of the early British activity in the interior Southeast was catching Indian slaves. Although such slaves had been found to be impractical for the British colonies of the eastern seaboard, chiefly because they found it so easy to escape to their own people with the help of the surrounding free Indians, the early South Carolinians soon discovered that they could trade Indian slaves for black ones in the islands, and thus supply themselves with the labor force they needed at small cost to themselves. Snell (1972:11), a student of South Carolina Indian slavery, reckons that the first Indian slaves thus exported may have been some Cusabos transported as early as 1671. In spite of opposition by the Proprietors in England, Carolinians continued to do the same with any Indians who gave them trouble and soon with any Indians brought captive to them by Indian allies.

The British could engage in this lucrative trade by exploiting the native institution of captive adoption. Among the Indians of the Southeast, as in most of the continent, captives taken in warfare were often kept and adopted into the tribe to boost its numbers. It is difficult to say how "aboriginal" this practice was, because the character of Indian warfare in precolonial times is unknown. What is known is that the turmoil of demographic disruption had left many tribal groups with a need to add to their population or at least to keep their numbers constant, and one way to do that was not to kill a captured enemy but to adopt him – or more frequently her – in the place of some lost member of the tribe. In the case of women and children, the adoption was complete and generally nondiscriminatory; in the case of men, perhaps less so. Thus a native practice of taking captives and keeping them already existed.

If they could be persuaded to undertake slave-catching, tribes with firearms enjoyed a huge advantage over those whose arms were limited to the bow and spear. For the Carolinians who would dominate this trade, Dr. Henry Woodward had begun both the push westward – even, according to Nairne (1988:50), offering trade to the Chickasaws as early as the 1680s – and the slave trade, which his friends the Westos supplied. Records are incomplete for Indian slaves kept in or transported out of Charles Towne (Snell 1972:appendix 1): there is little mention of slaves taken west of the Mobile River prior to 1700, yet the French found the tribes there already terrorized by Indian allies of the British in 1699.

Only passing references suggest the situation west of the Appalachians. Slaving activity must have begun through the early alliance with the Lower Creeks while they were still on the Chattahoochee, and through them with the Upper Creeks on the Tallapoosa – Nairne's Talapoosies. The record does show that Woodward had established a Kasihta trade as early as 1677 (Snell 1972:21). After the destruction of the Westos in 1680, the chief intermediaries to the west became the Savannahs, a Shawnee band that had recently moved into the Carolina back country; such early activity may have been reflected in the migration of the Quasate and Tubani and several other towns that Delgado reported had fled the depredations of the British and Shawnees. But it was probably not until 1690, when the Lower Creeks made the temporary move to Ochese Creek (the Ocmulgee) that gave them their English name, that Europeans began to make aggressive links far to the west. No records say more than that by the time of Welch's push to the Mississippi in 1698, permanent trading stations had been established among the Upper Creeks, specifically the towns settled on the Tallapoosa River and at the Coosa-Tallapoosa forks.

The British, or at least Thomas Nairne, referred to the Upper Creek towns collectively as the "Talapoosies," as they called the Lower Creeks "Ochesses." In default of traders' reports, specifying the towns that favored or were favored by the Carolina traders is difficult, in part due to the dominance of the slave trade: at this early stage it remained less than respectable, for all its profit, and the traders who incited slave-catching forays simply did not make records of their efforts. We do know that the Mobilians and other residents of the Mobile River area, as well as the Choctaws, complained of raids by the Alabamas just at the turn of the century, well before Nairne had conceived his grandiose plan of a massive attack by these same Indians. British allies among the Upper Creeks would in any case be more of a threat to the tribes of the Mobile delta because of their easy access to the region via the Alabama River.

Seventeenth-Century Overtures to Contact

At the beginning of the period discussed in this chapter, the forming Choctaw confederacy was strong enough not only to ward off attack but also to drive other groups away from the Tombigbee region, as Delgado was told. Serious attacks upon the Choctaws were not possible, pending a more complete penetration of the interior by Europeans and the arming of their enemies with firearms. One of the first objectives of Welch and others of his ilk in their earliest approaches to the tribes of the upper Tombigbee and Yazoo/Mississippi Valleys was to develop a slave trade, and one of the major victims of that trade would be the Choctaws. Conversion of the Chickasaws to trading partnership, with a permanent trade house among them, was the key to intensifying the slave trade in general and may have been the beginning of direct pressure on the Choctaws. French contacts with the Quapaws and other tribes of the Mississippi invariably brought with them reports of marauding by the Chickasaws, at dates early enough to imply that when the Chickasaws began their trade with Woodward's men they attacked the people of the trans-Mississippi exclusively. The evidence is very thin, but the Chickasaws may not have dared attack the Choctaw confederacy until the English traders came among them and equipped them with a large number of guns; they may even have required English leadership on the raids, such as Tonti observed in 1702, to persuade them to undertake such forays.

Extant records suggest that British allies could have enslaved no more than several hundred Choctaws before the coming of the French in 1699, since later and apparently more intensive efforts netted only a few hundred Choctaw captives (Snell 1972:appendix 1). Ironically, slave raids from the east may have set the final seal on Choctaw unity, as the Chickasawhays, the important group that moved west into the southern half of the Choctaw "homeland," were driven out of the Mobile River valley (Rowland and Sanders 1927–32, 1:156–57; Galloway 1994).

Choctaws in the Seventeenth Century

By the end of the seventeenth century the Choctaws can be said to have emerged into written history, as the Spanish, English, and French began to observe them. No historical document describes how they arrived, but at least the location of their homeland is known, if I have not yet proved who the Choctaws were. Their domain is roughly defined by the locations of the polities that surrounded them: Chickasaws and Chakchiumas to the north, Natchez and Tunicas to the west, Alabamas and Mobilians to the east, and a welter of "small tribes" – Pascagoulas, Biloxis, Acolapissas – to the south. Like many of their Eastern Muskogean neighbors who had been jostled onto the stage of history by European encroachment, many of the Choctaws had *moved* to be where they were, some from the Tombigbee Basin to the east, some from the lower Pearl to the west.

Just past the end of the century, as Henri de Tonti became the first documented European to visit the Choctaws, a slight hint of their social organization emerges in his observation that more than one chief was needed to speak for them in the meeting with Iberville on the coast. The remarkable list of villages made at that meeting, however, suggests that the Choctaws themselves did not yet define the Chickasaw-hays and Sixtowns peoples as part of their group, and this may be the best evidence of these groups' late addition. Apart from a few scattered observations Choctaws made to Frenchmen over the following few years, what I have presented up to this point is all that the historical and archaeological records have overtly to tell about Choctaw origins. Clearly, it is not enough for proof. I therefore turn to other evidence to strengthen the case – evidence not obviously available because it is the evidence of pattern.

CHAPTER SIX

The Cartography
of Early Contact

There is nothing more ordinary or easier than to make maps; nothing more difficult than to make acceptable ones. A good geographer is all the rarer because it is necessary that nature and art be united to create one. – Jean Nicolas Bellin, cited in Pierre François Xavier de Charlevoix, *Histoire et description generale de la Nouvelle France*

The interpretation of early maps is often undertaken by the archaeologist and ethnographer with a light-hearted innocence that must sometimes strike the historiographer as pathetic. – Philip Phillips, James A. Ford, and James B. Griffin, *Archaeological Survey in the Lower Mississippi Alluvial Valley, 1940–1947*

MAPS AS EVIDENCE

Beyond limited behavioral observations, the specific data that early European explorers and traders offer on the Choctaws are lamentably thin, since the location of these native peoples delayed contact until the very end of the seventeenth century. Conditions as encountered by Europeans who penetrated the Southeast in the later seventeenth century were dramatically different from what available information, by then over a century old, had led them to expect. The cartography of the Southeast from 1500 to 1703 provides probably the best view of European thinking during that hiatus and perhaps a few more hints about the interior that may not be recorded elsewhere, but that cartography is useless without a disciplined critical approach. Today we are accustomed to general maps based on satellite photographs, which provide more empirical data; human error and prejudice have been to a large degree removed. Maps of the sixteenth and seventeenth centuries were nothing like these: they represented theories and purposes much more directly, and they borrowed heavily from one another. If they are to be of use today, we must understand the conditions of their making.

In the sixteenth century, European cartography emerged from a medieval depression that had restricted knowledge of the earth, as it restricted the other sciences, to a spiritual metaphor. The revival of the classic work of Ptolemy provided a starting place for the mapping of the land, and the crusades and pilgrimages of the late Middle Ages endowed the charting of the seas with greater importance. What did not change appreciably as the age of exploration began were the sources of information available to the cartographer: either he went to the spot and gathered the information himself, or, far more frequently, he depended on the written or oral narrative accounts and rare sketches of travelers, mariners, and explorers.

Travelers could provide very good information if they had the instruments, training, and motivation to do so. Using compass, astrolabe, and knowledge of celestial objects and time of year, one could ascertain one's latitude with a fair degree of accuracy. Determining longitude, however, was a different problem; it depended on knowing how far one had traveled in what direction. Direction was not a problem, but distance was, especially at sea or in difficult conditions such as deep forest or bad weather. Also, though the available instruments were not impossibly complex, they did require a habit of exactitude and an acquaintance with a fair number of astronomical facts that the average explorer generally did not have. The activity was perceived as so abstruse that, for example, Captain Juan de Añasco's companions on the Soto expedition did not place much confidence in his claims of competence with astrolabe and cross-staff (Garcilaso de la Vega [1605] 1951:510,600).

Much more reliable were the observations of mariners, whose very lives depended upon their skill in the "haven-finding art." By the sixteenth century the portolan sailing charts of the Mediterranean had considerably improved mariners' ability to identify and note where they were – until they went to a place where they had never been. Even then, a method was available: chart the coastlines and then establish the winds, currents, and seasonal variations (Brown 1949). For this reason, pilots were the early leading lights of exploration in the Gulf of Mexico (Weddle 1985) and the authors of the first sea charts of the Gulf and Caribbean.

We should remember that accurate mapping of the surface of Europe itself only began in the sixteenth century, so the cartography of the New World was created at a time of changing methodology. Once some kind of outline was defined for a land mass by coastal reconnaissance, cartographers strove to fill the two-dimensional space thus defined. Cartographers (or perhaps their royal employers) preferred bad information to no information, and this remained true as exploration of the New World proceeded. The variable quality of the data that may be reflected on these maps and the difficulty of interpreting it call for a closer consideration of this language in which historical maps "tell" something.

We can assume that most maps are good-faith attempts to represent what the cartographer believes to exist in the world. Maps can, of course, be false or embody wishful thinking, but in principle the western European map is supposed to be a faithful picture. It is not, however, a literal portrayal, nor does its maker believe it to be such; instead it is made up of a symbolic repertoire that ranges from the iconographic to the purely arbitrary (Robinson and Petchenik 1976:61). One danger in interpreting maps is that of confusing these levels of representational literalness. Added to this is the problem of identifying just what is being represented – did the cartographer intend to interpret the data or merely to identify locations? Thematic, interpretive mapping is by no means a recent phenomenon (Robinson and Petchenik 1976:116); medieval mapping was, in fact, almost entirely interpretive.

In short, maps have meaning that is not transparent; interpretation depends upon the degree to which cartographer and map reader agree on the meaning of the graphical conventions used. A map is therefore a semiotic structure, and the task of the map reader is to interpret its symbolic vocabulary as commentary on the space it represents. Of interest to the present study are the location of Indian groups and any other data about them that the maps may reveal, so the particular focus here is on the conventions used to portray them and the meaning of those conventions.

"Convention" may be something of a misnomer: the system of symbols used in map making is even today only a set convention within specific institutions, such as national survey offices or map-publishing firms; there is no universal set of conventions, merely a loose agreement on the degree of stylization of given objects at given scales. In the Renaissance, when the cartographic art was changing rapidly, there were likewise no explicitly agreed conventions, but cartographers' usages were known to their fellows, and New World maps of the sixteenth century must be seen as part of this very large tradition. We must understand this context in order to specify the representational level of the symbolic systems that appear on New World maps.

Robinson and Petchenik (1976) have vehemently asserted that language, which is processed sequentially, and the cartographic image, with its simultaneous, nondecomposable gestalt quality, are incompatible. They argue that the symbolic projection that constitutes a map is in no way translatable into the "discursive" projection of verbal description – or vice versa. If this is true (and many aspects of their argument are quite persuasive), then the fundamental problem of understanding early maps of the Americas lies at the very point of their making.

The shores of the New World were mapped more or less directly, by pilots working with astrolabe, compass, cross-staff, sailing chart, and lead line. Aside from a few well-documented anomalies, the portrayal of the coastlines improved steadily over time as sailing charts made their way into the hands of royal and then commercial cartographers. But the picture of the interior did not show such steady improvement. However ill suited they may have been as a vehicle for geographic knowledge, exploration narratives were by and large what the early cartographers got to work with.

Cartographers were quite aware of the shortcomings of narrative sources for their purposes, as was eloquently expressed by Nicolas Sanson d'Abbeville *fils*, who observed in the introduction to his 1693 text on geography, "Although nearly all the narrative accounts are full of . . . errors, most of them do not hesitate to castigate maps for error, and to accuse geographers of ignorance, as if maps drawn up on the basis of narratives did not depend on the good faith of travelers, and as if geographers were responsible for the negligence of some travelers, the lack of capacity of several, and the ignorance of most of the others" (Sanson d'Abbeville 1693:97; translation mine). Cartographers accordingly had to extract relevant information from the narrative sources, in order to transform sequential information to simultaneous spatial information.

Renaissance mapmakers would not have been wholly unfamiliar with such a transformation. Cassirer (1957:450) has argued that it took a "spiritual transformation" to enable primitive humans to emerge from their topological space of known paths through the environment and to comprehend that environment in the symbolically constructed Euclidean space of a two-dimensional map. But Renaissance Europeans – and people today – made use of both sorts of portrayal simultaneously, using both one-dimensional route maps and two-dimensional area maps, so surely a cartographer of the day could work a similar transformation upon narrative data. He had the outline of the coast and the mouths of the rivers that emptied into the sea. Explorers of the interior would supply more or less accurate starting and ending points for their journeys, and between those points they would describe towns, mountains, swamps, forests, river crossings, and even river journeys. Some of those rivers would inevitably be the same ones that emptied into the sea at the coasts, and the explorers would frequently try to label them as such. Additional, corroborating information could include estimated rates, distances, and directions of travel, though its usefulness would depend upon the observer's reliability. Finally, in the best case, the cartographer might be supplied with one or more sketch maps of all or part of the region explored, or he might have the opportunity to question expedition participants. All these sources could help compensate for the limitations of narrative reports.

To understand how closely a given map approximates what the explorers saw, we must reconstruct the process by which the map was made – or at least the information that it embodied and the paths along which that information flowed to reach the cartographer. The modern observer is both handicapped and aided in this analysis, having better knowledge of the land's topography, but living at a time when many changes have taken place in the land and its people and when the preconceptions that conditioned the Renaissance cartographic vocabulary are obsolete. Although some of the narrative sources mapmakers used may be available, the modern observer does not share the linguistic competences and semantic fields of their authors as the mapmakers did and thus cannot reconstruct exactly what cartographers "made" of these narratives. She therefore must attempt to reconstruct the meaning of cartographic "codes" using the evidence of the map (the encoded document) and sometimes part of the information source thus encoded. She will probably never have access to all the information that went into any early map, and thus her interpretation of its code will always be faulty. Still, she is not alone; the very lack of cartographic convention and the failure of maps to portray exploration accurately meant that even contemporaries, explorers in the field whose very lives might depend upon the value of their maps, repeatedly cursed the failure of those maps to correspond with reality (cf. Iberville 1981:60).

The point is that very few of the maps now available are privileged; cartographers almost always had to construct them from less than ideal evidence. They must thus be subjected to a fairly well-defined suite of analytical questions – a "deconstruction," an "*explication de carte*." This process should include an examination of the physical map itself where possible, to determine those aspects of its creation perceptible in the paper, ink, printing, and so forth; an investigation of the cartographer, to discover what one can of his education and training as a cartographer and his connections and acquaintances; and, most important, a study of the possible sources of the information embodied in the map, including explorers' reports, printed narratives, and especially other maps.

SOTO AND THE INTERIOR

European mapping of the Southeast began with its discovery. This early mapping was done by ships' pilots (Weddle 1985), and details made their way to the hydrographic office Spain had set up in 1503 in the *Casa de Contratación* in Seville to control the mapping of the New World (Brown 1949:142–44; Delanglez 1945:17–32). All pilots had to obtain from the *Casa* a license to sail; they had to use its sailing charts, to record anything new on those charts, and to turn in the marked charts upon their return. The Pineda voyage of 1519, although it did not make its single long stop along the northern Gulf coast, had the charting of the coastline as one of its major purposes, and it did indeed yield a manuscript map of the coast that provided the earliest notations of general shape and river mouths but named only a few landmarks (see figure 3.1).

As activity in the Gulf of Mexico increased with the exploitation of Mexican mines, the treasure fleets needed more accurate maps and charts. Additional river and bay names began to appear on the Spanish master sailing chart, or *padrón general*, within a few years, together with the standard portolan stippling convention indicating that shallow water was known to be present along the northern Gulf coast (Cumming 1958:94). One such example, believed to reflect in greater detail the findings of the

6.1. Ribero map of the Gulf of Mexico, 1529. Placenames along the coast of the "Tiera de Garay" from east to west (names in italics are in red on the original): R: de la Paz, R: estapara, *B: de Jua Ponce*, de alaya, Motas, *R: de la cocibcion*, *R: de s: Juan*, Costa tessa, R: de fazallones, cañoveral, donde aquí descubrio garay, *R: de nieves*, R: de baxas, medanos, *R: de flores*, Ancones, motas del salvador, marpeqña, Ostial, *R: del espu sto*. Courtesy of the John Carter Brown Library at Brown University.

Pineda voyage because it portrays the "Tiera de Garay," was drawn in 1529 by Diego Ribero, a Portuguese who had worked for the *Casa* for some time and had been responsible for supplying official maps and charts to the Spanish-Portuguese junta that met in Badajoz/Elvas in 1524 to determine the location of the Line of Demarcation (Stevenson 1909). This map (figure 6.1) is crowded with names along the northern Gulf coast, and it marks some six rivers from Apalachee Bay in the east to the much-debated Río del Espíritu Santo, probably the Mississippi. Until the "de Soto" map of about 1544 (figure 6.2), however, no surviving map attempted to characterize the interior of the Southeast.

Barbara Boston's study (1941) of the "De Soto Map" established fairly conclusively that it was drawn at the *Casa*, where Alonzo de Santa Cruz was royal cosmographer; it was found among his papers, and he may even have drawn the map himself. It clearly reflects that institution's tradition: the names of coastal features and rivers correspond closely with those found on contemporary sailing charts and world maps from the same source. It can be compared with both Alonzo de Santa Cruz's 1542 world map (Dahlgren 1892) and that of Sebastian Cabot of 1544 (figure 6.3), both also thought to reflect the contemporary version of the *padrón general*. All three use nearly

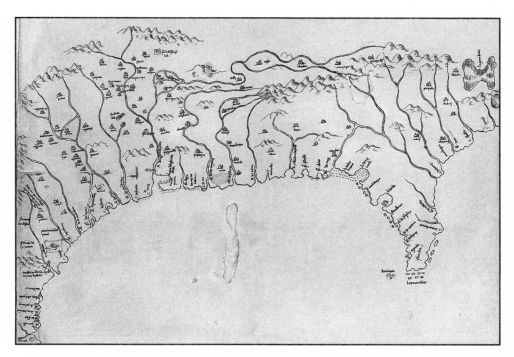

6.2. The so-called De Soto map of 1544, attributed to Alonzo de Santa Cruz (Archivo General de Indias, Seville; reproduced from a tracing in the J. P. Bryan Map Collection). Placenames along the Gulf coast from east to west: aguada, R. de Capay, R. de ranoas, b. de Ju poçe, fermallones, b. hoda, areobaxo, b. de miruelo, b. de los baxos, [unnamed river], c. de miz, p. chico, p. fodable, b. y Rio de navjdad, arenales, R. de vieles, R. de flores, R. de los angeles, c. th mo, matos del salvador, R. baxo, mar pe queña, baya del espiritu santo, R. del espiritu santo, c. de cruz, C. de fierto, R. de motañas. Courtesy of the Center for American History, University of Texas at Austin.

identical nomenclature for the rivers and bays of the coast yet are somewhat at variance with the Ribero maps reflecting the earlier version of the *padrón*. Notable additions on all of them are the Río de los Angeles and the Río de Navidad. These additions were not made from the new Soto evidence, however, since Santa Cruz's 1542 map already had them; instead, the evidence of Santa Cruz and Cabot and other maps also drawn from *Casa* sources (Delanglez 1945:25–30) confirm that the structure of rivers they portray was already established on the *padrón general*, possibly from the Narváez expedition evidence, and thus probably before Soto's departure. Hence, the *padrón* gave explorers a rough idea of the shape of the region they were attempting to traverse. As they proceeded, they had only to take account of common-sense models of hydrology and geology to proceed toward the gold and precious minerals they desired, as Oviedo y Valdés ([1526] 1959:108–9) explained in his *Natural History*: "For your Majesty must remember the maxim, and it certainly appears to be true, that all gold originates in the hills and tops of the mountains and that the rains gradually wash it out and carry it down the rivers and other streams that

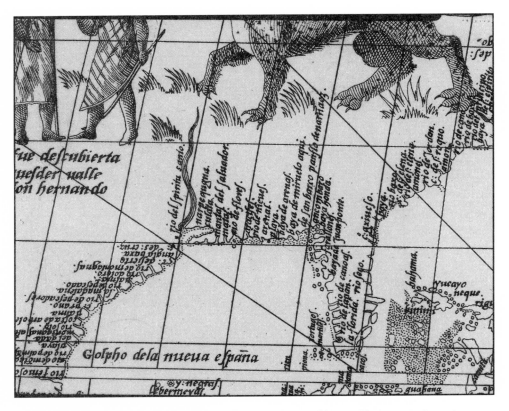

6.3. Detail of the Gulf coast from Sebastian Cabot's 1544 world map. Placenames along the coast from east to west: rio de lapan, rio de canoas, bayaan Juan ponte, fgralloncs, baya honda, ancombaxo, de san barco panflo de narnaez, baya de miruelo aqui, baya de arenas, playa, arenal, rio de nieves, aractses, rio de flores, matas, mantas del salvador, culata, narpequgna, rio del spiritu santo. Courtesy of the Newberry Library.

arise in the mountains. However, gold is often found on plains, far removed from mountains. When this happens usually large quantities are found in that area. For the most part, however, gold is found on the slope of hills and in the bed of rivers and streams." As long as they could find rivers that might reasonably emerge on the coast, they were performing a sort of "inland coasting," taking advantage of the known to guide them through the unknown.

The greatest interest of this 1544 "De Soto Map," as Boston (1941) says, is its portrayal of the interior, with the names of Indian groups located along a newly defined hydrography. Boston's careful tabulation of sources shows that the names were drawn for the most part from what she believed to be the complete account of Ranjel that Oviedo used, although Santa Cruz almost certainly knew also of Biedma's account. The names, however, are not enough here; what entitled the cartographer to create the spatial configuration he did? Did he have better narrative versions than are known today, or did he exploit the personal knowledge of living individuals and thus create, in this map, evidence of value beyond that of the narratives?

The rivers in the central Gulf region had already been named: Navidad, Nieves, Flores, Angeles, Espíritu Santo – from east to west. Until the creation of this map, as far as is known, these rivers were no more than names applied to river mouths by coasting pilots, yet the map displays a full-blown hydrography complete with mountain ranges to provide the rivers' sources. Delanglez (1945:62) argued that this map did embody privileged information: not the original account of Ranjel but a fuller account, perhaps including field notes, kept by Biedma, who as one of the royal officers of the expedition was obliged – as Ranjel was not – to report to the *Casa*. Delanglez nevertheless maintained that the interior hydrography was still a matter of guesswork – the rivers in question had surely not been charted – and that thus the map's only information of real interest is the town names not found in any extant narrative. It seems to me, however, that although assuredly the hydrography bears little resemblance to reality, if the map does contain some privileged information, we must also accept the possibility that it represents a real Spanish cognitive map of the interior, the graphic exemplar of a thesis, and perhaps with its help we may reconstruct something more of the rationale of the expedition as it proceeded.

The focus here is not the whole of the Southeast but only, as in chapter 3, the central section from Chiaha to Quizquiz and southward along the Mississippi. To investigate the relationship between narrative and map, I have first constructed the graphic equivalent of the narratives: a strip map, or itinerary, indicating towns (named and unnamed) and river crossings or rivers indicated as between towns. The result is shown schematically in figure 6.4. If this itinerary is superimposed on the Santa Cruz map by "following the dots" from one town to another, several facts become apparent (see figure 6.5). First, the hydrography is not wholly imaginary except in the cognitive sense; instead, it is an attempt to *rationalize* the narrative evidence. The river crossings on the map may help clarify the itinerary; their appearance is presumably dictated by the need to match the number of crossings mentioned in the narratives. Biedma referred to the rivers at Xuale, Chiaha, and Quizquiz as the *rio de Espiritusanto* in his summary report. Delanglez (1945:59–61) has argued that the mapmaker's effort to portray Biedma's decription virtually necessitated the appearance of an eastern branch of the Río del Espíritu Santo on the Santa Cruz map. The choice of the Nieves, Flores, and Angeles Rivers for the placement of the remainder of the itinerary is easily explained as a matter of dead reckoning; I would guess, furthermore, that Angeles and Flores arise in the same mountains as Nieves because the expedition had to cross three rivers from Tali to Coça, and that Flores has an eastern branch on the map because of the extra river crossing between Ulibihali and Tuasi.

6.4. Hernando de Soto itinerary from Chiaha to Quizquiz as a strip map (data from Biedma and Oviedo/Ranjel). Number corresponds with location on figure 6.5; B = Biedma "Province" name; town symbols are those that appear on the Alonzo de Santa Cruz 1544 map in figure 6.2.

1	B	Chiaha
		5-6 villages
		RIVER
		village
		RIVER
		village
		RIVER
		village
2	B	Coste
		RIVER
3		Tali
		RIVER
		RIVER
		RIVER
		Tasqui
		villages
4	B	Coça
		Talimachusy
5		Itaba
		RIVER
6		Ulibihali
		village
7		Tuasi
8	B	Talisi
		Casiste
		Caxa
		Humati
		Uxapita
9	B	Athahachi
10	B	Piachi
		fenced village
		villages
11	B	Mabila
		Talicpacana
		Moçulixa
		RIVER
		Zabusta
12		Apafalaya
		RIVER
13	B	Chicaça
14	B	Alimamu
		swamps?
15	B	Quizquiz
		RIVER

6.5. Schematic tracing of Alonzo de Santa Cruz 1544 map with Hernando de Soto route traced through named towns. Rivers: (*a*) Río del Espíritu Santo, (*b*) Río Baxo, (*c*) Río de los Angeles, (*d*) Río de Flores, (*e*) Río de Nieves, (*f*) Río de Navidad.

Thus I believe the hydrography was deduced from the number of known rivers at the Gulf of Mexico in conjunction with river crossings and direction of travel; it is a picture of where the officials of the *Casa* thought the Spaniards had gone. How well does it stand up as a picture of the Spanish conception of the landscape of native polities? To the extent that Spanish prejudice and desire made all groups they saw into autocratic chiefdoms, it stands up very well. The map's scale prevented it from portraying all places mentioned in the narratives, but it does not exclude a single "province" named by Biedma, who thought most thoroughly in *encomienda* terms (and named the fewest towns).

The convention by which the places are portrayed is worth investigation as well. Each named place is represented by what seems to be a tiny "town" icon: a group of two or three rectangular buildings with such features as doors and roof detail. Nothing like this had appeared on the sailing charts modeled on the *padrón general* – these charts had not portrayed the interiors of countries – but it was not an unfamiliar symbol. More or less naturalistic portrayals of towns had been appearing on maps since Roman times, and during the late medieval and early Renaissance periods they had been a regular feature of itinerary or strip maps. Late medieval portolan charts of the famous Mallorcan school sometimes portrayed important or legendary cities in the margins of the chart rather than on the spot where the cities were located. In fact, the notion of marking inland locations on a map at all was rather new in the mid–sixteenth century, and iconographic symbols were adopted from the pictures in these earlier forms. What emerged as the standard symbol in the most influential atlases of the day was the schematized drawing of one or more towers grouped behind a small circle meant to be the actual location mark. On European maps this symbol could be more elaborated for the more important towns and differentiated to identify re-ligious establishments or castles. Where the scale was large enough it might become a naturalistic drawing, but it was clearly the convention of choice for representing a named population agglomeration (see Dainville 1964:217–21; Smith 1985:20).

The simplification of the 1544 Santa Cruz map drawn by Hieronymo Chiaves and printed by Ortelius in 1584 (figure 6.6) showed similar symbols for Indian sites, moving closer to the convention in the rest of the Ortelius atlas by adding the further elaboration of tiny towers. Santa Cruz's symbols had not been exactly alike, but they did not differ from one another substantially. The Ortelius print shows greater differentiation in the symbols, but it does not agree with the importance accorded to the various towns in the narratives and must be assumed to be aesthetic or purely fortuitous. Cornelius Wytfliet's widely copied 1597 simplification of Chiaves's map showed further elaboration of the castle symbol, adding more towers, drawing them in a more naturalistic style, and continuing the arbitrary differentiation in complex-ity. Mercator used this same symbology on his planisphere of 1569 and on all the maps of his Duisberg atlas. Clearly the "fortified town" symbol for this use had become a convention on Spanish maps of the sixteenth century.

Symbology for Indian towns on other maps of the period suggests that although the appropriate icon might differ, the notion of using a single representational device was widespread. Thus the White–De Bry 1590 map of Virginia portrays such towns as oval palisade fences, an interesting adaptation of the symbol from Tudor maps of England, where it signified deer parks (Dainville 1964:199–200); Le Moyne's 1591 map of Florida shows towns as a single, apparently oval, thatched house. The icon-ographic symbols had wide influence in maps of the succeeding seventeenth century wherever the scale of the maps allowed, and in each case they had clearly become conventional: one sign was chosen to stand for an Indian town. There are a few exceptions – for example, Marc Lescarbot's 1612 map of the region of Laudonnière's Huguenot colony shows naturalistic, very differentiated European-style buildings for Indian town symbols and is more reminiscent of a contemporary estate or prov-

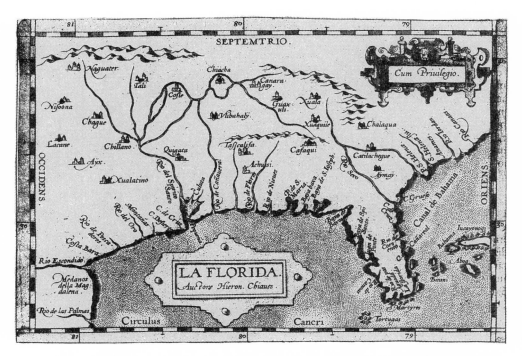

6.6. Ortelius's printed version of Chiaves's map, 1584. Courtesy of the Mississippi Department of Archives and History.

ince plan – but such maps are rare, and they represent a convention of sorts in any case, since they do not portray native architecture.

The Santa Cruz map and the Soto narratives that fed it thus seem to have set a mode of "seeing" for the region of concern, with both map and narrative establishing a view of Indian polities that admitted of no significant differentiation among them. Since the Santa Cruz map introduced the sixteenth-century "town" convention to portray the southeastern polities, Garcilaso's excesses were not required to establish the notion of these polities as well-organized provinces, and the reports from the Luna and Pardo expeditions of much-reduced glory in the interior were not enough to dislodge it. The Santa Cruz–Chiaves–Wytfliet family of maps, then, portrays inaccurate hydrography and an erroneous conception of social organization across the polities of the Southeast; these maps demonstrate graphically the early explorers' idea of one "standard Indian polity." They represented the Spaniards' reality, and they shaped the cognitive map transmitted to their colleagues who followed. Most material of these effects was their influence on seventeenth-century mapmakers, whose work in turn shaped the conceptions of other explorers.

We might logically imagine that some maps must have begun to incorporate further discoveries as the expeditions of Luna and Pardo revealed that changes were taking place in polities the Spaniards recognized as identical to those visited by Soto.

217

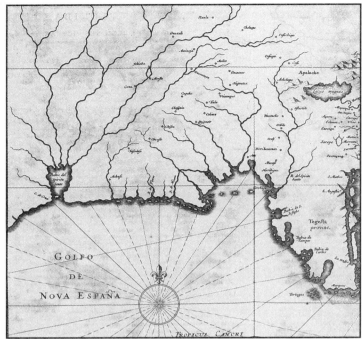

6.7. (*a*) Joannes de Laet's *Florida et regiones vicinae*, 1630; (*b*) Nicolas Sanson *père*'s *Amerique septentrionale*, 1650; (*c*) Nicolas Sanson *père*'s *Le Nouveau Mexique et la Floride*, 1656; (*d*) Pierre DuVal's *La Floride*, 1670. (*a*) courtesy of the John Carter Brown Library at Brown University; (*b*) courtesy of the Newberry Library; (*c*) and (*d*) courtesy of the Edward E. Ayer Collection, Newberry Library.

c

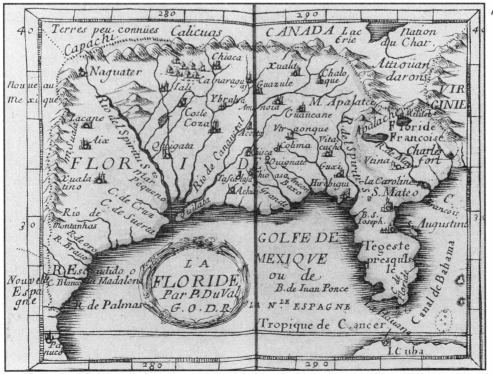

d

Luna's failure, however, had shifted Spanish interests to the Atlantic coast and away from the Gulf, while Pardo's journeys marked a beginning for the long-lived view of the interior beyond the Appalachians as undifferentiated "back country." The narratives that portrayed these expeditions were not widely available, either. What was available, soon after the turn of the seventeenth century, caught the imagination of Europe and set the cartography of the region back dramatically: Garcilaso's romance of Soto, printed in 1605.

The Spanish mapmakers and those they influenced held to the image popularized by Ortelius and Wytfliet, but the popularity of the Inca's literary romance was immediate and widespread, and it brought a new conception to the geography of the Southeast, one clearly not connected to any real information. Delanglez (1945:81–95) has outlined the story of the group of maps that reflect this influence and their relationships, from Johan de Laet's atlas of 1625 (figure 6.7a) to the very influential Sanson maps of 1650 (figure 6.7b) and 1656 (figure 6.7c) down to the map of Sanson's pupil Du Val in 1679 (figure 6.7d). The odd new portrayal of the interior hydrography introduced by de Laet, which emptied no fewer than six major rivers into a "Bahía del Espíritu Santo" at the northwestern end of the Gulf of Mexico, placed town names quite arbitrarily and is thus completely useless for locating Indian polities. Nicolas Sanson then borrowed the bay and its rivers from de Laet, duplicating the placement of town names almost exactly but adding river names from John Blaeu's maps based on the Spanish sea charts. On his influential map of 1656 Sanson further embroidered the landscape with a set of duplicated town names derived, Delanglez (1945:88) thought, by superimposing the Chiaves nomenclature on the de Laet hydrography. Du Val then followed this model almost slavishly.

One change nevertheless makes some of this erroneous development forgivable: a move away from the iconographic convention for town locations. This shift may have been partly due to a general increase in information on maps, forcing a more economical representation, but it likely owed something to another manifestation of seventeenth-century neoclassicism: the Ptolemy atlases, still being reprinted, used a simple circle convention to locate places. De Laet and Sanson both used undifferentiated small circles to anchor their place names (Du Val's use of the older sixteenth-century fortified-town symbols simply signals his "quotation" of the Chiaves map's nomenclature). Sanson's son, strongly influenced by Richelet's 1670 condensed translation of Garcilaso, made a new map in 1674 that reflected it (figure 6.8). Even Garcilaso's manufacture of high civilization in the Southeast did not have sufficient influence to counteract the trend toward an arbitrary convention, and most of the town locations on this map remain indicated by circles; in the area of interest, only the replicated Cofitachequi ("Cofachique," "Cofaqui"), Coça, and Tascalussa are marked otherwise, by a simple "multiple building" symbol.

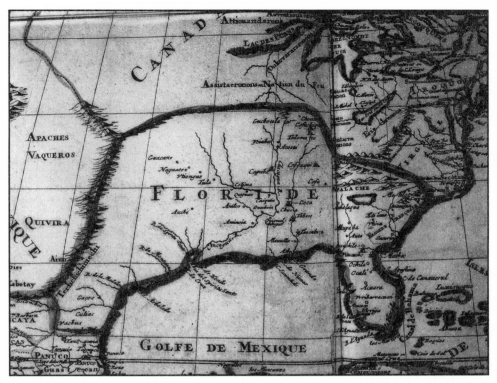

6.8. Nicolas Sanson *fils*'s *Amerique Septentrionale*, 1674, as reproduced in an atlas of 1692. Courtesy of the Edward E. Ayer Collection, Newberry Library.

A clearer explanation for this differentiation may be sought in the theoretical writings of Sanson *fils*, which included considerations of the kinds of polities represented by the peoples of the Americas. In 1681 he published an introductory text on geography that serves as a useful commentary on his and his father's maps and those of his contemporaries (Sanson d'Abbeville 1693). For example, he explained the convention in use for the representation of European towns:

> Towns are marked on the general map of the earth on one sheet by a simple circle; on the maps of the earth on several sheets, and on those of the five parts of the world on one or several sheets, the circle of the most important towns is amplified by several towers; on less general maps, as of a large region or a large kingdom, where several towns are amplified, the capitals are distinguished from the others by their size; on maps of one province on one sheet, where all the towns are portrayed, they are distinguished by different sizes, large, medium, and small; and on special maps that portray all the parishes, the large towns are ordinarily shown in plan or else are much amplified with several towers and bell towers, and the other towns are treated in proportion. Towns where there is a market are larger than simple parishes, and villages where there is a parish are

marked by a bell tower, at the top of which is a cross, the other villages that lack them being only simple villages or hamlets. (Sanson d'Abbeville 1693:73–74, translation mine)

Sanson *père*'s beautiful atlas, published in 1658 but containing maps dating as early as the 1630s, shows that his son's theoretical essay reflected the work of his house reasonably well, so it is worth turning again to the Sanson maps just discussed to see how the conventions are used on them. Both the *Amerique Septentrionale* of 1650 and the *Nouveau Mexique et La Floride* of 1656 appear in this atlas; the first uses circles alone for native towns in the Florida region, though circles with towers represent some Mexican towns. On the second, however, two native towns (Naguatex and Guxi) in the Spanish part of Florida and six in the French (Hustaqua, Anataqua, Utina, Potano, Edelano, and Saturiba) are represented by circles with towers, with the rest appearing as simple circles. The towns marked with towers may be those where some European presence had been established (as seems to be the case in Mexico), for the Spanish St. Augustine and St. Matheo towns on the east coast of Florida are also so marked. Sanson *fils*'s later text about Florida in his geography handbook (Sanson d'Abbeville 1693:201) recognized four different polities of the region (Apalache, Coca, Cofachiqui, and Quiqualtangui) as "small kingdoms," yet none of these are marked with towers on his father's earlier maps. His own 1674 map does reflect this thinking, however, with several Indian towns marked, including two of the listed polities.

Another convention in the Sanson atlas (not mentioned in Sanson *fils*'s text) recognizes a problem of American exploration. On several maps of South America, specifically of Peru and Brazil, interior tribes known only by names and vague location were represented by the name alone followed by a period. More settled parts of both areas show the circle and circle plus tower conventions; both maps date to 1656, clearly indicating that, even before Marquette and Jolliet, European cartographers had seen a need for some distinctive way to represent hearsay knowledge that had never been mapped. Thus the development of conventional location marks through the seventeenth century retained and regularized the circle plus tower usage, while map-makers searched for a new convention to represent "barbarian" social agglomerations and hearsay evidence. Cartographers remained dependent upon the Soto narratives for their portrayal of the interior Southeast, however, and they continued to believe in a uniformity of culture among its inhabitants:

The air is so temperate there [Florida] that old people 250 years old are often seen, and children of five consecutive generations. The land is fertile there, and full of fruit trees, and its towns the most populous of all of America. Its Apalatci mountain provides excellent copper. Its principal river is that of the Holy Spirit,

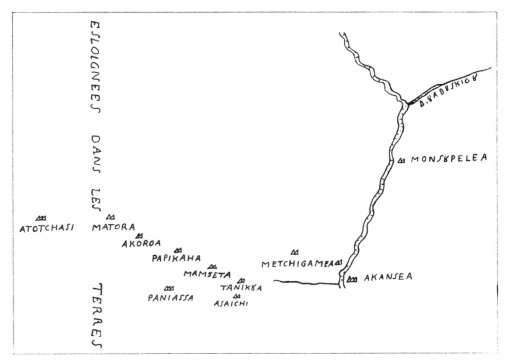

6.9. Tracing of a portion of Father Jacques Marquette's sketch map of the Mississippi, 1673–74 (original in Collège Sainte-Marie, Montréal).

which empties into the Gulf of Mexico, and its coast is very inconvenient to large vessels, because the sea has very little depth there. The hinterland there is held by the savages, governed by Paraoustis who are their lords. These savages worship the sun and the moon; and although they make war on one another, the Spaniards have not been able to subjugate them. They have the skill to enter into battle and to retire after having discharged their arrows. They have public places where they assemble for the distribution of grain that they give to every family that needs it. (Du Val 1670:56–57; translation mine)

FRENCH EXPLORERS AND THE MAPPING OF THE INTERIOR

In the year of the Sanson *fils* map this fantasy about the interior Southeast, which had endured for more than a century, began to be displaced. In 1673–74 Louis Jolliet and Father Jacques Marquette made their fateful journey down the Mississippi as far south as the Arkansas River, establishing at least one clear fact: that the Mississippi flowed south and emptied into the Gulf of Mexico. Manuscript maps executed by both Marquette and Jolliet (figures 6.9 and 6.10), though never printed, asserted their belief in this fact clearly, and their accounts were persuasive enough that map-

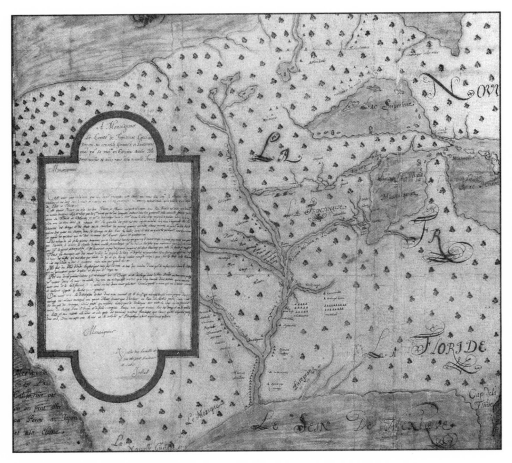

6.10. Jolliet's map of the Mississippi, 1674. Courtesy of the John Carter Brown Library at Brown University.

makers began to think in terms of a north–south flowing Mississippi with a "bay of the Holy Spirit" fed by fewer and fewer rivers and located east of it. For the remainder of the seventeenth century and the first quarter of the eighteenth, maps would portray a series of hypotheses as the shape of the interior Southeast gradually came into focus. Remnants of the old data would persist to fill blank space, but they would be squeezed out over time as more facts became available.

With the manuscript maps of the two French explorers a new convention for Indian villages appeared: a shaded triangle. In neither case is the triangle an analogue for an Indian lodging; the majority of Indians they met lived in permanent wattle-and-daub houses. Perhaps more to the point, on localized European maps of the period this triangle symbolized small peasant hamlets (Dainville 1964:228). Marquette's manuscript map uses a triangle to anchor Indian names, but Jolliet's work goes further. On the Jolliet map the draftsman has used multiple triangles, one for each village, to indicate Indian groups whose general location and number of villages were known. Most of the groups the map portrays are not southeastern; nevertheless, it is important because the use of multiple symbols to represent magnitude where location is unknown was widely adopted during the half-century of exploration to follow. Knowledge of this new practice – the conventional symbol as an arbitrary position and magnitude marker – serves as a tool for understanding what the explorers saw and resolves the confusing and false impressions created by the more representational town symbols.

This shift in convention seems to characterize another shift: to directness of observation, for one thing, and to a new dependence on Indian sources for quantitative information about tribes not seen and for direct cartographic intelligence (De Vorsey 1978; Lewis 1986; Waselkov 1989). The arrival of French explorers, who appear, on the basis of surviving evidence, to have been more inclined to produce manuscript maps and sketches than their Spanish predecessors had been, meant huge leaps in knowledge as exploration proceeded, backed by a new determination in Europe to stake claims to strategic lands by planting settlements. The French strategy of using voluntary Indian labor to extract furs is expressed cartographically in a more detailed representation of interior peoples as well as of the lands they inhabited.

The next major exploratory effort, that of La Salle, not only opened up the Mississippi but spurred the English and Spanish into new efforts as well. The "opening of the Mississippi," however, had more to do with reshaping concepts than it did with actual exploitation, and the process was reflected in a flurry of cartographic activity. In the 130 years that separated the major exploratory efforts of the Spanish and the French, progress in European cartography had begun to accelerate, and the eighteenth century would usher in a revolution in the application of scientific methods to cartography.

The period from 1670 to 1700 was crucial to French interests in the southern part of North America, as it was the beginning not only of sustained exploration but also of more frequent direct contact with native peoples of the interior Southeast. But since these peoples had already suffered seriously from disease and their relationships to one another and to their environment had altered, the maps reflecting this contact have no privileged view of what had happened in the years since first contact; our best hope is to find information that dates as early as possible in the period of "second contact," before the next wave of European disease and the effects of sustained contact.

During this brief period conflicting traditions and views were at work in the formation of the cartographic corpus. The progeny of the original Alonzo de Santa Cruz map of 1544 had had long to multiply and prosper, and at least some data on this map had become very deeply rooted in the minds and atlases of European cartographers through the odd reworkings of de Laet and the Sansons. For example, Echegaray, a Spanish inspector on his way to New Spain to examine financial records, responded with a memorial and map to the news of La Salle's colonization attempt. He claimed that his data came from the Apalachee Indians, and he said that two great rivers flowed into the "Bay of Espíritu Santo," one leading to the Movila region and one to New Spain. The countryside around the bay produced fruits like those of Spain and livestock in plenty, including a wool-bearing animal (Dunn 1917: 22–23). Echegaray's map, however much he believed it owed to Apalachee Indians, betrays a very confused notion of the hydrography of the interior that conflates the Alabama-Tombigbee and the Mississippi (figure 6.11), but it may also reflect Indian knowledge of the Alabama-Tombigbee system and its near connections with the Tennessee-Ohio system. Echegaray believed that La Salle had navigated from Canada to the mythical lake he portrayed and then down one of the rivers to the bay.

I have shown how the Sanson firm persisted in this tradition, but with the reports of the Mississippi brought back by Marquette and Jolliet new information and a new attitude were introduced into the mix. First, some native Canadian French cartographers were equal in skill to most of their fellows in France. Second, there was a newly awakened royal interest in the possibilities offered by the Mississippi, and Parisian cartographers and map publishers were not slow to grasp that fact. Third, much better knowledge of world geography was available, and the mathematical methods that supported it were widely taught and understood.

The consequences for the cartography of Indian settlement were mixed. Because of drastic improvements in the measurement of the earth, the outline of the coasts began to look very good indeed, and the unrelenting efforts of Canadian explorers and missionaries had yielded a very accurate representation of the Great Lakes region. Unfortunately, this spotty accuracy leads the casual viewer to believe erroneously that much of the other information about the interior is based on fact. On the other hand, improvements in cartography meant that many of the explorers, like Marquette and Jolliet, had been exposed to the kind of critical thinking that enabled them to make sketch maps of their travels. For although Europeans of the late seventeenth century were still limited to travel accounts for their information about southeastern North America, they were beginning to view them not with medieval credulity but in the new scientific spirit that would pervade the Enlightenment.

Several mapmakers beginning to benefit from this new knowledge had direct connections with exploration in the New World. Two of these men were working in Canada as the results of western and southerly explorations began to be available. One of them, Hugues Randin, was an engineer, assigned to the Canadian governor during the 1670s, who had done some limited wilderness exploration and knew La Salle. He produced a map of eastern North America for Frontenac (figure 6.12)

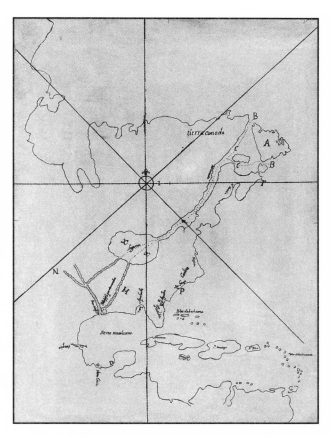

6.11. Echegaray's map of North America, 1686 (Archivo General de Indias, Seville; reproduced from a tracing in the J. P. Bryan Map Collection). Courtesy of the Center for American History, University of Texas at Austin.

giving usually only the names of tribes, but he also used the multiple-symbol device, and the symbol he used was a tiny squarish hut. These huts are not precisely representational, since when they are used in multiple they do not represent a number directly; presumably agglomerations of the symbol signified "many."

Randin's map does not add new information for the region of interest here, but it does show how persuasive an existing cartographic model could be; he summarized the discoveries of Marquette and Jolliet and connected their river (here called the "Buade") to a de Laet/Sanson-style Bay of the Holy Spirit on the Gulf. Back in France, the enthusiastic Abbé Bernou was more reserved when he prepared a summary map in 1680–81. Knowing already of La Salle's exploration plans, he left the entire Southeast virtually blank from the Ohio to the Gulf and from Texas to the Florida peninsula (figure 6.13). It would be La Salle's task to bring back the data required to get the Mississippi River right. The Bernou map suggests what French government thinking must have been as La Salle began his explorations: that the old Spanish information was not worth preserving, that it was too old to be of any use.

The Canadian mapmaker whose work has been most intimately connected with the La Salle journeys, Jean-Baptiste Franquelin, did not entirely share this view.

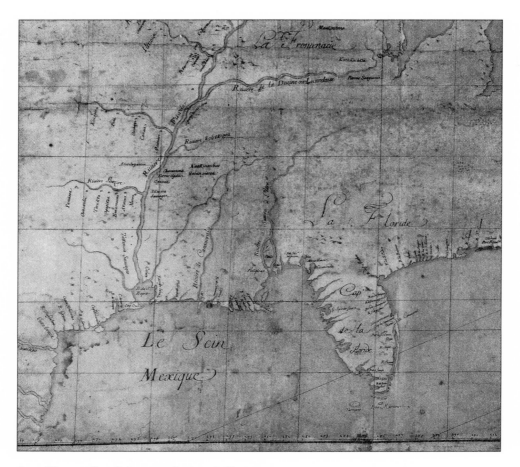

6.12. Hugues Randin's map of 1674–81(?). Courtesy of the John Carter Brown Library at Brown University.

Rather than leave blank an area that had been partially explored, in 1681 he drew a map virtually identical to Randin's, in which the Mississippi emptied directly into the "Baye du St Esprit" (figure 6.14). His map implies a remarkable degree of consensus in favor of the Marquette-Jolliet-Randin model of a Mississippi that flowed southward without significant changes in direction; it also emphasizes the dramatic change brought about by the new evidence of the La Salle exploration.

La Salle's reports had confirmed that the Mississippi did not empty into a huge bay, but they had not offered any evidence as to the existence or nonexistence of such a bay. The mapmakers thus took the mouth of the Mississippi to be further west than the Bay of the Holy Spirit, yet they continued to show the bay on their maps (where it would eventually metamorphose into Mobile Bay). What they did with the course of the Mississippi to compensate ranged from the ingenious to the bizarre. According to Delanglez (1943a), Franquelin copied and refined a sketch map made by La Salle in 1683 or 1684 (see figure 6.15a), and on this map the Mississippi makes a drastic

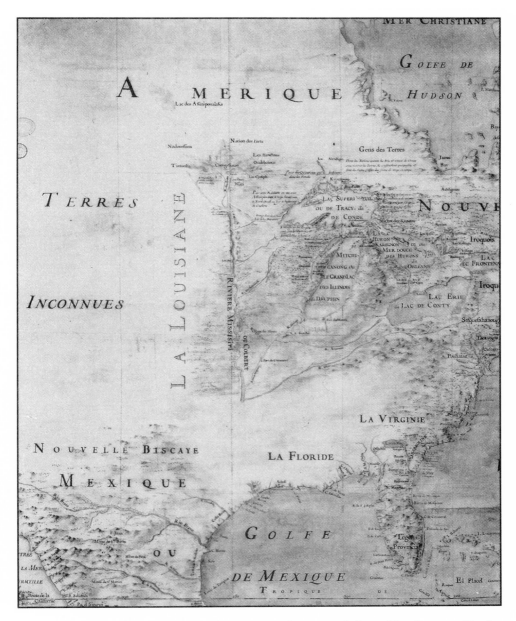

6.13. Abbé Bernou's *Carte de l'Amerique septentrionale et partie de la meridionale . . .* , 1680–81. Courtesy of the Bibliothèque Nationale de France, Paris.

detour to the west between the Chickasaw Bluffs and the Red River, then empties into the Gulf of Mexico through a bird-foot delta situated well west of the notorious bay, which is shown directly south of Lake Michigan. The engineer Minet who was sent on La Salle's second expedition drew a similar map around 1685 (figure 6.15b).

Both of these maps are interesting for their hydrography, but they are more rele-

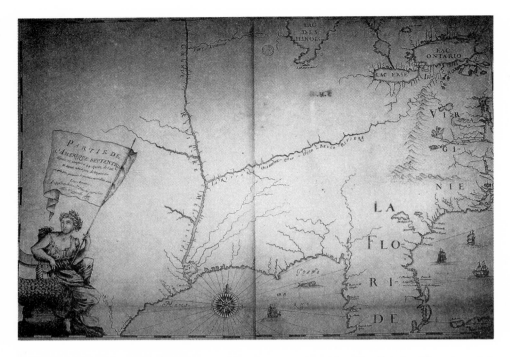

6.14. Jean-Baptiste Franquelin's *Partie de l'Amerique septentrionale*, 1681 (Service Historique de la Marine, Vincennes, cartes, recueil 66, no. 4; reproduced from a photostat in the Karpinski Series). Courtesy of the Newberry Library.

vant here for their new evidence of Indian settlement. The Franquelin map introduced a new convention: a dotted line around the lands of several known native groups of the Old Southwest. Only a tracing of this map survives, but it suggests that a tower symbol was used to indicate towns. Though the Yazoo Basin has been turned on its side, "les Cicaça" are shown at its northern border, just as La Salle met them in 1682 (Stubbs 1982a); the "Akansea" are shown occupying a region of convoluted hydrography that includes the lowlands west of the Mississippi as well as part of the southern Yazoo Basin, and the "Tounica" and "Yasou" occupy the eastern edge of the basin. The "Taensa" are shown west of the river and south of the Akansea. The lower end of the Mississippi is missing, as the map was torn, but text on the map states that east of the Mississippi, north of the Gulf, and west of the great bay "there are . . . many savages whose names are not known." Franquelin's map retains the old Spanish data: on the bay's one remaining river (du Saint Esprit, of course) is the town symbol for Coça, while Tascaluça appears on the next river east and Chisca on the next, in almost perfect agreement with Sanson's 1656 map. Franquelin's subsequent printed portrayals of the region followed the same pattern but removed the Spanish nomenclature and hydrography east of the bay. Only the "Pays de Chicacha" remained in position between the upper Yazoo and the bay. Minet's map, though it avoids making

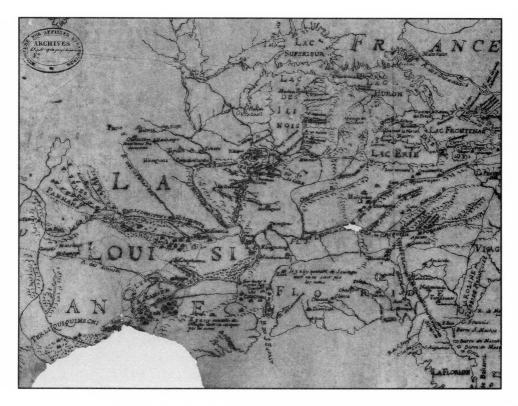

6.15. (*a*) D'Anville copy of Jean-Baptiste Franquelin's *Carte de la Louisiane En l'Amerique Septentrionale . . . ou sont decris les Pays que le Sieur de La Salle a decouverts . . .* , 1684 (Ge DD 2987, No. 8782). Courtesy of the Bibliothèque Nationale de France, Paris.

a choice by calling both the Mississippi and the river emptying into the bay by the Spanish "Choucagoua," uses fewer of the old Spanish towns, as newly discovered peoples and places crowd them out.

Another solution to the problem of the river's course was set forth by the celebrated Italian cartographer Coronelli. He showed the Mississippi as a predominantly north–south river beginning well west of Lake Superior and ending far south on the Texas coast. In his 1684 manuscript sketch for the maps that were to follow (figure 6.16a), Coronelli showed details and notes regarding the Indian groups La Salle had met, including the earliest known list of names for the Chickasaw villages and the alternative name of "Oughilousa" for the elusive Quinipissas (which Franquelin showed as two villages in 1685). He must have obtained this information from the La Salle expedition, either from a manuscript now lost or from oral testimony given while Coronelli was in France to execute the great globes he made for Louis XIV (Pelletier 1982). On this sketch Coronelli did not often portray villages, but when he did he used a sort of "pup-tent" symbol (notably for the Taensas clustered around their cut-off lake). Clearly he had also read an account of the voyage, for his under-

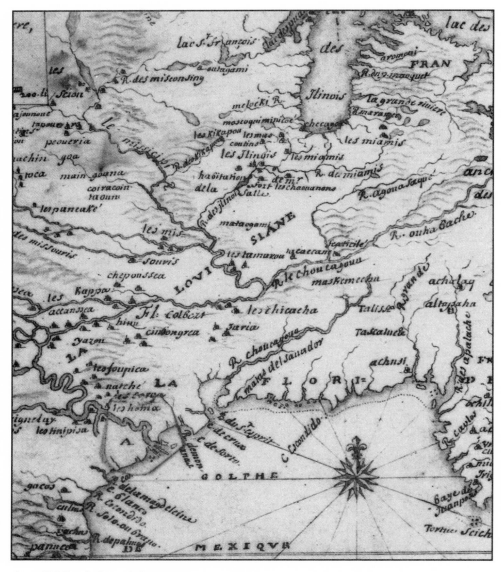

6.15. (*b*) Minet's *Carte de la Louisiane*, 1685 (Bibliothèque du Service Hydrographique c 4044-4; reproduced from a photostat in the Karpinski Series). Courtesy of the Newberry Library.

standing of the location of the Quapaw villages vis-à-vis the Arkansas and Mississippi Rivers and the Yazoo Basin accurately reflects the narrative accounts now extant. Subsequent globes (1683, 1688, 1696; see figure 6.16b) by Coronelli simplify these data somewhat but do not change the hydrography established in this sketch. And although Coronelli did keep the blessed bay, he confined all the dubious Spanish Florida evidence beyond a dotted line and omitted native names from that area.

This conflict over the interior geography of the Old Southwest could only be solved with new evidence. Although La Salle's next journey to reach the Mississippi from the Gulf was not destined to provide it, Tonti's various journeys to find La Salle did begin to fuel cartographers' speculations. Several extant sketches, harking back to the north–south Jolliet model but incorporating information from Tonti about the Indians of the lower river, foreshadow the effects of massive injections of information that were soon to come. In France, scientific cartography was progressing under the brilliant Cassini; his student and colleague Claude Delisle and his sons were to revolutionize the mapping of America.

Claude Delisle is said by some to have been more historian than cartographer, and later in the eighteenth century it was popular to undervalue his house's work as "armchair cartography" that depended in the old-fashioned way on travel accounts rather than on scientific survey and mapping. This evaluation has some truth to it, yet the Delisle Papers preserved in the French archives (Isnard 1915; Delanglez 1943b) show how much more can be made of traditional sources when a scientific attitude informs their use. Claude Delisle and his sons were called upon to accomplish mapping tasks of vast scope: the Americas and Russia. In neither case has complete mapping by terrestrial survey *ever* been carried out; satellite data is the source for modern maps of areas so large and underpopulated that many regions have not been visited in living memory. Joseph-Nicolas Delisle, the astronomer son who undertook to map Russia for the imperial government in 1728, expounded the methodology used previously by his father and brother in the Americas when he described his plan of work: "to gather together all Russian maps, manuscript or engraved, naval journals and travel accounts, to collect the greatest possible number of astronomical observations, and, before using these different sources of information, to submit them to a severely critical examination" (Isnard 1915:44; translation mine).

That this was exactly the way Claude and his more famous son, Guillaume, proceeded is abundantly clear upon examination of the Delisle Papers. This collection, organized and systematized by Joseph-Nicolas himself after the deaths of his father and brothers and his own return from Russia, contains working notes, maps copied from other authors, narrative travel accounts, working map sketches and drafts, final map drafts ready for the engraver, and proof copies of engraved maps. Its coverage is worldwide, and the material for North America is quite complete, as shown by Delanglez's (1943b) collation of Claude's list of sources for one map with the extant materials. The Delisle papers are valuable because they enable us to detect the sources of new information as it appears on their successive maps.

This new information came thick and fast at the turn of the century. The 1696 draft *Carte de la Nouvelle France et les Pays Voisins* and two related pieces (figure 6.17a–c) show that the Delisles began their work on North America with a conception

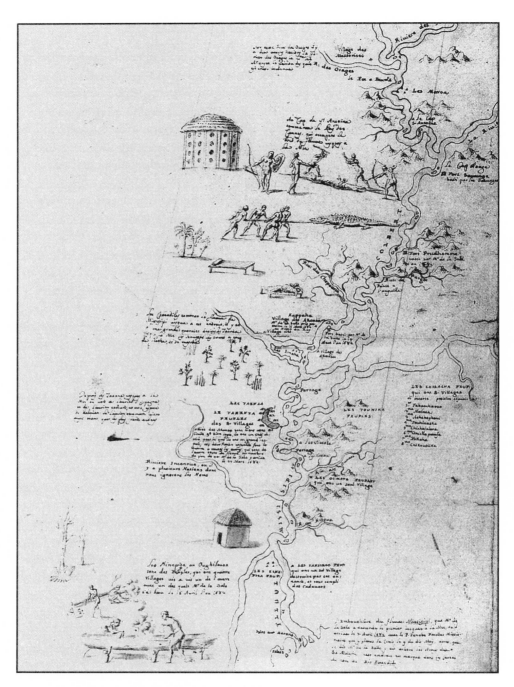

6.16. (*a*) *Left* Coronelli's manuscript sketch of the Mississippi, 1684; (*b*) *Right* Coronelli's globe gore, 1696. (*a*) courtesy of the Map Collection, Yale University Library; image enhancement courtesy of the Engineering Research Center for Computational Field Simulation, Mississippi State University; (*b*) courtesy of the Mississippi Department of Archives and History.

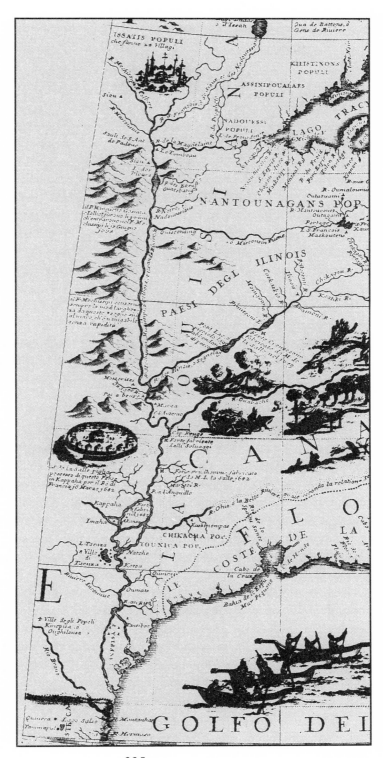

6.17. (*a*) *Left* Delisle 1696 draft, AN 178-32 (Marine 6JJ 75¹ pièce 128¹); (*b*) *Top, right* Delisle 1696 draft (blank cartouche), AN 178-31 (Marine 6JJ 75¹ pièce 128²); (*c*) *Bottom, right* Delisle, *Carte de la Nouvelle France et des pays voisins*, 1696, AN 178-29 (Marine 6JJ 75¹ pièce 130). Courtesy of the Archives Nationales, Paris.

borrowed from Coronelli, and they ignored the Spanish nomenclature to a great extent as he had done. Apparently, however, only a few maps deriving from this concept were printed around 1700 (Schwartz and Taliaferro 1984; Historical New Orleans Collection 1986) before the Delisles seriously altered the shape of the lower Mississippi based on information from Iberville's first 1699 journey to the Gulf of Mexico.

Iberville's information changed two major aspects of the Delisle map: the configuration of the western end of the Gulf coast and the hydrography and nomenclature for peoples of the interior. The former information came from experienced sailors and pilots spending enough time in the area to obtain a better knowledge of its absolute location and its physical configuration. The latter information tapped a major new source, first used by Marquette and Jolliet and now exploited systematically for the first time in the Gulf region: Indian informants.

Lewis (1986) has pointed out several methods by which we may recognize unacknowledged Indian contributions to European maps; he mentions the straight

236

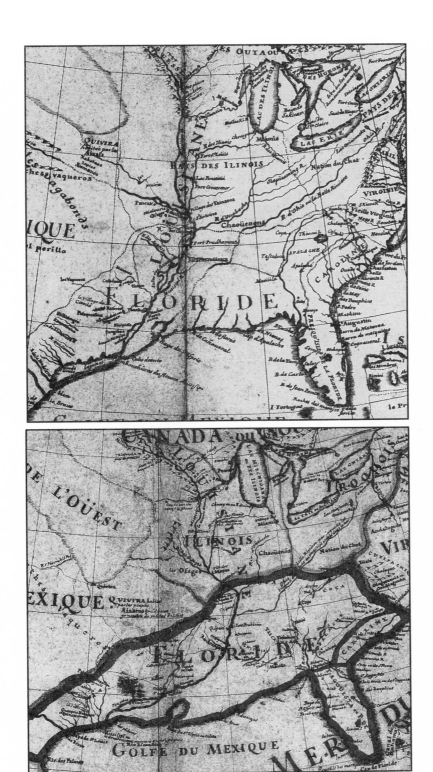

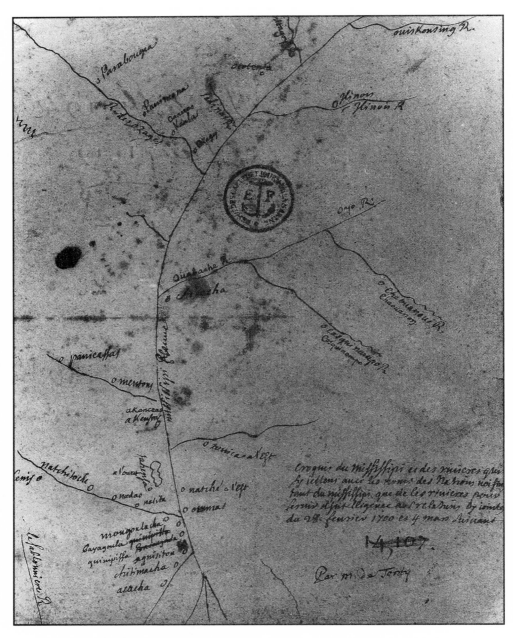

6.18. (*a*) *Left* Sketch map of the Mississippi attributed to Henri de Tonti, 1700, AN 194-1,19 (Marine 6JJ 75² pièce 249); (*b*) *Right* Delisle's *Partie du Mississipi et rivieres adjacent*, ca. 1700, AN 194-1,33 (Marine 6JJ 75² pièce 250). Courtesy of the Archives Nationales, Paris.

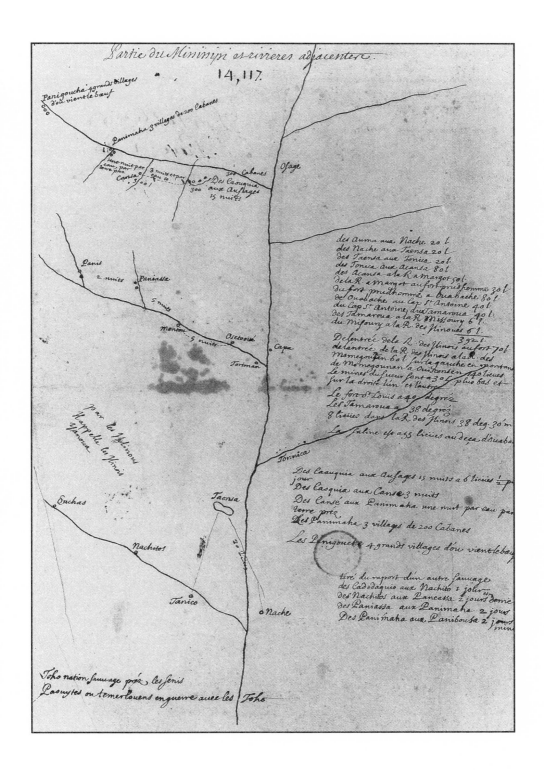

Partie du Mississipi et rivieres adjacentes.

14,117.

Panigoucha 4 grands villages
d'ou vient le bauf

Panimaha 3 villages de 200 Cabanes

une nuit par
eau par
terre près
Canse

3 nuits et par
eau 10

300 Cabanes

300

Des Caouquia
aux Aufages
15 nuits

Osage

Panis

2 nuits

Paniassa

5 nuits

Mentou

5 nuits

Oscotové

Torimän

Capa

par les Ilinous
s'appelle les Ilinois
Yamoua

Tonnica

Enchas

Taensa

Nachitos

Tanîco

Nache

des Auma aux Nache 20 l
des Nache aux Taensa 20 l
des Taensa aux Tonica 20 l
des Tonica aux Acansa 80 l
des Acansa a la R. a Margot 30 l
de la R. a Margot au fort prudhomme 30 l
du fort prudhomme a Ouabache 80 l
de Ouabache au Cap St Antoine 40 l
du Cap St Antoine du Tamaroua 40 l
des Tamaroua a la R. Missoury 40 l
du Missoury a la R. des Ilinoues 6 l

392 l

De l'entrée de la R. des Ilinois au fort 70 l
de l'entrée de la R. des Ilinois a la R. des
Momegouïen 60 l sur la gauche en montant
de Momegounan a Ouikonsen 140 lieues
Le mines d'argent sont a 3 ou 4 plus bas et
sur la droite l'un et l'autre

Le fort St Louis a 40 degré
Les Tamaroua a 38 degré
8 lieües dans la R. des Ilinois 38 deg. 30 m

La Saline est a 55 lieües au deça d'Ouaba

Des Caouquia aux Aufages 15 nuits a 6 lieües ½ p
jour
Des Casquia aux Canse 3 nuits
Des Canse aux Panimaha une nuit par eau par
terre près
Des Panimaha 3 villages de 200 Cabanes

Les Panigoucha 4 grands villages d'ou vient le bau

tiré du raport d'un autre sauvage
des Cadodaquio aux Nachito 1 jour
des Nachitos aux Paneassa 2 jours demi
des Paniassa aux Panimaha 2 jours
Des Panimaha aux Panibousa 2 jours
min

Toho nation sauvage près les Senis
Paouytes ou temerlouens en guerre avec les Toho

239

conception of the Mississippi and its tributaries found on Coronelli's map as possibly reflecting a schematized style of native depiction of hydrography. In view of Coronelli's undoubted use of materials derived from Marquette and Jolliet (and probably from Franquelin's 1681 *Partie de l'Amérique septentrionale*) and the changes in these sources' representation of tribal location, this possibility is quite likely. As the lower Mississippi was increasingly traveled by explorers more and more in touch with local Indians, this "fish-spine" model for the Mississippi returned to enter the lists against the exaggeratedly sinuous portrayals of Franquelin and Minet. Such drawings are attributed to Tonti (*Croquis du Mississipi*, 1700; see figure 6.18a), the most experienced European Mississippi traveler before the coming of the Le Moynes, and to others he escorted (Archives of the Seminary of Quebec, SQ, nos. 41 and 43; see also Jacques Bureau's 1700 sketch of the Mississippi River, Chicago Historical Society), and they retain the schematization of the Mississippi mouth that brings it flat against a straight east-west shore – a practice cited by Lewis (1986:15) as characterizing Indian maps – when Tonti knew from personal experience that the river made a considerable bend to the southeast. The Delisles apparently also made such a map at one point (*Partie du Mississipi et rivieres adjacentes*, figure 6.18b); it shows the course of the river and its main tributaries from the Missouri to the Red River confluence, and the profuse notes that accompany it include lists of tribal names that can be matched point for point with testimony from the Taensa guide Iberville picked up at the Oumas; according to Iberville's testimony (1981:70–76), the guide drew a map that covered the river and its tributaries and inhabitants from about the Red River to the Arkansas. If the Delisle map is not a draft of that Indian map, then it reflects Delisle's reading of Iberville's logs exactly.

Because of the overwhelming importance of the Delisles's work, we need to understand their procedures for evaluating and assimilating evidence and to trace in detail the development of information on their maps about Indian tribes. As has been seen, they first collected all available maps, journals, travel accounts, and astronomical observations. Their map sketches show that they had a precise method of converting narrative evidence to cartographic depiction: they drew a conventionalized outline of the region covered by the narrative and then marked on that sketch the relative locations and dates of events together with any mentions of distance. In this way they constructed a primitive triangulation using distances (converted from inferred days of travel where no other evidence was available) that permitted them to place locations in the interior working from more precisely known locations on the coast (many of whose latitudes, at least, were known from explicit observations). To assure the relative accuracy of the distances, they sought testimony from different observers that covered the same region: the collection includes some thirty maps of the St. Lawrence and upper Great Lakes region, for example – many of them identical

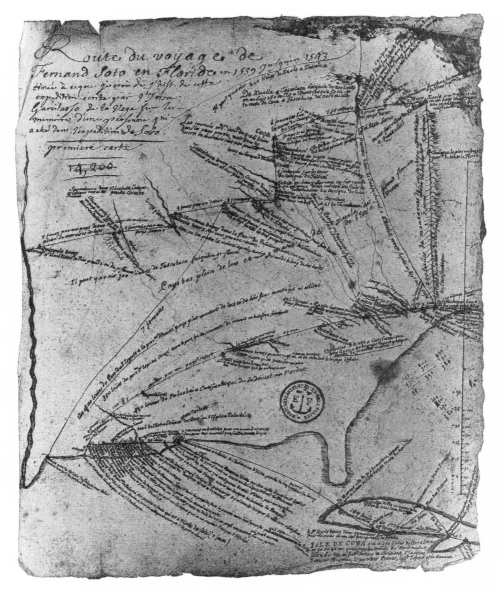

6.19. Delisle's sketch map *Route du voyage de Fernand Soto en Floride . . . premiere carte*, AN 192-1,11 (Marine 6JJ 75² pièce 231C). Courtesy of the Archives Nationales, Paris.

outline sketches – drawn from explorers' accounts; twenty-three of these systematically set forth the geographical information from the *Jesuit Relations*, year by year. Data from narrative accounts of the Southeast were more scarce, but the Delisles systematically exploited what they could find: there are Delisle sketches tracing the explorations of Verrazano, Walter Raleigh, John Smith, Narváez, Ponce de León, Ayllón, Soto (figures 6.19, 6.20), Ribaut, and Laudonnière.

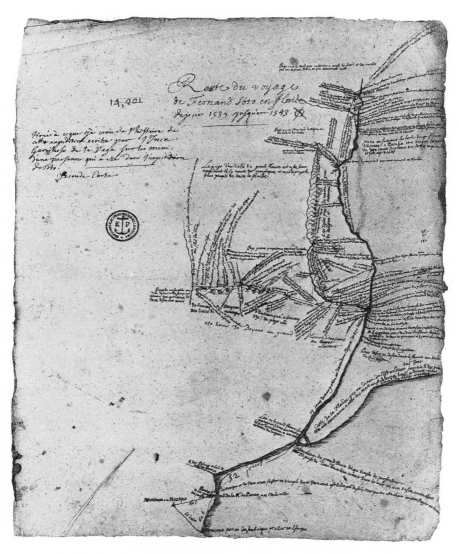

6.20. Delisle's sketch map *Route du voyage de Fernand Soto en Floride . . . seconde carte*, AN 192-1,14 (Marine 6JJ 75² pièce 231B). Courtesy of the Archives Nationales, Paris.

Another procedure the Delisles followed was to copy out all or part of the maps of other cartographers, not because they could not get sustained access to the originals (the Delisle house had royal patronage at least from 1702) but because no other method could better familiarize a cartographer with the information and the decisions of another. To this end they copied Spanish portolan charts of the coastlines; maps of Franquelin, Sanson, de Fer, Minet, and English mapmakers; sketches by Iberville, Remonville, Le Maire, and Dumont de Montigny; and possibly the maps of Indian informants as well. This wide variety of maps from practiced and unpracticed hands provided them with additional information to collate.

The Delisles also had access to a very precious resource: the explorers themselves. Their use of these men can be seen in the manuscript part of the collection, which includes not only extracts from published sources but correspondence and journals of such men as Tonti, Joutel, Iberville, and Le Sueur. Among this material can be found lists of questions, arising, for example, from narrative sources, that were to be put to the explorers by letter or in person. Iberville's logs reflect cartographic concerns, as they record inland latitude sightings all along the rivers he explored, and the Delisle papers contain further interviews with the explorer upon his returns to France.

All these sources were used in a series of extraordinary sketches, drafts, and finished maps from 1696 to 1718. Many of these are worthy of individual monographs; here I will deal only with the area of interest unless data elsewhere on the map can help us to date it. I have already considered the productions that date to 1696 and that reflect the Coronelli configuration for the Mississippi. Interestingly, the Delisles apparently never seriously considered the Franquelin-Minet conception of the twisted river, although the extreme westward curve on the first Coronelli-style draft (AN 178-29, not pictured here) may reflect influence from that model. Until 1984 these drafts were thought to be nothing but drafts, but we now know that the Delisles had enough confidence in that configuration to engrave and print some copies of it in 1700. Changes were made, however, for a reengraving that duplicated this map except for several alterations in the Mississippi and its tributaries and the Gulf coast. Since this is the first printed map on which the name of the Choctaw tribe appears, the source of the information (and thus its likelihood of accuracy) are important.

The information came from Iberville, of course, but more precise identification of the source is possible. Schwartz and Taliaferro (1984) argue that some of these data were available to the Delisles as early as 1699 but that for political reasons they proceeded with the printing of what they knew to be an outdated map (figure 6.21a). The 1700 "second state" of this map, however, shows the location of Fort Mississippi, established on the 1700 voyage, so it is apparently up-to-date to that extent (figure 6.21b). And while the "first state" shows the Red River with a dotted hypothetical lower course that connects with the Mississippi at about Vicksburg, the "second state" shows it joining a brand-new Marne River (mentioned by Iberville on his second voyage, 1700) just before emptying into the Mississippi. The first state shows only sparse Spanish data (Maouila on a "Nieves" River, Aute, Tascaluca, and Coça on a long river at the eastern end of the north Gulf coast) and La Salle's Sicacha east of the Mississippi; the second state adds the Tonica (on a new Yazoo), the "Chaqueta" indicated by a circle on the east side of the Tombigbee above the fork, Mobila within the fork, and Tascaluca and Coça moved slightly westward but not on a river, although their previous river remains in place. This new information appears

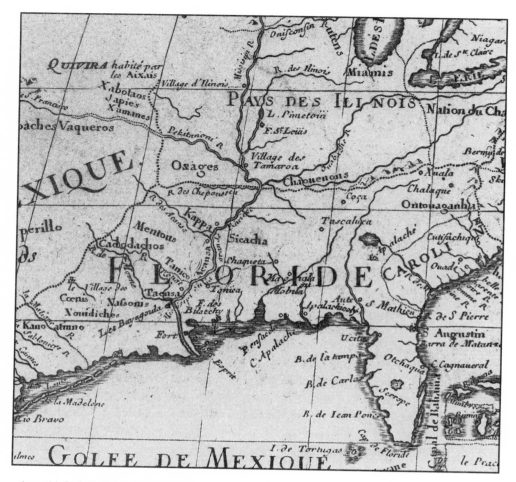

6.21. (*a*) *Left* Delisle, *L'Amerique septentrionale*, 1700, first state (THNOC acc. no. 1985.230); (*b*) *Right* Delisle, *L'Amerique septentrionale*, 1700, second state. (*a*) courtesy of the Historic New Orleans Collection, Museum/Research Center; (*b*) courtesy of the Library of Congress.

on a sketch map in the Delisle collection that also shows the location of "44 villages of the nation of the Chaquetas."

This sketch map (figure 6.22) is worthy of attention first for its portrayal of the hydrography. It contains the first realistic views of the lower Mississippi, Mobile Bay, the Tombigbee, and (surprisingly) the Pascagoula delta and river. The map must date from before 1701–2, since it shows Fort Maurepas on Biloxi Bay (founded 1699) but not Fort Louis north of Mobile Bay (founded 1702). Delisle did not mark overtly the extent of his informants' knowledge, but this is plainly visible in the conventions used to mark the locations of the Indian nations. The old-fashioned symbol of a single building with a tower on a slight rise depicts the Quinca, Tacapa, Tcheiou, Anilco,

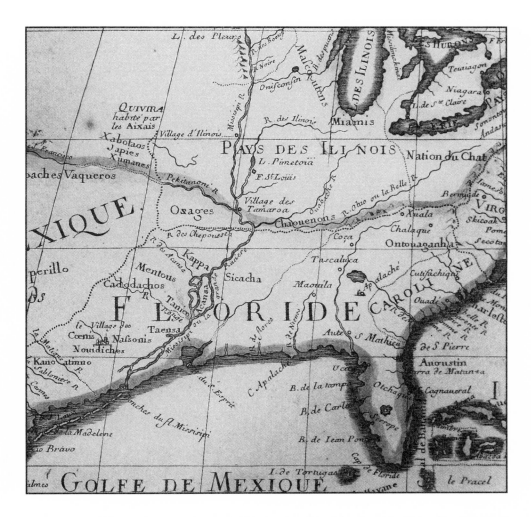

and Cheloels, most more legendary than real. The names of most other nations, those actually known to informants, are preceded by the definite article. The sources of the names are various. Some were named by Iberville's Indian informant: Theloel, Amylcou, Chycacha. Anilco had been present on maps of the Southeast from de Laet, as had Capaha (Tacapa?). Tcheiou probably refers to the Tioux, also mentioned in Iberville's journal. The Quinca remain unexplained, and the others seem rather randomly placed.

The Indian groups with whom Iberville had contact or of whom he received clear information are *not* randomly placed, but some are more directly represented than others, notably "les nadchers" shown with ten "house" symbols (the number of villages named in Iberville's log) located north of the Red River (called Sablonnière here) and east of the Mississippi, and the "44 villages de la nation des chaquetas," shown with exactly forty-four such symbols located on the west side of the Tombigbee and north of a large fork in the Pascagoula. Within that fork are the Capinans

245

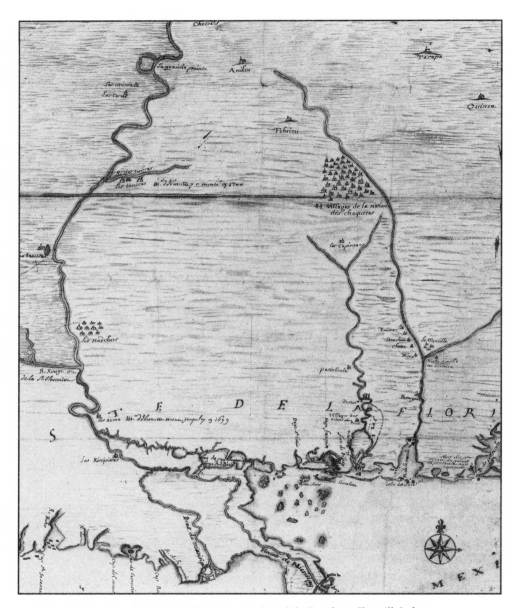

6.22. Delisle sketch of the lower Mississippi and Mobile Bay from Iberville's data, ca. 1700, ASH 138bis-1,5. Courtesy of the Archives Nationales, Paris.

(one house) and further down the Pascagoula the Pascoboula (replicated on the Mobile River as Pastogoula) and Biloxi (noted as abandoned). The tribes on the Tombigbee-Alabama-Mobile system are also shown in some detail, reflecting some of the same information Levasseur had obtained. The Aepatanis and Mogoulacha are placed on what may be meant as the Coosa River. West of the lower Tombigbee

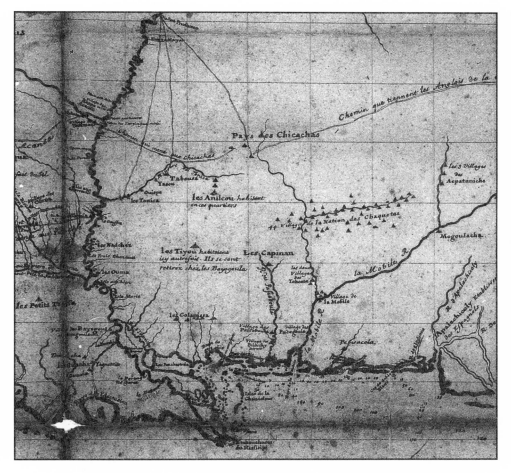

6.23. Delisle, *Carte des Environs du Missisipi par G. de l'Isle Geographe*, 1701, AN 193-12 (Marine 6JJ 75² pièce 253). Courtesy of the Archives Nationales, Paris.

above the forks are the Tounia (Tohomé?; two houses), the Etouchoco (one house), the Choila (one house), and the Minco (one house); in the forks is La Movilla (four houses) and east of the Alabama River at the forks is "Old Movilla or [?] Michica." Obviously the location of the Choctaws is of greatest interest here, but the cartographic fate of the other inhabitants of the Pascagoula and Tombigbee-Alabama watersheds is also of interest as a check on the persistence of this data in the face of additional information.

Further information was certainly forthcoming, for Iberville made yet another voyage, and his younger brother Bienville explored along with the redoubtable Le Sueur. A related group of three maps resulted, all dated to ca. 1701 (figures 6.23, 6.24, 6.25) and all manifesting a remarkable change in the location of the Choctaw villages. Because these three maps have been stored in separate archival series, they

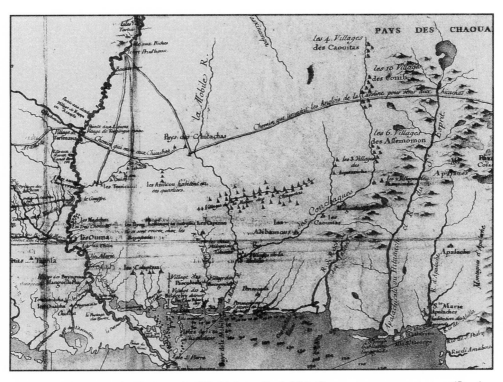

6.24. Delisle, *Carte des Environs du Missisipi par G. de l'Isle Geogr.*, 1701, BSH C4040-4 (Service Historique de la Marine, receuil 69, carte no. 4). Courtesy of the Service Historique de la Marine, Vincennes.

have never before been brought together so that the repetition of this change could be obvious. These maps also contain many additional changes, most of them clear additions to knowledge, and they are not by any means exactly alike: I presume that figure 6.23, although it is engraved and not manuscript, represents the first draft of southeastern North America using the new information because it is relatively sparse for that region. Figure 6.24, also engraved, repeats this information and adds more. Figure 6.25, a manuscript map still retaining many of the features of the other two, is a new beginning for the next iteration in the mapping of the Southeast. Although other relationships suggest that the sequence was not simply linear, all three maps agree on moving most of the forty-four Choctaw villages, first shown in the sketch just discussed, across the Tombigbee, to be strung out along a newly added river where the Black Warrior ought to be. Two of the maps actually repeat the full forty-four symbols.

One might conclude that somehow the order of the Delisle maps cited so far has been reversed and they are wrongly dated – it is hard to imagine the Delisles adding retrograde information. But the content of the maps belies this suspicion: the 1700

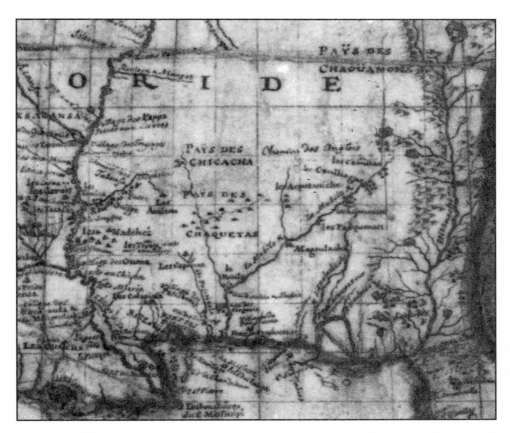

6.25. Delisle 1701 draft (no cartouche), ASH 140-4; reproduced from a photostat in the Karpinski Series. Courtesy of the Newberry Library.

printed second state (figure 6.21b) is clearly marked 1700; the sketch (figure 6.22) explicitly cites Iberville's 1699 and 1700 explorations; the three 1701 maps represent a dramatic increase in the quantity and accuracy not only of data about the Indians but of hydrography as well. The Delisles could have assumed that the Choctaws lived on an eastern Tombigbee fork, perhaps thinking of the Pascagoula drainage as occupied by the Capinans. Another possibility is that not all the Choctaws had yet settled on the upper reaches of the Pascagoula. A potential hint of this is on the sketch: Etouchouco, a village shown just west of the Tombigbee-Alabama forks on the sketch (figure 6.22), was still the name of a river among the Choctaw villages in 1729 (Rowland and Sanders 1927–32, 1:94); by then the name was attached to the region of the upper Chickasawhay River. The somewhat confused account in later French documents of the wanderings of Chickasawhay villages under the pressure of slave raids does imply that their movement was westward (Rowland and Sanders 1927–32, 1:156–57). This apparent cartographic anomaly (soon corrected) could reflect some such information given to the French, but proving it would require finding something in the Delisle papers that could have been responsible for the impression.

Even if we cannot solve these problems conclusively with the data at hand, other relevant information appears on the maps. The locations of the other tribes portrayed closer to the Mississippi are virtually identical on the three maps: the Ouma and Natchez on the Mississippi; the Tonica, Ouispe, Yazou, and Tabousa up the Yazoo and, after a sharp turn south, the Anilcou at its source; the Colapissa at the sources of several small rivers flowing south into Lake Pontchartrain and Mississippi Sound; and the Bilocchy (village destroyed), Pascoboula, and Capinans up the Pascagoula, with the Tiyou between Natchez and Capinan (where the Pearl River ought to be). The detail along the Yazoo, new since the sketch, can be traced to Iberville's log (1981:73) and to the narratives of the missionaries who visited there and started a mission in 1699. The Tiyou are indicated as having "formerly" lived in the new map location but having withdrawn among the Bayougoulas; this information must have come from Iberville's logs as well (1981:143). The Colapissa do not appear on the sketch at all, and indeed their presence was not suspected until Sauvole began to explore the Pearl River after the first French fort was established at Biloxi.

Another feature of some interest is the data regarding trails and routes. The sketch (figure 6.22) showed none, but the 1701 "sparse" engraving (figure 6.23) indicates a path from Charles Towne to the Chicachas; three paths from the Prudhomme Bluffs to the Chicacha, Tabousa, and Tonica; a path from the Quapaw trade house to the Chicachas (not linked to the English one); a path from "Baye St. Louis" (Matagorda Bay) to the Quapaws; and a route from Mexico City to Matagorda Bay. All were shown as double dotted lines. The second engraved 1701 map (figure 6.24) repeats all those routes, using a double solid line; the Chickasaw trails still do not connect and in fact terminate at different town symbols. This map also notes for the first time that the Tennessee-Ohio is the "route taken by the French to reach Carolina" (cf. Crane 1916 and Galloway 1991b). The 1701 "next-iteration" draft (figure 6.25) shows only the two Chicacha paths as a single dotted line, presumably because its scale is much smaller, but it indicates the sea route of La Salle in 1684–85. Though some of the information comes from Iberville, most details seem based on the missionaries' reports, Jean Cavelier's journal, and Joutel.

The three 1701 maps reveal a fairly dramatic evolution in the Delisles's thinking about the region's hydrography, and the first interesting detail may reflect an Indian source once more. The 1700 maps (both states) contained an unlabeled river at the extreme eastern end of the northern Gulf coast. Figure 6.23, thought to be the base map of 1701, shows merely a small river there called River of the Apalachees. The second 1701 map (figure 6.24), however, has an additional river, drawn in great detail and called "Apalachicoli, ou Hitanachi ou R. du St. Esprit" (for the long history of this last name at the *eastern* end of the Gulf see Delanglez 1945). Many of its tributaries spring from the "tadpole" lakes that Lewis (1986) has shown often mark Indian-derived hydrography, yet no Indians are indicated as inhabiting it; the Apalachees revert to their own smaller river, almost identical to the one on figure 6.23. The Delisles, having taken over the name of the Apalachicola as one of the names of this new river, renamed the Apalachicola to St. Roch or Indian River. This new river (presumably the Chattahoochee) has an interesting history: it moves east one river on the "next-iteration" draft (6.25), disappears entirely on the 1702 map (6.28), and then reappears in 1703 (6.29a). Complexities like these make the chronological placement of map drafts difficult, since some of the drafts were almost certainly being created simultaneously, embodying alternative "explanations" of fragmentary data.

The transformations in the depiction of the Alabama river system also exhibit alternative developments, beginning with the data obviously taken from the sketch. On figures 6.23–25 the Aepataniche and Mogoulacha are still located on the now obvious Coosa, but their numbers of symbols are reversed and the Mogoulacha are now south of the fork. La Mobila, represented again by four symbols, is in the Tombigbee-Alabama fork. On figure 6.23 a segment of the "Mobile" River (now known as the Alabama) stretches nearly directly northeast from the Tombigbee (unnamed here) forks to the Appalachians, with only one significant tributary. The Mogoulacha are placed opposite that tributary, followed by the "two villages of the Pasquenan," "6 villages of the Assemomon," "10 villages of the Conihaque," and "four villages of the Caouitas." The "next-iteration" draft (figure 6.25) places the new river *east* of the Appalachians and thus keeps this configuration, but being of smaller scale, it omits the numbers of villages. The second engraved map (figure 6.24) retains all these details, but because it has to fit the new river in *west* of the Appalachians, it has the "Mobile" River of the two other maps (6.23 and 6.25) – now renamed "River of the Conchaques" because "La Mobile" is reserved for the Tombigbee – turn almost due north opposite the Pasquenan villages. In addition, it adds groups of Alibamons and Caouitas between the two major forks.

These maps raise several questions. First, what was the source of this detailed information about the Alabama River inhabitants? No known Frenchman went this early among all the peoples mentioned. The 1700 sketch map showed nothing further east than the Coosa River fork, reflecting no additional information from Iberville's logs. Instead, the data must have come from Indian informants who reported to Levasseur when he explored the Mobile delta (Levasseur 1981; Villiers du Terrage 1922). The lack of exploration accounts from the interior east of the Mississippi becomes obvious when the portrayal of that area is compared with the great detail shown north of the Red River that reflects Bienville's journal of his journey from the

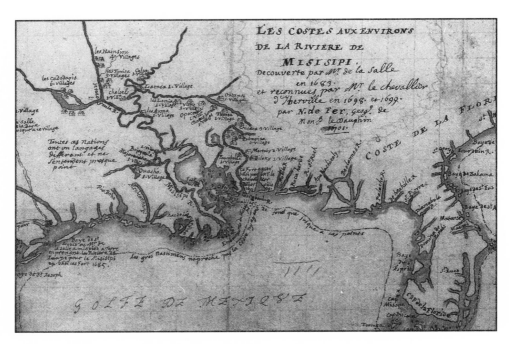

6.26. Nicolas de Fer, *Les Costes aux environs de la riviere de Misisipi*, 1701 (Service Historique de la Marine, receuil 69, carte no. 5). Courtesy of the Service Historique de la Marine, Vincennes.

Taensa to the "Yatache" and that is even legended as such on the "sparse" engraved map (6.23) and the engraved map (6.24; cf. Iberville 1981:146–56).

The influence of another man's map across this trio is additionally illuminating, suggesting that seemingly arbitrary changes may actually reflect dialogue with a source. A 1701 manuscript map by Nicolas de Fer, or a tracing of it, *Les Costes aux environs de la Riviere de Misisipi* (figure 6.26), claiming to cover La Salle's discovery in 1683 [*sic*] and Iberville's rediscovery in 1698–99, is part of the Delisle collection. Its hydrography of the lower Mississippi is related to and even more convoluted than that of Franquelin and Minet but does substitute Mobile Bay for the Bay of the Holy Spirit. Of more interest to the Delisles, de Fer drew an odd arrangement of two large islands through which flowed the Apalachicoly River to the west and the Beloannes River to the east, making the figure of a rough rectangle with the gulf for its southern edge and a diagonal river from northwest to southeast. This precise arrangement appears on two of the 1701 Delisle maps (6.23 and 6.25), but on the third (6.24) this unlikely hydrography has been rationalized so that this feature becomes the delta of the single River St. Roch – which de Fer had also indicated, west of his Apalachicoly-Beloanne construction.

The three related Delisle maps, then, show their cartographic thinking in process. The maps do not represent similar degrees of certainty, nor, presumably, does any one of them represent their final views on the data. These working versions are just

6.27. Tracing of BSH c4040-4 indicating explicitly French-explored areas as of 1700.

that, yet without them we would not know the cartographers' practice of trying and then discarding various possibilities. Two things become abundantly clear, however: except for explicitly explored areas (shown on a tracing of BSH c4040-4 in figure 6.27) the data on tribal locations came from Indian informants; and although the Delisles felt free to move the (presumably inferred) rivers around, they did not move the tribal locations *as referenced to those rivers* without concrete information. This habit makes the mystery of the Choctaws' placement on the Black Warrior even more tantalizing, since it implies that although the data may not have reflected a fact, the Delisles *believed* that it did.

They did not, however, continue to believe the accuracy of this location. By the time they made the 1702 *Carte du Canada et du Mississipi* (figure 6.28), they had reverted to the conception of the 1700 sketch, placing the "Chakta ou Indiens a tête

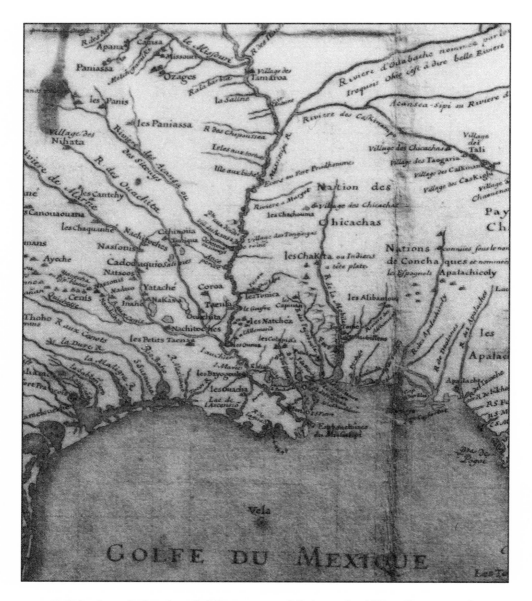

6.28. Delisle, *Carte du Canada et du Mississipi*, 1702 (Ministère des Affaires Etrangères, Service Géographique; reproduced from a photostat in the Karpinski Series). Courtesy of the Newberry Library.

plate" west of the Tombigbee (Mobile) and removing the eastern branch entirely. If the 1701 date for the three related maps is correct, however, this map also includes several other features that are oddly "retrograde." The elaborate Apalachicoli/Hitanachi/Holy Spirit construction has disappeared, replaced by a long and simplified Apalachicoly with a derationalized hydrography at its mouth. In this version the river has Indians; the large general legend "Nations known under the general name of Conchaques and called Apalachicoly by the Spaniards" appears on its upper reaches with an artistic scattering of tower-dots below it. All of this takes up so much room that the Tallapoosa branch of the Alabama River (now "River of the Alibamons") has been eliminated entirely with all its tribes – but the shift of the Conchaque appellation from the Alabama River implies that the cartographers believed they had got these Indians on the wrong river in 1701. Other tribal distributions remain generally the same, except that the Anilco, a legacy of Soto, have disappeared entirely, the Tioux have made their retirement, the Tabousa have disappeared from the Yazoo and the Pascagoula from the Mobile delta, and the Colapissa are now shown on a named but attenuated Pearl River. The configuration of the Ohio has been simplified considerably, and the peninsula of Florida is shown without a long peninsula that appeared on its east side in the three 1701 maps. Since in some aspects it relates more directly to the "sparse" engraving (6.23) than to the second engraved version (6.24), it is more accurate to think of this map as belonging to another family – expressing an alternative conclusion.

The most famous of the early Delisle maps was published in 1703, and it has been the subject of a number of analyses (Delanglez 1943b, 1945; Cumming 1958:172–73; figure 6.29a). Unlike the 1702 map, for which no precise draft can be found, several previous maps are relevant to that of 1703. It clearly owes some of its information to the two versions of *Carte des Environs du Missisipi* of 1701 (figures 6.23 and 6.24), particularly to the latter version, with its detailed and many-named Apalachicola River. From these maps also come the three mountain ranges (rather than two in 1702) shown to the east of the Rio del Norte, and the hydrography of the Ohio River. The Tallapoosa River is reintroduced as the eastern branch of the Alabama (called River of the Conchaques in 1703) although drawn in the style of the 1702 map. The 1702 change that restored the Choctaws to the west of the Tombigbee holds, but the Colapissa have again been placed on a river emptying into Pontchartrain. The Anilcou, Tioux, and Tabousa have disappeared entirely. The 1703 maps preserve the doubling of the Caouita location and introduction of the Alibamons found in the second engraved 1701 version (6.24), but the Conihaque and Assemomon have vanished. Overland trails are excluded from the 1703 maps, perhaps showing further influence of the 1702 map.

At least one manuscript draft exists for 1703, entitled *Carte du Mexique de la Floride et des terres des Anglois en Amerique avec les Isles Adjacentes* (figure 6.29b). This map incorporates substantially everything the engraver used. In addition, there is an extant inventory headed "Livres memoires Cartes imprimees ou M. S. dont on s'est servi . . ." in Claude Delisle's handwriting, which lists the sources used (Delanglez 1943b). Besides giving the sources for the 1703 map, the inventory reflects the 1703

6.29. (*a*) *Left* Delisle, *Carte du Mexique et de la Floride*, 1703; (*b*) *Right* Delisle, *Carte du Mexique et de la Floride*, draft, AN 193-6 (Cartes et Plans NN 173/01, Archives Nationales, Paris; reproduced from a photostat in the Karpinski Series). (*a*) courtesy of the Mississippi Department of Archives and History; (*b*) courtesy of the Newberry Library.

state of the Delisles's cartographic library concerning the Americas and thus offers valuable evidence of materials that could have been consulted for earlier maps.

We must keep in mind that the Delisles did not always use all their information, nor did they value all information equally. The evolution of Delisle maps from 1696 to 1703 suggests that their first concern was to get the Mississippi right, but that they could not achieve that goal until Iberville identified the river's mouth and adequately measured its location. The same event led almost immediately to the correct outline for the French-explored coastal region. Until that time plenty of information about the interior was available from Spanish accounts, but they had no real reason to use it because there was inadequate political motivation for interest in the region. Indian and European trails likely appeared on the maps of 1701 because they reflected the tensions of a precarious and threatened foothold; presumably the increased certainty of the French presence by 1702 and 1703 led to the exclusion of such trails on maps from those years. In addition, the degree of accuracy of Indian locations clearly reflected the intensity of French activity in a region: hence the Choctaws were placed on the Black Warrior until 1702, when Tonti, having been among them, supplied the

Delisles with data to place them properly (Galloway 1982b). The later work of the Delisles and other European mapmakers reflected the growing European interest in the region by providing increased detail about village locations; for the present purposes, however, the Delisle data up to this point are sufficient, for their work shows the fairly quick French grasp of the situation in the Southeast once they entered into immediate contact with it.

Oddly, the Spanish seem to have made no comparable mapping effort, in spite of having beaten the French to the Gulf coast in 1698 and in spite of their continuous settlement at Pensacola over the same period. Their small fort at Pensacola was, however, always seriously undermanned, underfed, and subject to revolt by its soldiers, many of whom had been pressed into service from Mexican jails (Ford 1939; Leonard 1974). Thus, although the Spaniards did carefully map the bay and harbor, they did little toward establishing contact with the hinterland, and in 1704 English destruction of the Spanish mission at Apalachee greatly reduced the likelihood of further Indian alliance by virtually destroying the tribes allied with Spain, thus eliminating their ability to make use of Indian informants in mapping the interior.

Considering the British interest in the trans-Appalachian interior, disappointingly few maps reflect the earliest English contact with the region, due not to a lack of native informants and allies but to a lack of education, since many traders sent into the interior were barely able to write, much less convey geographical information

systematically. Nor were they obliged to report what they found; the English penetrated the interior primarily through the efforts of independent and sometimes illegal entrepreneurs for whom geographic and ethnographic information was part of
trade secrecy; in this they paralleled the French voyageurs, who likewise reported
little such information.

That relevant information existed is demonstrated by a map drawn ca. 1708 by
Thomas Nairne, who traveled into the interior in that year with traders to forge an
Indian alliance to expel the French (Nairne 1988). This map (figure 6.30) is a very
small-scale inset to another map, but it clearly represents sources independent of the
Delisles. Mobile Bay has succeeded the Bay of the Holy Spirit as recipient of no
fewer than three rivers: the Chacta (Tombigbee), Pedegoe (Black Warrior), and
Movila (Alabama). The Choctaws are west of the Tombigbee and about the same
latitude as the Red River (Red and Arkansas conflated) on a very distorted Mississippi. Most of the larger Indian populations are also noted (presumably reflecting
English trading interests in the region), among them Natchez, Yazoo, Chickasaw,
Pensacola, Tallapoosa, Koasati, and "Chattahuchee," and trading paths appear. Anyone who wishes to decry the "armchair cartography" of the Delisles should compare
their 1703 map with this one; such a comparison exposes the advantage that accrued
to mapmakers who had access to distance measures and knew how to exploit them
scientifically. Nairne's depiction of the Chattahoochee River is more accurate – the
Delisles continued to use their odd 1701 construct until they got better information
from Father Le Maire in 1716 – but the remainder of Nairne's map is clearly distorted by his sense of the direction of his route.

CHOCTAWS ON MAPS, 1500–1703

I hope the foregoing analyses have shown that European maps of North America
from the sixteenth through eighteenth centuries are not directly usable as spatial
information from their ostensible dates of composition. Like nearly all representational maps, they are compendia of information gathered from many sources and,
except for the earliest ones, from many periods. Hence, to use them as a source of
information for events or states of affairs at any given date, researchers must subject
them to systematic analysis no less rigorous than textual sources require. In fact,
because maps convey so much more information than texts – since even their blank
spaces are significant – and because they convey it in a deceptively representational
way, they actually require more vigilance. All these maps must be seen as part of a
continuing debate through which the geography of the Southeast slowly emerged,
and no single such map can be taken out of that context at face value.

The early examples I have discussed, those related to the *padrón general* of the *Casa*

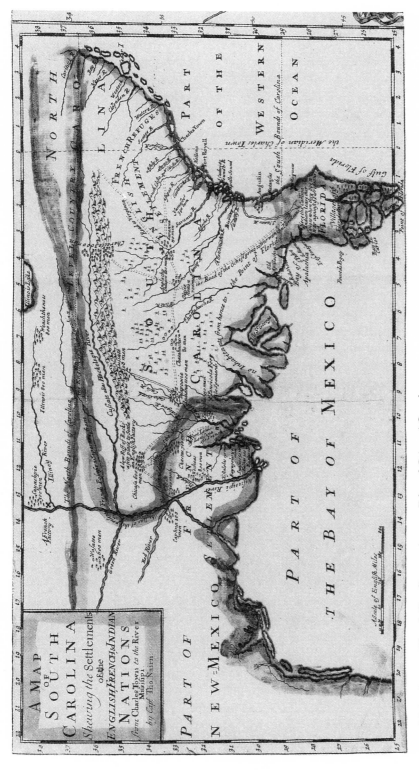

6.30. Nairne's map of South Carolina. . . , inset to Edward Crisp, *A Compleat description of the province of Carolina*, 1711. Courtesy of the John Carter Brown Library at Brown University.

de Contratación, had little concern with the interior and were more closely related to the portolan charts first developed in the Mediterranean for the benefit of mariners. This method of charting was generalized to newly explored areas of the Caribbean and eventually to the Gulf of Mexico. Harbors and rivers were marked primarily so that mariners could determine their location as well as find shelter during stormy weather and fresh water as needed. As pilots became more familiar with the northern Gulf coast, information was cumulatively added to the *padrón general*, and it in turn was the basis for new explorers' maps.

The innovation of most historical interest here is the addition of data for the interior. Understanding those additions is not straightforward either, however, because mapmakers, in addition to using information from explorers, drew upon their own ideas of how land and population groups ought to be portrayed. Through the *encomienda* and *repartimiento* systems, which assigned tribute to the conquistadors from existing native population units, the Spaniards attempted to assimilate what they found in the New World to the hierarchical feudal system of the Old. In the system the Spaniards knew at home, the important points on any map were the fortified towns where every important landowner had a townhouse and sat on a council that managed the region for which the town was a central place – market and governmental center. To these Spaniards the interior countryside was properly conceived as a tiled surface with city-states at the center of each tile.

Likewise, Spanish cartographers had common-sense models for how geographical features were related to one another. Mountains were most commonly found in the interior of a land mass; streams were known to arise in mountains and to join into rivers as they flowed down into lowlands to the sea. In addition, certain precious metals and gems were associated with mountains. Given the mapmakers' knowledge of the Iberian Peninsula's Pyrenees and the Italian peninsula's Alps, it is not surprising that they tended to manufacture a fence of mountains hedging off the upper reaches of the peninsula of Florida from the rest of the land mass, whether or not the explorers' evidence implied such a barrier.

If the mapmakers of Seville began with information they understood, from personal experience and from the mariners who were establishing navigational landmarks, they soon found themselves dealing with textual reports, unaccompanied by maps and ill suited by their very nature to supply the kind of information needed for understanding the geography of the interior. Part of the problem indeed was that the information was not prepared for the purpose of geographical mapping, nor was it directly destined for the mapmakers. The conquistadors worked under contract with the Crown; the only reports that came officially to the *Casa* would have been reports from the royal officials who went with every expedition to ensure that the contract was carried out and the king's share was duly paid. Although mapmakers might actively solicit other information, until the land was conquered there was little point in attempting to map it and nobody to pay for the mapping.

I have already discussed why the narrative accounts of conquest were poor sources for cartographic data: their descriptions of topography and distance had to serve literary ends when they were embedded in actual histories, and they were just as likely to partake of literary allusion or pathetic fallacy as to portray observations genuinely. Both first-person accounts and secondhand histories are essentially opaque geographically; indeed, most of the accounts are replete with avowals that they should not be held accountable for geographical data, because most of the authors expected that the land would be conquered and occupied and therefore better known in very short order.

At best, then, the early maps of the southeastern region should be seen as embodying hypotheses based upon the limited information available to the mapmakers at the time. Alonzo de Santa Cruz thus placed rivers and fortified town symbols and mountains on his map of 1544 using untested new data and common-sense rules about hydrography, geology, and polity location to create a hypothesis of the interior that he knew must bear only a tenuous relationship to the facts. Santa Cruz obviously did not try to prepare his hypothesis as one would do today, combing all accessible accounts for distance measures and attempting to project those measures onto the map; the point of his map was not accuracy but the creation of an impression, that of a populous and prosperous interior, no longer a *terra incognita* but not a tamed and regulated country either.

Do any of these early maps offer information not available from the narrative accounts? The only way to detect any additional source would be through additional polity names not reported in known sources or systematically different spellings from those used in known sources. Neither of these kinds of evidence is apparent on the maps examined for this study, all of which owe their names to known and in fact printed sources – Garcilaso and Elvas and translations of them. The only significant departure from these sources is the occasional fanciful duplication of names, distributed at random to fill in blank spaces.

In the Delisles's work with a narrative source for the Soto expedition it is now possible to see what a cartographer's graphical thinking about such data would look like, and it is clear that it looks nothing like what Santa Cruz produced (see figures 6.19 and 6.20). Furthermore, their sketches are overt hypotheses, replete with textual speculations of their own. Most interestingly, they represent a clear acknowledgment, as early as the eighteenth century, that the evidence of the narratives was insufficient to reconstruct a map, while demonstrating the lengths to which cartographers of the eighteenth century were willing to go to produce what amounted to no more than a decorative feature on their maps.

In fact, sixteenth-century maps have almost no additional information to offer about the Choctaws or their ancestors, both because no Spanish explorer traversed the later Choctaw homeland to confirm its emptiness and because the portrayals of native polities on maps of the period are so conventionalized that the map of the southeastern interior bears more resemblance to contemporary maps of Europe than to the state of affairs the early explorers encountered (compare figures 3.3 and 6.2).

It is our misfortune that this state of affairs did not improve until cartography became radically transformed at the turn of the eighteenth century, after the Choctaws became known to history. The French focus on the interior, which followed their interest in establishing claim to the Mississippi Valley and thus an interior bulwark against the aspirations of the coastal British colonies, advanced knowledge dramatically as increasingly specific questions were asked of the explorers' data. Success depended in part upon increasing amounts of data, but more important was increasingly *appropriate* data, as exploration came under greater control from the Crown of France than that of Spain had ever exercised. As a result of this control, cartographers directly questioned explorers, who gathered carefully specified detail when they were in the field. A more realistic intent to claim and occupy the land directed explorers' efforts.

In the eighteenth century the Indians also played a far more important part in providing information. Spanish explorers hardly endeared themselves to their native hosts, who, not surprisingly, supplied little useful information to them. British traders took another approach and French explorers still another, both respecting the tribes' power and economic importance and the information they could supply. This new attitude appears graphically on the new maps in their move away from the conventionalized "walled-town" symbol found on sixteenth-century maps to a more naturalistic use of multiple "hut" or "cottage" symbols to indicate village numbers. And although Indian mapping conventions were very different from those of Europeans and were not by any means as directly representational as the eighteenth-century conventions aspired to be, traces of Indian mapping practices visible in French maps of the early eighteenth century attest to their influence. Hence the shapes and directions of rivers often first appear portrayed by Indian conventions, becoming "Europeanized" over time, and the numbers of town symbols coincide with native informants' counts, conveyed through textual descriptions.

Maps were thus improving by focusing more closely on witnesses: European cartographers started with hypothetical reconstructions inherited from the early explorations and then gathered data as new explorations took place, updating areas the new explorations covered. When explorers used these new maps they were able to concentrate on *terrae* still *incognitae* and to gather more detailed information on areas already mapped, both from Indian informants and from new exploration. The process became more logical and repeatable – more scientific, in a word.

This scientific spirit, coupled with the use of native informants, offers the one real clue to Choctaw origins to come out of the Delisle house's blizzard of cartographic production in the early eighteenth century: the "Choctaws" are placed on what is now called the Black Warrior River on a map that simultaneously portrays the later "homeland" as empty of settlement. In the absence of additional evidence we would have to assume that the picture is an accident of misinformation; additional evidence does, however, support its claims.

It is a story that archaeology has already confirmed, a settlement situation that was true in late prehistory. The negative evidence of the early explorers also confirms this placement: neither Soto nor Luna heard of a powerful nation in the region in question. Finally, a mark remained on the land as a traditional name. From 1718 on, the Delisles called one river the Black Warrior because someone, perhaps Le Maire (1716, in Cumming 1958:184), thought that Soto had met Tascaluça there. Apparently, however, that was not its real name. Its original name was preserved briefly, as a label for towns on the Coosa, on Delisle 1701 and 1703 (figures 6.23, 6.29a) as "les Aepaetaniche"; variations of the name appeared in maps and texts of the British – better informed through their Alabama and Chickasaw allies – labeling what later became known as the Black Warrior:

> Pedegoe (Crisp/Nairne 1711, in Cumming 1958:179–80)
> Pedoge (Popple 1733, in Cumming 1958:198–200)
> Patagohatchee (Atkin 1753)
> Patagahatche (Mitchell 1755, in Cumming 1958:223–24)
> Potagohatche (Adair 1775).

Halbert and Swanton (Swanton 1931:57) reported that some of the eastern Choctaws were also known as the "Ahepat okla" or "Haiyip atokolo" in the late nineteenth century, but this name had a similar application in the eighteenth century, and indeed Delisle's transcript of Iberville's 1702 census of villages includes Ahipata bita Brugoula (Kernion 1925; see table 5.1). The name was all but submerged when the group became part of the "Eastern Party" known to the French and English (but see Rowland, Sanders, and Galloway 1984 4:276,283). As for "Tascaluça," that name had disappeared entirely as the name of a people by the eighteenth century and was preserved only as a place name. The "Pafalaya" province and its accompanying town names, of course, had vanished without a trace.

CHAPTER SEVEN

Ethnic Boundaries from Material Evidence

[T]he Yazoos and Koroas after the attack went to find the Ofogoulas who were three or four leagues from there occupied with making earthen jars in which to put their bear grease that they traded to the French. – Joseph Christophe de Lusser, journal, 1730, in Rowland and Sanders 1927–32

It is probable that in the absence of documentary evidence most cases of ethnicity would be difficult to verify archaeologically: they would appear primarily as distinctions of wealth, status, and other indications of social class. – Jeffrey P. Brain, *Tunica Archaeology*

CHOCTAW ETHNICITY

European observations from the first 150 years of contact with the Indians of the Southeast testify that great turmoil had occurred and demographically damaged groups had reorganized, but the details are still difficult to specify. The only certainty is that the Choctaws did not appear under that name in the documentary record until the latter half of the seventeenth century, and that when they did they emerged apparently from nowhere to be portrayed as an enormous force and serious threat to any European aspirations. If, as the evidence seems to imply, the Choctaws did not become a coherent group until the seventeenth century, then the documentary evidence just reviewed is all or most of what will ever exist referring to the historical events of the period, and it is not enough to support even a simplified picture of what happened. Further evidence about Choctaw origins will have to come from other sources. Telltale traces of ethnicity among the early eighteenth-century Choctaws may provide a key. By 1700 we know the location of the people the Europeans called the Choctaws; what we want to find out is which people called *themselves* Choctaws, and why.

So far I have taken only a very general look at the ethnic situation in the Southeast during the protohistoric period. When looking at the material record I have used the "culture" labels archaeologists use to draw their own boundaries. I have used tribal names with reference to the documentary record, but only as European observers applied them. Contemporary Europeans used the names they heard and did not try to define precisely where one name ceased to be a valid label and another began. This is just as well; if they had appeared to be more exact (as in fact Adair did) they might have been more persuasive, though their categories for detecting ethnicity were certainly worse than ours.

To advance a strong argument about Choctaw tribe formation, however, more specificity is necessary: I must choose specific signifiers of ethnicity and examine them closely. In chapter 2 I discussed the two great spheres of the Plaqueminian and Moundvillian culture complexes (and their prehistoric subdivisions) and attempted to suggest something of the process that brought these subdivisions into protohistory variously as chiefdoms or segmentary tribes. In the context of that overview I only suggested how Choctaw origins related to these two traditions. The present chapter pursues the material evidence in more detail to see if stylistic similarities can suggest more direct connections over time.

Archaeologists assume, at least as a working hypothesis, that distinctive material culture patterns are coterminous with coherent cultural groups. They are less willing, however, to pronounce them adequate markers of ethnicity, for two reasons: first, as the quotation from Brain above implies, intracultural patterns are as likely to reflect rank as ethnicity (and the same pattern may reflect rank in one context, ethnicity in another), and second, ethnicity is a slippery notion, as much a matter of belief as of practice. Finding ethnicity, then, requires looking at a variety of cultural features, some of which appear only partially if at all in the material record.

The anthropological concept of ethnicity is complex; it depends not on one or two cultural features, nor on the way those features fit together, but rather on how the people participating in that culture emphasize some of its features as markers of ethnicity. Ethnicity is therefore not an attribute that can be completely decided by genealogical facts, because it is less about actual genealogical relationship than about conventions of boundary maintenance as understood by one particular social group (Barth 1969:25). What it signifies, quite simply, is who belongs to what group, as seen by the people who belong to a group and those contemporaries who do not; it therefore has internal and external, visible and invisible aspects.

The Choctaws did not exist as an ethnic group, even if disparate populations had come together in the "homeland" area, until they *decided* that they existed as a group. They had to enact rituals or ceremonies of solidarity for their own benefit and to adopt modes of corporate behavior that led others to recognize their existence. If therefore the Choctaws were an amalgam of groups, the cultural markers that signaled the differences among those constituent groups had to be eliminated or redefined as insignificant or insufficient to the definition of "Choctaw." In this latter case, variant cultural markers such as pottery styles might still coexist happily, demoted to signify, for example, moiety or lineage affiliation. Other old markers would have to be altered, redefined, or replaced by new ones in order to establish the new ethnic boundary around "Choctaws."

This chapter offers a look at the distribution across the Choctaw "homeland," and across the southeastern region, of two kinds of material evidence from archaeology: pottery types and mortuary ritual. Both have been taken at various times as markers of ethnicity; both have been rejected as such. What I am interested in here – and also in the next chapter, which explores documentary evidence for the nonmaterial markers of alliances, language, and origin myths – is pattern; by superimposing pattern on pattern as the evidence accumulates, I hope to elucidate some common lines that will define cultural boundaries. Where multiple boundaries in these data coincide, I will define the tribal groups of the turn of the century; where subsets of features defy these boundaries, I will use these overlaps to suggest the ethnic derivation of this "new" people, the Choctaws, and how they came together.

CERAMIC TYPES IN THE CHOCTAW HOMELAND

Pottery types provide some tantalizing hints about Choctaw ethnicity (see chapter 2), but as yet the evidence from the east-central Mississippi "homeland" is too sparse and too poorly controlled temporally to present more than a part of what will certainly become a more fully developed picture. Nor is the evidence of ceramics trustworthy in the absence of other information: archaeologists are aware of too many cases of stylistic copying by unrelated groups – for example, many of the Creek tribes seem to have intentionally standardized their pottery types as the confederacy formed in the seventeenth and eighteenth centuries (Smith 1987:141–42). Nevertheless, for a long time pottery was thought to define Choctaws archaeologically, and since new data suggest a less monolithic tribal organization in the protohistoric and early historic periods than was previously assumed, I think it is important to discuss it here.

Archaeologists of the culture-historical persuasion in the Southeast have long assumed, without analysis, that women made pots (cf. Phillips 1970:23). Since kinship was probably reckoned matrilineally during the Mississippian period and since residence is assumed to have been matrilocal, pots were therefore considered a good marker of ethnicity. Because the potters rarely moved – matrilineages promote stable residence patterns for females – pottery types would tend to exhibit continuity over time. Where a "foreign" pottery type appeared among an assemblage not normally associated with it, archaeologists supposed that a woman had, exceptionally, married into a group and persisted with her ancestral styles; if much of this intrusive pottery was evident, invaders were thought to have set up housekeeping. Relying on these assumptions, archaeologists were soon speaking of pottery types as though they reproduced on their own, because the genealogy of pots seemed so much easier to trace than that of people.

Yet some ethnographic evidence suggests that men made pots too (Rowland and Sanders 1927–32, 1:99–100), which meant that where men married into matrilineal households, they might transfer pottery styles. Furthermore, we know that some classes of pottery were traded as containers for specific products or as markers of high status. Cultural anthropologists have argued that pottery decoration was not a genetic inheritance but a meaningful and expressive medium, with various reasons for transmission or conservatism. Still, those breeding pots never lost their appeal, as repeated disclaimers attested (e.g., Gifford 1960:346), because potsherds were so abundant on archaeological sites, so resistant to destruction, so temptingly groupable.

I do, in fact, group them for my purposes here. First I use ceramic evidence to discuss the meager clues to the protohistoric and early historic Choctaw occupation of the homeland area. I then relate that evidence to the pottery assemblages of other early historic tribes to see if Choctaw ceramic styles share elements with those of their neighbors in such a way that the neighbors in question may be seen as having become "Choctaw."

One fact cannot be reiterated often enough: by far the largest part of the Choctaw homeland area (bounded by the Pearl River to the west and north, the Tombigbee to the east, and the Leaf-Pascagoula system somewhat more vaguely to the south) was uninhabited during the Mississippian period. Archaeological survey has repeatedly shown that despite healthy populations in the Archaic and Woodland periods, and in agreement with the notion that Mississippian populations required broad and fertile floodplains, there was no permanent occupation by Mississippian peoples within the region, although modest populations belonging to a "prairie" adaptation lived on its northern border, around and northeast of the Nanih Waiya site. Thus where these new "Choctaws" established a settlement, the remains of their material culture either represent the first occupation on the site or are clearly discontinuous with what went before.

The archaeology of the region occupied by the historic Choctaws is still so underdeveloped that any conclusions as to resemblances or relationships must be tentative. The 1980s saw a dramatic advance in archaeological studies of the region, however. Before the excavation of the Tombecbé fort site in the early 1980s, archaeologists habitually and without much thought labeled as Choctaw the single pottery type Chickachae Combed, described by Henry B. Collins in 1926, named by George

Quimby in 1942, and defined by William Haag in 1953, although Moreau Chambers (1935) thought it unlikely to date from the early colonial period. Collins had found the type on known nineteenth-century sites located through information obtained from Henry Halbert, who agreed with Swanton in believing in immemorial Choctaw residence in the homeland area. And since no archaeological investigation was carried out in the region from Collins's day until the 1970s, that flawed model had gained the dignity of age without having been tested. Hence when legal requirements and modest development demanded archaeological reconnaissance in the 1970s, researchers adopted that model, so that Chickachae Combed ceramics were taken to signify Choctaw villages unequivocally (e.g., Tesar 1974; Atkinson and Blakeman 1975; Atkinson 1976; Penman 1977, 1978).

The increased survey activity meant increased collections, however, establishing one new fact about the sites being labeled as Choctaw: shell-tempered plain coarse pottery was consistently found in conjunction with the Chickachae Combed, which was characterized by a hard, compact, sand-tempered paste. Archaeologists multiplied the varieties of this coarse plainware, defining as Mississippi Plain the varieties *Wilson Pasture* (Tesar 1974:114; Atkinson and Blakeman 1975:12), *Como* (Atkinson and Blakeman 1975:14–15), and *Enterprise* (Penman 1977:23). The distinctions among these are slight, depending on the size of the shell inclusions and the presence or absence of sand temper.

Further detail was added to the Chickachae Combed type definition, too. Phillips (1970:65), referring to Ford's (1936) published historic samples from Mississippi and Louisiana, established two varieties, *Chickachae* and *Nick*, both characterized by multiline (combed) curvilinear and rectilinear incised motifs, but the second distinguished by a lack of sand in the paste. Penman (1977), carrying out surveys in the southern part of the homeland region, attempted to restrict the *Chickachae* name to rectilinear designs, assigning *Chickasawhay* to the curvilinear motifs. He recognized an additional variety, *Jasper*, characterized by freehand incised motifs sometimes mixed with combed motifs, and a Chickachae Plain *var. Souinlovey*, a hard sandy plainware covered with red slip. Atkinson (1976:40-41), who had obtained further samples similar to Penman's in the southern region (Atkinson and Blakeman 1975), defined a new variety of Chickachae Combed, *Ocobla*, when he found combed sherds tempered with grog (crushed pottery) and fine shell on sites near the headwaters of the Pearl. Although these archaeologists were somewhat vague about temporal assignment of these types, all agreed that they pertained to a whole that could be labeled "Historic Choctaw," and all still thought in terms of a single Chickachae type (see figure 7.1).

The Tombecbé excavation changed all that. James Parker's excavation showed that the Tombecbé site, where the French had built a fort and supply depot on the

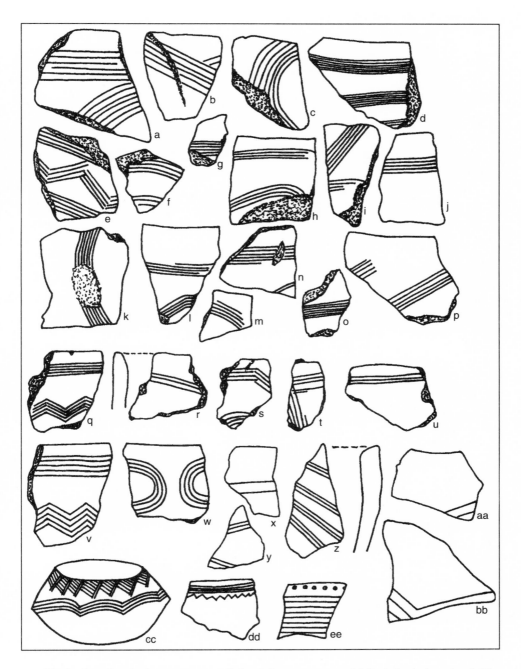

7.1 Chickachae Combed pottery types defined from east-central Mississippi sites. (*a–p*) The original pottery examples as reported by Collins (1926:figure 1); (*q–u*) combed pottery from the Nanih Waiya mound site (Ford 1936:figure 5, a–e); (*v*) Chickachae Combed, *var. Chickachae*; (*w*) Chickachae Combed, *var. Nick* (Philips 1970:66); (*x, z, aa*) Chickachae Combed, *var. Ocobla*; (*y, bb*) Chickachae Combed (Atkinson 1976:figure 8); (*cc*) Chickachae Combed, *var. Chickasawhay*, reconstructed pot; (*dd*) Chickachae Combed, *var. Chickachae*; (*ee*) Chickachae Combed, *var. Jasper* (Penman 1978:figure 2).

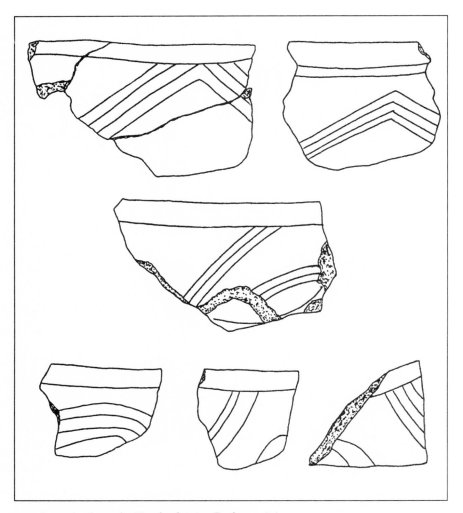

7.2. Ceramics from the Tombecbé site (Parker 1982).

Tombigbee River in 1736 to support their first Chickasaw war, presented a sealed context dating certainly from 1736 to 1763 that had been a major contact point for French-Choctaw trade. Reviewing the aboriginal pottery from the site, however, Parker (1982:71–72) noted that it shared only "design motif similarity" with the defined Chickachae Combed types, since it was shell and grog tempered and characterized by freehand incised designs, and that this lack of similarity might have chronological significance. It was then suggested that the Chickachae Combed type could well date from the mid– to late eighteenth century and be a product of contact, as it was decorated using trade combs (Galloway 1984). The Tombecbé assemblage, then, might be interpreted as early colonial Choctaw pottery (see figure 7.2).

Subsequently, two surveys in the eastern part of the homeland area on a western

Table 7.1 Blitz's Choctaw Ceramic Complex (Voss and Blitz 1985: table 1).

Type	Temper	Vessel Forms
Fatherland Incised	fine grog/sand/shell	simple bowl, jars
Chickachae Combed	fine sand	simple bowl
Kemper Combed	fine grog/sand/shell	simple bowl
Nicked Rim Incised	fine grog/sand/shell	simple bowl
Bell Plain	fine shell	simple bowl
Mississippi Plain	coarse shell	simple bowl, globular jar
Unclassified Plain	fine grog/sand/shell	simple bowl
Unclassified Plain	fine sand	simple and carinated bowl

tributary of the Tombigbee in Kemper County, carried out by John Blitz and Jerome Voss (Voss 1985; Blitz 1985; Voss and Blitz 1988), found more of this pottery in association with village and farmstead sites and thereby demonstrated that the pottery at Tombecbé was in fact Choctaw. Blitz (1985) worked this data into a "Choctaw ceramic complex," which he attributed to a Choctaw phase occupation dating from 1750 to 1850, while indicating that the temporal span of any single pottery type might overlap these dates on an earlier or later end. Table 7.1 gives an outline of the types named, as modified somewhat by Voss and Blitz in 1988, and the decorated types are illustrated in figure 7.3.

Blitz's work has helped to establish heterogeneity for at least the late Choctaw assemblage, but as he himself was fully aware, the nature of his sample – surface collections from mostly disturbed sites in a single region of the homeland area – prevented him from sequencing the various types from that sample or determining whether they represented any sort of spatial variant compared to the rest of the Choctaw homeland.

I have some worry also as to the prejudicial effect of classifying the freehand incised type on grog-, sand-, or shell-tempered paste as "a variety of [the Natchez type] Fatherland Incised" (Blitz 1985:75), when the "real" Fatherland Incised is based on an *Addis* paste that includes organic materials and has never been defined as including sand. Phillips (1970:38) classified the Addis ware as Baytown Plain, *var. Addis*, and described its range as limited to the Mississippi Valley; Williams and Brain (1983:92) remarked that "the 'organic' nature of *Addis* is diagnostic and widely sortable." Nor are the so-called Fatherland sherds from the sample particularly identifiable in terms of decorative motifs with Fatherland varieties from the type site or its region.

Instead, what Blitz has defined here is a different grog-tempered ware with sand inclusions, upon which freehand incised ("Fatherland Incised" and Nicked Rim Incised) and combed (Kemper Combed) decorative motifs were executed, in opposition to a sand-tempered ware (Chickachae Plain) upon which a combed (Chickachae

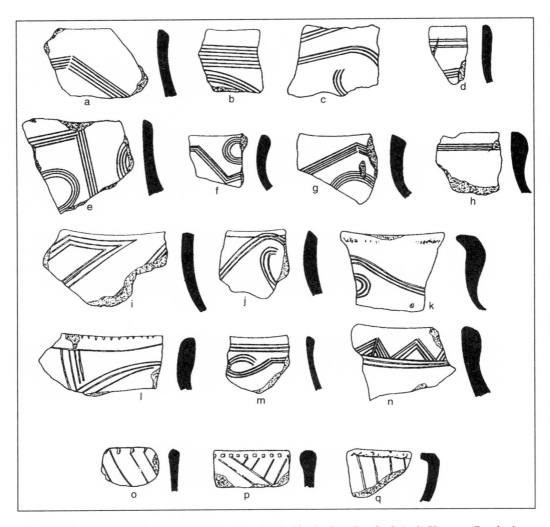

7.3. Ceramics from Kemper County survey. (*a–d*) Chickachae Combed; (*e–h*) Kemper Combed; (*i–n*) Fatherland Incised; (*o–q*) Nicked Rim Incised (from Voss and Blitz 1988:figures 3 and 4). Reproduced courtesy of the Society for American Archaeology from *American Antiquity* 53(1).

Combed) motif was executed. Blitz did not originally include the Unclassified Nicked Rim Incised types in his Choctaw complex presumably because the decorative motifs of "rim area punctations and lines incised vertically from the rim are common ceramic attributes in the Protohistoric period across the central Gulf Coastal Plain" (Blitz 1985:76), but subsequent reevaluation led to its inclusion.

Additional work with the pottery sample gathered by Blitz and Voss, as well as many of the other samples mentioned, has led to a number of observations. Voss and Mann (1986:52–54), in a study of stylistic variation in the execution of decorative designs, found that most of the sherds from a western division site were combed, whereas most of the sherds from two clusters of eastern division sites were freehand incised. They suggest that this difference may be ethnic or temporal, with the combed motifs as the later majority preference marking an increase in the Choctaw confederacy's solidarity. Blitz (1991:9–10 and his figure 3) has pursued further studies with Choctaw ceramics, and he has suggested that the eastern sites may have a temporal sequence of types, with the Nicked Rim Incised type predating 1736, the freehand Fatherland Incised type lasting at least from 1736 to 1763, and the combed types postdating 1763. These are interesting preliminary efforts at the kind of analyses necessary to resolve unanswered chronological and distributional questions, but the database is still much too slender to permit secure conclusions.

Further analysis of Choctaw pottery from recent surveys and excavations was carried out by Timothy Mooney (1991), who looked at materials from surface collections and one excavation in Lauderdale County in the eastern Choctaw region and from surface collections and excavations at the southern Chickasawhay site. The Chickasawhay site contained a very wide range of pottery types, as would be expected of such a crossroads: it was at the crossing of the east–west Natchez–Mobile delta and the north–south Chickasaw–Mobile Bay trails and was an important center of French-Choctaw interaction in the eighteenth century. Those connections were directly reflected in the ceramic wares found at the site. It yielded impressive amounts of what Blitz had called Nicked Rim Incised, which probably represents a range of varieties, as Mooney (1991:89–94; see figure 7.4) was able to show with this larger sample; some are very similar in design motifs but not in paste to the Doctor Lake Incised varieties described by Fuller, Silvia, and Stowe (1984:225–26) from the Tombigbee-Alabama forks region. Chickasawhay collections were dominated, however, by large majorities of genuine (that is, identifiable with Lower Mississippi Valley Natchezan types) Addis Plain and Fatherland Incised sherds.

These Mississippi Valley types far outnumbered both Chickachae Combed and Kemper Combed at Chickasawhay, in a context of European trade goods dated securely to the middle of the eighteenth century. Two sites further north and east in Lauderdale County, both dated to the nineteenth century, showed these two combed types outnumbered by dramatically soaring counts of European-made pearlware; Kemper Combed ceramics were clearly still preferred to Chickachae Combed, which did not occur at all on one site. Even more recently, a newly discovered site from another Tombigbee tributary in Kemper County, Harrison #4, has shown majority representation of the Doctor Lake–like incised types in a context without European trade goods and with shell-tempered plain pottery (Carleton, pers. comm. 1992; see figure 7.5), emphasizing the eastern connection and the early date. Although these recent studies cannot be conclusive for the reasons cited earlier, they do provide comparative information both temporally and spatially, and they supply data

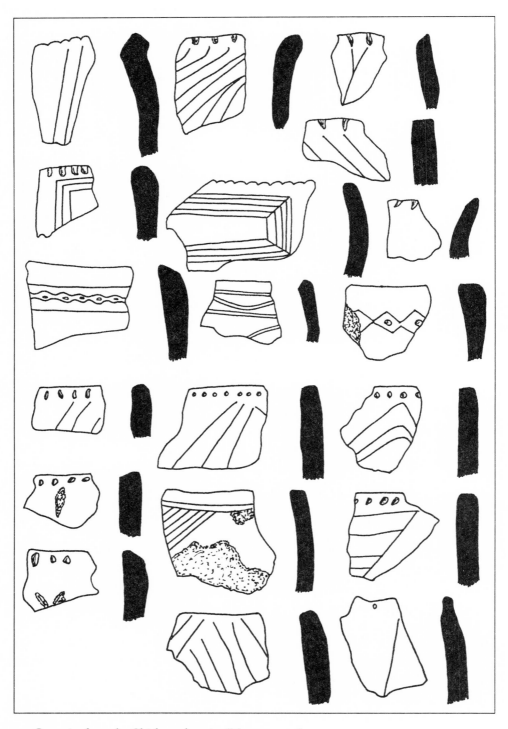

7.4. Ceramics from the Chickasawhay site (Mooney 1991).

7.5. Ceramics from the Harrison #4 site, Kemper County.

for arguing much more strongly for external influences and connections for Choctaw pottery types.

The work done so far with Choctaw ceramics has thus provided us with some information. First, although coarse cooking-pot pottery is dominated by the shell-tempered Mississippi Plain – almost certainly reflecting the common tradition of the Tombigbee/Mobile Valley and the Gulf coast – two tempering modes seem to be present in the early Choctaw assemblage of decorated pottery, one dominated by crushed pottery and a second by sand. Both tempers had been used earlier in the Tombigbee Valley, but the use of sand temper proved to be a historic-period revival of a usage that was very old in the region. Both tempers are used in pottery decorated with multiline curvilinear motifs – often the same motifs, and with strong similarities to the Natchezan decorated pottery tradition – and over time freehand incised motifs seem to have given way to combed motifs. Such early eighteenth-century Choctaw pottery as can now be identified, most of it from the eastern and southern settlements, seems to blend several traditions, sharing aspects of both Natchezan and probably Alabama River traditions with strong suggestions of Pensacola as well. The pottery of the western Choctaws in the eighteenth century remains almost unknown, and more information is needed from the south and even the east before certain connections can be asserted. The Choctaw types do, however, appear to represent a more mixed tradition than those of their neighbors, and they suggest clear links to the east and to the west.

MORTUARY PROGRAMS

Mortuary ritual is part of what the majority of cultures consider their most profound rite of passage – the nexus at which a society's myth of permanence meets the inevitable recognition of the transitoriness of the individuals who comprise it – so such ritual should come close to reflecting the values and some of the most significant symbolic repertoire of a culture. Students of early man consider reverent disposal of the dead to be one of the first indicators of a growing intelligence in the precursors of humankind; science fiction writers have speculated that consciousness of mortality may be fundamentally responsible for many of the manifestations of culture in the first place.

Interestingly, however, the serious anthropological literature on death is comparatively sparse, and the most profound insights so far about the cultural treatment of death were attained shortly after the beginning of the twentieth century in and around the Paris circle of Emile Durkheim, the great student of the sociology of religion. The theoretical framework came from Arnold van Gennep's work that introduced the phrase "rite of passage" – it covers all manner of social transitions, but he established the structure common to them all: a tripartite sequence of "preliminal rites (rites of separation), liminal rites (rites of transition), and postliminal rites (rites of incorporation)" (van Gennep 1960:11). Van Gennep recognized that there could be many variations in the emphases placed on the different phases depending upon the nature of the passage being observed. In the case of funerals, he observed that "the rites of separation are few in number and very simple, while the transition rites have a duration and complexity sometimes so great that they must be granted a sort of autonomy. Furthermore, those funeral rites which incorporate the deceased into the world of the dead are most extensively elaborated and assigned the greatest importance" (van Gennep 1960:146).

One of Durkheim's students, Robert Hertz, wrote a study specifically focused on death that was published slightly earlier than van Gennep's work, but it went barely noticed even after being translated in 1960, until Huntington and Metcalf (1979) undertook to explore its implications. Hertz's study is of particular interest here because his focus was upon not just death but the problem of temporary disposal of the dead, which is so common to the Southeast and a prominent feature of historic Choctaw mortuary practice; he even cited the work of the eighteenth-century observer James Adair for examples of southeastern burial practices. Hertz did not devote attention to what van Gennep would call rites of separation; his essay instead concentrated on the latter two phases of the funerary rite, and he concluded that the motivation behind the sequence of temporary burial (or other temporary disposal), exhumation, and final burial lies in specific beliefs about the afterlife and the fate of the deceased in it.

According to Hertz (1960:32–38), the provisional burial or deposit of the body for a period of months or years is a direct result of a cultural requirement that the corpse decompose to a skeletal condition. The waiting period is characterized by other behavioral requirements due to the vulnerability of the corpse, the discomfort of the dislodged soul, and the "pollution" inhering in material things and in the deceased's relatives. Hertz's (1960:48) real insight was in relating this complex of behaviors to the idea of death as a process, terminated only by complete bodily dissolution, whose obverse is the transition or rebirth of the soul into the new deathless body of the afterlife. This period of provisional burial, then, corresponds with van Gennep's rites of transition.

The final transfer of remains to a permanent burial place thus represents the incorporation phase. The corpse is ordinarily placed with those of its ancestors and the soul is seen as gaining peace through its admittance to the land of the dead. The final burial rite is also important for its effect on the living mourners, who are thereby reincorporated into the community (Hertz 1960:49–72). An important aspect of this phase is the extinguishment of some of the deceased's roles and obligations and the transferal of others so that the society remains capable of reproducing itself (Goody 1962).

Hertz points out that this understanding of the symbolic value of the rituals connected with the several phases of the mortuary process helps to explain the variation in it – and sometimes even the exclusion from it – that is occasioned by death in unusual circumstances. John Middleton (1982:143) has considered what he calls "bad deaths," which "take place when the psychical elements of the person do not disperse properly and at the same time, or they do so at a wrong time or in a wrong place." Such deaths occur through accident or misfortune, and they lead to variant practices of purification "to remove the impropriety of the death and to produce the situation which enables the deceased and his living kin to start the various processes of transition and transformation properly" (Middleton 1982:145). Such distinctions can help to explain one dimension of variation in mortuary practice.

Because patterns of variation expose the kinds of differences that may be understood as ethnic, we must first distinguish kinds of variation that do not indicate such a boundary. Van Gennep has shown how to segment the process into meaningful units, whereas Hertz has provided a way to interpret aspects of each segment in terms of metaphysical belief and its material expression. Neither considered another important aspect of mortuary ritual, now thought to be one of the most significant for the study of social structure: the body of the deceased is also a social object, and its treatment can reflect on the milieu from which it came.

Many of the Muskogean groups did practice provisional burial, but most did not practice it exclusively and a few may not have practiced it at all. Some scholars have seen the source of such differentiation on the plane of social organization. Bloch and Parry (1982:20–21), for example, have observed that exogamous social formations, which distinguish between kin and affines (kin by marriage), are likely to map that distinction onto the permanent bone and transient flesh of the corpse respectively, and to separate them after death. Endogamous systems, on the other hand, are likely to maintain the corpse as a whole, or at least to package it as such, even if they do practice double burial. Hence the effects of this variation in systemic marriage principle can partly explain the single/double burial dichotomy.

However the remains may have been processed, archaeologists have studied their disposition and accompaniment at ultimate interment for clues to social structure, generally accepting the materialist assumption that the treatment of the body in death reflects its treatment in life – that is, that differential post-mortem treatment reflects a difference in rank (Binford 1971). What the archaeologist sees, however, is at best the result of the final stage of funerary ritual, not the ritual itself, and of that result only what remains after many years of burial. Furthermore, cultures may choose to honor the deceased by *not* accompanying a burial with offerings or marking it especially. Thus, though burials are full of detail that may be significant for social structure and ethnicity, interpreting such incomplete evidence is difficult.

Material remains can, at least, tell us how the burials were arranged and where they took place. With regard to arrangement, Binford's principle of difference in life equaling difference in death not only testifies to an assumption about ranking; it also implies that the attitude of a society toward its past is straightforward. If the society has no ideological reason for denying differences among its members, interpretation is simple. Burials unaccompanied or accompanied by simple everyday items – thought to be needed by the soul, presumably – would characterize egalitarian societies, while ranked or stratified societies would bury a distinguished class of rulers with objects far from the usual requirements of life, symbolic in some sense of the exalted rank of the deceased. The accompaniments of the grave would cause the world of the dead to mirror the world of the living and would concretely structure the past that the world of the dead represents. But where a society chooses not to reflect the world of the living in that of the dead, mortuary evidence alone cannot reveal this contradiction.

The location of burials, on the other hand, has a more direct relationship to the world of the present because it becomes a feature of the cognitive landscape, "an idealised material map of the permanent social order" (Bloch and Parry 1982:35). On the scale of the village, the location of tombs, charnel houses, or cemeteries serves to define the relationship of the dead to the living directly. Tombs and burial areas also serve among many peoples as markers of identification with their land (Chapman and Randsborg 1981:17). Chapman (1981:81; also Morris 1987) has remarked upon the use of formal burial areas in Greece to support land claims when a dispersed settlement pattern fails to make such a nodal statement, and I would suggest that this issue is material here in light of the predominantly dispersed settlement patterns of early historic western Muskogean groups.

As researchers concerned with these issues have pointed out, the rites of mourning and especially of the final deposition of the corpse serve to transfer aspects of the deceased's social persona to living members of the group and thus to perpetuate the group. In Western societies the major emphasis is on economic issues, and there are certainly economic considerations to be dealt with in these rites, as Goody (1962) has shown. Woodburn (1982:205–6) makes a distinction between what he terms the "immediate-return" hunter-gatherer societies, which bury simply and have little or no consideration for the future, and the "delayed-return" ranked or stratified groups, which plan for the future and bury in more complex ways. Within such groups it becomes necessary not only to manage the structure of the past in the tomb but to assert the immortality of the social order by transferring its theoretically unchanging roles to the living.

Prehistoric Patterns from Archaeological Evidence

Because the remains of mortuary practices are in good part material, I look first at the prehistoric practices of the groups discussed in chapter 2 in an attempt to begin tracing patterns of continuity. A difficulty to be faced immediately in attempting to reconstruct mortuary ritual from material remains is that, although it may be possible to reconstruct in part what final depositions looked like, reconstructing ritual and the associated values and attitudes, or reconstructing even the totality of the material remains, is impossible where there is no documentary or oral witness. The vicissitudes of both archaeological data recovery and the original site formation processes mean that great gaps will exist in the recoverable data. Chapman and Randsborg (1981:12–13) have summarized many of the problems of this kind that have appeared in archaeological and ethnographic studies: the nonpreservation of objects or materials important in the material representation of mortuary practices; the relative survival potential of different methods of disposal; the systematic exclusion from the grave of possessions or offerings to the dead; the simultaneous appearance in the archaeological record of multiple phases of a single mortuary activity and multiple patterns of mortuary activity over time. The only hope of a corrective here is the careful evaluation of the full pattern of archaeological remains left by the system under consideration, so that missing data in the mortuary evidence can be accounted for elsewhere (as for example the casual disposal of the corpses of infants in village middens complementing the lack of infant burials among those of adults).

Detailed examination of the archaeological record with such problems in mind has already offered suggestions to define its limits. John O'Shea's (1981) analysis of Plains mortuary practices in the historic period, meant to elucidate the effects of site formation processes on the quality of the subsequent archaeological record, offers a useful framework for considering the evidence at hand regarding Muskogean mortuary practices. He distinguished two kinds of social differences that might be demonstrated in mortuary practices: "horizontal differentiation," or kin-based differences, and "vertical differentiation," or differences in social rank. O'Shea used ethnographic data to create a model to predict the kinds of archaeological evidence that would indicate the various kinds of differentiation.

A similar model can be suggested here. Table 7.2 indicates the range of social categories suggested by the literature on southeastern chiefdoms and tribal groups, together with a list of suggested archaeological attributes. Both the categories creating the differentiations and the artifact types suggested for them are theoretical generalizations, hypothetical correlation classes that may or may not reflect social or archaeological reality, but they do offer at least a starting point for a comparative analysis of mortuary archaeology.

Very little archaeological evidence indicates exactly how the secondary processing of the body was carried out. Ethnographic evidence from the world over suggests that the options ranged from temporary burial in the earth to exposure on a scaffold to temporary enclosure above ground in some sort of container. Only the first of these options is likely to leave any recognizable trace, and indeed such evidence

Table 7.2 Predicted Archaeological Attributes of Social Categories for
Southeastern Chiefdoms and Tribes (after O'Shea 1981).

Social Category	Sex	Age	Frequency	Symbolic Designators	Spatial Designators
Vertical (Rank) Differentiation					
Chief	M	Adult	Lowest	Supralocal prestige symbols; wealth	Yes
Ranked males	M	Adult	Low	Local prestige symbols; wealth	Possible
Ranked females	F	Adult	Low	Local prestige symbols; wealth	Possible
Ranked subadult	M/F	Subadult	Low	Local prestige symbols	Possible
Priest/doctor	M?	Adult	Low	Local prestige symbols; ritual implements	Possible
Craft specialist	M?	Adult	Low	Tools of restricted types	No
Horizontal Differentiation					
Gender	M/F	Potentially all	100%	Gender specific artifacts	No
Age	M/F	All of "common" rank	80%?		No
Moiety	M/F	All	100%	Possible formal differentiation	Possible
Clan	M/F	All	High	Possible specific supralocal symbols	Possible
Circumstantial	M/F	All	Low	Alternative burial treatment	Possible
Deviants	M/F	Adult	Low	Alternative burial treatment	Possible

appears for several sites and periods in the region of interest. Empty burial pits found
in the protohistoric/historic Natchez temples excavated by Chambers and Neitzel
clearly indicate exhumation for further processing as the documents suggest (Neitzel
1965; see Brown 1971:105). Empty pits in the mounds at Moundville, which contained artifacts thought to correlate with high rank, seem to indicate the same conclusion (Peebles 1974:185). Even at the modest single-mound site of Lyon's Bluff, an
alligator skull–accompanied burial that consisted solely of skull fragments, hand
bones, a few ribs, and some vertebrae, all resting in roughly anatomical order at the
bottom of a pit cut into a previous nearly congruent pit, is a suggestion of this
practice for at least an elite (in this case perhaps a shaman), probably datable to the
earlier end of the Mississippian sequence at the site (Galloway n.d.c).

If temporary burial was in fact a widespread solution to the processing problem,
then we need some way to distinguish, in a set of contemporary flesh burials, those

that are temporarily interred from those that are permanently interred. Some spatial factor seems likely to give the desired clue, but this is a matter for further archaeological research. The possibility exists, of course, that only when a site was abandoned under truly disastrous circumstances did families fail to complete the processing of the bones of their dead (Neitzel 1965:84–85); if that is true, apparent mixed burial practice on protohistoric sites may indicate abandonment due to disease or other disruption. Multiple secondary burials probably do not offer the same indication, however, since they are much more likely to have resulted from the periodic emptying of a charnel house.

An additional type of evidence likely to be correlated with secondary processing is the so-called Southeastern Ceremonial Complex of exotic objects and symbols; they appear at some late Mississippian sites, including Moundville, and incorporate symbolism of skulls and longbones. This correlation is strengthened by the increase in the practice of secondary processing toward the end of the prehistoric period in the Tombigbee Valley; at the same time, stylized versions of the skull and longbones were among the few Southeastern Ceremonial Complex motifs that persisted into the protohistoric, sometimes decorating the very ceramic urns containing skull/longbone burials (Sheldon 1974; Stowe 1989). Arguments for cultural continuity in these cases are uncontested, but it is not clear whether this broadened use of the skull and longbone symbolism indicates a kind of democratization of the ideology of lineage inheritance that may be represented by the symbolism of the Southeastern Ceremonial Complex (cf. Huntington and Metcalf 1979:101).

A thorough study of the mortuary practices of the protohistoric peoples of the region is impossible because only rarely is anything even approaching the full range of mortuary evidence available from any single site or group of sites. Accordingly, all I attempt to show here is the methods of disposal of the dead, how those methods are distributed through the region, and how archaeologists have interpreted differentiations within single sites or groups of sites. Below I examine data from the great Plaquemine mound sites in the Yazoo Basin and Natchez Bluffs regions, including Winterville, Lake George, and Emerald, and data from Moundville and culturally related sites, including the Summerville-phase sites on the Tombigbee River and "Burial Urn" sites on the Alabama River and in the Mobile-Tensaw delta, divided into Sheldon's (1974) three groupings.

Plaqueminian Mortuary Practice

Burial practices among groups of Plaquemine culture are not fully defined because few of the sites have been excavated, and though some paramount sites have been investigated, few smaller ones are known. Furthermore, researchers have not systematically sought mortuary remains in the Mississippi Valley, where they have most frequently been revealed to archaeologists only after having been vandalized. Thus nowhere in the region has the full range of burial practice, both synchronic and diachronic, been uncovered. In addition, it is as yet difficult to establish an unbroken trajectory of Plaquemine cultural development. Here, restricted by the evidence, I look at data from the Coles Creek–based Winterville and Lake George sites on the lower Yazoo and the Plaquemine Mangum and Emerald sites on the Natchez Bluffs; the Natchez evidence from Fatherland and the Tunica burials from Angola are discussed in the section on historic mortuary practices.

Yazoo Basin. Data from the Late Mississippian period in the lower Yazoo Basin may grant some perspective through which to view the thinner data for the same period further south. In the lower Yazoo Basin the two significant mound sites, Winterville and Lake George, have yielded larger burial populations than are found further south, 24 in the case of Winterville (from Mound B) and some 180 in the case of Lake George (from Mound C). Both sites include flesh burials, skull burials, and bundle burials. The burials from Lake George date from the Coles Creek Aden II and Kings Crossing II periods, while those from Winterville date from the later Plaquemine Winterville II and "Mississippianized" Lake George phases; since both sets of burials came from separate phases of substructural ceremonial mound usage, they may be viewed as a roughly chronological sequence. Because all these burials were found in mounds, however, they are not representative of the whole population (see the appendix for burial data cited in this section).

If there is any trend in the burial data from these sites, it is a decided increase in the incidence of secondary processing and a decrease in primary burials over time. Another interesting feature is that the Coles Creek–period evidence from Lake George exhibits a high frequency of multiple infant flesh burials. Evidence from elsewhere (see below) shows that infants are seldom treated in any way other than flesh burial, yet this practice is frequent enough here that when such burials are subtracted from the sample the overall importance of flesh burial through the Aden and King's Crossing phases is significantly reduced, and the trend in favor of secondary processing remains stable. The infants in question at Lake George were sometimes simply buried in a group and sometimes associated with the burial of a single adult, but both practices suggest possible ceremonial sacrifice, echoed to the south at Emerald.

Natchez Bluffs Plaquemine. An extensive cemetery from Emerald would be useful, but unfortunately we know of none. Instead there are two groups of burials, one group found in recent excavations around the base of a secondary mound on Emerald's crest, the other found disturbed by the digging of the relic hunter Perrault in the nineteenth century (Steponaitis 1974). Of nineteen burials all but one disturbed one were certainly flesh burials. A group of sixteen Foster or Anna phase burials was striking: in three burial pits around the base of a midden mound infant groups (of three, four, and seven) were interred, while a fourth contained another infant and a juvenile. The burials exposed by Perrault, three adults dated to the Emerald phase, had with them five Southeastern Ceremonial Complex limestone effigy pipes and pottery vessels indicating a Foster or Emerald phase date.

These burials show no indication of any secondary processing, yet all these burials may well be anomalous, the earlier child burials because they represent some ceremonial placement of specially selected individuals, the later adult burials because they represent a narrow elite. The Ring site, which apparently represented a cemetery of the Emerald phase (Brown 1985), could possibly have supplemented the Emerald data, but only two burials (both extended) were complete enough for a description of their form – still not enough evidence to prove that flesh burial was the habitual form of burial in the period immediately preceding the development of the historic Natchez.

The Mangum site north of Natchez on the Natchez Trace may supply the missing range of burial treatment. The site is in fact a cemetery only, and it is famous for the eponymous repoussé copper plate depicting a bird-man figure found by a farmer with an adult burial, connecting the Foster-phase Plaquemine site with the Southeastern Ceremonial Complex (Steponaitis 1981:12–13). This burial, thought to be a male because it was accompanied by a second adult who had the remains of a fetus in her pelvic region, was extended, as were eleven more skeletons said to have been found by the same farmer (Cotter 1952:65). Professional excavations in 1951 uncovered twelve more extended burials and one possible bundle, and a second excavation season in 1963 revealed another copper plate and at least seventy-four more burials, of which about 54 percent were bundles or disarticulated piles of bones (Bohannon 1963; Dailey 1974).

Bohannon believed that the site represented a single period, and that the bundled burials were remains that had been dug up to make way for the extended ones. This, he felt, accounted for the "stacked" appearance of some of the burials, with bodies and bones piled on one another in a single pit; in fact he distinguished only twenty-four grave-pits for the seventy-four burials. Many of what he called bundle burials represented masses of bones belonging to several people, but the burials he excavated show what seems to be a normal age distribution, with most child deaths either in infancy or after weaning, all adult female deaths during childbearing years, and most adult male deaths in the twenties or in the late thirties to early forties. The proportion of disarticulated burials is quite evenly distributed. Hence the routine procedure was apparently initial flesh burial, followed later by excavation of fleshless remains, followed by reinterment. The general lack of grave goods at Mangum might suggest a "commoner" cemetery, except for the two very rare repoussé copper plates, which suggest elite burials. Yet without additional knowledge of the community whose dead are buried at Mangum, we can do little but note the importance of secondary burial in the Natchez Bluffs region in the Foster phase.

Plaqueminian Summary. Jeffrey Brain (1979) has remarked, in connection with a study of Winterville burials, that burial form may have an ethnic connection in the Lower Mississippi Valley: that flesh burial seems to be connected with "Mississippia-nization," influences coming from the north into the Yazoo Basin, whereas tempo-rary deposition in a charnel house (as implied by the burial groups especially in the Coles Creek phases of the Lake George site) is a "southern" feature associated with the Coles Creek culture. The data examined above seem to contradict this hypothe-sized trend in the lower Yazoo Basin, suggesting perhaps a strong Coles Creek "survival." The Natchez Bluffs evidence, especially from Mangum, strongly sup-ports secondary burial practice, but who was buried in what way is still not evident. Nearly all the burials in this analysis, omitting some unknown portion of those from Mangum, are probably elite burials, with the exception of burials made to accom-pany elite burials. If some of the Mangum burials are those of ordinary people, secondary processing may have been as frequent or more frequent for them. This will be of material interest in the examination of historic Natchez phase practice.

Moundvillian Mortuary Practice

The Moundville sphere of influence included several cultural variants distributed about the Alabama-Tombigbee drainage (see chapter 2). Except for Moundville itself and the Summerville sequence, however, reliably phased data are hard to obtain, so the danger of comparing noncontemporaneous data is always present. This problem is particularly severe, for example, with the enormous Alabama River phase sites in the Montgomery area so efficiently vandalized by the gentlemanly antiquarians of the Alabama Anthropological Society in the first quarter of the century. Their im-pressionistic descriptions indicate that they found a preponderance of secondary burials of ranked individuals with the burials of "non-persons": "whole skeletons or isolated skeletal parts – usually skulls – that are used as ritual artifacts" (Peebles and phases. Thus for the Coosa-Tallapoosa forks region the evidence amounts to spec-ulation narrowly reinforced by a small amount of modern excavation on these heavily damaged sites.

Moundville. The Moundville site itself is no model of clarity as far as our understand-ing of mortuary practices is concerned. Moundville enjoyed the early attentions of such luminaries as C. B. Moore at the turn of the twentieth century, who in his usual style excavated mound burials there in search of decorated pottery and other artifacts with scant concern for the form of burial employed. In fact the work at Moundville from 1840 to 1941, extensive as it was particularly in the WPA-era excavations, had not been formally reported and could not be explicated stratigraphically until the pottery from eighty-seven (of more than three thousand) recorded grave groups was seriated, enabling that from many others to be assigned to phases (Steponaitis 1983: figure 25). Of these eighty-seven graves, fully a fourth had no description of the burial (Peebles 1979a), so although Peebles (1971:80–84) was able to distinguish ranking in the spatial organization of burial patterns and in the objects included within the mound burials as opposed to those not placed in mounds, he could not at that time distinguish a temporal sequence of burial form, since the Mississippian occupation at Moundville had still not been broken up into phases.

In Peebles's more extended analyses of the Moundville burials for his studies of social organization (Peebles 1974; Peebles and Kus 1977) this problem was still present. Despite a range of variability in burial form – extended, flexed, bundle, skull – most of this variability could be accounted for by the accompaniment of burials of ranked individuals with the burials of "non-persons": "whole skeletons or isolated skeletal parts – usually skulls – that are used as ritual artifacts" (Peebles and Kus 1977:439). That is, the extended inhumation burial form was almost ubiquitous; ranking was interpreted on the basis of spatial distribution (the mounds being considered the most favored location) and the inclusion of specific artifacts. Yet there was evidence – the empty pits mentioned earlier containing elite grave goods – that at least some of the secondary bundle burials, which accounted for 9.4 percent of the sample Peebles analyzed, were those of important people. More to the point, there was no indication that secondary burial was ever "democratized" at Moundville. Where such burials occurred in cemeteries rather than mounds, the grave goods and location identified them as cemeteries of an upper class.

In other words, Moundville provides no evidence of a temporal trend toward increasing the practice of secondary burial among all social ranks. Peebles's analyses, though not meant to delineate phases at the Moundville site, indicated a striking uniformity in burial form at least through the subsequently defined Moundville II and III phases from which most of the burials were taken. Powell (1988:85) observed that "the majority of burials for which information exists are single primary interments, with the arms placed parallel to the long axis of the body or (less commonly) crossed over the trunk. Secondary deposits of remains were occasionally encountered but were not common." Again, however, the small size of the seriated sample and its failure to overlap usefully with the extant skeletal material compelled her to analyze the skeletal series as a single synchronous sample. Indeed, the single example of a bundle burial dates early in the seriated sequence, to early Moundville II. The remaining fifty-five burials whose form is known were nearly all flesh burials – the rest were skull or "trophy" burials. If elite burials of whatever period were accorded extended processing and multiple burial events, the evidence that would have demonstrated as much is gone.

Work now in progress (V. Steponaitis, pers. comm. 1993) will extend the implications of the ceramic seriation to the complete range of burials, but it is unlikely to show a trend in burial form for several reasons. The fact that the protohistoric Alabama River phase does not occur at Moundville surely accounts for some of this homogeneity. In addition, evidence for the Moundville site is skewed because it represents what was done at the paramount site of a multilevel chiefdom. Other sites within the Moundville sphere of influence must provide "the rest of the story" and a view of the trajectory into the protohistoric period.

Other Sites on the Black Warrior. Unfortunately for the present inquiry, the evidence from other sites on the Black Warrior is inconclusive. The only one that has received any significant excavation and reporting is the White site. Paul Welch (1991) has recently reevaluated the burial evidence from this Moundville III–period single-mound site, one of six subsidiary to Moundville during the Moundville III period, and has dated the burials mostly to late Moundville III. The original excavation of this site, which took place in the 1930s, did not include very sophisticated recording procedures, and the forms of the burials can only be inferred from Welch's presentation of the data. Only seventeen of the twenty-nine burials can be judged with any degree of confidence to be extended flesh burials; in fifteen cases the notes provided information on the orientation of the burial, and in two additional cases the placement of artifacts near some anatomical feature suggests extended burial. Poor preservation seems to account for the notes' silence on the rest, but it is also possible that the excavators did not note the form of burial because it was the same across all burials and all of them were extended.

The contents of the graves were far from uniform, however. The burials were accompanied with artifacts in eight or nine cases, and in the richest of these a child was buried with shell beads, a rare copper ornament, and two pottery vessels, indicating the ascribed status of hereditary rank. If White was representative of secondary centers during the last Moundville phase, the evidence points to a mortuary practice that was undifferentiated as to form but highly differentiated as to content, repeating to a degree the pattern at the central Moundville site.

The greatest recent excavation interest along the Black Warrior has been in protohistoric-period Alabama River phase sites (Sheldon 1974:140–51; Curren 1984b). Although these sites have demonstrated a clear bias in favor of secondary burial, they have not demonstrated continuity with the preceding Moundville phase on the same sites, for the simple reason that transition to the Alabama River phase on the Black Warrior also included a change in settlement pattern. Minor Moundville phase sites have been surveyed extensively (Bozeman 1980) but not excavated in detail, so we do not know what burial program – if any – was used at subsidiary sites in the Moundville chiefdom.

The purely Alabama River phase material from the Black Warrior is apparently unequivocal, although as Sheldon (1974) has observed of all Burial Urn sites, the frequency of primary burial is probably underrepresented due to the interests and frequently the methods of the excavators. Both the Foster's Ferry and Lon Robertson sites suffered from unprofessional attentions, but both yielded a clear predominance of urn burials, apparently not skewed in the direction of infants and small children and none of them accompanied with grave goods (Sheldon 1974:140–51). Excavations at the single-component Moody Slough and Big Prairie Creek sites conducted by Curren (1984b) demonstrate that secondary burial methods dominated overwhelmingly, for all age groups. No burials were accompanied by the rare and symbolically rich grave goods that would indicate ascribed ranking.

Although more research is necessary, especially on long-term Moundville phase occupations, before results can be considered conclusive, a definite shift in mortuary program evidently occurred on the Black Warrior over time, distinctly coinciding with a change in settlement pattern and probably social organization. The change in mortuary program coincided with the protohistoric period, and it consisted of more intensive use of secondary burial methods for adults, children, and sometimes infants. Curren's excavations have shown that urn burial may have been preferred for infants, whereas adults were more often interred in bundles enclosed in containers of perishable materials. Urn and bundle burials, which are often multiple, suggest possible charnel house assemblages, and although extended and flexed burials occurred, we have no way of knowing if they were intended to be permanent.

Lubbub Creek Archaeological Locality. Excavations at the Lubbub Creek Archaeological Locality have fortunately supplied a very clean and well-analyzed set of data that offers a continuous trajectory from Late Woodland into the protohistoric period for a residential group whose close association with the Moundville chiefdom is clear from its use of the same pottery types and cultural equipment. But Lubbub was not abandoned in the protohistoric period. The Summerville sequence of phases at Lubbub (which parallels Moundville phases) has a fourth segment, related to the Alabama River phase, that develops smoothly from the preceding phase. In fact, the number of burials (eighty-two) from a separate precinct in the excavated portion of the site indicates that the Summerville IV (protohistoric) phase was by far the most populous at the site. Also, whereas preceding phases showed no secondary processing at all, a dramatic predominance (90 percent) of urn and bundle burials suddenly emerged, suggesting that the few flesh burials are likely either anomalous or temporary burials (Peebles 1983b, 2:appendix A).

Lyon's Bluff. The Lyon's Bluff site is quite similar to Lubbub Creek in its location off a Tombigbee tributary and its long-term relationship with the Moundville polity. Extensive excavations in the 1930s and 1970s still remain underreported, but field notes for the earlier excavations and limited published data for the later ones can provide a few generalities. Although the thirteen burials recovered in the 1930s are next to impossible to date, all but one were flexed flesh burials. All the known burials are from the occupation midden area around the mound, and many of them seem to have been associated with house patterns; Marshall (1986) has suggested that during the Lyon's Bluff and Sorrells phases (ca. A.D. 1200–1550) infants, at least, were commonly buried beneath house floors along the walls, while adults were buried outside the houses. Only very few of the recovered burials were accompanied with any grave goods, all utilitarian objects. The one exception to all of these statements was Burial 11, interred in a pit lined with turtle shells and containing the skull of an alligator; the long bones of this individual seem to have been dug up for reburial (Galloway n.d.c). The unusual arrangement of faunal remains suggests a special treatment that parallels the extended secondary processing the missing remains probably received (cf. Brown, Kerber, and Winters 1990:273).

The pottery assemblage from the site relates it to the Moundville hegemony during most of its lifetime, but there are significant connections with the central Mississippi Valley toward the end of the sequence. The site is therefore thought to represent a simple chiefdom that maintained some independence from Moundville. Apart from the single alligator skull burial, there are no known burials with significantly distinguished accompaniment. Also, although subfloor burials are known from Moundville, the practice departs from the usual Moundville, White, and Lubbub practice of inhumation in specifically designated areas.

Mobile Delta and Alabama River. For burial urn sites from the Tombigbee, Mobile delta, and Alabama River region, Sheldon's work (1974) contains a useful summary of earlier excavations in the region; Curren (1984a) has expanded this summary for the lower Tombigbee, and Fuller, Silvia, and Stowe (1984) have done the same for the Tombigbee-Alabama forks region. Although little of the work is modern and the sample is far from representative of the regional population, the data clearly suggest a shift from flesh burial to secondary processing, since in most cases Fuller, Silvia, and Stowe identify sites with flesh burials as sites with earlier Woodland or early Mississippian components. The occurrence of historic European artifacts – sixteenth-century

Spanish to eighteenth-century French – with some of these burials brings the late Doctor Lake pottery complex and the "Ginhouse Island Mortuary Complex" of urn burials into the historic period to be identified directly with the Mobile delta historic tribes. This historic connection is interesting in the context of the investigation of ethnicity here because one of the marker pottery types, Doctor Lake Incised, seems related to both Pensacola Incised, *var. Pensacola*, and at least the "Nicked Rim Incised" material found on eighteenth-century Choctaw sites (Fuller, Silvia, and Stowe 1984: 225; see also chapter 6).

Sheldon's summary of burial modes (1974:246–56) highlights the variability of interment practice in the Lower Tombigbee–Alabama region, but he states that the apparent bias in favor of urn burial is probably based upon amateur interest and activity; he opines that flesh burials – extended or flexed – were probably most frequent, particularly if that category includes flesh burials with inverted vessels over the head. And although sexing of these burials is generally doubtful, there is no doubt that the bodies of children were far more frequently placed in a burial urn than inhumed without one. The urn burials were of two types, flesh burials of children or secondary bundle burials of adults, placed in an urn and often covered over with another before burial in a pit. Sheldon also notes that secondarily processed bundle burials may be of all ages and sexes and are frequently found in multiple lots, sometimes with an inverted vessel.

Sheldon identified three clusters of burial urn sites: on the Alabama River, at the junction of the lower Tombigbee (Mobile) and Alabama, and on the lower Black Warrior. He rejected social stratification or kinship groups as explanation for the variety of interment forms on those sites and instead suggested, on the basis of burial urn pottery type variation and the distribution of interment forms, that the variety of burial forms might reflect ethnic variation. He pointed to the increasing frequency of bundle burials moving westward along the Alabama to the Tombigbee junction, paired with the increasing dominance of Pensacola pottery types and a clustering of small, low burial mounds containing bundle and urn burials at the Tombigbee-Alabama forks (Sheldon 1974:26,80,257–58). Although better temporal control and a more representative sample would likely clarify this picture greatly, Sheldon's suggestions have not been seriously challenged.

Moundvillian Summary. It seems clear that in the Moundville cultural sphere there were several widespread trends. The first is from more varied to less varied burial forms, apparently related to a decline in ranking, since the second correlated trend is from a wide to a narrow range of burial accompaniments. By the late prehistoric Alabama River, Summerville IV, and Mhoon phases, all these related groups seem to have settled on two alternative burial forms: flesh burials, extended or flexed; and secondary bone burials, enclosed in inorganic (ceramic) or organic (basketry?) containers. In at least some instances the flesh burials could perhaps represent the first stage of a secondary burial process, since in several cases secondary burials show overwhelming predominance; where excavation has been to modern standards (as at Lubbub) this predominance is clearly the terminal end of a trend.

Historic Patterns from Documentary Evidence and Archaeology

Mortuary practices among the region's historic tribes are obviously better documented, for the Europeans who came into contact with the tribes described them to some degree. We need to be sure that the descriptions apply to the period of interest, of course, and since most of the more elaborate descriptions come from the late colonial period or even the nineteenth century, in every case here the earliest account will be the most favored. An additional problem arises from the fact that mortuary practices are so universally connected with religious beliefs and taboos that the Europeans probably did not see the complete rituals or understand the practices they saw; in fact, several witnesses (notably Adair) were candid about the difficulty they experienced in being allowed to observe burial rites. Hence the material and overt behavioral aspects of an observation are again important because they are much less susceptible to ethnocentrism than the interpretive aspect.

The goal is to find patterns that systematically distinguish burials according to specific criteria within each culture, and to determine as well the larger pattern of consistencies across the cultures. A degree of commonality is to be expected, for most of the tribes enjoyed unquestioned cultural links. We do not know, however, how far back those links went or how close they were; discontinuity may help establish those degrees. The tribes are the Choctaws and their neighbors: Tunica; Natchez, Taensa; Bayougoula, Houma, Pascagoula, Biloxi, Acolapissa; Mobile, Tohomé; Creek, Alabama; Chickasaw, Chakchiuma.

Tunicas. Jeffrey Brain (1979) has studied the premodern history of the Tunicas tirelessly for more than twenty years, and one reward for this quest has been the opportunity to record and analyze the material correlates to historical descriptions of eighteenth-century Tunica burials. Although archaeologists did not see the burials looted to uncover the "Tunica Treasure" when they were dug up from the Trudeau site, it is possible to reconstruct a tradition that consisted almost exclusively of flesh burials with elaborate material accompaniment. Nor was this tradition a new one; evidence backtracking from that late eighteenth-century site to the Portage de la Croix location and then to the village sites on the lower Yazoo (where the Tunicas lived side by side with Yazoos, Coroas, and Ofogoulas) indicates that the pattern had been continuous since before Father La Source observed in 1699 that "they inter their dead . . . and in the evening they weep over the grave of the departed and make a fire there and pass their hands over it, crying out and weeping" (Shea 1861:81). Father Davion, the Tunica missionary, unfortunately did not provide a fuller description, but the archaeological evidence could not be clearer.

Natchez. The French description of this burial complex is well known from the published early French accounts of it and the studies of MacLeod (1928) and Brown (1971). Brown has summarized the complex succinctly, setting out first MacLeod's attributes for the Natchez-Taensa complex:

1. Primary burial phase by inhumation and scaffold burial that is differentiated by status and rank. It is composed of burial in a platform mound, in individual scaffold platforms, and in grave pits.
2. Reburial in mortuary houses as secondary burial for selected individuals.
3. Final interment in unspecified locations as tertiary phase.
4. Central mortuary house on platform mound for high ranking individuals; local village mortuaries for the others.
5. Mortuary house of the central village is the tribal temple, in which the sacred fire, the stone ancestor figures and other ritual objects for the well-being of the tribe are housed.
6. Mortuary house custodians are also the temple guardians, and are assistants of the presiding priest of high status ("Master of Ceremonies").
7. The mortuary house custodians are flesh strippers (see Swanton 1911:160). (Brown 1971:103)

In brief, the chiefly Sun family was accorded special treatment, being buried within the mound for a time to allow the flesh to rot, then exhumed, with the remains placed in a container in the temple for an unspecified time; the ultimate fate of the chiefly remains is unknown. According to MacLeod, the corpses of the rest of the people, possibly even including those sacrificed to accompany the Suns in death, were scaffolded for a time and then went through the bone house–to–mass burial process. Brown has articulated this scheme into a table (given here as table 7.3) showing the types and phases of burial according to the documents and the archaeological evidence from the excavations of Chambers and Neitzel at Fatherland. Brown's citations show that most of the documentary evidence comes from several observers, who in many cases corroborate each other, thus improving our confidence in their assertions. Three of the observers were visiting missionary priests (Gravier, LePetit, and Charlevoix) and one a long-term resident (Du Pratz); two sources record fleeting visits (Iberville, *Marin* logs), and two reflect extended visits (Penicaut, Dumont de Montigny).

Table 7.3 J. Brown's (1971) Analysis of the Natchez Burial Procedure by Phase and Social Segment. Reproduced courtesy of the Society for American Archaeology from SAA Memoir 25.

Primary Burial	Secondary Burial	Tertiary Burial
I. In the temple portico: *Inside:* chief, members of chief's family. *Outside:* high ranking officials (DM, DP, P) (Swanton 1911:141, 145, 157)	Placed on temple shelves: cleaned and wrapped in cane baskets or placed in chests* (G, C, DM, F) (Swanton 1911:158–161)**	Removed from temple: not observed.
II. On individual house-shaped platforms: "principal servants" (LP) (Swanton 1911:143) in local village (DM) (Swanton 1911:157).+	Placed on temple shelves (?): "principal servants"?, referred to as being carried to temple of own village after immolation ceremony (DP) general comment (DP) (Swanton 1911:143, 149).#	Removed from temple (?): not observed.
III. Pit burial: "ordinary servants" immolated during funeral (LP); placed in pits with "arms and clothes" after immolation (C) (Swanton 1911: 142–143).	Existence unknown.	

*The high ranked status interments in the temple were accompanied with new immolations (DM) (Swanton 1911:156).
**Also the Taensa (LP) (Swanton, 1911:269).
+The mode of burial recorded among the Acolapissa (P), Bayogoula (DI, LM), and the Houma (LM) (Swanton 1911:275–77, 282, 287).
#Reinterment of the platform burials recorded among the Acolapissa (P) (Swanton 1911:282).
Sources (in Swanton 1911): C = Charlevoix, DI = D'Iberville, DM = Dumont, DP = DuPratz, G = Gravier; LM = "Le Marin" Journal, LP = LePetit, P = Penicaut.
Note: The table has been reset, but the content has not been altered.

With all this corroboration, however, even Brown's elegant analysis cannot hide the fact that the actual archaeological evidence is missing for the tertiary burial of important people and the possible secondary burial of the "ordinary servants." Brown's analysis also omits the mortuary treatment of ordinary people. According to Father Le Petit, such people received a flesh burial in the earth accompanied by firearms, a kettle, and food; this treatment is virtually the same as the historic Tunica pattern repeated at Trudeau and other sites.

Thus Brown's analysis, by implying that the Natchez/Taensa mortuary program described by the sources was a unitary phenomenon, obscures some unsolved problems about Natchez mortuary practice. First, there is as yet no Natchez phase evidence for the disposal of infants sacrificed at the death of a chief, although the phenomenon is amply documented and although multiple infant burials are common in preceding Coles Creek and Plaquemine phases on the Natchez Bluffs and in the lower Yazoo Basin. Furthermore, not only is the documentary evidence cited by MacLeod and Brown not unitary (some witnesses certainly described the Natchez, while others described possible non-Natchezan people), but the eighteenth-century

Natchez were themselves inclusive of one or more refugee groups (see Brain 1982); the "social segments" of Brown's interpretation may well obscure ethnic differences. This mixture of Natchez and possible non-Natchez evidence may account for some of the disparity Brown observed in the formal analyses of the burials from Fatherland Mound C (Brown 1971:table 5) and in the burial attributes derived from documentary sources (Brown 1971:table 6). Clearly, however, one of the main problems lies in the fact that the spatial distinctions noted in the written sources – an indication of corresponding spatial distinctions in the world of the Natchez dead – have not yet been observed on a Natchez site. A few farmsteads and hamlets in the countryside have yielded flesh burials that are at least accompanied by Natchez artifacts (Brown 1985; Barnett 1986), and these data may begin to fill the "commoner gap."

Small Tribes of the Lower Mississippi and Gulf Coast. The French described these groups, which included the Bayougoula and Houma on the Mississippi and the Acolapissa, Biloxi, and Pascagoula on the coast, relatively well at an early date, simply because these were the first representatives of the sedentary southeastern Indians they met. Furthermore, since at first contact or soon afterwards these tribes were suffering from epidemics of European disease or lethal raids by Chickasaw slave-catchers, the French had an opportunity to observe at least partial mortuary patterns.

When Father du Ru visited the Houmas in 1699 with Iberville's party, the chief had been dead for two months and his body was still lying in his cabin, where the Jesuit said it would lie until the flesh rotted, after which the chief's possessions would be disposed of, his house burned, and the bones taken to the temple and venerated as in life, being given a share of French presents. Du Ru was appalled by the mourning ceremonies, which included blowing tobacco smoke over the body on its bier, offering food, and ritually purifying female mourners through their excessive indulgence in black drink and subsequent vomiting (du Ru 1934:27–29).

On the same trip Iberville (1981:63) observed the results of epidemic at the Bayougoula village, where he saw seven-foot platforms all around the village, bearing dead bodies "wrapped in cane mats and covered by a cane mat shaped like the roof of a house. This stinks badly and attracts many buzzards." Du Ru (1934:20) added that when he entered the temples of the Bayougoulas and Mongoulachas he saw "many rows of packages piled one on the other . . . the bones of dead chiefs which are carefully wrapped in palm mats." Neither directly made such observations of the Acolapissas; du Ru (1934:27) only indicated that when a chief died among them a dozen of what the priest termed "his most loyal friends" committed suicide to be buried with him.

Although the French observed drastic population diminution among the Biloxis and Pascagoulas around 1700, they did not report mortuary practices, and it was left to the somewhat imaginative Dumont de Montigny to make purported observations datable to more than thirty years later; Dumont attributed to these tribes an elaborate mummification practice for dead chiefs, whose bodies were first smoked and dried and then propped up like statues, first to receive food offerings and then to stand around the interior of the temple (MacLeod 1928:211).

The documentary evidence thus suggests that secondary processing was practiced almost universally in some form and for all ranks, although chiefs received spatial distinction in the preservation of their remains in the communal temple. The archaeological evidence for these tribes is so sparse that in most cases we do not even know of a site that can reasonably be connected with them (see Davis 1985a; Brown 1976), much less material evidence of mortuary practice. For none of these tribes is there even a complete documentary description of such practice for all segments of the population. Father du Ru evidently decided early on that the coastal tribes he saw were very uniform in their cultural features, and he only described something when it departed from what he had seen before; the information that he saw these groups in south-to-north order is therefore important, possibly accounting for the lack of detail on the curation of chiefly burials among the Houmas and the expanded detail on mourning among those same people. Similarly, it is not clear whether Iberville's observation of the scaffolding of the Bayougoula dead described the means by which their chiefs became du Ru's "many rows of packages." The only certainty, then, is that although the picture is nowhere complete, it always includes secondary processing.

Small Tribes of the Mobile Delta. The lifeways of these small groups, which include the Mobilians, Tohomés, and Naniabas, were poorly described in spite of their early contact with the French at Mobile. Penicaut ([1723] 1953:11) attributed the pile of bones the French encountered on Dauphin Island to the Mobilians, reporting that "as the manner of savages is to gather together all the bones of the dead, they had carried them to this spot." All such a report can testify, however, is that perhaps the Mobilians or some other precontact Mobile Bay tribe emptied their charnel house into a mound on the island. A more pertinent connection for the tribes of the Mobile delta is with the urn burials discussed earlier for the region, the "Ginhouse Island Mortuary Complex" of the Tombigbee-Alabama forks region, and thus with secondary processing for adult burials along with primary deposition of infants in urns.

Alabama and Creek. Traditions among the historic Alabamas and Upper Creeks are difficult to deal with because, until modern times, most English-speaking writers have thought of them as a homogeneous amalgam; fortunately, the French and the Spanish did not, but because they did not live among them as the British did, there is little early historic description of burial practices on the upper Alabama River and at the Coosa-Tallapoosa forks. The evidence that does exist suggests that the historic Upper Creeks, Alabamas and Koasatis alike, followed the same customs as the Chickasaws.

The only early French account of Alabama practice is from the sometimes fanciful Bossu, dating to the mid-1730s. Bossu observed simply that the Alabamas buried the bodies of their dead in a sitting posture, surrounded with their possessions and supplied with tobacco and paint, but he added that suicides were deprived of burial and cast into running water (Swanton 1928c:397). Adair's description of Chickasaw and Upper Creek burial is, except for some details, subsumed under a general description of burial practice in the region, which is based on a description of the sole funeral that Adair saw, that of the chief of the refugee Chickasaw village settled among the Creeks; I have placed that description under the Chickasaw heading below. Presumably the outward and public aspects of Upper Creek burial practice, which Adair must have seen simply in the course of his business, did not contradict the general lines described there: for a natural death in the village, flexed flesh burial under the floor of the decedent's house, accompanied by most of his or her possessions, after a brief mourning period; for a death while hunting or at war, scaffolding in the woods until the flesh rotted, after which the body was fetched home and buried in the usual manner (quoted in Swanton 1928c:389–90).

The Alabamas and Upper Creeks have long been considered the heirs of the burial urn cultures of the Alabama-Coosa-Tallapoosa forks area; at least these descriptions do not conflict seriously with a version of the urn burial practice that included flesh burial for adults. But the historical descriptions may be incomplete. They are very late, and they clearly pertain to a period when the native groups of the region had had contact with Europeans for nearly a hundred years, so the lack of a mention of urn burial is not surprising.

Chickasaw. Chickasaw burial practices were described earliest in 1708 by the British Indian agent–trader Thomas Nairne. According to Nairne (1988:48-49), a Chickasaw dying at home would be dressed in his best and buried beneath his bed in the floor of his house. A post decorated with the possessions of the deceased man or woman would be planted at the door and mourners would weep regularly around it, after which it would be pulled up. The mourning period was a year for a man, six months for a woman, and four months for a child. Nairne mentions no other rite for unusual deaths, but he notes that if a man had been killed in war the post would be saved for the torture of an enemy captured for revenge.

The more famous account of alleged Chickasaw practice, by James Adair, is dated considerably later (late 1740s?) and suffers from Adair's desire to prove Indian descent from a lost Hebrew tribe. His description also has severe limitations: he only witnessed a single burial, because the Indians were "unwilling we should join with them while they are performing this kindred duty" (Adair 1775:180). Also, he witnessed this ceremony in the "Ooeasa" town of refugee Chickasaws and Natchez among the Upper Creeks (Adair 1775:319), where traditional practices might have been altered. Additional information presumably comes from Adair's observations of several tribes; Swanton (1928c:389–91) presents these observations as a synoptic account of the practice of *all* tribes of the region. Hence these data must be used with reservation.

Adair said that the body of the Ooeasa chief was prepared within his house; brought outdoors and propped up with his possessions for a brief mourning period; carried three times around the house with chanting by the chief mourner; and buried sitting, facing east, with face paint and all his best possessions, under the floor of his house in a deep grave covered over with logs and bark. In the section on mourning Adair (1775:187) stated that Chickasaw widows had to mourn for three years, spending the first month weeping at the warrior's "mourning war-pole," which was set in the earth at the door of the house and decked with weapons that hung until they rotted – implying that such a pole would remain set for some time. Mourning for women, Adair (1775:189) suggested, was limited to three months among all the tribes. He claimed that all the tribes, "if they have not corrupted their primitive customs," went, after the flesh had rotted off on a scaffold, to collect the bones of relatives who had died in war away from home (1775:180). In another place he described the use of scaffolding for a warrior killed while hunting on Choctaw land, yet on a similar occasion he described a burial under a pile of logs secured with saplings (Adair 1775:323n,338).

Only limited archaeological excavation has been conducted on Chickasaw sites in the vicinity of Tupelo, Mississippi, but, along with information from the uncontrolled digging of relic hunters, it amply confirms the practice of burial beneath the floors of houses, and since the burials are nearly always found along the walls, presumably also beneath the bed of the deceased. Nearly all the burials are flexed to some degree, which may indeed mean that they were buried sitting up and that the weight of the soil has pushed them over into a flexed position. Because houses most frequently have several burials beneath their floors, it seems that they were not abandoned after a burial. Among all the rather sketchy excavations of the remains of post holes, however, no one has been able to distinguish holes that may have contained mourning poles.

The bundle burials one would expect to find as a result of the secondary processing Adair suggested, however, raise a problem not addressed by Adair's remarks. Bundle burials were found by Spaulding (1940) at MLe18, by Jennings (1941) and Chambers (Chambers Collection) at MLe14, and recently by a University of Mississippi excavation at Meadowbrook (Yearous 1991); the majority of them were single adult individuals. Other bundle burials are difficult to explain, such as the one containing an adult and two children (Jennings 1941) at MLe14, a second containing an adult and an infant from MLe18 (Spaulding 1940), and three adult-child bundles, one containing two adults, from the Meadowbrook site (Yearous 1991). One such burial from one site would have been anomalous, and clearly they differ from the single-adult bundles that seem to be the norm for bundle burials, but the similarities among these five burials suggest that they may mark an anomalous or "bad" death, perhaps death in childbirth or from European disease.

In general, however, given the limited excavation, the number of single-adult bundle burials does not seem too many to be accounted for by Adair's explanation (seven of thirty-three at MLe14, two of thirteen at MLe18), particularly considering that MLe18 is now thought to be the Ackia village the French attacked in 1736 (Atkinson 1986) and nearly all the excavated burials are from the eighteenth century, when the Chickasaws were constantly on a war footing with their neighbors. Also, the three groupings of houses (to a total of twelve) revealed by the digging of collectors showed only one possible bundle, probably a child, out of twenty-seven burials. These excavations were primarily guided by topographic clues, surface scatters, and metal detector prospecting, but they do seem to have been exhaustive in examining the whole of each house interior.

Secondary processing may also be suggested by the frequent tightly flexed burials usually assumed to be primary, and perhaps by a very few bundle burials: if the bones were still joined by tendons when bodies were removed from scaffolds, then they could be flexed tightly and appear to be flesh burials. The same possibility may also account for occasional bundle burials found with many of the bones in anatomical order but bundled more tightly than they could have been in the flesh. Jennings (1941) noted an example in a burial from MLe14 that seems to reflect the latter case, and several of the burials uncovered elsewhere by collectors were reportedly "extremely tightly flexed."

This evidence may warrant the conclusion that apart from missing a possible anomalous treatment for the remains of women and children dead in childbirth or for victims of European disease, the historical sources do give a reasonable picture of the behavioral side of Chickasaw mortuary ritual. It was a unitary practice of flesh burial that reserved secondary processing for anomalous deaths. Interestingly, there seems to have been no spatial distinction between these burial types: both flexed and bundle burials were interred beneath house floors. The apparent lack of such associations for any of the burials at MLe18 (Spaulding 1940:2) and for some of them at Meadowbrook (Yearous 1991) may only have been due to the deep plowing and erosion in the area that has destroyed house patterns, since Jennings (1941) noted on other sites that the burials were found at considerable depth beneath the floors, deeper than post holes were sunk (as they would presumably have to be if the houses were to remain habitable), and the burials at MLe18 and Meadowbrook were found in house-sized groupings.

Chakchiuma. Although European colonial documents do not mention Chakchiuma mortuary ritual, certain sites in the Starkville region have been circumstantially identified as having a Chakchiuma connection (Atkinson 1979). Burials recovered from the Rolling Hills site included bundle burials of adults and children, urn burials of infants, and a few flexed burials that may not have dated to the historic period. Bundle burials were found in multiples (seven adults and a juvenile, four adults and a juvenile, and an adult and two children) and accompanied by European trade goods.

Choctaw. The realm of mortuary ritual is the only one in which Swanton had to acknowledge that his "indefinite" Choctaws needed yield to no one for complexity and gruesomeness. Europeans and their American successors were so struck by the process that they described it over and over with fevered fascination, so plenty of ethnographic description is available; the data are so detailed and explicit that it is the only example from North America that figured in Hertz's (1960) treatment of secondary burial. Because the descriptive data are so voluminous, however, we must be particularly careful to use the earliest possible information, which is, unfortunately, rather thin.

The earliest complete account, the so-called Anonymous Relation manuscript held by the Newberry Library (see Swanton 1931:243–58 for a segment), probably dates to after the 1730s. In it the narrator describes the process of scaffolding, final bone preparation, and curation in the charnel house:

> As soon as he is dead his relatives erect a kind of cabin in the shape of a coffin, directly opposite his door six feet from the ground on six stakes, surrounded by a mud wall, and roofed with bark, in which they enclose his body all dressed, covering it with a blanket. They place food and drink beside him, giving him a change of shoes, his gun, powder, and balls. They say that it is because he is going into another country, and it is right that he have everything he needs in his journey. They believe that the warriors go to war in the other world, and that everyone there performs the same acts that he did in this. The body rests in this five or six months, until they think that it is rotted, which makes a terrible stench in the house. After some time all the relatives assemble ceremoniously and the honored woman of the village who has for her function to strip off the flesh from the bones of the dead, comes to take off the flesh from this body, scrapes the

bones well, and places them in a very clean cane hamper, which they enclose in linen or cloth. They throw the flesh into some field, and this same flesh stripper, without washing her hands, comes to serve food to the assembly. This woman is very much honored in the village. After the repast, singing and howling, they proceed to carry the bones to the charnel-house of the canton, a cabin with only one covering in which these hampers are placed in a row on poles. The same ceremony is performed over chiefs except that instead of putting the bones in hampers they are placed in chests locked with keys in the charnel-house of the chiefs. (Swanton 1931:170–71)

Although Swanton then proceeded to quote from several additional eighteenth-century sources, little else was added except details about the charnel houses: that they seem to have been divided by "tribes"; that they were located away from the villages; that villagers visited them for specific ceremonies once a year; and that when they were filled the bones were brought out and interred in a mass grave. Scarce references to Choctaw mortuary practices in other early eighteenth-century French sources add little more, mostly to the effect that the final curation process for a chief (referred to in French as *désossement*, or "boning") was an occasion for celebration and feasting and important political activities among the leaders of the tribe, the chiefs of which were expected to attend (Rowland, Sanders, and Galloway 1984, 4:282,284).

The sources differ on other details: whether the scaffolds were burned, the sex of the mortuary specialist, whether that individual used a knife or fingernails to strip the flesh, whether the skull was painted red, and the nature of the container for the bones. These details, if they are not simply idiosyncratic, may be attributable to ethnic variations within the Choctaw nation. Since none of the sources is specific on the location of its observations – representing them as applying to the whole tribe – identifying these variations with any specific ethnic subgroup is not now possible.

The known archaeological evidence for Choctaw mortuary practice does not contradict these descriptions (the few known flesh burials of Choctaws can be dated firmly to the nineteenth century), but the evidence consists of several ossuary mounds: two at the Nanih Waiya mound site, a group in Clarke County (east of the "homeland"), and a group in Wayne County (south of the "homeland"; see Collins 1926:90–94). In any event, only the final deposition of bones from charnel houses would be archaeologically recoverable except in very unusual circumstances.

Interpretation

The first step in interpreting this evidence is to review the universal sequence of mortuary ritual and to look at how the examples fit into it. When a person dies, the pollution introduced by death has to be purified and the soul released through an initial process, and in many cultures that entails protecting the remains until the soul is felt to be free. If this process does not include the permanent interment of remains, the survivors must do something to prepare them, which means packaging the remains in some way. If interment is not to be immediate, the survivors must provide for the curation of the remains for some period of time, and this phase may incorporate veneration of the remains. Eventually, however, the remains must be returned to the earth if they have not gone completely to dust.

All societies define "good" or "normal" deaths for which they provide an ordinary treatment in death, which may vary with the rank of the decedent. Most societies also feel the need to cope with "bad" or "anomalous" deaths, deaths due to causes that the society does not understand or that it chooses to deny; in either case, these deaths usually have some suspected special danger or pollution connected with them, and the treatment of the victims of such deaths may require extraordinary effort or may entail the drastic course of casting the body aside without ceremony – and thus excluding the dead person from the other world entirely.

The work of mortuary ritual is not simply the duty of the family, except under a broader definition; the work is carried out by many persons having defined social roles with respect to the decedent in order to ensure the perpetuation of the social role that person occupied. Thus the family, the lineage, the moiety may be involved. But because the pollution introduced by death can be damaging to those who are of the same kind as the decedent, such tasks may instead be carried out by their opposite numbers: the other moiety, a paired clan.

To show how these considerations apply to the possible interpretation of mortuary practices as markers of ethnicity, the distribution of those practices in space and time is important. Table 7.4 presents the mortuary forms from both historic and prehistoric evidence in the same sequence as in the discussion above. Seen in that way, it presents some problems for establishing the continuity of late prehistoric and historic populations, because in several cases the historic evidence presents significant modification over the evidence for the prehistoric period. Choctaw practice especially indicates a distinctive "leveling" of mortuary activities, providing the entire population with the same lengthy postmortem treatment. The problem is to attempt to explain it.

There are several dimensions of variability in mortuary practice. The first is of course sociopolitical: important people qualify for more expenditure than do unimportant people. Because that expenditure does not necessarily correlate with the time the soul needs to reach the other world, however, secondary treatment is not the only way in which the deceased person may be honored. Another way to make that expenditure is to deposit valuable items in the grave of an important person, thus taking them out of circulation and reinforcing the value of similar such goods re-

Table 7.4 Summary of Burial Types in the Study Area, Late Prehistoric to Early Historic Periods.

Region	Period	Primary	Urn	Bundle	Skull
Yazoo	Coles Creek	X		X	
	Plaquemine	X		X	X
	Historic (Tunica)	X			
Natchez Bluffs	Plaquemine	X		X	
	Historic (Natchez)	X		X	
LMV & Coast	Historic			X	
Mobile	"Burial Urn"		X	X	
BW/Alabama	Moundville III	X		X	
	Alabama River	X	X	X	
	Historic (Alabama)	X		?	
Tombigbee	Summerville	X		X	X
	Sorrells	X			
	Historic (Chickasaw)	X		X	
	Historic (Chakchiuma)	?	X	X	
	Choctaw			X	

Key: LMV = Lower Mississippi Valley, BW = Black Warrior

maining in the possession of other important people, including an heir. So although lengthy secondary processing was a popular option for southeastern chiefs (as witness the tireless use of the Natchez as a model for chiefdoms by southeastern archaeologists), it was not the only one, and the Coles Creek evidence from Lake George even suggests that infant sacrifice, for example, could be substituted for it almost entirely.

What other reasons might lead to disparate burial programs? Some statement of identification, a sign of ethnicity – whether of family, lineage, or moiety – must be involved, but ethnographic evidence suggests that markedly divergent practices, incorporating processes that demanded a large difference in expenditure of effort, would inevitably be converted into sociopolitical distinctions, as it may have been among the Natchez to the extent that "stinkard" was equated with "flesh burial." In a situation such as that enjoyed by the Chickasaws, where lineal development in roughly the same place over time entailed perhaps the rise and decline of a simple chiefdom, the simplification of mortuary practice, limiting extended treatment to those who had met with an unusual death, would harmonize well with the aspirations of group members who enjoyed virtually equal access to resources. Finally, ethnic identification within a multiethnic group striving for equality would probably have to depend upon minor variations that would rarely survive in the archaeological record and that might even be missed in ethnographic description – the kinds of variation suggested by the variant descriptions of eighteenth-century Choctaw mortuary practice.

As a spatial distribution, this summary of evidence shows that secondary processing certainly seems to be more frequent in the focal southern Mississippi area than elsewhere. When the data are examined as a temporal distribution, however, it is possible to suggest that the variability may have started out as a distinction in rank, just as Binford (1971) said it should. As chiefdoms declined, however, the mortuary ritual that previously served to reproduce a ranked ordering of social persons was simplified, apparently in two steps. First, both forms were retained, but one was assigned to "normal" deaths, while the other was assigned to "anomalous" deaths. And generally speaking, the form that was assigned to "anomalous" deaths – deaths in childbirth or war – was the longer one that provided more opportunity for purification of pollution. Eventually, a single form became universal as European influences began to prevail. This trajectory goes a long way in explaining the mortuary practices of the Tunicas, the Natchez, the Alabamas, and the Chickasaws, but the Choctaws are an anomaly: they "simplified" to one mortuary practice, but in "simplifying" they chose the more complex mode of treatment.

We can hypothesize that the Choctaws, attempting to amalgamate several populations from east, west, and south – all of whom practiced secondary burial for important individuals – adopted as their single burial form the one that all had used for their important people. Their extremely odd migration myth suggests a reason for this choice, as will be discussed in the next chapter; some of the arguments that will make that clue believable require a brief look at what the burial of the dead has to do with a people's relationship to the land they live on.

Places of burial are no accident. In numerous examples throughout the world, they are chosen to reflect the relationship of social groups to their land (Bloch and Parry 1982:34–35). The Chickasaws and Tunicas did not just bury their dead in the ground; they buried them under the floors of their houses or in the environs of their houses. The ultimate disposal of secondary burials, after curation in ossuaries, was in the earth too, and when it was done these southeastern people often created an above-ground marker on the landscape by heaping up the bones of the dead as an announcement of the perpetuity of their community. The bones of ancestors, in other words, functioned to structure the world of the living by structuring the supernatural world of the dead; by placing the bones of ancestors one established a settlement charter.

A famous example of this practice comes from Madagascar, where the people spend enormous amounts of money and time constructing monumental tombs that are the most significant buildings in the landscape (Bloch 1971). These tombs certify and perpetuate the claims of specific lineages to specific places, and even people who move far away will spend a great deal of money to prepare the body of a dead loved one and to carry it back to the ancestral tomb. Similarly, a recent study of mortuary practices in classical Greece has suggested that as the notion of the *poleis* began to take form, and citizenship was defined in terms of landholding, the places of burial in a Greek city-state grew to define the structure of the city-state more surely than the places of settlement of its people, which might have to be spread over the countryside (Morris 1987).

This notion of burial place as settlement charter has a ready-made example in early colonial North America in the case of the Hurons, who practiced an egalitarian mode of secondary processing much like that of the Choctaws, except that the bodies remained in a village cemetery consisting of scaffold tombs instead of being removed from their scaffolds and enclosed in an above-ground charnel house structure. Whenever the Hurons relocated large villages to be near more fertile land or better forest resources, they held a "Feast of the Dead" for the final burial (in a large common grave near the village) of the bodies from the village cemetery and from those of any satellite villages. The abandoned village was then thought to constitute a village of the dead, who would continue to make use of the fields and forest abandoned by the living (Trigger 1976:85–90,147). As I hope to show, some of the proto-Choctaws may have done something analogous, except that they knew, as they moved into the new homeland, that they would not be returning to the places they were leaving. The evidence for such a "second foundation" through a mass burial may be much more accessible than the burials are.

CHAPTER EIGHT

Ethnic Boundaries from Documentary Evidence

As to the Chatkas, I suppose, that being very numerous, they have been able to preserve their own language in great measure; and have only adopted some words of the Chicasaw language. – Antoine Simon Le Page Du Pratz, *The History of Louisiana*

What can be reconstructed of a protolanguage is thus comparable to the visible part of an iceberg; only a greater or lesser percentage is recoverable in spite of the certainty that the reality was both quantitatively and qualitatively much richer. In this respect historical linguistics is like archaeology. – Mary R. Haas, *Language, Culture, and History*

In this chapter, still in search of markers of ethnicity, I examine several specific types of information, all of which are available only through European reports but most of which Europeans would have had no particular reason to falsify or distort. The first comes from the reports of Frenchmen and Englishmen at the turn of the eighteenth century and into its first decade: the intertribal relationships observed at that date. The evidence for the second, the distribution of languages and dialects, comes from the same sources, but it is complicated by the problem of the "Mobilian" or "Chickasaw" trade language. With the third, migration legends, we are even less fortunate, for the earliest dates to 1735, and most were not collected until the nineteenth century; these require serious critical examination before they can be evaluated and interpreted.

INTERTRIBAL RELATIONS, 1700

In the context of the face-to-face cultures of the seventeenth-century Southeast, kinship relations or the lack of them were likely to exert a powerful influence over alliances and enmities. Research on trading networks among small-scale chiefdoms and tribal segments led by big-men has shown that long-distance trade almost never followed a single trajectory between distant points except in unusual circumstances (as along the Mississippi River, for example); instead, kinship links from village to village enabled goods to be passed along to their destination. In the disruption that followed European contact, such links likely remained the only armature for reconstructing the communication network that crossed the region; and by marrying into this network to exploit it, Europeans preserved evidence of its existence.

To make use of the network they had to understand how it worked, and intertribal relations are therefore among the most frequently noted features of Indian society in contemporary accounts. Europeans needed the alliance of Indians and, given the presence of Europeans and their possession of desirable goods, Indians also sought European alliance, creating fictive kinship with these new people as the mode of their diplomacy. Thus, studying the way the Europeans were woven into the existing fabric of intertribal alliances may permit analysis of that fabric.

Examining these problems in spatial terms – viewing these "ethnic" features as spatial distributions – can be helpful. What is already "known," it turns out, is subject to the same difficulties that have been encountered all along; for a start, it is difficult even to visualize any of these problems except in terms of Swanton's 1911 map of tribal distributions, which portrays an ethnographic present that never existed. To move at least to a map that was attempting to portray a moment in time, I here refer to a distribution of tribal names taken from Delisle's 1703 map of the Southeast (figure 8.1).

In previous chapters I have explicitly questioned the validity of certain European representations of Indian intertribal relations, particularly those that suggested that Indians would ask Europeans for help in whipping "allies" or "tributaries" into line, and I have shown why such portrayals were so much in the interests of the Europeans that they are untrustworthy. Here, therefore, I try to state clearly what kind of evidence I consider acceptable as indicating bona fide intertribal relations.

By no means should we assume that intertribal relations in the year 1700 or thereabout reflected anything except the already much altered conditions in the interior at that time. I believe that examining those relations is worthwhile, however, because if the Choctaws did come together in the seventeenth century, then I think it likely that some of those relationships may reflect longer habit.

All the evidence to be used was related by Europeans, so here also nothing is privileged as an early and firsthand native source. But here also we can consider behavior rather than commentary, and this will be the rule of thumb: warriors who hunt together are probably allied, and if an Indian of one tribe is said to be living among another tribe, though this may indeed be the case, we should not exclude the possibility that his mother may have been married into it to seal an alliance, and the Indian mentioned was merely retaining her ethnicity.

It is fortunate that the Frenchmen who first began extended contact with the Choctaws at the turn of the eighteenth century considered themselves so ill-informed. Without access to any unpublished Spanish sources, these Frenchmen had

Chickasaws
Chakchiumas
Caskinampo
Chickasaw
Village
Caouitas
Conchaques
Yazoos
Ouispe
Tunicas
Choctaws
Aepataniche
Alabamas
Caouitas
Koroas
Taensas
Natchez
Capinans Tohomés
Mobilians
Oumas
Acolapissas Pascagoulas
Bayogoulas
Ouachas

0   miles   200
0   kilometers   200

8.1. Location of southeastern tribes ca. 1700 (data from Guillaume Delisle, *Carte du Mexique et de la Floride*, 1703).

no detailed idea of the tribes they would encounter north of the Gulf coast apart from those La Salle and Tonti had met on the Mississippi River. Their ideas of tribal structures and groupings had been formed on the basis of more than a hundred years of fur trade with the tribes of French Canada, and they were very different from the Spaniards' Aztec- and Inca-influenced ideas of "provinces." They expected to see ad hoc groupings and power struggles, and they knew that the only way to detect what was going on was to observe sharply.

Mississippi River Tribes

The early information gathered by both La Salle and Iberville on the Mississippi River depended heavily upon Indian guides – in La Salle's case, first a Quapaw and then a Taensa escort; in Iberville's case, a singularly well informed Taensa who allegedly even drew maps for him. These biases do color the evidence to a certain extent – and may account in some measure for the distinctly Natchez-centered view of the lower river – but they also introduce a much more detailed view of the region and its interconnections; and those interconnections seem not to have included the Choctaws to any significant degree.

The French explorers of the late seventeenth century found the Oumas located north of their famous *baton rouge*, a presumed boundary marker with their enemies the Bayougoulas to the south. The French observed that in their fights with the Bayougoulas the Oumas could call on the "little Taensas," a Natchezan tribe located west of the Mississippi near the Red River (Iberville 1981:122–23). Beyond implications that they and other Indians of the lower part of the valley had suffered from raids by the Chickasaws, there is little indication of Ouma relations to the east (Bowman and Curry-Roper 1982).

In the view of both La Salle and Iberville, the Natchez were most closely affiliated with the Taensas to their north, on the west side of the Mississippi, sharing nearly all cultural features, including language, religion, and material culture. The two groups seem to have been peers in the late seventeenth century, although archaeological evidence is much more extensive for the Natchez than for the Taensas, suggesting that this was not always the case. If the Natchezan peoples of the lower valley were the heirs of the Quigualtam chiefdom of Soto's day, then the Taensas, possibly identified with Guachoya or Anilco, might once have been tributary; if they were not the Quigualtam people, we know even less. But neither in the questionable Spanish accounts nor later is there any suggestion of significant alliance to the east by any Mississippi River group. The La Salle accounts suggested that the Natchez did hold some alliances with tribes further south along the Mississippi, specifically the Quinipissas, but by 1700 the European accounts no longer mentioned that relationship; the Quinipissas, also known as the Mongoulachas, had merged with the Bayougoulas.

Most documentary and archaeological studies of the Natchez have concluded that they had become multiethnic in some sense well before the end of the seventeenth century, and this development is connected hypothetically with the depopulation of the Yazoo Basin due to European disease (Ramenofsky 1987; Brown 1985). The "outsiders" in this new combination were, by the eighteenth century, known as the Tioux and Grigras, thought to have been of Tunican extraction; if they were, their relations with the Quapaws were probably none too good, reflecting the decided enmity between the Quapaws and the tribes of the lower Yazoo Basin, including the Tunicas.

In 1682 a group of Coroas was an important part of the Natchez conglomerate, yet in 1700 there was no such group reported by that name among the Natchez. There was, on the other hand, a group of Coroas located among the tribes on the lower Yazoo River. Several recent studies have suggested that "Coroa" was a name applied to Tunican peoples in the lower Mississippi Valley (Jeter 1986; Kidder 1988), who played a significant part as intermediaries between the lower valley and Caddoan groups to the west. Thus the "Coroas" of the La Salle expedition could possibly have become the eighteenth-century Tioux. In either case, however, the intertribal link that is suggested is toward the west of the Mississippi.

The Tunica grouping on the lower Yazoo at its confluence with the Mississippi was an important force at the start of the eighteenth century. Enmity clearly existed between the Tunicas and the Quapaws, who viewed them as the most significant tribe on the lower Yazoo. Just as clearly, as Father Davion learned, there were ongoing relations between the tribes of the lower Yazoo – the Tunicas, Yazoos, and Coroas – and the Chickasaws of the upper Tombigbee drainage.

Brain (1988) has argued for some time that the Tunicas were the historic-period heirs to the sixteenth-century chiefdom of Quizquiz that the Hernando de Soto expedition saw. If that was the case, the internal dynamics of the region had been seriously altered in the interim. Soto's expedition had come upon the Quizquiz people totally unawares, thus suggesting to some researchers that a no man's land marked at least competition if not enmity between the Yazoo Basin chiefdoms and the Tombigbee Chicaça people – and probably enmity, since the Chicaça people had had a whole winter to warn their western neighbors about the Spaniards and apparently had not done so. This observation from the documents is not contradicted by the presence of trade goods from the central Mississippi Valley – the painted polychrome vessels of the (probably non-Quapaw) "Quapaw" phase – found at modest sites on the Tombigbee (Sheldon and Jenkins 1986), since no materials suggest a comparable Tunican connection. In fact this clear trade connection between the middle Tombigbee and the far northern Yazoo Basin and trans-Mississippi amounts to another argument against Quizquiz having been located that far north, if we are to believe that Quizquiz was not warned.

Gulf Coast Tribes

As I have shown, European contacts with tribes of the western Gulf coast before the coming of the French were, apart from the sporadic slight contact of the documented expeditions, apparently limited to undocumented shipwrecks, since deep draft ships could not directly reach the coast. The earliest contacts made by Iberville's expeditions were with tribes found along the coast west of Mobile Bay. Most of these groups were in the grip of two miseries, perhaps connected: epidemic European disease and Chickasaw slave raids.

The Pascagoula estuary and delta had apparently been thickly populated, for on it lived the three "villages" of the Biloxis, Moctobis, and Pascagoulas (Iberville 1981: 92), although by 1699 they were decimated by illnesses. We know little of the Moctobis beyond their name; they are assumed to have been Siouan, like their neighbors the Biloxis. As the archaeology suggests, however, the Pascagoulas were culturally related to the natives of the Mobile bay and delta, who, as I have argued, had important Choctaw connections. It may therefore have been no accident that it was the Pascagoulas who first told the French about the powerful Choctaws of the interior, who, they said, consisted of forty-five villages and were being preyed upon by British allies in slave raids (Sauvole [1699–1701] 1969:35–36). Subsequently, after Iberville sent men into the interior with a Pascagoula chief to visit the Choctaws, Tohomés, and Mobilians, it was the chief of the Pascagoulas and a chief of the Mobilians from the Mobile delta who brought the first Choctaws to visit the French on the coast (Iberville 1981:141–43; Sauvole [1699–1701] 1969:40–41).

According to a visiting Bayougoula chief who met Iberville while hunting with a band of his men on the coast, his calumet dance to Iberville had cemented French alliance with a large range of tribes: the Mougoulascha (Mougoulacha), Ouascha (Washa), Toutymascha (Chitimacha?), and Yagueneschyto ("big country" in Choctaw; tribe unknown) west of the Mississippi, and the Bylocchy (Biloxi), Moctoby, Ouma, Pascoboula (Pascagoula), Thecloel (Natchez), Bayacchyto ("big bayou" in Choctaw; tribe unknown), and Amylcou (Soto's Anilco? – never mentioned by the French again) east of the Mississippi (Iberville 1981:47–48). This list suggests wide-ranging native alliances, but either the chief was inflating the influence of his own tribe or the Frenchmen misunderstood his assertion, since, as I have already said, there was enmity between the Bayougoulas and Oumas. It does, nevertheless, suggest some alliances for the Bayougoulas stretching into the hinterland of the Pearl River to the east, since "Bayacchyto" would become "Bogue Chitto," long the name of a major southwestern tributary of the Pearl. Father du Ru and a party sent by Iberville visited the Acolapissas, who lived in several villages on the lower Pearl River, in 1700, when two of their villages had been destroyed by the Chickasaw slave raiders and fifty people carried off to be sold to Carolina.

The behavior of the Bayougoulas, Mougoulachas, and Acolapissas was a symptom of the turmoil in the region. By the time Iberville visited, the Bayougoulas had assimilated La Salle's mysterious "Quinipissas" in the persons of the Mougoulachas, who had formed a sort of duplex village with them including its own chief and temple. Yet within a year they had apparently killed or at least attacked and driven out the Mougoulachas, replacing them with Acolapissas and Tious (Iberville 1981: 143). The Oumas and Tunicas would reprise this same strange theme of hospitality and takeover some seven years later (Brain 1988:31).

Ethnic Boundaries from Documentary Evidence

Mobile Bay and Alabama River Tribes

In 1699 Iberville (1981:143) observed, having talked with some Choctaws and Tohomés, that the English arming of the Indians of the interior had put the Choctaws at war with "all the other nations to the north and east of them." This is a particularly interesting remark: since the Choctaws of the Mississippi "homeland" area were certainly at peace with the tribes of the Mobile delta to the east, it implies that those tribes were considered in some sense Choctaw rather than "other nations." Charles Levasseur (1981) visited the tribes in question, the Mobilians and Tohomés, in 1700; he reported that they were friendly with one another – as Delgado had seen in 1686 – and that the Tohomés traded salt to the Choctaws. Furthermore, when Tonti traveled among the Choctaws and Chickasaws in 1702, two of his guides were Mobilian and Tohomé (Galloway 1982b:167), perhaps implying that this trade was not only widespread but even gave them safe passage as far as the Chickasaw territory. Yet the Mobilians and Tohomés were cruelly exposed to the British-sponsored slave raids of their neighbors to the north and east, as Iberville (1981:169–70) observed when he traveled into the delta in 1702 and saw deserted settlements "almost everywhere."

Levasseur also supplied, via a "Maugoulacho" informant living among the Mobilians, a curious list of thirty-six nations on the Alabama River, some of them echoing Delgado's lists of chiefs met at Tiquipache, Culasa, and Tabasa in 1686. Levasseur's informant indicated that some among these Alabama River tribes, having been armed by the British, were hostile to the others, especially the Pensacolas to the southeast and the Mobilians to the west, but the very presence of the informant from one of these nations indicates, as did Delgado's evidence, that contacts from the Mobile delta with the Indians of the Alabama, Coosa, and Tallapoosa Rivers to the east were not infrequent. Iberville's (1981:173) pronouncements at treaty talks with the Chickasaws in 1702 indicate that the French singled out the Alabamas and the "Conchaques" as the chief among the slave raiders from the east – and thought that the Chickasaws might have some influence over them.

Tribes North of the Choctaws

The Chickasaws were the most important tribe to the north of the Choctaws, and archaeological and documentary evidence attests to their presence in that region (with their position steadily altered as they moved northward up the Tombigbee watershed) from 1540 until the early 1700s (Johnson 1990). La Salle's meeting with Chickasaws along the Mississippi, and the reaction of other tribes further south when one of them accompanied him down the Mississippi, indicate that even at that time their reputation was far-ranging and dangerous, for by the time Father Davion settled with the Tunicas in 1699 a British slave-trader had been resident among them for several years, his presence presumably only reflecting the increased volume of the trade that the British had begun fostering years before.

When Henri de Tonti was sent to bring in Choctaw and Chickasaw chiefs for parleys at Mobile with Iberville in 1702, the Chickasaws and their allies and near neighbors the Chakchiumas were actively taking Choctaw slaves, and the Chickasaw emissaries to Mobile apparently needed a good deal of protection from their Choctaw escort to come safely through Choctaw country on the way. When Iberville spoke to them at the treaty talks, he mentioned five hundred slaves taken from the Choctaws and eighteen hundred Choctaws killed – but also eight hundred Chickasaw deaths at the hands of Choctaw defenders (Iberville 1981:172). Yet the evidence is not entirely straightforward, for Tonti also observed that the Choctaws had built up a stock of hides to trade (possibly with the English through the Chickasaws), and some Choctaws, Tonti's escort among them, clearly favored extinguishing the enmity between the two tribes (Galloway 1982b).

The presence of Chakchiumas on the slave raids and the existence of a Chakchiuma village between the Choctaws and Chickasaws may be somewhat misleading; since Tonti made no effort to bring a Chakchiuma chief with him to Mobile, and since other observations indicated that Chakchiumas were also living on the upper Yazoo River at the same period, the French may not have seen the Chakchiumas among the Chickasaws as a separate nation, or that location may not have been the nation's primary one. At any rate, in the early 1700s the Chakchiumas were inimical to the Choctaws to some degree.

Father Davion's observations of the upper Yazoo River help to complete this round of tribes. As relayed through the writings of others, we hear of several other tribes (also seen as allies of the Chickasaws) on the upper Yazoo: the Ofogoulas, Ibitoupas, and Taposas. These tribes seem to have been pretty insignificant at the time, and they all subsequently merged with other tribes. The Ofogoulas, who are thought to have been Siouan like the Biloxis and the Quapaws, made up a group with the Tunicas and Yazoos, while the Ibitoupas and Taposas apparently lived near the Chakchiumas on the upper river. Nothing is said directly about any of these nations' relations with the Choctaws, but if place names are any guide, some Ibitoupas may have later amalgamated with the Choctaws (Galloway 1982c).

The Choctaws as a Confederacy

"South of the Chycacha," Iberville (1981:74) said in 1699, "all the nations are at peace with one another." If this can be taken to mean that a sort of "Greater Choctaw

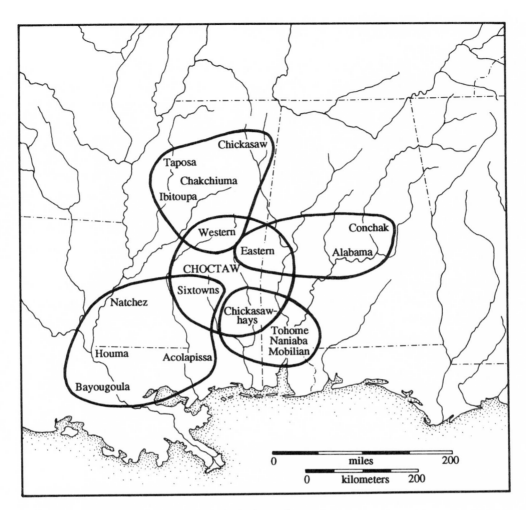

8.2. Intertribal alliance relations ca. 1700 in the study area.

Federation" existed, it may provide a clue to the process of amalgamation. When Tonti went south with Choctaw chiefs for the treaty talks with Iberville, he took *three* Choctaw chiefs to speak for the nation, and one among them had specified that he did not speak for any but the people of his own village group (Galloway 1982b:163). This external evidence alone suggests that the Choctaws consisted of more than one segment in 1700, so the segmentation that held good throughout the eighteenth century and into the nineteenth had its beginning at least this early.

Conditions Affecting Intertribal Relations

By the time of first sustained contact, Europeans had already done much to alter intertribal relations in the interior, but some constants break through this litany of domino-effect enmities effected by the Chickasaw and Alabama slave-catchers.

313

By 1700 the British had not only set up what would become a full-fledged trade emporium at the Coosa-Tallapoosa forks; they had gone beyond their native intermediaries to move a trade outpost into the Chickasaw village agglomeration on the upper Tombigbee to siphon wealth in the form of deerskins and human slaves out of the deep interior. Meanwhile, the French had made first contact down the Mississippi and at the coast, had communicated their desire to settle among the tribes of the Mississippi Valley, had perhaps created a temporary trade outpost among the Chickasaws (Galloway 1991b), and had certainly established several missions in the Mississippi Valley. The effects of these apparently ephemeral presences on people whose lives had already been significantly disrupted were beginning to take hold, but they were still being felt in native terms to some degree; new institutions were not yet necessary to deal with them.

Instead, leaders among the tribes trading with the Europeans were attempting to control that trade just as they had controlled external prestige-goods trade in the aboriginal context. They could not, however, control it as hereditary chiefs had done before the coming of Europeans, because they could no longer control the desired materials for reciprocation. The Europeans wanted not the craft objects whose manufacture the chiefs could control, but only the raw material of deerskin or slaves, and both were available to any warrior who was able to catch them. Big-men or chiefs who wished to maintain their status or build upon it, therefore, had to cooperate with the Europeans to limit to their own supporters the availability of the high-technology means of production (guns and ammunition) that enabled a warrior to compete successfully for the trade. They could not, however, stop anyone who could make and use a bow and arrow from profiting to some degree (except as they could persuade the Europeans to refuse to trade with individuals), so in the long run this trade in raw materials would tend to weaken central control of native groups where any remained or threatened to arise.

To maintain their power and influence or simply to defend themselves against the depredations of their armed neighbors, chiefs and big-men had to maintain old alliances and in some cases forge new ones. Clearly, also, the European intrusion was having an effect upon alliances, so that the beneficiaries of the British trade found themselves allied against its victims. Alliances were still being made through kinship, so strategic marriages were the method of choice to form them. This is one reason for the repeated references to Indians of one polity living with another polity – when these Indians were not traders, they may have been native to the polity in a physical sense but still belonged to their mother's polity through the matrilineal kinship of the Southeast.

A deeper current to these alliances exists, however, that is not entirely explained by European pressures: common ethnicity, a consciousness of sharing identity through a common (if mythical) past or origin and through identifiably distinct cultural practices. Thus the Natchez are allied with the Taensas on the lower Mississippi, and they in turn have connections with the Oumas and Bayougoulas, whose pottery plainly shows strong influence from Natchezan models, whatever their linguistic affiliations may have been (Jeter 1989:241–42). Hence the Tunican tentacles reached out through the lower Yazoo Basin and to the south and west through the Coroas, another Tunican people. The peoples allied with the Choctaws are those of the coast and the Mobile delta, the same people who knew, feared, and spoke of them to the Spaniards fifteen years earlier, but who now found in them a powerful ally or buffer against pressures from the east. These peoples also shared certain pottery styles and mortuary rites with them, and language as well.

LINGUISTIC VARIATION AND BOUNDARIES

Language has been more often – and more erroneously – equated with ethnicity than perhaps any other cultural feature. Language is not inextricably tied to the praxis of culture, and it can easily change in a generation or less if demographic upheaval takes place; thus it is not a good ethnic indicator. Yet if its speakers are left in peace or isolated by geography or politics, it is so conservative that it may be understandable after a thousand years. Anthropologists approach language with caution because of this double-edged quality: if language variation matches ethnic variation as otherwise predicted, they are glad to use it; if it does not, they consider that they must explain the dissociation.

Linguistic Boundaries

A first step in using linguistic evidence is to understand what a linguistic boundary is, and that is perhaps best explained by looking at how students of American Indian languages have arrived at the distribution map of southeastern languages shown in figure 8.3. Linguists are handicapped just like historians because of the lack of very early vocabularies and texts in the native languages of the Southeast. This deficiency does not, however, thwart historical linguists who want to know the history of the modern Indian languages, because by comparing related languages – seen as related because of common vocabulary items and sometimes grammatical features – and by using principles of sound change over time, they can postulate the genealogical relationships among the modern languages and even reconstruct theoretical common "protolanguages" out of which they developed. Using the methods of lexicostatistics, which purport to provide information about how long related languages have been independent of one another by examining their shared features, they are even able to add some kind of temporal scale to this reconstruction. What linguists cannot say is *where* these languages were spoken at any time before the present or recent past; they must depend upon historical or archaeological witnesses for this information. Figure 8.3 therefore has no defined boundaries because it is based upon the random remarks of Spanish, French, and British observers.

That is not to say that there are no methods for establishing language boundaries. The distinctions between related languages amount to differences in pronunciation, grammar, and vocabulary; within the languages similar kinds of differences define dialects; and the individual variations of a single speaker can be defined as an idiolect. A living language or dialect has a statistically dominant median of distinctive features that defines it with respect to other languages or dialects; a map of feature distributions can define with reasonable precision even the dialect boundaries within a language. Without access to a broad range of speakers in every possible location, however, as is the case with languages in the historical past, such a precise map of language distributions is not possible.

Linguistic Prehistory of the Southeast

Languages always change over time. If any language were spread out in a flat plane with a uniform distribution of speakers, all the dialects and eventually all the daughter languages would imperceptibly grade into one another. But such a picture omits the other features of human life in a varied environment, where people do not spread out uniformly over a landscape that does not uniformly provide for their needs, nor do they remain organized in single families. People organize themselves in groups and concern themselves with group as well as individual goals, and although language as a means of communication is a fundamental tool that enables them to do so, it is also a tool that its users modify for specific needs, including the need to distinguish themselves from others. In short, languages change over time, accidentally and intentionally, so that eventually even related languages can become mutually unintelligible.

Such was the case in the Southeast. Modern archaeological thinking now holds that most of the southeastern Indian groups descended from Mississippian predecessors in the region, and that the Mississippian cultures in turn mostly developed *in situ* from Woodland-period predecessors. Thus it should come as no surprise that most of the Indians of the Southeast at the time of European contact spoke languages belonging to the same language family: Muskogean. Furthermore, lexicostatistical comparison of the daughter languages they spoke has suggested that Proto-Muskogean began to subdivide some three thousand to thirty-five hundred years ago, at or around the end of the Archaic period and well before agricultural sedentarism began to demand more fixed locational identification (Witkowski and Springer 1979). This

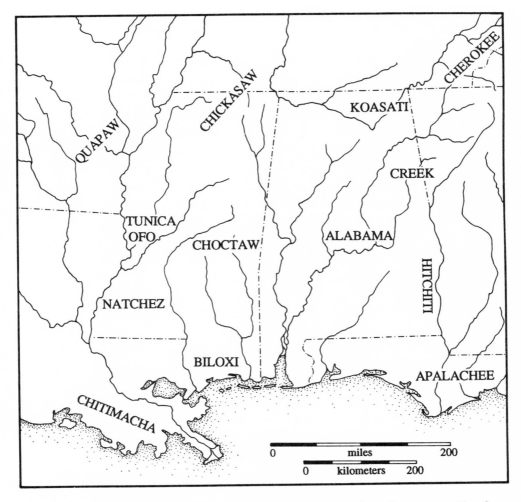

8.3. Location of Indian languages in southeastern North America about the year 1700 (data from Crawford 1975:facing p. 1).

means, given the number of different languages spoken historically, that the few multilevel Mississippian polities in the region east of the Mississippi probably spoke different but often related languages.

Mary Haas's (1978:291) reconstruction of the history of the Muskogean language family (figure 8.4a) divides Muskogean into Eastern and Western groups. Eastern Muskogean is further subdivided into Old Creek, Old Hitchiti, and Old Alabama; the latter is closest in similarity to the sole representative of the Western branch, Old Choctaw. The subdialects descended from Old Choctaw are New Choctaw and Chickasaw. Old Alabama, on the other hand, developed into three separate languages, New Alabama, Koasati, and Apalachee. Old Hitchiti developed into New Hitchiti and the subdialect Mikasuki, while Old Creek developed New Creek subdia-

317

lects, including New Creek and Seminole. More interesting, perhaps, Haas's (1956) long-sustained work on Atakapa, Chitimacha, Natchez, and Tunica – the language "isolates" – has found that Natchez and Tunica in particular probably shared a common ancestor, the hypothetical protolanguage "Gulf," with Proto-Muskogean.

More recently, Pamela Munro (1987) has proposed a slightly different view of the Muskogean language relationships (figure 8.4b) that groups the family differently at the higher levels in order to account for some specific innovations, making Choctaw and Chickasaw Western Muskogean, grouping them with Alabama and Koasati (and presumably also Apalachee) as Southwestern Muskogean, grouping all those with Hitchiti and Mikasuki as Southern Muskogean, and leaving Creek and Seminole to their own Northern Muskogean group, only related to the others at the Proto-Muskogean level. Further detailed work by Martin (1992; see figure 8.4c) has supported Munro's reconstruction and added suggestions of external linguistic relationships through studies of vocabulary and structural borrowings.

These genealogical diagrams are very provocative, and one might be tempted to assign some of the language names to real people and be done with it. With full awareness that language need have nothing to do with other markers of ethnicity, one may speculate on a scenario beginning in the Mississippian period, when it would not be excessive to identify Western Muskogean speakers of "Old Choctaw" with the Mississippian horizon on the Tombigbee watershed, to see in the speakers of "Old Alabama" the people who dwelt on the Alabama River and in the Mobile delta and the central coast, and to identify the speakers of "Old Hitchiti" and "Old Creek" as the people who occupied the lands south and east of the lower salient of the Appalachians. If the Moundville people were as reluctant to have anything to do with the peoples east of them as the absence of material evidence of such contact suggests (Peebles 1986:32–33), we might reasonably assume that they were also liable to maximize language differences along with everything else.

If we can make such identifications for the late Mississippian period, the transformation of minor chiefdoms of the upper Tombigbee and the central hills of Mississippi into the dispersed, hunting-oriented "prairie cultures" of the protohistoric period could be seen as the moment when the Chickasaw dialect became an entity on its own. "New Alabama" might then be equated with the burial urn horizon of the Alabama River phase. Clearly Munro's reworking of the relationships, by bringing Alabama into close connection with Choctaw and Chickasaw, expresses the close relations known from the early historic period for these peoples.

Although these identifications are certainly tentative, there is nothing tentative about the identification of the Natchez language with the people of the Natchez Bluffs region who built Anna, Emerald, and eventually the Grand Village of the Natchez. The protohistoric trajectory of Tunica speakers east of the Mississippi is

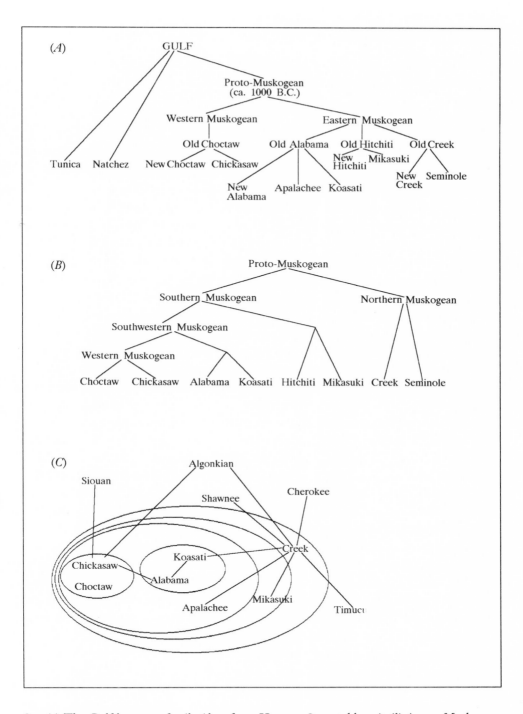

8.4. (*a*) The Gulf language family (data from Haas 1978:251,table 12); (*b*) A new Muskogean family tree (data from Munro 1987:figure 3); (*c*) Areal and genetic relations in the southeastern United States (data from Martin 1992:22).

now also well enough established to identify them with the people of specific phases at Winterville, Lake George, and Haynes' Bluff.

The Choctaw Problem

What linguistic effects would then characterize the influx of populations into the Choctaw homeland region in the sixteenth and seventeenth centuries? The "natives" – that is, the Nanih Waiya people – had been in all likelihood speakers of Old Choctaw, before they had gradually differentiated themselves from their Chickasaw neighbors to the north to speak the New Choctaw dialect. The "incomers" from the east, then, would be perhaps other speakers of New Choctaw and speakers of New Alabama, while those from the southwest would be Natchezan speakers. So except for the southerners, the people who would make up the new Choctaw tribe would have spoken mutually intelligible languages and would not have needed to make any changes in order to communicate; and since the Moundville polity had prehistoric contacts with the peoples of the Yazoo Basin and Natchez Bluffs regions, there were at least trading contacts and whatever linguistic arrangements they implied with Natchezan peoples.

What would then happen to the language? Later evidence shows that the tribal divisions of 1700 remained on the three watersheds of the Pearl, Chickasawhay, and Sucarnoochee (although their towns made some slight movements), and part of this stability was due to the matrilineal pattern of residence organization. The marriage rule of the Choctaws was exogamous between lineages and moieties, and it stands to reason that such an arrangement would have been adopted from the first by a new coalition whose constituents' prior habit had been exogamous. Since children would be fostered in the households of their mothers, less homogenization of language would occur over time than would have in a patrilocal arrangement where the primary caregiver was removed from her ethnic context. Barring a conscious effort to adopt a single dialect or language, if the people settled on separate watersheds their languages would tend to remain localized and not to be leveled into a single dialect over time, and the Choctaws would not likely have spoken one single dialect in the early eighteenth century. In fact they must not have done so, since the Choctaws in Mississippi do not speak one dialect today (P. Kwachka, pers. comm. 1991), and this distinctiveness has been reported frequently since the eighteenth century. The question then becomes what dialects were spoken in the early eighteenth century and what roles those dialects played.

I have already drawn attention to the natural desire of peoples to mark external boundaries between themselves and "others" by emphasizing their differences; this tendency is likely to be even more marked for societies in a state of stress or for newly formed groups, both of which apply in the Choctaw case. Among constituents of the Creek confederacy, a dramatic change to a uniform pottery style seems to correlate very closely with the formation of that confederacy (Smith 1987), which suggests that in certain situations cultural changes may even be made consciously. The Choctaw language could therefore have been a minority dialect that achieved an artificially inflated visibility through being used as a boundary marker or a sort of "court language" for external dealings of the confederacy. This use of "genuine" Choctaw in formal situations is amply attested in the records of relations between the Choctaws and their European and Indian neighbors during the eighteenth century (Galloway 1987).

The "Mobilian" Question

When the French first arrived in the coastal region in 1699, they found that many of the tribes they met, from Mobile Bay to the lower Mississippi River, were able to speak or understand what seemed to them to be a single dialect (Iberville 1981), which the French most frequently called "Mobilien." British traders, entering the same region via an inland route and making their first and most significant contact and alliance with the Chickasaws, referred to it as "Chickasaw" (Adair 1775). After initial impressions had passed, both recognized that what was so widely spoken was a simplified jargon or trade language (Du Pratz 1758), but the names stuck. And because the French and English explorers and traders depended upon it to be understood, having made their first contacts with people who probably spoke one of its parent dialects, even the names of some of the lower Mississippi tribes have come to us in "Mobilian" guise when those may not have been their names at all.

Studies by James Crawford (1978) and Emanuel Drechsel (1979, 1992) have established more facts about this trading language, both the certainty of its existence and its character as a jargon rather than a complete language or dialect, but because the large majority of the source materials Drechsel used in his reconstruction were collected only in the twentieth century, among small, displaced, isolated, and marginal populations of Indians and mixed-bloods in Louisiana, his characterization of the language probably could not have applied in the early eighteenth century. Furthermore, the behavior of both the French newcomers and the Indians clearly indicates that Mobilian was not used, either intertribally or between Indian and European, in formal or important situations (Galloway 1989b). Since groups define themselves and emphasize their differences from others in just such situations, the Mobilian trade language is not of great interest here except for having been identified so closely with both Chickasaw and Mobilian: that emphasis implies in turn the near identity of those two languages, both thus dialects developing from Old Choctaw. This reconstruction fits well with Drechsel's (1992:18) present thinking about

Mobilian's prehistoric existence: he acknowledges that the languages represented by the surviving evidence may have been spoken in the region of Moundville's hegemony only. Interestingly, it also suggests that Europeans did not perceive the language of informal contacts in the region of Choctaw dominance as being based on the New Choctaw dialect.

French Interpreter Distribution

Of more interest to the early French explorers, who while establishing contacts were not much interested in the informal contacts that an interlanguage facilitates, was the possibility of communicating with some fluency and command of nuance through interpreters. These first explorers found native institutions in place for dealing with formal intertribal communication. In the early eighteenth century the *fani mingo* institution served this purpose among the Chickasaws and Choctaws: tribes would adopt an advocate within a neighboring tribe, and his duty would be to argue in favor of what became in a sense his adopted tribe whenever war threatened to break out. Under other names such an institution may have been widespread as a means of dealing with intertribal relations throughout the Southeast, connected with the fictive kinship mechanisms of the calumet ceremony. No specific evidence indicates that the *fani mingo* or calumet chief would also be capable of speaking the language of the tribe whose interests he represented, but in several instances this is implied (Galloway 1989a).

The young French boys so eagerly sought by Indians of the region to learn their language quite likely fit into such a native institution. Since intertribal alliances were made by creating real kinship ties, the sons of women married into another tribe to cement an alliance stood a good chance of obtaining bilingual proficiency and a knowledge of different customs but retained the rank to which they were entitled through their mothers in their native tribe. It is also possible that the leaders of tribal groups fostered their nephews with the leaders of allied neighboring groups. Young men who had gone through either preparation would be highly qualified to serve as interpreters and diplomats.

Another piece of evidence also fits well with the hypothesis of the native importance of interpreters. At one point in the Louisiana colony's history Indians brought complaints that traders were being used as interpreters and that this was offensive: the speaker for any chief was a man of rank and dignity, whereas the interpreters used by the French were of low rank and lived by somewhat questionable trading practices. The colonial official reporting the need for interpreters suggested that the interpreters be given officer rank (Rowland, Sanders, and Galloway 1984, 4:100). It is by no means certain that the speaker for a chief – who presented the chief's speeches at home as well as among foreigners – had also to be an interpreter, but this example does suggest that the Indians had a model for what rank an interpreter should have, and that it was comparable with that of an officer.

The French government clearly did not intend that the boys sent to learn Indian languages should converse in the Mobilian trade language, nor was that what those boys learned. From the beginning, French governors chose specific tribes – Choctaw, Chickasaw, and later Natchez, Alabama, Tallapoosa – to receive these boys; they were chosen because of their perceived importance to French policy, or their possible threat to it (Galloway 1987). That the boys were sent to learn specific languages and that they thus fit into a preexisting Indian model together support an emphasis on language differentiation in external relations.

What dialect, then, *was* spoken in external relations? It was not that spoken by the southern incomers, the Sixtowns people of the upper Chickasawhay watershed: the French officer Régis du Roullet was told in 1730 that his interpreter, who spoke Sixtowns "Choctaw," was not linguistically competent for carrying out serious negotiations with the Great Chief on the subject of establishing a trading post (Rowland and Sanders 1927–32, 1:22,171; see Galloway 1987:163 n.61). It was not that spoken by the eastern Choctaw incomers whose eighteenth-century leader was known as "Alibamon Mingo": when the Alabama chief Tamatlé Mingo attended a meeting of chiefs of the whole Choctaw nation in order to persuade them not to break with the French in favor of the English, he did not speak his native Alabama language but apologized for his poor Choctaw (Rowland, Sanders, and Galloway 1984, 4:288). Régis du Roullet's "incompetent" interpreter was in fact capable of making himself understood in most of the villages he visited, but Régis's embassy was not taken seriously. And Tamatlé Mingo could well have spoken Alabama and been understood, but he wanted to achieve a serious effect, and by speaking Choctaw he was able to do so.

Choctaw Language as Boundary Marker

Choctaw as the emblematic language of the confederacy may, therefore, have begun as the language of the Nanih Waiya people, the "hosts" of the confederation and the only natives of the core region, becoming the language of the nation only gradually, through use as a boundary marker in formal situations. Furthermore, if its hegemony, aided by the prestige lent it through dealings with Europeans and by eventual codification by nineteenth-century missionaries, was as recent as the sixteenth or seventeenth century, then traces of the incomers' languages should still be present in the dialects spoken by modern Choctaws.

Although a dialect geography of the modern Mississippi Choctaws is in the planning stages (P. Kwachka, pers. comm. 1991), no study is available at present that would provide an outline of these traces. Swanton (1915:ix) remarked in his introduction to Cyrus Byington's dictionary of the Choctaw language that "anciently there were several Choctaw dialects, but only one of these, that of the Sixtowns Indians living in the southern part of the old Choctaw country, differed to any considerable degree from the standard, or Longtown, dialect spoken in the western part of the Nation. Moreover, this difference seems to have been confined mainly to certain words, involving but very slightly the language as a whole." Byington included some Sixtowns words in the dictionary, and Swanton further remarked that his coeditor, Henry S. Halbert, himself a fluent speaker of Choctaw, had "let certain doubtful words and sentences stand as in the original manuscript, with the idea that they may represent certain dialectic or archaic variations which have escaped him" (Swanton 1915:ix). Only systematic examination of modern dialect evidence will reveal any dialectal affinities with Alabama or Natchez, but I consider such results likely.

MIGRATION AND ORIGIN LEGENDS

Most versions of the migration and origin legends of the southeastern peoples were, unfortunately, collected very late, some by missionaries and early settlers, the rest by ethnographers who believed they reflected epic wanderings. Because they were collected well after the tribes had passed through such demographic upheaval that most detailed prehistoric tradition had to have been lost, and because the individuals who collected them had very big axes to grind, migration legends may be nearly useless for telling us how the historic tribes originated in the depths of prehistory. But because they may combine with other cultural practices to affirm historical agreement on events of the protohistoric period, and because they frequently establish a charter for polity formation, I consider them another possible source for information on the constituent ethnicity of the Choctaws.

Migration legends, although they may purport to be history, are nearly always as much "just-so stories" – etiological myths explaining the origins of cultural practices – as they are the histories of actual migrations (Vansina 1973:158–59). As discussed in chapter 2, most historical tribes of the region of interest developed virtually *in situ* from Woodland-period origins; their migrations were intraregional and dated to the late prehistoric and protohistoric periods (Brain 1979; Smith 1987). Thus the flush of migration legends belonging mostly to the Muskogean tribes in the interior Southeast must pertain historically to the relatively recent period of the sixteenth and seventeenth centuries when the region was in such turmoil and the historic tribes were in formation. If this is so, then they should help reconstruct what happened.

As etiological myths pertaining to social entities, the migration legends explaining the formation of southeastern tribes must explain also the origins of their political economies, establishing their claims to nationhood through cosmological references and claims to land through geographical ones. Interestingly, the few southeastern migration legends attested at a relatively early date specify relationships with specific historic neighbors, and nearly all of them specify a chthonic or earth-emergence origin near or in the region of their historic residence. This may also prove useful for addressing questions about origins, but it already introduces an element of distortion, increasing the likelihood that what is portrayed is not "what happened" but "what should have happened to get us where we are (or want to be) today."

I have already discussed the perils of dealing with any historical text as a text, and the considerations that must be given to the relationships between historical texts. As Vansina (1973) has pointed out, the transmission history of any oral tradition is equally complicated. Oral traditions become available through what he terms a "chain of transmission," beginning with the observer of the fact or event that underlies the tradition, passing through a chain of hearsay testimonies, and ending with what becomes the final testimony that is written down by a literate witness and that thus enters the written historical record. "A tradition," Vansina (1973:21) says, "should be regarded as a series of historical documents, even if the documents are verbal ones." Thus, we must pay careful attention to what we can learn of an oral text's transmission history.

Furthermore, for the southeastern material – collected well after the newly dominant literate Anglo culture had enveloped the bearers of tradition – many of the informants could have had access to and been influenced by earlier versions of their own or others' legends that had already been collected. And finally, because the dominant culture was in fact dominant and its representatives saw it as inevitably so, we must expect large doses of interpretation and other distortion at the collection stage.

Although many of the recorded versions of origin and migration legends purport to be in the words of the native informant, these "final testimonies" do not preserve the language or much of the rhetorical structure of the oral testimony, and in the majority of cases what exists is even overtly paraphrase. Thus much of the evidence that might have signaled a genuine oral tradition and what genre it represented – oral formulae and the like – is gone. It would be very useful, for example, to know if any of these traditions were handed down in a fixed, memorized form (as opposed to improvised narrative), which generally tends to be more conservative in preserving information as formulated by the first observer; but except for a single example, which seems by external evidence to have had this character, we cannot now tell which is which.

To discuss the migration legends of the Creeks, Alabamas, Chickasaws, and Choctaws, I must present condensed versions of them as narratives, as they are generally too long to be presented in full. These legends were not recorded in the words of their bearers and are already summarized to some extent, so I feel no qualms about reducing them to basic elements. Because I am most interested in the traditions collected earliest, and not in how they might have evolved later, I will not present versions that are either repetitions of earlier versions or obvious later elaborations, particularly since most versions of extant migration legends were published by Swanton at some time or other and are available in print elsewhere.

Migration legends are not preserved for all southeastern tribes, and indeed only two are well preserved – those of the Kasihtas and the Choctaws – although early hints and late evidence allow us to suggest something for the Chickasaws and Alabamas. The Tunica legend that Mary Haas (1950) collected relatively recently from one woman obviously tells the story of Tunica migrations only since their contact with the French, while the Natchez legend as told to Du Pratz ends by asserting that the Natchez did not know from whence they ultimately came, only that they warred with some "ancients of the country" and with some "warriors of fire," interpreted by Du Pratz as the Spaniards (Swanton 1911:182–84). Thus we can only reach a suggestion of what the tribes thought about their own genesis, some of it historically verifiable, some of it not.

Creek Migration Legend

The Kasihta migration legend, that belonging to one of the dominant tribes of the Lower Creeks, is the earliest preserved; it dates to 1735, when a Kasihta chief named Tchikilli, head chief of the Lower Creeks, told it to Governor Oglethorpe of the newly created Georgia colony. The legend was said to have been translated and inscribed on a buffalo skin to be sent to London, but the skin and the translation were lost. Until an English translation also dating from 1735 surfaced in 1931 (Pennington 1931), the legend was thought to have been preserved only in a German translation published in 1735 as part of a colonist-recruitment effort. This German translation provided the basis for a lengthy study of southeastern linguistics and ethnography by Albert Gatschet in 1884 (Gatschet 1884, 1888). Here, however, I have used the place-name spellings from the original English translation.

According to the legend, the Kasihtas emerged from the earth in the west but decided to move on when the earth ate their children. They traveled eastward across a muddy river to a blood-red one that emerged from a thundering and smoking mountain, where they met three other tribes from whom they learned about the use of fire and herbal medicines. Offered four fires from the cardinal directions, they chose the one from the north to add to the fire they had already obtained from the mountain. They also acquired a ceremonial war club to carry into war by sacrificing a child to it. Here also they found the four herbs used for the Busk ceremony and learned that women in their menses must stay apart from that ceremony. The four nations then gathered, and disputing which was oldest and which should rule, they decided to set up four posts: each nation would go to war to see which could first cover its post in scalps. The Kasihtas were first in this contest, followed by the Chickasaws, the Alabamas, and finally the Abihkas.

Next the legend describes the attacks of a giant blue bird or eagle. They tricked the bird into fathering a rat upon the image of a woman, and the rat then told them how to kill the bird; eagle feathers were thenceforth considered sacred. The Kasihtas next continued eastward alone until they came to a white path, which they followed to a Coluosa Hutche creek. They crossed it to find the Coosa town, where they sacrificed another child to trap and kill a lion that was attacking the Coosa people every seven days, thus establishing for themselves a commemorative six-day fast in preparation for war. Again they departed, after four years, to the "Nowphawpe" or Callusie Hutche River, where they lived by hunting and gathering for two years; they then proceeded past Owatunha River and Aphoosapheesaw River, after which they came to a Moterelo mountain where they found people. Shooting white arrows toward them to ascertain their goodness, they received red ones in return and found the houses deserted, so they attempted to follow the river. On a mountain they found more people in a town who shot red arrows at them. They attacked the town and killed all but two of the flat-headed people; in pursuing the survivors they killed a white dog and came at last to a town of Pallachacula (from whom, the legend claims, the eighteenth-century Yamacraw Tomochichi was descended), who gave them black drink, buried their tomahawk, gave them white feathers, and proposed to live together with a common chief. One group settled on one side of the river and became Kasihtas; the other on the other side became Kawitas.

This legend clearly has two elements: the migration story and a series of explanations of ceremonial practices current among the Creeks in the eighteenth century. The abundance of elements pertaining to this latter topic may be due to the context in which the legend was declaimed, a solemn peacemaking with Oglethorpe. The first part, up to the finding of the white path, is a sort of prologue to the story, which establishes the Kasihtas in certain of their fundamental ceremonial practices (the use of four specific medicines in the Busk, ritual separation of menstruating women, the establishment of the New Fire, the use of wooden war clubs, the ceremonial significance of eagle feathers) and sets up their relationships as senior to the western Muskogean Chickasaws and Alabamas and the eastern Muskogean Abihkas. The second part of the story, in which the Kasihtas go on alone, sets out a series of migrations following a white (or peaceful) path to the Coosas, for whom they killed a marauding lion and in the process secured important war medicine; to an unnamed flat-headed people, whose deaths led them to a white dog that they also killed; and to a final settlement in common with a Pallachacula people, who gave them the supremely important ceremonial black drink, as Kasihtas and Kawitas.

Gatschet and Swanton did not agree completely on the interpretation of the migration. Gatschet (1884, 2:61–67) thought the first two rivers were east of the Mississippi, while Swanton (1928c) felt that the first river was the Mississippi and the Kasihtas were portrayed as literally crossing the Mississippi and joining the Chickasaws, Alabamas, and Kawitas somewhere in the upper Tombigbee region. Both agreed, however, that the second part of the legend referred to the Alabama-Coosa-Tallapoosa region where the Upper Creeks were settled and the Chattahoochee River area where the Lower Creeks lived in the eighteenth century. I think the first part is meant to be more mythical – it includes the derivation of fundamental elements of Creek ceremonialism – and therefore less specifically connected with any geographical feature, especially since it establishes the Kasihta relationship with tribes who were only marginally parts of the Creek confederacy and who were linguistically distant from the eastern Muskogean groups named in the rest of the legend (Chickasaws, Alabamas). Clearly, however, the second part of the legend refers to the protohistoric and early historic wanderings of the Creeks, perhaps including in legendary form the resistance they encountered when they moved temporarily onto the Ocmulgee, Oconee, and Savannah drainages in the seventeenth century (Smith 1987).

Tchikilli's version of the Kasihta migration was not the only one preserved by a native informant: Taskaya Miko related a version of it to Benjamin Hawkins ([1798–99] 1848, 1:81–83), apparently in the last years of the eighteenth century. This account is almost entirely a history of the early Creek confederacy, told in terms of the Kasihta, Kawita, Chickasaw, and Abihka. Its similarities to Tchikilli's version are apparent.

At a location with two mounds, west of Weocoofke and at Wechatehatche Aufuskee, the Kasihtas, Kawitas, and Chickasaws had no fire when they were visited by four men from the cardinal directions, who made fire for them and taught them the use of the four major medicine plants and perhaps several others. Then the three groups chose ruling clans. When games with Indians from the west turned violent, with ball sticks being exchanged for war clubs and bows and arrows, the three tribes allied and went to war. After this they went east and met with the Abihka on the Coosa River, and they all agreed to battle for four years to see who would bring the most scalps. As a result, the Kasihtas won the first rank, followed by the Kawitas, Chickasaws, and Abihkas. The Chickasaws and Abihkas thus became younger brothers to the Kasihtas and Kawitas; the Abihkas and Chickasaws achieved roughly equal rank, with the Chickasaws perhaps leading slightly.

Next, settlements began, first on the Coosa and Tallapoosa; then they went to the Chattahoochee, where they drove out a flat-headed people who occupied the mounds of the region. Then they spread to the Ocmulgee, Oconee, Ogechee, and Savannah Rivers, where they met the whites who drove them back inland. The

Kasihtas and Chickasaws remained closely linked, with the Chickasaws (who were given their first chief by the Kasihtas) settled on the Savannah River; and the Kasihtas were able to make peace between Chickasaws and Creeks in "the late war" when no one else could.

We know lamentably little about the circumstances under which this version of the legend was collected; the informant, Taskaya Mico, was chief of "Apatai, a branch village of Kasihta." There is no way of knowing if he had become acquainted with Tchikilli's version through Hawkins, but given Hawkins's education at Princeton, his interest in the scientific study of languages, and his possession of the works of French and Greek historians as well as those of Adair and Bartram and a collection of "travel journals, geographies, gazeteers, atlases, and maps" (Henri 1986:35), Hawkins may have seen a version of it, as it was preserved in a German travel journal. If, on the other hand, Taskaya Mico's version was not in any way affected by Tchikilli's (except as a lineal successor), and if the text now extant is plausibly what Hawkins was given, then this legend is independent confirmation of Tchikilli's, much reduced in complexity and much rationalized. Some of the differences may be related to how the account was elicited, which was certainly a less ceremonial context than that in which Tchikilli had delivered his.

As Taskaya Mico tells it, fire and medicine herbs were acquired in much the same way, but the tribal relationships are slightly different, including the Kawitas explicitly from the beginning instead of the Alabamas but retaining the Chickasaw relationship and retaining the lowest rank for the Upper Creek Abihkas. This segment seems to compress Tchikilli's opening with four tribes and eventual movement to the Coosa so as to account for the presence of the Abihkas, since the eastward movement seems to include an explicit crossing of the Mississippi. The subsequent movements are explicitly located to the areas that were in fact the path of the Creeks' movements in the seventeenth and eighteenth centuries. A strong emphasis is placed upon the Kasihta relationship with the Georgia band of Chickasaws, presumably referring so explicitly to a recent incident (the "late war") that discovery of the referent might explain the reason for the telling of the legend. Since Hawkins was directly concerned with the land claims of the eastern tribes, the legend may have been told to him to justify the specific Chickasaw settlement claims to the Savannah.

The final version of the Kasihta migration legend to be examined here was related by the Frenchman Milfort, a friend of the Creek chief Alexander McGillivray (Swanton 1928c:40–46). This highly romanticized and indeed fictionalized version of a general "Moskoqui" migration from northwest Mexico (!) to eastern Alabama/western Georgia contains only one addition significant to our interest here, which is that in conquering and populating the region occupied by the Creek confederacy, they displaced the Alabamas, who took refuge around Mobile Bay and among the Choctaws before the French engineered a peace that enabled them to settle on the upper Alabama River as part of the confederacy. The tale as told by Milfort is so full of patent absurdities and historical error even where historical events are cited that it would be foolish to give it credence, but the idea of enmity or dissimilarity between the eastern Muskogean Creeks and the western Muskogean Alabamas, as well as the latter's connection with the Choctaws, fits with what is known from other sources and reinforces the notion of an Alabama-Choctaw connection.

Alabama Creation Legend

The Alabamas were not of sufficient number or interest to warrant early collection of their legends, and the only authentic legend is as late as 1847, collected by Schoolcraft from Alabama elder Sekopechi after the Alabamas had been removed west of the Mississippi. This legend represents a rather simple version of the earth emergence myth with a migration spliced on, indicating that the Alabamas came out of the earth between the Alabama and Cahaba Rivers, moved to dwell at the junction of the "Tuscaloosa" and Coosa Rivers, and then moved again to settle at the Coosa-Alabama junction. Schoolcraft paraphrased his source throughout, concluding that "they claimed the country from Fort Jackson to New Orleans for their hunting-grounds" and "they are of the opinion that the Great Spirit brought them from the ground, and that they are of right possessors of this soil" (quoted in Swanton 1922:191). The only problem with this account of Alabama movements, as Swanton saw it, was the identification of the Alabamas' intermediate home; believing that the Alibamu of the Soto narratives were the historic Alabamas, he judged that "Tuscaloosa" meant "Tombigbee" and that "Coosa" meant "Alabama."

Yet the import of this simple origin account is surely not the precise locations of the Alabamas' intermediate dwelling places, but their claim to specific tracts of land "from Fort Jackson to New Orleans," which would require that an intermediate point or two be specified. Certainly it may legitimately be taken to indicate an Alabama attachment for such a tract, particularly the parts of it from the lower Tombigbee to the Alabama-Coosa-Tallapoosa junction. The fact that this is the very area defined by the Alabama River phase pottery tradition and the burial urn mortuary practice makes it an obvious reiteration of patterns already seen.

Chickasaw Migration Legend

James Adair was so taken by the Chickasaws that he liked to attribute to them his generalizations about common southeastern Indian practices, and the case of migration legends was no exception. Thus Adair (1775:352) was probably borrowing from the Choctaw migration legend when he placed the Chickasaws as coming from the west with the Choctaws and Chakchiumas. Bernard Romans ([1772] 1961:69), like Tchikilli, was probably trying to account for their widely scattered settlement centers when he outlined a migration from the west to the Ohio and thence to the upper Tombigbee.

A version that Schoolcraft (in Swanton 1928b) collected from an anonymous informant in the mid–nineteenth century (after Removal) claimed that the Chickasaws came from the west with a large dog to protect them, led eastward by a leaning pole. The dog was lost in the Mississippi (Swanton rationalized this to "in the state of Mississippi"), but the pole led them across the river to the region of Huntsville on the Tennessee River. They then split into two bands, one going east to settle with the Creeks as the Cushehtah (Kasihta) and the other west to the Chickasaw Old Fields. A second post-Removal version was collected from a woman named Molly Gunn, who simply brought the Chickasaws alone from the west to the Chickasaw Old Fields on the upper Tombigbee, led by a leaning pole and accompanied by a large war dog.

The Chickasaw legends thus fairly clearly only attempt to account for the several settlement loci of the Chickasaws in the eighteenth and early nineteenth centuries, with the mythical "from the west" element tacked on to the beginning to account for the Chickasaws' not being native to the upper Tombigbee region, which has now been confirmed. The leaning pole seems to be an accretion from the Choctaw legend (below), since it is not present in the earliest versions or in the versions of the Creek myth that include the Chickasaws.

Choctaw Creation and Migration Legends

As with their mortuary ritual, the Choctaws need bow to no one for the profuseness and detail of the extant versions of their migration legend. Unfortunately the earliest versions are pitifully vague. The French chronicler of the Natchez, Du Pratz (1758, 2:216–17), says a tradition of a massive and rapid migration to empty land led the Choctaws to claim to have emerged from the earth. Bernard Romans ([1772] 1961: 71) echoes the earth-emergence tradition when he says they emerged from the earth from a hole "between their nation and the Chickasaws." Adair, as I have said, claimed that a single tradition referred to the Choctaws, Chickasaws, and Chakchiumas as having come from the west. But there is no single extended version of any Choctaw migration legend from the eighteenth century.

The earliest nineteenth-century versions of the legend were reported by settlers and entrepreneurs interested in Indians. Catlin's version dates from the 1830s and is a simple, unattributed paraphrase. Catlin (in Swanton 1931:10) says that long ago the Choctaws migrated from the far west (far west of "the great river and the mountains of snow"), led by a great medicine man who carried a red pole that he planted in the earth every evening and found pointing east every morning. One day the pole stood straight at a place called Nahnewaye, where the Choctaws settled. This version contains all the basic elements of the migration myth to be found in later accounts, and is probably as close to its original version as we are likely to get.

A second version was elaborated by Gideon Lincecum (1861), an early settler in the Mississippi Territory who claims to have come to know the Choctaws well during the four years he lived in their country, 1822–25. But Lincecum appears to have been an accomplished con artist, replacing the homeopathic remedies of a medicine-show scam with mysterious Indian cures that the same manuscript validates by attributing them to a sort of forest residency with a Choctaw medicine man. And if this romantic claptrap were not enough, Lincecum dresses the Choctaw migration legend up in the same Spanish conquest–Aztec alliance garb that Milfort had fancied, making it the migration of Muskogee, Chickasaw, and Choctaw nations. The sacred leaning pole is there, but its use is bound up with a constant battle for supremacy between the traditional priests (who were vigorously opposed by Lincecum's friend Pushmataha in his own day) and the idealized hero leader.

But Lincecum does more, casting doubt upon the whole of the version he reports. The entire unpublished manuscript is entitled "Traditional History of the Chahta Nation, translated from the Chahta by Gideon Lincecum, 1861" (Lincecum 1861). In it he tells a vast story, from creation through the introduction of all possible customs and ceremonial practices (including nothing that could not have been known to a nineteenth-century witness) through migration, and the entire history of the people down to the death of his alleged informant Chahta Immataha (Lincecum apparently did not know that this name was an honorific title, not a personal name). In the true tradition of sixteenth-century romances, Lincecum claims to be the mere amanuensis of the old man, visiting and staying with the ailing elder in his woodland hut and constantly claiming authenticity for his account because of its unsophisticated simplicity: "if the tradition took higher grounds, we should be suspicious that the old man's narrative was not reliable."

Indeed the old man's narrative is not reliable. He recalls events in the dim mists of time with crystal clarity, down to fine details of political wranglings between civil and religious leaders on the migration and even a vision (Lincecum dates it to 1823) in which he saw "all the Chahta people cross back over the big river again and settle in a far off country, that he had never seen . . . having white men for their leaders, they crossed back over the great river Mississippi on fire boats, all very safely." Apparently, however, the old man had only very generalized and attenuated traditions for the whole of the colonial period (the events of which are very well documented, but to which documentation Lincecum had no access), although that period contained intertribal and even intratribal wars of immense importance to the Choctaw people. What the evidence of the narrative suggests to the critical reader, in short, is that either the old man existed and was pulling Lincecum's leg, or Lincecum, seeking literary fame in his Civil War exile in Texas, added to his real knowledge of contemporary Choctaw history and customs – and to authentic knowledge about customs and remedies passed on to him by a single elder Choctaw – the fruits of his reading in the history and travel literature of the period to create a vast panorama of the effects of white conquest on the Choctaws, from Cortés to Removal.

Swanton (1931:11–27), although characterizing Lincecum's narrative as "worthy of a Spanish chronicler, and in fact recalling the Fidalgo of Elvas," was eager to use Lincecum's account of the migration not for the migration proper, which he could see was derivative, but for the account of the etiology of Choctaw burial practice, which occurs at the point where the pole stands straight up at Nanih Waiya and the civil chief triumphs over the "lazy Isht ahullos" (priests) by persuading the people to divest themselves of the "useless dry bones" of their ancestors that they have been carrying for the duration of the epic migration and to bury them at the spot, thus creating the immense Nanih Waiya mound (which of course is not a burial mound at all). The extended version contains a clear rhetorical parallel drawn between this tale of the triumph of innovation (interment) over traditionalism (veneration of physical remains) and contrasting descriptions of the post-Christian Choctaw rite (interment, followed by the cry and the joyous pole-pulling) and the traditional one (a gory description of the activities of the bone-strippers, the most elaborate and intentionally repugnant description of this process now extant). The "mound-building" segment of the account, which was published separately with a little contextualizing information in 1904 (Lincecum 1904) and which was all that Swanton had seen in 1931, also explains Lincecum's interpretation of the Woodland-period burial mounds that he had observed in the region as the burials of hunters or warriors killed away from home. However, the extraordinary gaps in Lincecum's alleged informant's memory discourage the belief that the carrying of the ancestral bones, which is the main addition Lincecum has made to the migration legend, is a genuine part of the tradition – however useful its connection with Choctaw mortuary ritual might be.

Three versions of the Choctaw migration legend are connected with Christian missionary activity, and all three are not only rather brief and to the point but understandably reminiscent of the Israelite flight out of Egypt, with the oracular pole serving the place of the pillar of fire. The Reverend Alfred Wright (1828:215–16) published a version in the *Missionary Herald* that brought the Creeks, Chickasaws, and Choctaws (in that order) from far in the west. The Choctaws were led by a great leader and prophet who carried a pole that he planted in the earth every night, with his medicine bag hanging on it. The pole leaned eastward every morning until they reached Nanih Waiya, where it remained upright. The source of this tradition seems to have been a certain "aged interpreter" who also opined that few modern Choctaws recalled this tradition because they wished to forget that when they arrived they had to drive out the existing inhabitants. This tradition nevertheless does not appear to be a single unified story in the sense of Vansina's "testimony"; instead, it seems rationalized from several sources.

Cushman (1962:18–21), the son of a missionary to the Mississippi Choctaws who grew up as a boy in Choctaw country, reported two versions of the legend. One is his own retelling of what Choctaw elders had allegedly told the missionaries around 1820. He depicts the Choctaws emigrating from a land of oppression under the brothers Chahtah and Chikasah like, Cushman says, the Jews from Egypt under Moses and Aaron. A pole produced, after much prayer, by the "chief medicine man and prophet" was set in the ground each night, to be found leaning toward the east each morning until the "great multitude" crossed the Mississippi and finally arrived at a land where the pole rested upright. There they built a large mound that they called Nunih Waiyah. Some years later, Chahtah and Chikasah disagreed on some unspecified matter, so the two segments of the tribe decided to separate; the land taken by each was decided on the fall of a pole, which allotted the north to the Chickasaws and the south to the Choctaws.

Cushman also reported a version he attributed to the Reverend Israel Folsom, a native Choctaw missionary. Folsom said that following the Cherokees and Muscogees and led by the prophet warrior Chahtah, the Choctaw people migrated from the distant west. Chahtah carried a long staff and planted it in the earth at every encampment in front of his "wigwam"; it signaled their direction of march by inclining, only signaling a stopping place by inclining "backward." At that place, called Nunnih Waiya, the Choctaws built a strong fortress. At length their numbers multiplied until the Yazoos and Chakchiumas split off from them.

Henry Halbert (1899b), a long-time educator among the Mississippi Choctaws, reported another version an early settler obtained from a clerical Folsom, this one the Reverend Peter Folsom, who attributed it to his father and dated it to 1833. Again the migrants came from the west in separate divisions led by the brothers Chahta and Chikasa and a great prophet who carried a pole that he planted in the front of the camp at the end of each day. The pole was found leaning every day in the direction of march until they reached Nanih Waiya, where it stood upright. It rained that night and for several days, and the Chikasa group, having failed to learn of the pole's new message, had continued on, leaving no trace behind them, eventually settling on the upper Tombigbee.

These "clerical" versions agree on the leaning pole and the destination of Nanih Waiya, but only two of four agree on the Choctaw-Chickasaw brother leaders, while

Wright articulates the intertribal relationship as a Creek–Chickasaw–Choctaw sequence and Israel Folsom derives the Chakchiumas and Yazoos from the Choctaws. It is difficult to know how much rationalization stands in the way of whatever nugget of living legend may be buried inside, for clearly none of these even purports to be the faithful transcription of a Choctaw informant's words, and each interjects a narrator's comments. The two Folsoms, both Choctaws, might be presumed to be ideal informants, but Peter apparently reported that his father told him the legend when the two visited Nanih Waiya after his graduation from boarding school and just three years after Removal, implying that he had not himself been socialized as a Choctaw.

This circumstance brings up a powerful element that had to lie behind most of the extant early versions of the Choctaw migration legend: most of them purport to have been collected by the decade before Removal and some shortly after, but nearly all (except the very early eighteenth-century mentions) were published at dates that meant they were finally shaped by the knowledge of Removal. The missionaries especially tended to favor Removal as protecting the Choctaws from the deleterious effects of having frontier whites as neighbors, so it is not surprising that most of them remark on the fine lands to the west of the Mississippi that the Choctaws passed up because of the leaning pole, since these were the same fine lands to which the Choctaws were being evicted.

Traveler Charles Lanman (1856:457–59) attributes another late origin myth to Peter Pitchlyn, a well-known mixed-blood leader who died in 1881. Pitchlyn's version reportedly portrayed the Choctaws as emerging from under the sea, after which they walked along the shore seeking a place to settle until they met with sickness and their prophet advised them to enter the wilderness. On the day appointed for the start of their journey, the prophet's staff was found leaning northward. They followed it for many days until they reached and crossed a large river into a beautiful country; they built mounds along the way to express their delight and eventually settled in that region. As they multiplied it was necessary for some to depart from that land, and thus the Chickasaws, Cherokees, Creeks, Shawnees, and Delawares emerged from the original Choctaw tribe, and the Choctaws built a great city called Yazoo. Swanton (1931:31) passed over this version with the dry comment that it is "the only version known to me which brings the Choctaw from under the ocean"; he clearly did not think it very consequential.

A related theme is the earth-emergence tradition that, like the early accounts (from Du Pratz and Romans), saw the origin of the Choctaws at Nanih Waiya. Halbert (cited in Swanton 1931:35–36) collected a late version of this myth, attributing it to Isaac Pistonatubbee around the turn of the century; it is very elaborate, and brings the Muskogees, Cherokees, Chickasaws, and Choctaws out of Nanih Waiya in that order, with the last of the four deciding to stay where they emerged. Both traditions – earth-emergence and migration – were clearly in circulation in the 1720s, when Du Pratz heard of them; both are still alive and well today.

Migration Legends as Oral History

What is most striking about the Creek origin legends is that, viewed as a group in connection with what is known of the tribes' late prehistory and protohistory, they seem to reflect specific historical trajectories; they speak in mythic mode about real events that happened in the sixteenth, seventeenth, and eighteenth centuries, at least for all but the Choctaws. Could the Choctaw legend reflect historical events also?

The Creek legends clearly pertain to the origins of their confederacy and its division into the Upper and Lower Creeks. They emphasize population movements, underlining the correctness of the story Marvin Smith (1987) has put together for the beginnings of the core Creek groups. Thus the Creek myths are historical and refer to the protohistoric period.

The Alabama myth is just as obviously representative of the earth-emergence type of origin legend, so common worldwide as an assertion of claim to land. A more interesting proposition, given that the Alabamas may have been among the inheritors of the traditions of the Moundville hegemony, is the suggestion that a chthonic emergence myth may be connected with mound-building (Knight 1989). The Alabama myth's migration segment outlines a multiple-phase migration that may reflect either separate migrations of several groups or a single migration of one group, but that in any case probably has a base in historical fact.

The Chickasaw legend is interesting because some of its migration element was probably borrowed by Adair from the Choctaw legend to explain the linguistic connection between the two tribes; the rest of it had to explain the origin of the Chickasaw settlement on the Tennessee River (the "Breed Camp" of the British traders) and the presence of a Chickasaw settlement in South Carolina, which may have dated from Woodward's day. Most of the elements from this fragmentary tradition, however, seem to date from the eighteenth century, when the gradual movement of the Chickasaws up the Tombigbee drainage was culminating in the settlement around Tupelo, which is prominently mentioned in the myths as the "Chickasaw Old Fields."

The Choctaws have origin myths with two contradictory traditions: migration and earth-emergence. The migration legend dominates our thinking because it was most frequently collected and elaborated, and it had several functions. In all its versions and in common with the Creek myth it emphasizes intertribal relationships, both genealogical (with Creeks, Chickasaws, and Chakchiumas) and political (Cherokees and Yazoos). More important, however, it provides a supernatural charter for those who migrated to the east-central Mississippi "homeland" location, since some superhuman force guided the leaning pole. Furthermore, since it is clearly connected in theme and even in specific reference to the Creek migration myth, there may be some reason to link it with a constituent element of the Choctaws who came not from the west but from the east.

The parallel earth-emergence myth, sometimes told together with the migration story, provides a similar supernatural charter for those who built Nanih Waiya and had their origin in the region. It is related thematically to other Muskogean earth-emergence myths, a theme limited in the Southeast to Muskogeans (Lankford 1987:112). Finally, the odd "sea-emergence" myth attributed to Peter Pitchlyn might not be wholly out of place if viewed in the context of close relations with and partial adoption of some Pensacola peoples from the south.

It is very tempting to rehabilitate Lincecum's account of the carrying of the bones and their burial at Nanih Waiya, as Knight (1989) has done in his discussion of mound ceremonialism. The account would allow us to suggest that in-migrant proto-Choctaws, all practicing secondary burial for their elites, simply brought along the as yet unburied packets of their elites' bones to bury in the new place in order to claim it. Certainly most of the Choctaws' neighbors who might possibly have provided populations for the new confederacy had such a practice in the protohistoric period, so it would not be unreasonable. Furthermore, it would explain why the Choctaws, unlike all their neighbors, adopted the expensive practice of secondary processing not just for elites but for everyone: in a weirdly prophetic way, it would ensure that in any future migrations the Choctaws would be able to carry the bones of *all* their ancestors. If the Lincecum version of the legend has anything in it beyond Lincecum's own fertile imagination, I am inclined to believe that it is this use of the ancestors' bones.

CHAPTER NINE

Choctaw Tribe Formation

[H]istory . . . having grown old in embryo as mere narrative, for long encumbered with legend, and for still longer preoccupied with only the most obvious events . . . is still very young as a rational attempt at analysis. – Marc Bloch, *The Historian's Craft*

[T]o offer interpretations without acknowledging their uncertain ground would be less than candid, while to state only what is certainly known would be to leave unexplored what matters most. – Inge Clendinnen, *Ambivalent Conquests*

To adhere dutifully to the Aristotelian unities and finish this study satisfactorily, I would now have to provide neat closure by assembling all the suspects and revealing how the murder was done, like the detective in a classic mystery. Unfortunately, the mystery remains unsolved, at least if the solution is to be fully acceptable to answer for real lives. After a long and sometimes painful process of sifting evidence, the reward of a solved puzzle is to be deferred once again. A good deal of this lack of resolution is due to the ambiguity of the evidence; a good deal of it is due to my own ambivalence toward the evidence. Were I to wait until I was completely satisfied that the evidence was sufficient for a solution, this book would not see the light of day for at least another ten years. And the time to a solution may be shortened if other investigators are invited to consult on the case.

THE NATURE OF THE ENTERPRISE

The whole project has been difficult because I have been trying to construct a moving picture out of a series of stills, stills taken with different kinds of cameras at different shutter speeds, using different compositional principles and with very different filters attached. I myself am caught between history and anthropology, using the glimpses of a few documented events and the synthetic configurations of archaeological "cultures," bound together none too securely with theories of social change, in an attempt to tell what happened to several groups of people whose names I can never know.

I have not, nevertheless, made it into a story, although its constituent parts have been arranged in roughly chronological order; I have instead pursued different lines of attack as the nature of the sources dictated. Now that I have come to the end, however, I have set myself that task: to summarize what has been seen on the way and then to tell my version of what happened while European observers were elsewhere.

Neither history nor anthropology has provided perfect tools for this task. I cannot tell a narrative history of events because I have very few events to work with; as history, this would thus have to be a history of long-term trends, written with an awareness of the tension between this unconventional subject and the very conventions of the writing of history. Anthropology, with its notions of "cultures" and "ethnicity," is much more suitable, but only for looking at the subject as a synchronic phenomenon; for all the theoretical discussion of "social reproduction," anthropologists after all have not devised effective ways to write about how real cultures change.

To review the materials for this construction I survey the materials from the preceding chapters in a slightly different way, under the headings of diachrony and synchrony.

DIACHRONY FROM ARCHAEOLOGY AND HISTORY

Chapters 2 through 5 presented the available evidence for Choctaw tribe formation gleaned first from archaeology and then from history. The two perspectives overlapped one another, and the resulting text could be construed as a diachronic narrative only through convention, since it really consisted of a sequence of synchronic constructions bridged by interpolation. Still it was a sequence, a sequence of real detritus left by people whose lives it reflected only indirectly, overlaid by a sequence of brief encounters with strangers, told by the often uncomprehending strangers. Here I recapitulate and evaluate that sequence.

In chapter 2 I reviewed the archaeological evidence for the development of specific agricultural societies in the region of interest in late prehistory, relating them to the landscape in which they developed and to whose limitations they were subject. All this was of course constructed from the fragmentary material precipitate of a sequence of specific events, almost none of which can be deciphered from it. Instead I had to substitute the archaeological constructions of assemblages and cultures and to describe how they "intersected" and "interacted." Using ethnographic analogy, archaeological theorists have offered sociopolitical interpretations that seem to fit the evidence from the region rather well, and I used them to organize the evidence about the prehistoric Plaqueminian and Moundvillian neighbors of the comparatively empty region that historic Choctaws would later inhabit.

That theoretical framework permitted the construction of a rough sequence, a patchwork of evolution and cyclic near-stasis. I described a plausible scenario for how both the Plaqueminians and the Moundvillians, like their neighbors in the larger sphere of the Mississippian culture area of the Southeast and probably in symbiotic relationship with them, increased in population, became fully sedentary maize agriculturists, and in the process developed hierarchical sociopolitical structures. Some of the Mississippians, Moundvillians included, were apparently too successful, and their cultures devolved to less complex arrangements before Europeans appeared on the scene. Some, like the Plaqueminians, retained at least some of their sociopolitical complexity. And some others clung to a middle-of-the-road status, remaining at a modest level of population and complexity on the social and geographical margins of their more populous neighbors.

There are no people in this picture, only theoretical constructs, even though there are unique fingerprints in the clay of the pottery they made and rough deformities of arthritis, induced by the strains of agricultural work, on their bones. These were the people who once must have gloried in the power and prosperity their collective toil had built and then walked away from the grand pomps of mounds and earthworks and withdrew to their villages when people began to die of starvation and their leaders could no longer compel or justify the expense of sustaining a leader class. These were the people who turned to more intensive hunting in the uplands when corn yields in the bottomlands failed to live up to their promise in the long run. They were people who faced and adapted to the effects of their own alteration of the landscape.

The sparse archaeological evidence shows that these people could organize and reorganize in complex ways that they themselves invented; they could choose to honor some among them or not; they could expand, stressing their environment until it failed them, and then fall back on older subsistence activities that had remained in their repertoire for bad crop years. Though the principles of change in their societies are expressed in the neutral terms of theory, these people were themselves innovators and subduers of the earth who had confronted and accomplished change many times; they were in no sense passive victims.

One further detail of late prehistory is that none of these people found the region bounded by the Pearl on the west, the Tombigbee/Mobile on the east, and the Leaf River system to the south appropriate for living in full-time. The region remained a buffer between the greater systems to east and west, rich in game because it was not rich in arable soil.

At the very end of the fifteenth century, Europeans trying to break the Arab monopoly on routes to Far Eastern spices accidentally ran into the western hemisphere, bringing two old worlds together after a separation of more than ten thousand years. They quickly found reasons to be glad for the mistake, and, arrogantly assuming that they could take whatever they found, they proceeded to explore. By the time they began serious explorations of the southeastern interior, the riches of Mexico and

Peru had made them even greedier, while the microbes they unintentionally carried along with them had made conquest easy and thus increased their illusion of invincibility. The description these conquerors provided of the people and places they saw, in spite of its drastic bias, provides the first information about the nonmaterial culture of Southeastern Indians.

The Hernando de Soto expedition brought out of the interior of southeastern North America observations that had given them something of a shock. The peoples of the Southeast were not so monolithically organized as the Aztecs or Incas, and they were therefore nearly impossible to control. In some places powerful chiefs commanded obeisance for miles around, but in others scarcely a person in authority was to be found. In four years of exploration a well-armed expedition of more than six hundred failed to conquer anyone and was itself half destroyed, including its dashing leader, the hero of Cajamarca.

In the lands of the Florida peninsula and the piedmont east of the Appalachians they met with centrally organized chiefdoms and tried to proceed as they had in South America, by seizing the chief and forcing him to provide what they wanted. Sometimes, particularly when the natives had a good reason – such as the protection of crops – to wish the intruders quickly on their way, the Spaniards secured cooperation with this stratagem. At other times, however, it was less successful, meeting with open resistance at Apalachee and an ambush at Mabila. In the latter case, they may even have precipitated the formation of a larger confederation of power than the chief Tascaluça could have wielded without the threat of their presence.

Once the expedition passed into the Tombigbee Valley, however, the situation changed. Soto was unable to command bearers for the expedition's belongings and indeed met with repeated attacks and resistance. The Pafalaya and Chicaça peoples lived in modest dispersed villages and could not be got at through one chief. If they had ever been hierarchically organized, that was not the case in 1540.

The Soto expedition saw hierarchical centralization once more in the broad Mississippi Valley. In what is now Arkansas, Louisiana, and western Mississippi they encountered multilevel chiefdoms made up of many dependent towns and centered on the important sites with impressive earthworks that characterized the Mississippian and Plaquemine cultures in the valley. These chiefs were powerful enough, with their "armadas" of canoes, to dictate terms to the Spaniards, who were by then in a bedraggled state.

The earlier expeditions of Alvarez de Pineda and Panfilo de Narváez had hinted at the unattractiveness of the northern Gulf coast and the growing hostility of peoples whom Europeans were beginning to contact from time to time. These expeditions and that of Soto saw evidence that might be interpreted as indicating that European disease had begun to take dreadful tolls near the coasts of the southeastern region, while the interior still remained relatively untouched.

Some twenty years later the expeditions of Tristán de Luna and Juan Pardo told a different story. These expeditions saw in the interior increased evidence of the effects of European disease. The impact on the peoples of the region was serious enough to have virtually destroyed several of the large chiefdoms that had formerly been so powerful – notably that of the Black Warrior, Tascaluça. Their fine towns were nowhere to be found, and food was so scarce in some places that the Indians could barely feed themselves, let alone a horde of Spanish settlers.

Decreased population was not the only effect; polities had been disrupted fundamentally, and expeditions into the interior found different peoples and even different names. Where they found a familiar name, often the people did not behave as before. If the demographic effects of disease were not particularly marked in the central interior, on the still-populous Tombigbee watershed, that may only have been because, as elsewhere, the region had seen dramatic shifting of populations. Furthermore, the people the Spaniards did meet were none too welcoming on balance, having learned that Europeans could inflict damage overtly and also leave death invisibly behind them.

European disease and European violence gathered momentum during the seventeenth century, during which time the peoples of the interior must have felt a growing sense of encroachment from all sides as the English pressed from the east, the Spanish from the south, and the French from the west. The Spanish and English made permanent settlements in Carolina and Florida; the French mastered the Mississippi, the river that had buried Soto. European reports began to be more specific about the peoples of the interior, but they described momentary states of affairs that the next observer would contradict as native groups formed and broke apart, migrated and consolidated. As they began to establish permanent contacts with Europeans, the traditional cultures of the interior adapted to accommodate them as powerful foreigners.

Toward the end of the century came the first mention of the Choctaws by name, a mention that made it clear that this new group was living where no one had lived before and that it was too populous and too powerful not to have been forming for some time. The seventeenth-century textual data is not precise enough to write what happened as history, but even more significant population movements certainly occurred during the course of the century, leading to conflicts as well as consolidation. The European observers on the periphery of the region caught only occasional glimpses of these events.

SYNCHRONY FROM HISTORY AND ARCHAEOLOGY

The pseudo-diachronic flow of the history and archaeology just reviewed suggests that the Choctaws formed during the upheaval of the protohistoric period in a refuge area previously unpopulated, but it is clearly too general to provide a convincing thesis for what happened in their formation. I have attempted to go further in chapters 6 through 8 by making careful use of well-selected synchronic evidence, specific epiphanies that provide crucial facts for establishing the ethnic identity of the Choctaw peoples. These facts will still not describe "what happened," but, by linking the *dramatis personae* with their prehistoric ancestors, it allows for a more specifically peopled theoretical construct.

The discussion of the cartographic evidence in chapter 6 showed the degree to which maps also represent a constructed reality, an interpretation rather than a simple representation. I demonstrated how iconographic convention in sixteenth-century map-making tended to enshrine the mistaken notion that southeastern Indians were all organized as centralized chiefdoms at contact, when archaeological and historical evidence suggests otherwise. A tracing of Soto's route on the earliest map of the interior showed how that map, rather than the implications of the narrative accounts, was probably responsible for modern historians' placement of the battle of Mabila in the Mobile River delta. The information portrayed on sixteenth- and early seventeenth-century maps, before the late seventeenth-century transformation in map-making method, was shown to be more metaphor than reality.

Maps are nevertheless amenable to critical reading just as histories are, and the evidence of the seventeenth-century maps, taken chronologically, reflects the turmoil and population movements of the period in the real confusion that emerges once we have factored out plain ignorance and uncritical copying of earlier data. The maps confirm that populations moved, and they help somewhat in putting names to those populations. Toward the beginning of the eighteenth century, when European exploration in the region had begun again in earnest, maps began to embody the primary testimony of explorers, and their evidence became more reliable. I argued that symbolic representation on three Delisle 1701 maps and nomenclature on several later British maps capture the fact that the eastern division of the Choctaws came from east of the Tombigbee River.

In chapter 7 I discussed two very different kinds of archaeological evidence, both preferentially studied by archaeologists. Pottery survives in archaeological contexts because it is inorganic and must be literally pulverized to be destroyed. Burials come to the attention of archaeologists more frequently than any other kind of feature because of the natural human interest in death. Pottery is seen as a vital index of cultural change over time, whereas burials are held to be time capsules that permit the archaeologist to assert the simultaneity of objects found with them. Both these kinds of evidence accordingly have a long history of study behind them, hence a great importance in the theoretical discourse of the discipline. Here I studied them for indicators of ethnicity, but extracting such information is not straightforward.

In examining the pottery types associated with eighteenth-century Choctaw sites in the east-central Mississippi "homeland," I argued that ethnicity was visible in them because of a clear association of diverse types with sites attributable to neighboring ethnic groups. Hence the Natchezan Fatherland Incised type, found in particular concentration on the southern site of Chickasawhay, seems to point to a Natchez connection. Whether the proportional representation of this type on southern Choctaw sites will prove to suggest trade rather than residence remains to be seen, but its very presence is highly suggestive nonetheless. Similarly, the southern sites and, more important, the eastern sites show a consistently significant presence of a "Nicked Rim Incised" type whose design motifs are very closely related to the Doctor Lake Incised pottery of the Mobile delta, and quantities seem much too great to be the result of exchange alone. We still know too little of the northwestern sites to demonstrate any external connection or design influence.

The distribution of burial types through the region and through time from late prehistoric through historic periods represents an entirely different scale of evidence, and the uneven reporting of data seriously compromises its study. Further, as an examination of existing mortuary practices attests, many if not most of the significant ritual elements of burial are not preserved archaeologically. Still, a study of distribution does indicate some clear trends. The Choctaws' well-known burial rite, with its lengthy processing of the remains, temporary housing of cleaned bones in a charnel house, and final deposition in earthen mounds, was also used for specific kinds of burials by nearly all their eighteenth-century neighbors. By that century this form, which had started out in a very ancient past as the preferential mode of burial for high-ranking persons, had clearly become simply a mode reserved for anomalous deaths among most of the more egalitarian tribes that survived protohistoric-period upheavals. The Choctaws were exceptional in adopting for everyone the extended processing that had once been reserved for the elite, a trend that may have begun with the "burial urn" traditions of the protohistoric period in the Tombigbee/Alabama watershed.

Material evidence cannot alone determine ethnicity or culture, however. Archaeologists of necessity tend to see cultures as loci of overlapping trait distributions; indeed, some are so ceramicentric that they define cultures according to the percentage distribution of groups of pottery types. Social anthropologists speak of cultures as loci of interaction, attempting to capture a similar generalization about regions of nonmaterial sameness. The focus of social anthropology on actual people suggests the next direction in which to turn for further evidence, the place where much material culture gets its start but of which it is only an indirect indicator: the realm of communication.

Thus in chapter 8 I turned to the very late and imperfect evidence of language and myth. Historical linguists still debate the genetic relationships among the Muskogean languages spoken by the Choctaws and their neighbors, and the debate will continue pending further study of those languages at the level of language differences as well as of dialectal variation. What is certain is that Choctaw and Chickasaw are closely related, and that both are more closely related to Alabama than to the other Muskogean languages. This simple assertion is suggestive of social relationships by itself, but I have also adduced facts of social context from the early eighteenth century that argue that the "Choctaw" most studied by linguists – that is, the dominant dialect in Mississippi and Oklahoma in the nineteenth and twentieth centuries – is not the dialect that was spoken by most Choctaws in the eighteenth century or before, and possibly not the dialect spoken by most Choctaws at the time the evidence was gathered. "Choctaw," in short, was the "public" language, the "court" dialect of diplomacy and formal discourse in the eighteenth century. Because it reflected a connection with the only other natives of the region, the Chickasaws, it was probably the dialect of the west and center, the Nanih Waiya region of the Pearl River's headwaters that had continued to be inhabited by the participants in a modest polity as multilevel chiefdoms crumbled to east and west.

Why then the famous Choctaw migration myth with the leaning pole, if the western, "native" mode of self-presentation prevailed in language? In that myth the Choctaws and Chickasaws are intimately linked, but a look at the migration myths from the whole Muskogean world leads to the strong conclusion that the story they tell represents the conflation of the very ancient migration of all eastern peoples across the Mississippi with the very recent population displacements of the seventeenth century. Further, the simultaneous contradictory appearance of an earth-emergence myth among the Muskogeans, particularly the Alabamas and Choctaws, represents an assertion of claim to land that connects with mound-building traditions and leads full circle to the Choctaw burial rite, which makes those same assertions through the construction of landmarks with the bodies of Choctaw dead. I therefore suggested that the combination of the two themes in the Lincecum version of the Choctaw migration myth, which is otherwise so fancifully linked with supernatural Aztecs, may represent a nineteenth-century Choctaw etiological reasoning about their linkage to the east-central Mississippi "homeland."

None of this synchronic evidence is sufficient in itself to allow any kind of assertion of constituent ethnicity for the Choctaws, but together they build patterns of variation that I think cannot be ignored. I am persuaded by the patterns because they are so strong that they emerge in spite of the imperfection of the evidence.

Even to the eye of the lay person the pottery types I have pointed out as markers of ethnicity do not seem to go together; they pursue sometimes similar decorative ideas in very disparate ways, and even a cursory glance at their geographical distributions makes the Choctaw homeland occurrences obvious outliers. Still, migrating pots alone need not suffice as evidence when we have the remains of migrating people. Collected in the eighteenth and nineteenth centuries, the gruesome descriptions of the Choctaw rites add a dimension of variability that echoes that of the pottery, suggesting that the processes leading to communal burial expressed consolidation for the Choctaws while consoling the living with rituals that recalled an older uniqueness. The Choctaws similarly asserted unanimity by adopting a single dialect for "public" situations while continuing to speak distinct dialects in their villages, and without any sense of contradiction they cherish to this day the earth-emergence myth that makes a single claim to their homeland and the migration myth that brings a large and diverse people to that land.

All these kinds of evidence repeatedly assert ethnic linkages to what history called the Choctaws' neighbors: Chickasaws to the north, Alabamas to the east, Natchezan people from the southwest, and Mobile delta people from the southeast. If the "marrying out" of Choctaw women, who created "Choctaw" lineages with men of these neighboring tribes in the eighteenth century for purposes of political alliance, seems to go against the grain of the usual matrilineal and matrilocal practices of the region, it may be that most of these women and their lineages did not see them as "marrying out," but as reestablishing older lineage links severed by migration. But that suggestion must remain only a suggestion while I turn to the painfully uncertain task of articulating the scenario of Choctaw tribe formation that I expect the foregoing evidence to support.

HYPOTHESIS: THE MERGER OF DIACHRONY AND SYNCHRONY

I intend that my hypothesis for Choctaw tribe formation serve as a model that can be tested both against new evidence from the period I have examined and against the evidence that emerges in the documentary and archaeological record generated since full contact. The problem that arises is just how to express it. It must be narrative to the extent that it is diachronic; it must be schematic to the extent that it is synchronic. It must not only include the "what" but also attempt to explain the "how."

The notion of a social system moving through time has been formulated by Marxist anthropologists as "social reproduction," thus appropriating a whole realm of genetic and evolutionary metaphor (much as culture-historical archaeologists have done for pottery). One drastic difference between biological systems and social systems must be recognized, however: the evolution of social systems is Lamarckian – that is, their participants are not determined in their behaviors by their "genetic" inheritance of tradition: they can learn, and having done so, having changed their system, they can pass on to their children something new, not simply what they themselves inherited. Furthermore, because cultural systems are extrabiological, because they have a material component capable of "speaking" to their participants, the individual can interact with and change the culture in many ways. In short, given the inexact reproduction of cultures, it would be truly wonderful if they did *not* change over time, even if there were no impetus for it.

During the period I have considered there was, of course, plenty of impetus for change. First was the significant change in subsistence and social patterns wrought by the American "Neolithic Revolution" that brought corn agriculture to the southeastern woodlands, changed hunters and gatherers into farmers, and eventually created the necessity for a more complex social organization. Then came aliens that brought the demographic disaster of disease and strange new ways of creating and manipulating wealth and power that changed many farmers back into hunters. Whether interacting with close and distant neighbors in their own hemisphere to enhance their own prestige and security or providing raw materials to fuel someone else's empire, again to enhance prestige and prosperity, the native peoples of the Southeast were never hermetically sealed entities. Their changing patterns of interaction and thus of internal change were therefore very complex, but these two revolutions provide a useful focus for developing the hypothesis.

Mississippian "Evolution" and "Devolution"

Hierarchically organized Mississippian societies did not require an external push to come into being; they appeared as corn agriculture took hold and the big-men who used faction leadership to get things done discovered ways to perpetuate their own leadership. The adoption of horticulture and then agriculture as an increasingly important part of the subsistence base created a positive feedback cycle: a reliable, storable food source made population growth possible, and population growth in turn required the intensification of agriculture to assure that the food source would remain reliable and abundant. As a result, emergent Mississippian populations throughout the southeastern region moved to a deliberately simplified subsistence base and a more sedentary way of life. This trajectory was shared by population groups in the Mississippi and Tombigbee/Mobile Valleys, although the lower Mississippi Valley supported two distinct cultural styles, while the Tombigbee/Mobile was dominated by only one.

Because the river valleys appropriate for supporting large populations with corn agriculture were few, the leaders of these agricultural groups had to be concerned with many new issues that smaller-scale societies less closely bound to the land did not need to care about, such as defense, food storage and distribution, and planting times. In time these concerns became a full-time job, legitimated through kinship ties and belief system. Contact with other such groups permitted the communication of new ideas as it spurred competition, and it also apparently fostered a degree of regional unity in the belief system as it supplied leaders with sources of exotic goods with which to reward their followers and build their power.

Mississippian societies likewise did not need an external push to disintegrate. They were vulnerable through both their full-scale agriculture and their hierarchical organization. As population grew, agriculture was intensified until it occupied more and more time, but the corn crop that had provided plenty eventually depleted the available soils, while the needs of large populations deforested wide areas around their settlements, making it harder to supplement the diet by hunting and gathering. A point came when some of the river valleys could no longer support their populations, or when populations right at the edge of need experienced a run of bad years or even climatic change, and the people had to disperse or starve.

Hierarchical organization could not survive such levels of stress, either. As their societies' subsistence intensification activities began to yield diminishing returns, dissatisfaction could emerge in many forms, and leaders might have had to depend more and more on their preferential access to and control of the external trade that allowed them to distribute the objects that were the legitimating marks of rank. Thus they became vulnerable to the loss of such external contacts, whether to usurpation or to the trading partners' own collapse. When they could not solve the shortages and could not even demonstrate their power through sumptuary distinction, they could no longer command the tribute from their own people that kept them in power.

The results of all this would be a reintensification of hunting and gathering strategies and a redistribution of population. But just as resources were not the same everywhere in the region and societies did not grow at the same rate everywhere, so not all Mississippian societies reached this point of diminishing returns at the same time or in the same way. The greatest of all such societies and the first to emerge, Cahokia at the confluence of the Mississippi and Missouri, came apart in the fourteenth century. The multilevel Moundville chiefdom, confined as it was to a relatively narrow floodplain, began to disintegrate toward the end of the fifteenth century; chiefdoms of a similar scale on the lower Mississippi, nowhere near straining the carrying capacity of that extraordinary environment, were still fully functional in the mid–sixteenth century.

Simple chiefdoms on the small tributaries of the Tombigbee, such as that represented by the Lubbub Creek site, formerly in tributary or alliance relationships with Moundville, did not react immediately. Instead, freed of the overhead of their share of support for the primary center, they enjoyed a respite for a time. Others, like Lyon's Bluff and Nanih Waiya, that were probably involved in the external contacts to the west that dried up during the fifteenth century, decentralized along with

Moundville as their peoples dispersed over the uplands. The later Chickasaw people and, I believe, the western Choctaw group were among these latter peoples.

As Tainter (1988) has suggested, for all these peoples decentralization, to which archaeologists have referred lugubriously as the "Mississippian Decline," was a positive act, an act of economy that solved the problem of expensive overheads and restored a subsistence balance. In the eastern woodlands the Mississippian adaptation had simply added corn agriculture to a very rich repertoire of subsistence techniques that, even lacking full-scale corn agriculture, had already arguably built hierarchy in the Hopewell manifestation during the Woodland period. Turning away from Mississippian-style intensive dependence on corn agriculture simply meant a reassertion of parts of the Primary Forest Efficiency that had been so successful in the region for millennia. Just as people had continued to care for seed-bearing grasses all along, so they would continue to grow corn, beans, and squash; but they would depend less on them and more on the available forest resources, especially as they had to move away from exhausted fields.

European Contact and Disruption

There is no telling what might have happened to the peoples of the Tombigbee-Mobile region if they had been left alone; if many of their neighbors still retained organizational complexity, they might have fallen into tributary status to them or have been forced at some point to recentralize. Before that could happen, however, the alien invasion began.

Proponents of the concept of the European world system as an expansionist economic and political phenomenon that began to spread outward in the sixteenth century have seen the impact of European explorers and settlers on the western hemisphere as one in a series of steps that eventually spread a market economy worldwide. The Europeans were not, however, acting on an access of fellow-feeling, no matter how they used religion to rationalize their actions; they were acting to benefit themselves, and the native peoples they met could only avoid being expendable in the process by becoming necessary to the creation of wealth for Europeans.

Some effects of this expansion were unintended, the spread of disease and later larger alien species being the most important for the Americas. The sixteenth-century expansion of Europe created a common world disease pool for the first time, mixing European, Asian, and African germs in European bodies to produce a cocktail that turned out to be less lethal to them than to their new acquaintances. The natives of the Americas were most at risk, having been cut off from the rest of the human family for so long, and a huge proportion of their populations perished.

Nor, probably, did the Europeans realize that they would alter native notions of warfare by introducing truly lethal weapons and a totally alien spirit to revenge. With the exception of the Aztec and Inca state formations, western hemisphere natives had not pushed intergroup conflict much past the satisfaction of individual grievances; total war on the European model was foreign, and they more often used their limited metallurgy for ceremonial weapons than for functional ones. Flesh-slashing blades and projectiles driven by more than human force were unknown, and the very concept of reducing a human body to a lifeless bloody mass without any kind of direct personal contact was unthinkable.

Europeans did intend to introduce a market economy that allowed them to make a profit on exchange, particularly where extracting the raw materials they needed was most efficiently accomplished by farming the work out as piecework. Native North Americans were lucky that large amounts of precious metals were not found at first by Europeans. The fact that the only wealth that interested them came from the skins of animals that were available to all, however, meant that even had the population not been drastically affected by European disease, structures of power would have been seriously affected as chiefs found they could no longer control the goods tradable for indicators of status.

These three factors, disease, total warfare, and a market economy, led to a complex of changes among North American peoples that can be seen from an external perspective as the beginning of a process creating underdevelopment and dependency, but that view tells very little about what actually happened to real people to alter their way of life so drastically. Particularly in colonial-period North America, native people were not generally forced at gunpoint to do much of anything; the Europeans were too few. Europeans simply became another set of players in what initially seemed like continuing peer-polity interactions.

Had it not been for the American demographic collapse induced by European, African, and Asian diseases, they would have *remained* another set of players, unable to set aside the millions of people who already possessed the land. The demographic changes are therefore fundamental to this consideration of the emergence of the Choctaws, because without large-scale population loss many other changes would not have taken place or would have been more gradual.

It is reasonably simple to give a general outline of the processes that this population loss entailed. An initial effect was on the primary subsistence base, the corn crop. Although the European intrusions were certainly responsible for some expropriation and destruction of crops, which were thereby lost to the polities that produced them, in the interior such forays were few and short-lived, having little more effect than a bad crop year. The serious effects on subsistence crops resulted, again, from the effects of disease, as damaged populations were too weak and demoralized to plant, store, or harvest crops. If, as European observations suggest, the primary tasks of cultivation were assigned to women, and if those tasks were accordingly devalued (although we must remember that such a view echoes the mounted knight's view of the toiling peasant), then the need for everyone to undertake hard field work in order to avoid starvation must have had serious effects on notions of status and sexual division of labor.

Where hunting and gathering had not already assumed a renewed importance due to environmental stress, they undoubtedly came into greater play as contact with Europeans began, both because hunted and gathered foodstuffs did not require the care that decimated populations could not muster and because Europeans were willing to trade for the food and other products thus secured. In some instances, where increasing dependence on hunting and gathering had not begun before contact, people may have found themselves having to learn anew, if not the basic skills of such pursuit, at least the habits and distribution of the prey.

With their population diminished in this sudden way, some of the peoples of the region began to move and amalgamate their settlements with those of other survivors. Dobyns (1983) has spoken of the desire to restore the "proper size" for a village; this "proper size" is no more and no less than the required number to reproduce the society as the people understood it – enough nonrelatives for people to marry outside the incest prohibition, enough neighbors to perform the functions of the settlement. Thus the extensive amalgamation of peoples suggests how devastating the experience of massive disease mortality must have been.

Moving their villages was not some simple act of nomads folding their tents. The southeastern peoples had lived for many generations in much the same places, and although they were accustomed to seasonal hunts and other such temporary absences from their villages, they did not abandon the villages except when the surrounding fields had become too exhausted to support the necessary crops, and (as with the Hurons) they probably had important ceremonies connected with such abandonment. In the cases at hand, nothing so orderly could be carried out. If ceremonies existed, the people who knew their details were probably dead. If those people had survived, the rest may no longer have trusted the sacred order they represented, since it had been unable to stop the ravages of disease. A traditional move might not have been possible in any case, particularly if such a move was supposed to be prepared a long time in advance.

Probably the most serious aspect of abandoning a former settlement was the abandonment of the dead, whose interment had marked a structuring of the other world that guaranteed the rightness of settlement in this one. With a sudden and forced move, protracted secondary processing of dead bodies might not be completed; the dead who had not yet finished their journey to the other world might be given an untimely final burial in desperation. And if complex relationships with the ancestors had to be broken off, and the structures of the other world local to their village abandoned, the kin-based rank of elites that depended upon these relationships for its legitimacy could also disappear, all the more easily since the elites had little to do in the face of the desperately changed conditions.

In short, what was abandoned in all this turmoil was not only the villages but the "great tradition" of rank and the sacred, which depended on the esoteric specialized knowledge of the elites and in turn validated their existence. What could be preserved was the "little tradition": the subsistence technologies of planting, hunting, and gathering; the skills for making pottery, clothing, and houses from materials at hand; the small-scale rules of kinship that did not run to dynastic schemes. It was portable knowledge because it was what everyone knew, not just the specialists.

THE MOVEMENT INTO EAST-CENTRAL MISSISSIPPI

I have outlined in a general way what the processes of disintegration amounted to, whether engendered by internal instability or the unexpected attacks of invisible enemies. To propose just how people reconstructed their lives in new groups, I must offer a hypothetical reconstruction of what I think the proto-Choctaws in particular did.

They gathered in east-central Mississippi, ever afterward to be called the Choctaw "homeland"; and in a real sense it was, because there the group of people who would be called "Choctaw" assembled for the first time. The region had probably long been used for winter hunts by many groups – the people of the modest simple chiefdoms to the north, the people of the Mobile delta Bottle Creek chiefdom and its neighbors, possibly the Natchezan people living halfway down the Pearl River, probably some of the people of the coast – but its interior, south and east of the Pearl and west of the Tombigbee, had not been settled during the Mississippian period. Two major routes of trade and communication crossed it, one that went from north to south parallel to the west side of the Mobile-Tombigbee system and one that crossed from the Natchez region to the head of Mobile Bay. It was a region known to many people, but no one lived there.

Precisely because nobody permanently settled there during the Mississippian period, it probably served as a buffer zone used in common by many groups for such hunting as they did. With more than one group using it, however, game was likely less intensively hunted than it would have been were there no chance of encountering competing and perhaps inimical hunters. Game was thus probably abundant, and the region would be very attractive to people who needed to subsist on hunted and gathered foods or who wanted to exploit hunting to accumulate a surplus.

The region had an advantage for agriculture, too. The river and creek valleys were not wide and the renewal they received from annual flooding was not significant, but except for the Pearl and Tombigbee/Mobile Valleys on the borders of the area, they had probably never been farmed before. So although they were not the deepest nor the best of soils, at least at first they would have given very good crops compared with those yielded by longer-cultivated soils in the previously populated valleys.

The constituent peoples of the Choctaws settled on the three different watersheds with which they were already associated. The "prairie" people associated with Nanih Waiya and other sites like it settled on the headwaters of the Pearl River and just south of them, if they were not there already. They had come from a resilient small-scale chiefdom and were probably mostly intact as to lineages and leadership. They became what Anglo-Americans would later term the "Western Division."

Two groups settled on the significant southwestern tributaries of the Tombigbee – the Noxubee and the Sucarnoochee – during the seventeenth century. The first were people who had been connected with Moundville but had either been part of satellite, semi-independent simple chiefdoms such as the Lubbub Creek community or had belonged to actual subordinate chiefdoms within the Moundville system. They were the people Soto called "Pafalaya." The second group to settle west of the Tombigbee probably came from the upper Mobile delta. They were connected with the Bottle Creek chiefdom in prehistory; they later became "burial urn" people, probably identifiable with the abandoned villages seen north of Luna's "Nanipacana." From that expedition they had suffered the effects of prolonged exposure to European disease.

A second wave of people from the Mobile-Tensaw delta moved onto the Chickasawhay River at the turn of the seventeenth century because of slave raids by the English and their mostly Alabama allies. They had probably long used the lands for hunting. They came from the populous groups around the Bottle Creek chiefdom – the Nanipacana of Tristán de Luna – and they had also already been stricken by European disease when they moved into the homeland area.

The Natchezan people who abandoned the large chiefdom at Pearl Mounds around the time of contact probably began to occupy the upper headwaters of the Leaf and the western branches of the Pascagoula in the middle seventeenth century. They had been living on the lower reaches of the Leaf tributaries for some time, until the ravages of disease along the coast began to reach them.

HOW THE PEOPLE CAME TOGETHER

To say that thus and such a group moved into the Choctaw homeland area, as I have just done, is easy enough; the trick is to show how they made themselves into what looked to the French and the British like a unified tribal entity by 1700. We should remember that these constituent peoples did not see each other as the unimaginably

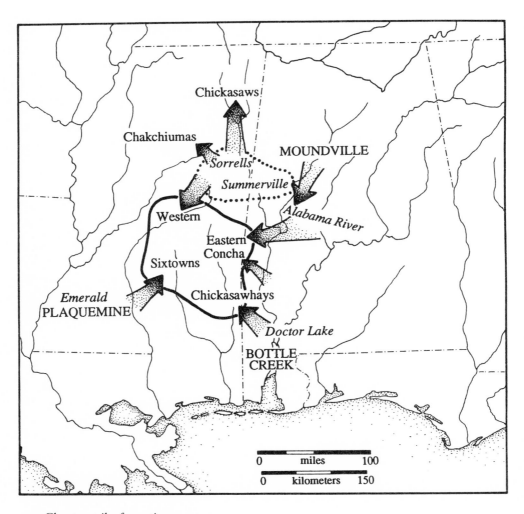

9.1. Choctaw tribe formation, 1500–1700.

strange and outlandish people the Europeans must have seemed; the European intrusion must have made all native southeastern peoples aware for the first time of their likeness to each other by giving them drastically different grounds for comparison. Except for the Natchezans the new "Choctaws" shared closely related languages; they had all without exception been agriculturists living on corn, beans, and squash supplemented by the game and gathered foods of rather similar environments; and they had all developed for millennia in the region, sharing an ancient conceptual patrimony.

Nor were they ignorant of each other's existence prior to gathering together in the seventeenth century. They were neighbors who had shared a hunting area reasonably equably (because none of them depended essentially on hunting for subsistence) and who were linked by trade and the communications of alliance. They all came from

354

polities that had evolved or devolved to roughly peer status when the European intrusion occurred, and their relations as a unified group would inevitably be governed by what their relations had been before they became a group.

Thus, as I have discussed, the peoples of the Tombigbee/Mobile would remain more closely linked within the new alliance, in the same way that they had formed an axis of trade and communication when Moundville and Bottle Creek shared dominance on the river system. Similarly, the Natchezan people of the Pearl would have had connections with the Nanih Waiya people of the Pearl, and although their greatest loyalties were to the west and north respectively they would form a second axis within the new tribal entity. These two alignments may go a long way toward explaining how a dual division emerged to structure the new tribe, and the subordinate position of the prairie people of Nanih Waiya with respect to Moundville may explain why the eastern alignment came to be connected with the Inholahta, white, peace, "elder brother" moiety, while the two western groups became the Imoklasha, red, war, "younger brother" moiety (Swanton 1931:76–79; Galloway 1982a).

The gathering of peoples in the homeland area was thus not some kind of desperate refugee rush; those of the new allies who had experienced serious disruption from the European intrusion had already buried the dead killed by disease where they were and had even begun to be involved in long-range connections that terminated at the coastal European settlements. The Choctaw genesis was probably preceded by visits, negotiations, possibly even marriages, as the peoples particularly of the Tombigbee/Mobile and the Leaf and lower Pearl began to realize that coastal encroachments were increasing and were empowering long-established enemies to the east of the Appalachian terminus.

As this process advanced, leaders who could see how to solve the new problems must have emerged to devise the kinds of new solutions that were possible when large chunks of tradition had been devalued and even lost. They would not have been working blindly. Most of the southeastern peoples must have known that many of their neighbors were in trouble and known where they themselves stood with reference to their neighbors. The leaders who arose in the midst of this turmoil must have done so because they could see advantage beyond it and thus devise a way forward.

Because direct contact with Europeans was so sporadic for natives of the deep interior in the sixteenth and seventeenth centuries, the immediate effects on the Indian people were mostly limited to the invisible illnesses that could be passed through indirect contact. In time, however, coastal groups in direct contact with Europeans began to be involved in trade as they were called upon to provision the new settlers, and the repercussions of the contact with the world system began haltingly to be felt, in the context still of native modes of managing exterior contact. Coastal tribes acted as intermediaries to bring raw materials out of the interior in exchange for some of the goods obtained from the Europeans. Because early exchanges in such a contact would not include useful items but would instead approximate the exotic prestige goods obtained through long-distance trade before, they could be monopolized by people in a position to control the trade. Hence at first European goods simply entered the trade arena as prestige goods. They promised a way for enterprising big-men to begin building toward chiefdoms again, with production beyond subsistence simply based upon another commodity.

Over time, of course, trade with Europeans would lead to the systematic distortion of boundaries as new commodities were exploited and of power relationships as new external trading partners were contacted. This external trade through intermediaries took on a significant new complexion when the Europeans began to demand, toward the end of the seventeenth century, another product of the interior: human slaves. The numbers of slaves taken and the violence with which it was done, made possible by European firearms technology, were unprecedented, even though at first the natives doubtless understood the practice in traditional terms. We know too little of the effects these slave-catching activities had on the political economy of the native groups who carried it out on the Europeans' behalf, but the effects on the victimized peoples must have been dramatic. For what was probably the first time ever in the region, acts of warfare were being perpetrated for the direct purpose of capturing (preferentially) women and children, and these acts frequently resulted in the deaths of men who tried to defend them. When the Indians of the interior learned that their women and children were being taken not to make up the numbers of their decimated neighbors but to give to the European intruders to labor for them or even to be sent beyond the sea never to return, the idea must have seemed unthinkable, paralyzing. And defense, without European arms, was impossible; the only recourse was withdrawal, and a substantial segment of the Choctaws moved into the homeland in just that way.

We cannot easily imagine what happened when the constituent peoples came together or precisely how they arrived at the solution of confederation, but some suggestions for a scenario follow from a few general principles. They must have helped each other from the start; the more "native" northwestern and southwestern segments must have given advice about the agricultural potentials of the small valleys of the region – information about which streams were intermittent and which were reliable water sources. But subsistence was perhaps the easiest requirement for the social reproduction of this new group, since all the constituent peoples were acquainted with the region in a limited way already. The really complicated issues to be worked out had to do with sexual reproduction: arrangements for who would marry whom.

It is difficult to hazard guesses at how many people belonged to the four segments – the western Nanih Waiya group, the eastern settlers on the Tombigbee tributaries, the southern people on the Chickasawhay, and the southwestern Natchezan people – but an arbitrary assumption that each segment represented one-fourth of the population of the united groups, together with another arbitrary assumption that in 1700 the Choctaws numbered twenty thousand, would suggest that each segment amounted to five thousand people. That would certainly be enough to maintain an autonomous society had the numbers indeed been that high, but some researchers (e.g., Thornton 1987) have suggested that by 1700 some southeastern peoples were already beginning a population recovery, so such a number may be too high. At the earlier date when nonresident people began to move into the region, their numbers might not have been large enough to sustain an independent society, particularly since those peoples likely entered the homeland area in small groups rather than all at once.

The universal taboo against incest requires that within the endogamous unit defined as a society some minimal set of exogamous groups is necessary to create a society capable of self-sustaining reproduction. By the end of the eighteenth century the dual division of the Choctaw confederacy bore that function among others, but I cannot do more than suggest what must have been the case at first. The Nanih Waiya people would probably have remained virtually intact and would have had no requirement to marry out unless their group had been drastically reduced in size by disease, which does not seem to have been the case. In fact, all four constituent groups could have remained autonomous if they were able to preserve intact villages, at least to the extent that they practiced the village endogamy that is common among matrilineal peoples so that males can manage their sisters' households without deserting their wives. Such a favorable scenario is not likely, however, because disease and other hazards of white contact had taken their toll and because the migrant settlers probably did not transplant entire functioning villages.

If no one group or only one group preserved adequately intact kin networks to continue with marriages according to its own prior arrangements, new arrangements had to be made quickly. Because people of high rank had likely made at least some alliance marriages with neighboring groups in the past, such a model may have been the basis for a new system. The easiest thing to do was to marry other people, other participants in the alliance. Not only would this avoid any problems of incest, but it would also tend to damp any residual enmity the four groups may have felt for one another. Exogamy was probably practiced by easterners marrying westerners and vice versa, as later evidence shows the moiety division tended to lie (Galloway 1982a). But if descent was reckoned through the mother and residence was in her household, as was later the case, then marriage would not be the only or indeed the most effective glue to stick the confederacy together, because the culture of its children would be dominated by the maternal households.

VARIEGATED ETHNICITY

The many different ways in which the constituent Choctaw peoples had to come together, the different surfaces that had to bond to make a whole, account for the interwoven markers of ethnicity in the culture of the eighteenth-century Choctaws. Each of the four groups made its contribution to what was eventually identified by outsiders as "Choctaw" culture and what in the course of time became so. How that happened can suggest some further aspects of the confederation process.

The Choctaw language was probably not spoken at first, or even in the eighteenth century, by all of the constituent peoples; it was rather clearly the language of the northwestern people of Nanih Waiya, and it was very near to the language of the Chickasaws. This, and the fact that the Nanih Waiya people were in some ways the "hosts" of the confederacy, may explain why it first gained ascendancy as the language of external diplomacy. The historical data demonstrate that the Chickasaws were the most powerful tribal entity in the region at the time of Choctaw tribe formation, enjoying particularly easy access to the "homeland" area via the Tombigbee River. Most of the intertribal diplomacy that had to take place early on, then, would have been with the Chickasaws, and the appropriate language would have been one that was very close to theirs.

By the end of the eighteenth century most of the Choctaws were making the style of pottery that came in time to be considered their only style: the curvilinear-incised "Chickachae Combed" pottery, named for the French spelling of the Chickasawhay river and village. A "genetic" relationship of this pottery to the decorative motifs of the Natchezan Fatherland series has long been suggested by archaeologists, and the thematic affinities of the types are undeniable. I think that the stylistic predominance of Chickachae Combed pottery is probably real for the later period, and I would suggest that it indicates the contribution of the Natchezan Sixtowns people to the confederacy. The means by which it spread to the other members of the confederacy are still unclear, unless it was used ceremonially in activities conducted for the opposite moiety, or it was consciously adopted as a marker of ethnicity for symbolic reasons not now recoverable. Curvilinear decorative motifs for pottery were in the repertoire of all the constituent peoples, which may reinforce the idea of symbolic significance. At any rate, this was the latest of the markers to be adopted by all the Choctaws.

The other striking marker of Choctaw ethnicity, the protracted processing of the bodies of the dead, should, in my opinion, be attributed on balance to the eastern people and their burial-urn tradition, and again possibly to a conscious decision, adopted early on. Equal treatment for the dead would have been increasingly practiced by the four constituent groups as they devolved or suffered depopulation, but the adoption of a lengthy processing, linked ideologically with the notion of the soul's long passage from one world to the next, would seem odd in a historical context of increasing uncertainty.

The answer may lie in the fact that members of the opposite moiety historically carried out the processing of the body. Because disease mortality may have continued to be serious during the early years of the confederacy, the performance of such a duty would have been freighted with significance as the other face of moiety exogamy. During the eighteenth century the processing of the remains of prominent leaders was occasion for mending quarrels and for tribal decision-making; attendance by a large segment of the tribe was apparently compulsory (Rowland, Sanders, and Galloway 1984, 4:282–83). Thus burial rites may have been an early method of building solidarity.

A further factor is the creation of ossuary mounds, which were built when a village charnel house was full. Mounds, with and without burials, had a long history in the region as markers of settlement charters, and adopting this custom to contain all the Choctaw dead must have had special significance for people who had been forced to abandon their dead unburied or with their journey to the other world incomplete. This elaborate treatment for the dead could also have promised the living some relief from contagion; to us now it seems an extraordinary expression of defiance against the forces of fragmentation the Europeans' arrival set in motion.

Because the migration of at least two (and probably three) of the four constituent Choctaw peoples was a significant part of their formation process, the migration legend was probably adopted by all the Choctaws because it reflected a recent historical experience, although in its echoes of the Creek myths it probably also reflects a contribution from the eastern peoples. The simultaneous adoption of the earth-emergence legend has a different basis. Probably the contribution of the western people, and not coincidentally identified with the Nanih Waiya area, the earth-emergence legend became a way of expressing the Choctaw settlement charter, just as their burial customs did; it is also not coincidental that huge ossuary mounds of probably tribal significance were established on the Nanih Waiya site.

VIEW FROM THE INTERIOR

These, then, are my ideas about the ethnogenesis of the historic Choctaw tribe in the sixteenth and seventeenth centuries. Some of these ideas can be tested, and I hope they will be. I have to confess at this point that of course all along I was cheating; these ideas were only possible because I know how the story came out, I know the details of telling incidents in the eighteenth century that make powerful suggestions about what had come before. I make no apologies for cheating in this way, since some of the original ideas so garnered had to be discarded when confronted with a microscopic view of the actual evidence for the earlier period. Some of those ideas, however, have made this whole enterprise possible.

My reading of the prehistoric evidence and of the sixteenth- and seventeenth-century evidence of history is my own, but like others who have interpreted it I have shaped the evidence by chiseling free those facets that might account for the object of my own interest, the formation of the Choctaws. Were it not for the need to account for their very significant existence in the eighteenth century, chiefdoms need not have fallen and disease might have run more rampant; the Choctaws thus have shaped history in their turn by requiring it to flow around them. If I have done nothing else, I have defined the limits of the place in space and time where the Choctaws began to become the people known to history.

I hope that I have also conveyed convincingly my sense that the Choctaws of the eighteenth century were not monolithic, whatever the Europeans who knew them might have thought. At least during the sixteenth and seventeenth centuries, "Choctaw" designated not so much a concrete referent as a locus of change. If full contact with Europeans and integration into a world economic system had not decentered entirely the political economy that had begun to develop in the confederacy, the Choctaws might have built themselves into a chiefdom again. In that sense the Choctaws as a *tribal* entity in the anthropological sense were affected by the new European players in the game of peer-polity interaction. By emerging into history, the Choctaws became encapsulated in European notions of nationhood and ethnicity and were increasingly affected by their own perception of themselves under that name. I think the results would likely have been very different had they continued to interact only with native peers, but if Europeans had never come to the Americas, or if they had not brought disease and rapine, the Choctaws as such would not have existed anyway. There is nothing to celebrate in the bully-boy mentality of colonizing Europeans, but southeastern natives were not exclusively their victims – they were not so passive as that. Instead, in the face of disaster, they innovated and built, making markers of difference into symbols of unity.

Appendix

Table A.1 Burial Type Sequence from Winterville and Lake George (Williams and Brain 1983; Brain 1989). Phases are in chronological order.

INFANTS INCLUDED WITH FLESH BURIALS:

Phase	Flesh	Bundle	Skull	Fragmentary
Burial Counts				
Aden II	27	0	3	4
Kings Crossing II	102	7	26	16
Winterville II	7	1	2	0
Lake George	3	3	0	8
Burial Percentages				
Aden II	79%		8%	11%
Kings Crossing II	68%	4%	17%	10%
Winterville II	70%	10%	20%	
Lake George	21%	21%		57%

INFANTS COUNTED SEPARATELY:

Phase	Flesh	Infant	Bundle	Skull	Fragmentary
Burial Counts					
Aden II	14	13	0	3	4
Kings Crossing II	67	35	7	26	16
Winterville II	7		1	2	0
Lake George	3		3	0	8
Burial Percentages					
Aden II	41%	38%		9%	12%
Kings Crossing II	44%	23%	5%	17%	10%
Winterville II	70%		10%	20%	
Lake George	21%		21%		57%

Table A.2 Burial Types from the Emerald Site (Steponaitis 1974).

Burial	Age	Form	Accompaniments
1	Adult	Extended	5 effigy pipes
2	Adult	Extended	Fatherland Incised bowl
3		Disturbed	Mazique Incised jar
4A,B,C	Infants(3)	Extended	
5A,B,C,D	Infants(4)	Extended	
6A,B	Infant(1) Juv(1)	Extended	Plaquemine Brushed sherd
7A–G	Infants(7)	Extended	

Table A.3 Burial Types from the Mangum Site (Bohannon 1963; Dailey 1964).

Burial	Age	Sex	Form	Accompaniments
1	Adult, 30	M	Extended	Addis Plain bowl on chest of adult
	Infant		Extended	
2	Adult, 20s	F?	Extended	shell disk
3	Adult, 35	M	Extended	
4	Adult, 22	M	Extended	celt, polishing pebble, mussel shells
	Infant, 1			below chin of adult on rib cage
	Child, 2		Extended	frog pot; near right side of adult
	Infant		Bundle	
	Adult, 20s	F	Bundle	
	Adult, 24	F	Bundle	Mass of bones overlying three primary
	Subadult, 14		Bundle	burials above
	Adult, 35	M	Bundle	
	Adult, 45	M	Bundle	
5	Child, 4		Extended	Addis Plain bottle
6	Adult, 42	M	Bundle	
	Adult, 25	M	Bundle	
7	Adult, 25	M	Extended	
	Adult, 18	F	Bundle	Burials stacked on top of one another; ex-
	Child, 9–12		Bundle	tended burial above bundled mass burial
	Child, 5–8		Bundle	above extended burial
	Adult	F	Bundle	
	Adult	M	Extended	celt and polishing pebble
8	Child, 4–5		Extended	
9	Child, 6–7		Extended	
10	Adult, 20s	F	Bundle	
	Child, 5		Bundle	
	Subadult, 16	F	Bundle	Bundle burial group stacked on top of ex-
	Subadult, 13	F?	Bundle	tended burial
	Child, 12		Extended	
11	Adult, 22	F	Bundle	
	Infant, 1		Bundle	
	Adult, 25	M	Extended	Bundle burial group stacked on top of se-
	Adult, 20	M	Extended	ries of extended burials
	Subadult, 13		Extended	
	Adult, 26	F	Extended	

Burial	Age	Sex	Form	Accompaniments
12	Adult, 38	M	Bundle	
	Infant, 3–4		Bundle	
13	Adult		Extended	
14	Adult, 22	F	Bundle	not completely disarticulated
15	Adult	M	Skull	
	Adult, 22	F	Skull	
16	Child, 2–4		Extended?	reburial, partially decomposed?
	Adult, 30	F	Bundle	
	Child, 1		Bundle?	completely disarticulated
17	Adult	M	Extended	Addis Plain bowl
18	Adult, 26	M	Extended	
19	Adult, 18	F	Extended	
	Adult, 28	F	Bundle	
20	Adult, 22	M	Extended	Addis Plain cup, elbow pipe, 6 arrow-
	Adult, 28	F	Bundle	points, shell bead
	Child, 5–6		Bundle	
21	Adult, 25	M	Bundle	
	Child, 4		Bundle	
	Unknown		Bundle	Group of bundle burials stacked above
	Adult		Bundle?	extended burial
	Adult, 24	M	Extended	
22	Adult, 20	F	Extended	
	Infant, 1		Extended	
	Adult	F	Extended	
	Child, 2		Extended	
	Child, 4		Extended	conch shell dipper
	Child, 2		Extended	
	Child, 5		Skull	
23	Adult, 30	F	Extended	
	Infant		Extended	beneath right shoulder of adult
	Adult, 18	F	Disturbed	
	Adult		Disturbed	
	Child		Disturbed	
	Child		Disturbed	
	Unknown		Disturbed	
24	Adult, 25 +	F	Extended	
	Adult	M?	Extended	crushed terrapin carapace
	Adult	M	Disturbed	

Table A.4 Moundville III Burials from the White Site (data from Welch 1991:table 3.7).

Burial	Age	Form*	Accompaniments
1			
2	3 yrs	Extended	Bowl @ right knee
3		Extended	4 bear teeth @ neck
4			
5	Adult male	Extended	Sandstone disk @ foot
6			
7	6' tall	Extended	4 bear teeth @ wrist
			sandstone disk @ hand
			paint, shells, etc.
8–13	Separate burials but no further information		
14	Infant		
15	Child		Shell pendant
16	2 yrs	Extended	Shell beads @ wrist, neck
			copper ornament on chest
			plain handled jar @ skull
			inverted on A1. R. Incised bottle
16a			
17	Infant		
18	6 yrs	Extended	Fragments of decayed wood @ feet
19	Infant	Extended	Sherd discoidal @ hips
20	Adult		
21			
22	Infant		
23			
24			
25			
26			
27			
28	Infant	Extended	Bowl @ left of skull

Note: The forms of burial were not indicated by the excavators nor by Welch but were inferred from the excavators' notes indicating the position of artifacts relative to the burials.

Table A.5 Burial Types by Age (Where Known) from
Black Warrior Protohistoric Sites (data from Curren 1984b).

Type	Child	Subadult	Adult	Total
BIG PRAIRIE CREEK:				
Bundle	5	2	5	12
Urn	3	1		4
Extended			2	2
Semiflexed		1	4	5
Flexed		1		1
Totals	8	5	11	24
MOODY SLOUGH:				
Bundle	4	5	8	17
Urn	8		3	11
Extended	3		1	4
Semiflexed			4	4
Flexed			1	1
Cremation	1			1
Unknown	2		5	7
Totals	18	5	22	45
BAKER:				
Bundle			1	1
Urn	3	1	5	9
Extended			2	2
Semiflexed			1	1
Flexed	1			1
Totals	4	1	9	14
LON ROBERTSON:				
Bundle			1	1
Urn	1		2	3
Extended		2	1	3
Flexed				0
Disturbed	1		1	2
Totals	2	2	5	9

Table A.6 Temporal Distribution of Burial Types at the Lubbub
Creek Archaeological Locality (Peebles 1983, 2:appendix A).

Period	Flesh	Bundle	Disarticulated	Skull	Fragment	Total
Miller III	1					1
Summerville I	12			1	1	14
Summerville II–III	8			2		10
Summerville IV	4	55	19		4	82
Mississippian	11			2	2	15
Unknown		1			3	4
Totals	36	56	19	5	10	126

Table A.7 Burials from 1934–35 Excavations at Lyon's Bluff.

Burial	Age	Sex	Form	Accompaniments
1	Adult	M	Flexed	
2	Infant			
3	Subadult?		Flexed	Whetstone
4	Adult	M	Flexed	
5	Subadult	F	Flexed	Shell spoon
6	Subadult	M?	Flexed	
7	Subadult	M?	Flexed	
8	Subadult	F?	Flexed	
9	Subadult		Flexed	
10	Adult	M	Flexed	
11			Dug up	Alligator skull, turtle shells
Bluff 1	Infant		Flexed	
Bluff 2	Adult			

Table A.8 Burial Types on Protohistoric Sites in the Lower Tombigbee-Alabama Area (data from Sheldon 1974; Fuller, Silvia, and Stowe 1984).

Site	Extended	Flexed	Bundle	Urn	Inverted Vessel	Skull	Unknown	Total
Tu4				2				2
Tu49	1	1		4				6
Tu93	1		2	11	2		2	18
Taskigi	X		X	5	1		X	9+
Pintlala	X	X	X	16	2		X	22+
Durand's Bend	21	2	2	20	1		2	48
Wx1	X	2		14	2		7	26+
Wx12	1			3				4
Matthew's Landing	8		8	2	3	3	7	31
Little River	1		2	2	3	1	X	10+
Bashi Creek			X	1			X	3+
Gaines' Landing	1			3			X	5+
Three Rivers	5	4	5	2	2	1	X	20+
Ginhouse Island	7	5	10	6	3	1		9
Hook's Plantation			5	2				7
Pine Log Creek	X	X						2+
Cut-off Mound			2					2
Doctor Lake				1				1
Bates Lake				1				1
Total	50+	16+	39+	95	19	6	24+	226+

Bibliography

Adair, James
   1775   *The History of the American Indians*. London: Edward and Charles Dilly.

Adorno, Rolena
   1991   The Negotiation of Fear in Cabeza de Vaca's *Naufragios. Representations* 33: 163–99.

Albright, Caroline
   1983   The Summerville IV Community. In *Prehistoric Agricultural Communities in West Central Alabama*, Vol. 1: *Excavations in the Lubbub Creek Archaeological Locality*, ed. Christopher S. Peebles, 309–90. Mobile: U.S. Army Corps of Engineers, Mobile District.

Altman, Ida
   n.d.   Biedma's Survivor Narrative. In *Historiography of the Hernando de Soto Expedition*, ed. Patricia Galloway. Lincoln: University of Nebraska Press, forthcoming.

Alvord, Clarence Walworth, and Lee Bidgood, eds.
   1912   *The First Explorations of the Trans-Allegheny Region by the Virginians, 1650–1674.* Cleveland: Arthur H. Clark.

Anderson, David G.
   1990   Stability and Change in Chiefdom-Level Societies: An Examination of Mississippian Political Evolution on the South Atlantic Slope. In *Lamar Archaeology: Mississippian Chiefdoms in the Deep South*, ed. Mark Williams and Gary Shapiro, 187–213. Tuscaloosa: University of Alabama Press.

Arnold, J. Bartolo, III, and Robert S. Weddle
   1978   *The Spanish Shipwrecks of 1554: The Nautical Archeology of Padre Island.* New York: Academic Press.

Atkin, Edmond
   1753   Historical Account of the Revolt of the Chactaw Indians in the late War from the French to the British Alliance and of their Return Since to that of the French. British Library, Lansdowne Manuscript 809.

Atkinson, James R.
   1976   *Cultural Resources Reconnaissance, Edinburg Lake, Pearl River Basin, Mississippi.* Mississippi State: Mississippi State University Department of Anthropology.
   1979   A Historic Contact Indian Settlement in Oktibbeha County, Mississippi. *Journal of Alabama Archaeology* 25 (1): 61–82.
   1985   A Surface Collection from the Chickasaw Agency Site, 22-CS-521, on the Natchez Trace in Chickasaw County, Mississippi. *Mississippi Archaeology* 20 (2): 46–63.
   1986   Post–Woodland Period Archaeological Phases in the Upper Tombigbee River Valley between Tibbee/Line Creeks and Tupelo, Mississippi. Manuscript.

Atkinson, James R., and Crawford H. Blakeman Jr.
   1975   *Archaeological Site Survey in the Tallahala Reservoir Area, Jasper County, Mississippi.* Mississippi State: Mississippi State University Department of Anthropology.

Bibliography

Atkinson, James R., John C. Phillips, and Richard Walling

1980   *The Kellogg Village Site Investigations, Clay County, Mississippi.* Mississippi State: Mississippi State University Department of Anthropology.

Avellaneda, Ignacio

1990   *Los sobrevivientes de la Florida.* Gainesville: P. K. Yonge Library.

Baca, Keith A.

1989   Archaeological Collections of the Mississippi Department of Archives and History. *Mississippi Archaeology* 24 (2) : 24–44.

Bannon, John Francis

1972   Introduction to *The Narrative of Alvar Núñez Cabeza de Vaca.* Barre MA: Imprint Society.

Barnett, James F.

1986   The Play Site (22-Ad-812): A Natchez Phase Burial in Natchez, Mississippi. *Mississippi Archaeology* 21 (2) : 3–11.

Barth, Fredrik

1969   Introduction to *Ethnic Groups and Boundaries: The Social Organization of Cultural Difference*, ed. Fredrik Barth, 9–38. Boston: Little Brown.

Bartram, William

1955   *Travels of William Bartram*, ed. Mark Van Doren. New York: Dover Publications.

Bass, Quentin

n.d.   Sociopolitical and Economic Aspects of the Mississippian Occupation in the Lower Tennessee Valley. Ph.D. dissertation, University of Tennessee.

Belmont, John S.

1967   The Development of Agriculture in the Lower Valley. *Southeastern Archaeological Conference Bulletin* 5:16–18.

1982   The Troyville Concept and the Gold Mine Site. *Louisiana Archaeology* 9:63–98.

Belmont, John S., and Jon Gibson

1988   Coles Creek Culture in the Lower Mississippi Valley: A View from the Inside Out. Paper presented at the 45th annual meeting of the Southeastern Archaeological Conference, New Orleans.

Berkhofer, Robert F., Jr.

1978   *The White Man's Indian: Images of the American Indian from Columbus to the Present.* New York: Alfred Knopf.

Binford, Lewis R.

1968   Archeological Perspectives. In *New Perspectives in Archeology*, ed. Sally R. Binford and Lewis R. Binford, 5–32. Chicago: Aldine.

1971   Mortuary Practices: Their Study and Their Potential. In *Approaches to the Social Dimensions of Mortuary Practices*, ed. James A. Brown, 6–29. Society for American Archaeology Memoir 25. Washington DC.

Blitz, John H.

1983   The Summerville Mound. In *Prehistoric Agricultural Communities in West Central Alabama*, Vol. 1: *Excavations in the Lubbub Creek Archaeological Locality*, ed. Christopher S. Peebles, 198–253. Mobile: U.S. Army Corps of Engineers, Mobile District.

1985   *An Archaeological Study of the Mississippi Choctaw Indians.* Mississippi Department of Archives and History Archaeological Report 16. Jackson.

1991   Choctaw Archaeology in Mississippi. Paper presented at the 24th annual meeting of the Society for Historical Archaeology, Richmond.

1993   *Ancient Chiefdoms of the Tombigbee.* Tuscaloosa: University of Alabama Press.

Bloch, Marc

1953   *The Historian's Craft,* trans. Peter Putnam. New York: Knopf.

Bloch, Maurice

1971   *Placing the Dead: Tombs, Ancestral Villages, and Kinship Organization in Madagascar.* London: Seminar Press.

Bloch, Maurice, and Jonathan Parry

1982   Introduction to *Death and the Regeneration of Life,* ed. Maurice Bloch and Jonathan Parry, 1–44. Cambridge: Cambridge University Press.

Bohannon, Charles F.

1963   The Mangum Site: A Plaquemine Necropolis in Claiborne County, Mississippi. Manuscript on file, National Park Service, Southeast Regional Office, Tallahassee.

Bolton, Herbert E.

1925   Spanish Resistance to the Carolina Traders in Western Georgia (1680–1704). *Georgia Historical Quarterly* 9:115–30.

Bolton, Herbert E., and Mary Ross

1925   *The Debatable Land.* Berkeley: University of California Press.

Boston, Barbara

1941   The "De Soto Map." *Mid-America* 23:236–50.

Bourne, Edward Gaylord (ed.)

1922   *Narratives of the Career of Hernando de Soto in the Conquest of Florida,* 2 vols. 1904. Reprint, New York: Allerton Book Company.

Bowman, Greg, and Janel Curry-Roper

1982   *The Houma People of Louisiana: A Story of Indian Survival.* Houma LA: United Houma Nation.

Boyd, C. Clifford, Jr., and Gerald F. Schroedl

1987   In Search of Coosa. *American Antiquity* 52:840–44.

Boyd, Mark F.

1937   The Expedition of Marcos Delgado from Apalache to the Upper Creek Country in 1686. *Florida Historical Quarterly* 16:1–32.

1948   Enumeration of Florida Spanish Missions in 1675, with Translations of Documents. *Florida Historical Quarterly* 27:181–88.

Boyd, Mark F., Hale G. Smith, and John W. Griffin

1951   *Here They Once Stood: The Tragic End of the Apalachee Missions.* Gainesville: University of Florida Press.

Bozeman, Tandy K.

1980   Moundville Phase Sites in the Black Warrior Valley, Alabama: Preliminary Results of the UMMA Survey. In The Moundville Archaeological Project, ed. Margaret Scarry, 26–40.

1983   Moundville Phase Communities in the Black Warrior River Valley, Alabama. Ph.D. dissertation, University of California at Santa Barbara.

Bibliography

Brain, Jeffrey P.

n.d.   The Coles Creek Culture in the Lower Mississippi Valley. Manuscript.

1971   The Natchez "Paradox." *Ethnology* 10:215–22.

1978a   Late Prehistoric Settlement Patterning in the Yazoo Basin and Natchez Bluffs Regions of the Lower Mississippi Valley. In *Mississippian Settlement Patterns*, ed. Bruce D. Smith, 331–68. New York: Academic Press.

1978b   Review of Hudson, *Southeastern Indians. American Antiquity* 43:310–13.

1979   *Tunica Treasure.* Papers of the Peabody Museum of Archaeology and Ethnology 71. Cambridge MA.

1982   La Salle at the Natchez: An Archaeological and Historical Perspective. In *La Salle and His Legacy: Frenchmen and Indians in the Lower Mississippi Valley*, ed. Patricia Galloway, 49–59. Jackson: University Press of Mississippi.

1984   The De Soto Entrada into the Lower Mississippi Valley. *Mississippi Archaeology* 19 (2) : 48–58.

1985   The Archaeology of the Hernando de Soto Expedition. In *Alabama and the Borderlands: From Prehistory to Statehood*, ed. R. Reid Badger and Lawrence A. Clayton, 96–107. Tuscaloosa: University of Alabama Press.

1988   *Tunica Archaeology.* Papers of the Peabody Museum of Archaeology and Ethnology 78. Cambridge MA.

1989   *Winterville: Late Prehistoric Culture Contact in the Lower Mississippi Valley.* Mississippi Department of Archives and History Archaeological Report 23. Jackson.

Brain, Jeffrey P., Alan Toth, and Antonio Rodriguez-Buckingham

1972   Ethnohistoric Archaeology and the De Soto Entrada into the Lower Mississippi Valley. *Conference on Historic Site Archaeology Papers* 7:232–89.

Brannon, Peter A.

1935   *The Southern Indian Trade.* Montgomery AL: Paragon.

Brasseaux, Carl, ed. and trans.

1979   *A Comparative View of French Louisiana.* Lafayette: University of Southwestern Louisiana.

Braudel, Fernand

1972   *The Mediterranean and the Mediterranean World in the Age of Philip II*, 2 vols., trans. Siân Reynolds. New York: Harper and Row.

Braun, David P., and Stephen Plog

1982   Evolution of "Tribal" Social Networks: Theory and Prehistoric North American Evidence. *American Antiquity* 47:504–25.

Brose, David S.

1979   A Speculative Model of the Role of Exchange in the Prehistory of the Eastern Woodlands. In *Hopewell Archaeology: The Chillicothe Conference*, ed. David S. Brose and N'omi Greber, 3–8. Kent OH: Kent State University Press.

Brose, David S., and N'omi Greber, eds.

1979   *Hopewell Archaeology: The Chillicothe Conference.* Kent OH: Kent State University Press.

Brown, Calvin S.

1926   *Archeology of Mississippi.* Oxford: Mississippi Geological Survey.

Brown, Ian W.

1976   A Reexamination of the Houses at the Bayou Goula Site, Iberville Parish, Louisiana. *Louisiana Archaeology* 3:193–205.

1980   *Salt and the Eastern North American Indian: An Archaeological Study.* Lower Mississippi Survey Bulletin 6. Cambridge: Lower Mississippi Survey, Harvard.

1985   *Natchez Indian Archaeology: Culture Change and Stability in the Lower Mississippi Valley.* Mississippi Department of Archives and History Archaeological Report 15. Jackson.

1989   The Calumet Ceremony in the Southeast and Its Archaeological Manifestations. *American Antiquity* 54:311–31.

Brown, Ian W., and Richard Fuller, eds.

1992   Bottle Creek Research: Working Papers on the Bottle Creek Site (1Ba2), Baldwin County, Alabama. Unpublished manuscript on file at Gulf Coast Survey, Alabama Museum of Natural History, Tuscaloosa.

Brown, James A.

1971   The Dimensions of Status in the Burials at Spiro. In *Approaches to the Social Dimensions of Mortuary Practices*, ed. James A. Brown, 92–112. Society for American Archaeology Memoir 25. Washington DC.

Brown, James A., Richard A. Kerber, and Howard D. Winters

1990   Trade and the Evolution of Exchange Relations at the Beginning of the Mississippian Period. In *Mississippian Emergence*, ed. Bruce D. Smith, 251–80. Washington DC: Smithsonian Institution Press.

Brown, Lloyd A.

1949   *The Story of Maps.* New York: Little, Brown.

Bushnell, Amy Turner

1989   Ruling the Republic of Indians in Seventeenth-Century Florida. In *Powhatan's Mantle: Indians in the Colonial Southeast*, ed. Peter H. Wood, Gregory A. Waselkov, and M. Thomas Hatley, 134–50. Lincoln: University of Nebraska Press.

Byington, Cyrus

1915   *A Dictionary of the Choctaw Language*, ed. John R. Swanton and Henry S. Halbert. Bureau of American Ethnology Bulletin 46. Washington DC.

Byrd, Kathleen M., and Robert W. Neuman

1978   Archaeological Data Relative to Prehistoric Subsistence in the Lower Mississippi River Alluvial Valley. *Geoscience and Man* 19:9–21.

Caldwell, Joseph R.

1958   *Trend and Tradition in the Prehistory of the Eastern United States.* American Anthropological Association memoir 88, Springfield IL. *American Anthropologist* 60 (6), pt. 2.

Carleton, Kenneth

1989   Eighteenth-Century Trails in the Choctaw Territory of Mississippi and Alabama. Master's thesis, University of Georgia.

Cassirer, Ernst

1957   *The Phenomenology of Knowledge.* New Haven: Yale University Press.

Chambers, Moreau B. C.

1932–35   Field Notebooks. RG31, SG4, Vol. 218, Mississippi Department of Archives and History.

1980   Oral History Interview OH 80-01, Mississippi Department of Archives and History.

Chambers Collection

1928–193?   Photographic and manuscript collection assembled by Moreau Browne Congleton Chambers and accessioned as part of RG 31, Mississippi Department of Archives and History.

Chapman, Robert

1981   The Emergence of Formal Disposal Areas and the Problem of Megalithic Tombs in Prehistoric Europe. In *The Archaeology of Death*, ed. Robert Chapman, Ian Kinnes, and Klavs Randsborg, 71–81. Cambridge: Cambridge University Press.

Chapman, Robert, and Klavs Randsborg

1981   Approaches to the Archaeology of Death. In *The Archaeology of Death*, ed. Robert Chapman, Ian Kinnes, and Klavs Randsborg, 1–24. Cambridge: Cambridge University Press.

Charlevoix, Pierre François Xavier de

1744   *Histoire et description generale de la Nouvelle France avec le Journal Historique d'un Voyage fait par ordre du Roi dans l'Amerique septentrionale*, Vol. 5. Paris: Rollin *fils*.

Chase, David

1982   Site 1Ds53: A Glimpse of Central Alabama Prehistory from the Archaic to the Historic Period. In *Archaeology in Southwest Alabama*, ed. Cailup Curren, 19–30. Camden AL: Alabama-Tombigbee Regional Commission.

Chatman, Seymour

1980   *Story and Discourse: Narrative Structure in Fiction and Film*. Ithaca NY: Cornell University Press.

Clarke, David L.

1968   *Analytical Archaeology*. London: Methuen.

Clayton, Lawrence, Vernon James Knight Jr., and Edward C. Moore, eds.

1993   *The De Soto Chronicles: The Expedition of Hernando de Soto to North America in 1539–1543*, 2 vols. Tuscaloosa: University of Alabama Press.

Clendinnen, Inge

1987   *Ambivalent Conquests: Maya and Spaniard in Yucatan, 1517–1570*. Cambridge: Cambridge University Press.

Cédula

1883   Real cédula dando facultad á Francisco de Garay. . . . In *Colección de documentos inéditos relativos al descubrimiento, conquista y organización de las antiguas posesiones españolas en América y Oceania*, 39:514–26. Madrid: José María Pérez.

Collins, Henry B., Jr.

1926   Archaeological and Anthropometrical Work in Mississippi. *Explorations and Field-Work of the Smithsonian Institution in 1925*. Smithsonian Miscellaneous Collections 78 (1) : 89–95. Washington DC.

1927   Potsherds from Choctaw Village Sites in Mississippi. *Journal of the Washington Academy of Sciences* 17:10.

1977   Oral History Interview OHP 184, OHP 185, Mississippi Department of Archives and History.

Cotter, John L.
1952   The Mangum Plate. *American Antiquity* 18:65–68.

Cottier, John W.
1970   The Alabama River Phase: A Brief Description of a Late Phase in the Prehistory of South Central Alabama. Appendix to *Archaeological Salvage Investigations in the Miller's Ferry Lock and Dam Reservoir (1968)*. University of Alabama Office of Archaeological Research Report to the National Park Service. Moundville.

Crane, Verner
1916   The Tennessee River as the Road to Carolina: The Beginnings of Exploration and Trade. *Mississippi Valley Historical Review* 3:1–18.
1956   *The Southern Frontier, 1670–1732*. Ann Arbor: University of Michigan Press.

Crawford, James M.
1975   Southeastern Indian Languages. In *Studies in Southeastern Indian Languages*, ed. James M. Crawford, 1–120. Athens: University of Georgia Press.
1978   *The Mobilian Trade Language*. Knoxville: University of Tennessee Press.

Cronon, William
1983   *Changes in the Land: Indians, Colonists, and the Ecology of New England*. New York: Hill and Wang.

Crosby, Alfred W., Jr.
1972   *The Columbian Exchange: Biological and Cultural Consequences of 1492*. Westport CT: Greenwood.
1988   *Ecological Imperialism: The Biological Expansion of Europe, 900–1900*. Cambridge: Cambridge University Press.

Culler, Jonathan
1975   *Structuralist Poetics*. London: Routledge and Kegan Paul.

Cumming, William P.
1958   *The Southeast in Early Maps*. Princeton NJ: Princeton University Press.

Cumming, William P., S. E. Hiller, D. B. Quinn, and G. Williams
1974   *The Exploration of North America, 1630–1776*. New York: G. P. Putnam's Sons.

Cunninghame Graham, R. B.
1949   *The Horses of the Conquest*. Norman: University of Oklahoma Press.

Curren, Caleb (Cailup)
1976   Prehistoric and Early Historic Occupation of the Mobile Bay and Mobile Delta Area of Alabama with an Emphasis on Subsistence. *Journal of Alabama Archaeology* 22 (1) : 61–84.
1982a   Mississippian Period Salt Processing Sites in Southwestern Alabama. In *Archaeology in Southwestern Alabama*, ed. Cailup Curren, 95–102. Camden AL: Alabama-Tombigbee Regional Commission.
1984a   Summary and Conclusions. In *The Protohistoric Period in Central Alabama*, ed. Caleb Curren, 238–48. Camden AL: Alabama-Tombigbee Regional Commission.
1986   *In Search of DeSoto's Trail: A Hypothesis of the Alabama Route*. Bulletins of Discovery 1. Camden AL: Alabama-Tombigbee Commission.
1987   *The Route of the Soto Army through Alabama*. Alabama De Soto Commission Working Paper 3. Tuscaloosa.

Bibliography

—, ed.

1982b   *Archaeology of Southwestern Alabama*. Camden AL: Alabama-Tombigbee Regional Commission.

1984b   *The Protohistoric Period in Central Alabama*. Camden AL: Alabama-Tombigbee Regional Commission.

Curtius, Ernst Robert

1963   *European Literature and the Latin Middle Ages*, trans. Willard R. Trask. New York: Harper and Row.

Cushman, Horatio B.

1962   *History of the Choctaw, Chickasaw and Natchez Indians*, ed. Angie Debo. Condensation of 1899 edition. Stillwater OK: Redlands Press.

Dahlgren, E. W.

1892   *Map of the World by Alonzo de Santa Cruz, 1542*. Stockholm.

Dailey, R. C.

1974   Osteological Analysis of the Human Skeletal Remains of the Mangum Site, Natchez Trace Parkway, Mississippi. Manuscript on file, National Park Service, Southeast Regional Office, Tallahassee.

Dainville, François D.

1964   *Le langage des géographes: Termes, signes, couleurs des cartes anciennes, 1500–1800*. Paris: A. and J. Picard.

Dávila Padilla, Agustín

[1625] 1955 *Historia de la fundación y discurso de la provincia de Santiago de México, de la Orden de Predicadores, por las vidas de sus varones insignes, y casos notables de Nueva España*. Madrid: Pedro Madrigal.

Davis, Dave D.

1984a   Protohistoric Cultural Interaction along the Northern Gulf Coast. In *Perspectives on Gulf Coast Prehistory*, ed. Dave D. Davis, 216–31. Gainesville: University of Florida Press.

—, ed.

1984b   *Perspectives on Gulf Coast Prehistory*. Gainesville: University of Florida Press.

Debo, Angie

1961   *The Rise and Fall of the Choctaw Republic*. Norman: University of Oklahoma Press.

De Certeau, Michel

1986   *Heterologies: Discourse on the Other*. Minneapolis: University of Minnesota Press.

DeJarnette, David L., and Steve B. Wimberly

1941   *The Bessemer Site*. Geological Survey of Alabama Museum Paper 17. Tuscaloosa: University of Alabama.

Delanglez, Jean

1943a   Franquelin, Mapmaker. *Mid-America* 25:59–60.

1943b   The Sources of the Delisle Map of America, 1703. *Mid-America* 25:275–98.

1945   *El Rio del Espiritu Santo*. New York: United States Catholic Historical Society.

DePratter, Chester B.

1983   Late Prehistoric and Early Historic Chiefdoms in the Southeastern United States. Ph.D. dissertation, University of Georgia.

DePratter, Chester B., Charles M. Hudson, and Marvin T. Smith

1983   The Route of Juan Pardo's Explorations in the Interior Southeast, 1566–1568. *Florida Historical Quarterly* 3:125–58.

1985   The De Soto Expedition: From Chiaha to Mabila. In *Alabama and the Borderlands: From Prehistory to Statehood*, ed. R. Reid Badger and Lawrence A. Clayton, 108–27. Tuscaloosa: University of Alabama Press.

DeRosier, Arthur H., Jr.

1970   *The Removal of the Choctaw Indians*. Knoxville: University of Tennessee Press.

De Vorsey, Louis, Jr.

1978   Amerindian Contributions to the Mapping of North America: A Preliminary View. *Imago Mundi* 30:71–78.

1982   The Impact of the La Salle Expedition of 1682 on European Cartography. In *La Salle and His Legacy: Frenchmen and Indians in the Lower Mississippi Valley*, ed. Patricia Galloway, 60–78. Jackson: University Press of Mississippi.

Dobyns, Henry

1983   *Their Number Become Thinned*. Knoxville: University of Tennessee Press.

Dowling, Lee

n.d.   Garcilaso and His Sources. In *Historiography of the Hernando de Soto Expedition*, ed. Patricia Galloway. Lincoln: University of Nebraska Press, forthcoming.

Drechsel, Emanuel J.

1979   Mobilian Jargon: Linguistic, Sociocultural, and Historical Aspects of an American Lingua Franca. Ph.D. dissertation, University of Wisconsin.

1994   Mobilian Jargon in the "Prehistory" of Southeastern North America. In *Perspectives on the Southeast: Linguistics, Archaeology, and Ethnohistory*, ed. Patricia B. Kwachka, 25–43. Athens: University of Georgia Press.

Dunn, William Edward

1917   *Spanish and French Rivalry in the Gulf Region of the United States, 1678–1702: The Beginnings of Texas and Pensacola*. University of Texas Bulletin No. 1705. Austin.

Du Pratz, Antoine Simon Le Page

1758   *Histoire de la Louisiane*, 3 vols. Paris: De Bure, Delaguette, Lambert.

[1774] 1976   *The History of Louisiana*. Baton Rouge: Louisiana State University Press.

du Ru, Paul

1934   *Journal of Paul du Ru*, ed. and trans. Ruth Lapham Butler. Chicago: Caxton Club.

Du Val, Pierre

1670   *Le Monde ou la Géographie Universelle*, 2 vols. Paris: Duval.

Eggan, Fred

1937   Historical Changes in the Choctaw Kinship System. *American Anthropologist* n.s. 39:34–54.

1966   *The American Indian: Perspectives for the Study of Social Change*. Chicago: Aldine.

Elvas, Fidalgo de

[1557] 1932   *Relaçam verdadeira dos trabalhos quem ho governador dom Fernando de Souto y certos fidalgos portugueses passarom no descobrimento da provincia de frolida*, trans. James A. Robertson, 2 vols. Facsimile. Deland: Florida State Historical Society.

Elbl, Martin, and Ivana Elbl

n.d.   The Gentleman of Elvas and His Publisher. In *Historiography of the Hernando de Soto Expedition*, ed. Patricia Galloway. Lincoln: University of Nebraska Press, forthcoming.

Erdrich, Louise

1988   *Tracks*. New York: Henry Holt.

Flannery, Kent V.

1968   The Olmec and the Valley of Oaxaca: A Model for Interregional Interaction in Formative Times. In *Dumbarton Oaks Conference on the Olmec*, ed. E. P. Benson, 79–110. Washington DC: Dumbarton Oaks.

Ford, James A.

1936   *Analysis of Indian Village Site Collections from Louisiana and Mississippi*. Louisiana Department of Conservation Anthropological Study 2. New Orleans: Louisiana Geological Survey.

Ford, Lawrence Carroll

1939   *The Triangular Struggle for Spanish Pensacola 1689–1739*. Washington DC: Catholic University of America.

Ford, Richard I.

1979   Gathering and Gardening: Trends and Consequences of Hopewell Subsistence Strategies. In *Hopewell Archaeology: The Chillicothe Conference*, ed. David S. Brose and N'omi Greber, 234–38. Kent OH: Kent State University Press.

Foret, Michael James

1990   On the Marchlands of Empire: Trade, Diplomacy, and War on the Southeastern Frontier, 1733–1763. Ph.D. dissertation, College of William and Mary.

Frankenstein, Susan, and M. J. Rowlands

1978   The Internal Structure and Regional Context of Early Iron Age Society in Southwestern Germany. *Institute of Archaeology Bulletin* 15:73–112.

Fried, Morton H.

1967   *The Evolution of Political Society*. New York: Random House.

Friedman, Jonathan

1975   Tribes, States, and Transformations. In *Marxist Analyses and Social Anthropology*, ed. Maurice Bloch, 161–202. New York: John Wiley.

Fuller, Richard S.

1985   The Bear Point Phase of the Pensacola Variant: The Protohistoric Period in Southwest Alabama. *Florida Anthropologist* 38 (1–2, pt.2) : 150–55.

Fuller, Richard S., Diane E. Silvia, and Noel R. Stowe

1984   *The Forks Project: An Investigation of the Late Prehistoric–Early Historic Transition in the Alabama-Tombigbee Confluence Basin. Phase I: Preliminary Summary*. Mobile: University of South Alabama Archaeological Research Lab.

Fuller, Richard S., and Noel R. Stowe

1982   A Proposed Typology for Late Shell Tempered Ceramics in the Mobile Bay/Mobile-Tensaw Delta Region. In *Archaeology in Southwest Alabama*, ed. Cailup Curren, 45–94. Camden AL: Alabama-Tombigbee Regional Commission.

Bibliography

Galloway, Patricia

n.d.a Ceramics from the Richard Site. Notes on file, Mississippi Department of Archives and History.

n.d.b The Incestuous Soto Narratives. In *Historiography of the Hernando de Soto Expedition*, ed. Patricia Galloway. Lincoln: University of Nebraska Press, forthcoming.

n.d.c Lyon's Bluff: The Chambers Excavations, 1934–1935. Report on file, Mississippi Department of Archives and History.

1981 Multidimensional Scaling for Mapping Ethnohistorical Narrative: Choctaw Villages in the Eighteenth Century. In *Coloquio Manejo de datos y métodos matemáticos de arqueología*, ed. George Cowgill, Robert Whallon, and Barbara Ottaway, 159–75. Mexico City: Unión Internacional de Ciencias Prehistóricas y Protohistóricas, X Congreso, Comisión IV.

1982a Choctaw Factionalism and Civil War, 1746–1750. *Journal of Mississippi History* 44:289–328.

1982b Henri de Tonti du Village des Chactas: The Beginning of the French Alliance. In *La Salle and His Legacy: Frenchmen and Indians in the Lower Mississippi Valley*, ed. Patricia Galloway, 146–75. Jackson: University Press of Mississippi.

1982c Historic Tribes in the Yazoo Basin during the French Colonial Period. Appendix to *Cultural Resources along the Yazoo River from Greenwood to Vicksburg, Mississippi*, ed. Samuel O. Brookes. Report submitted to U.S. Army Corps of Engineers, Vicksburg District.

1982d Sources for the La Salle Expedition of 1682. In *La Salle and His Legacy: Frenchmen and Indians in the Lower Mississippi Valley*, ed. Patricia Galloway, 11–40. Jackson: University Press of Mississippi.

1984 Technical Origins for Chickachae Combed Ceramics: An Ethnohistorical Hypothesis. *Mississippi Archaeology* 19 (2) : 58–66.

1987 Talking with Indians: Interpreters and Diplomacy in French Louisiana. In *Race and Family in the Colonial South*, ed. Winthrop Jordan and Sheila L. Skemp, 109–29. Jackson: University Press of Mississippi.

1989a The Chief Who Is Your Father: Choctaw and French Views of the Diplomatic Relation. In *Powhatan's Mantle: Indians in the Colonial Southeast*, ed. Peter H. Wood, Gregory A. Waselkov, and M. Thomas Hatley, 254–78. Lincoln: University of Nebraska Press.

1989b The Currency of Language: The Mobilian *Lingua Franca* in Colonial Louisiana. Paper presented at the 15th meeting of the French Colonial Historical Society, Martinique-Guadeloupe.

1991a The Archaeology of Ethnohistorical Narrative. In *Columbian Consequences*, ed. David H. Thomas, Vol. 3: *The Spanish Borderlands in Pan-American Perspective*, 453–69. Washington DC: Smithsonian Institution Press.

1991b Couture, Tonti, and the English-Quapaw Connection: A Revision. In *Arkansas before the Americans*, ed. Hester Davis, 74–94. Arkansas Archeological Survey Research Series 40. Fayetteville.

1994 "So Many Little Republics": British Negotiations with the Choctaw Confederacy, 1765. *Ethnohistory* 41:513–37.

————, ed.

n.d.d   *Historiography of the Hernando de Soto Expedition*. Lincoln: University of Nebraska Press, forthcoming.

1989c   *Southeastern Ceremonial Complex, Artifacts and Analysis: The Cottonlandia Conference*. Lincoln: University of Nebraska Press.

Galloway, Patricia, and Clara Sue Kidwell

1990   Choctaw Land Claims in Mississippi. Final performance report, National Endowment for the Humanities Grant No. RO-21631–88.

Gannon, Michael V.

1965   *The Cross in the Sand: The Early Catholic Church in Florida, 1513–1870*. Gainesville: University Presses of Florida.

Garcilaso de la Vega

[1605] 1982   *La Florida del Ynca*. Introduction by Sylvia-Lyn Hilton. Facsimile. Madrid: Fundación Universitaria Española.

1951   *The Florida of the Inca*, ed. and trans. John G. Varner and Jeannette J. Varner. Austin: University of Texas Press.

Gatschet, Albert S.

[1884] 1969   *A Migration Legend of the Creek Indians*. Vol. 1. Philadelphia: D. G. Brinton. Reprint, New York: Kraus.

[1888] 1969   *A Migration Legend of the Creek Indians*. Vol. 2. St. Louis: Albert Gatschet. Reprint, New York: Kraus.

Gearing, Fred

1962   *Priests and Warriors: Social Structures for Cherokee Politics in the Eighteenth Century*. American Anthropological Association Memoir 93, Menasha WI. *American Anthropologist* 64 (5), pt.2.

Geiger, Maynard

1937   *The Franciscan Conquest of Florida (1573–1618)*. Washington DC: Catholic University of America.

Gibson, Jon L.

1974   Aboriginal Warfare in the Protohistoric Southeast: An Alternative Perspective. *American Antiquity* 39:130–33.

Gifford, James C.

1960   The Type-Variety Method of Ceramic Classification as an Indicator of Cultural Phenomena. *American Antiquity* 25:341–47.

Giraud, Marcel

1974   *A History of French Louisiana*. Vol. 1, trans. Joseph C. Lambert. Baton Rouge: Louisiana State University Press.

Goody, Jack

1962   *Death, Property and the Ancestors: A Study in the Mortuary Customs of the LoDagaa of West Africa*. Stanford: Stanford University Press.

Greengo, Robert E.

1964   *Issaquena: An Archaeological Phase in the Yazoo Basin of the Lower Mississippi Valley*. Society for American Archaeology Memoir 18. Salt Lake City.

Haag, William G.

1953   Choctaw Archaeology. *Southeastern Archaeological Conference Newsletter* 3 (3): 25–28.

Haas, Mary R.
1950 *Tunica Texts*. University of California Publications in Linguistics 6 (1) : 1–174. Berkeley: University of California Press.
1956 Natchez and the Muskogean languages. *Language* 32 (1) : 61–72.
1978 *Language, Culture, and History: Essays by Mary R. Haas*, ed. Anwar S. Dil. Stanford: Stanford University Press.

Halbert, H. S.
1899a Danville's Map of East Mississippi. *Publications of the Mississippi Historical Society* 3:367–71.
1899b Nanih Waiya, the Sacred Mound of the Choctaws. *Publications of the Mississippi Historical Society* 2:223–34.
1902 Bernard Romans' Map of 1772. *Publications of the Mississippi Historical Society* 6:415–39.

Hally, David J., Marvin T. Smith, and James B. Langford Jr.
1990 The Archaeological Reality of de Soto's Coosa. In *Columbian Consequences*, ed. David H. Thomas, Vol. 2: *Archaeological and Historical Perspectives on the Spanish Borderlands East*, 139–52. Washington DC: Smithsonian Institution Press.

Hamilton, Peter J.
1910 *Colonial Mobile*. Boston: Houghton Mifflin.

Hann, John H.
1988 *Apalachee: The Land between the Rivers*. Gainesville: University Presses of Florida.

Haring, Clarence H.
1963 *The Spanish Empire in America*. First printing, 1947. New York: Harcourt.

Harris, Marvin
1978 *Cannibals and Kings: The Origins of Cultures*. London: Collins.

Hawkins, Benjamin
[1798–99] Taskana Mico's Creek Migration Myth. In *A Sketch of the Creek Country*, ed.
1848 William B. Hodgson, 81–83. Georgia Historical Society Collections 3, pt. 1. Savannah.

Helms, Mary W.
1979 *Ancient Panama: Chiefs in Search of Power*. Austin: University of Texas Press.

Henige, David
n.d. "So unbelievable it had to be true": Inca Garcilaso in Two Worlds. In *Historiography of the Hernando de Soto Expedition*, ed. Patricia Galloway. Lincoln: University of Nebraska Press, forthcoming.
1986a The Context, Content, and Credibility of *La Florida del Ynca*. *The Americas* 43 (1): 1–23.
1986b If Pigs Could Fly: Timucuan Population and Native American Historical Demography. *Journal of Interdisciplinary History* 16 (4) : 701–20.
1986c Primary Source by Primary Source? On the Role of Epidemics in New World Depopulation. *Ethnohistory* 33:293–312.

Henri, Florette
1986 *The Southern Indians and Benjamin Hawkins, 1796–1816*. Norman: University of Oklahoma Press.

Hertz, Robert.

1960   *Death and the Right Hand*, trans. Rodney Needham and Claudia Needham. Glencoe IL: Free Press.

Historic New Orleans Collection

1986   Acquisitions, Curatorial: Report on Acquisition of First State of Delisle 1700. *The Historic New Orleans Collection Newsletter* 4 (2) : 12.

Hodder, Ian

1986   *Reading the Past: Current Approaches to Interpretation in Archaeology.* Cambridge: Cambridge University Press.

Hoffman, Paul E.

1990   *A New Andalucia and a Way to the Orient: The American Southeast during the Sixteenth Century.* Baton Rouge: Louisiana State University Press.

Holmes, Nicholas H., Jr.

1963   The Site on Bottle Creek. *Journal of Alabama Archaeology* 9 (1) : 16–27.

Hudson, Charles M.

1976   *The Southeastern Indians.* Knoxville: University of Tennessee Press.

1987   *The Uses of Evidence in Reconstructing the Route of the Hernando de Soto Expedition.* Alabama De Soto Commission Working Paper 1. Tuscaloosa.

1988   A Spanish-Coosa Alliance in Sixteenth-Century North Georgia. *Georgia Historical Quarterly* 72:599–626.

1990   *The Juan Pardo Expeditions: Exploration of the Carolinas and Tennessee, 1566–1568.* Washington DC: Smithsonian Institution Press.

Hudson, Charles M., Marvin T. Smith, and Chester B. DePratter

1984   The Hernando DeSoto Expedition: From Apalachee to Chiaha. *Southeastern Archaeology* 3 (1) : 65–77.

1990   The Hernando de Soto Expedition: From Mabila to the Mississippi River. In *Towns and Temples along the Mississippi*, ed. David H. Dye and Cheryl Anne Cox, 181–207. Tuscaloosa: University of Alabama Press.

Hudson, Charles M., Marvin T. Smith, Chester B. DePratter, and Emilia Kelley

1989   The Tristán de Luna expedition, 1559–1561. *Southeastern Archaeology* 8 (1) : 31–45.

Hudson, Charles M., Marvin T. Smith, David J. Hally, Richard Polhemus, and Chester B. DePratter

1985   Coosa: A Chiefdom in the Sixteenth-Century Southeastern United States. *American Antiquity* 50:723–37.

Huntington, Richard, and Peter Metcalf, eds.

1979   *Celebrations of Death: The Anthropology of Mortuary Ritual.* Cambridge: Cambridge University Press.

Iberville, Pierre Le Moyne d'

1981   *Iberville's Gulf Journals*, trans. Richebourg Gaillard McWilliams. Tuscaloosa: University of Alabama Press.

Isnard, A.

1915   Joseph-Nicolas Delisle, sa biographie et sa collection de cartes géographiques à la Bibliothèque Nationale. *Comité des Travaux Historiques et Scientifiques, Bulletin du Section de géographie* 30:34–164.

Bibliography

Jaenen, Cornelius J.
1976 *Friend and Foe: Aspects of French-Amerindian Cultural Contact in the Sixteenth and Seventeenth Centuries*. New York: Columbia University Press.

Jenkins, Ned J.
1976 Terminal Woodland-Mississippian Interaction in Northern Alabama: The West Jefferson Phase. Paper presented at the 33d annual meeting of the Southeastern Archaeological Conference, Tuscaloosa AL.

1981 *Archaeological Investigations in the Gainesville Lake Area of the Tennessee-Tombigbee Waterway*, Vol. 2: *Gainesville Lake Area Ceramic Description and Chronology*. University of Alabama Office of Archaeological Research Report of Investigations 12. Moundville.

Jenkins, Ned J., and Richard Krause
1986 *The Tombigbee Watershed in Southeastern Prehistory*. Tuscaloosa: University of Alabama Press.

Jenkins, Ned J., and Teresa Paglione
1982 Lower Alabama River Ceramic Chronology – A Tentative Assessment. In *Archaeology in Southwest Alabama*, ed. Cailup Curren, 5–18. Camden AL: Alabama-Tombigbee Regional Commission.

Jennings, Jesse D.
1941 Chickasaw and Earlier Indian Cultures of Northeast Mississippi. *Journal of Mississippi History* 3:155–226.

Jeter, Marvin
1977 Late Woodland Chronology and Change in Central Alabama. *Journal of Alabama Archaeology* 23 (2): 112–36.

1986 Tunicians West of the Mississippi: A Summary of Early Historic Archaeological Evidence. In *The Protohistoric Period in the Mid-South: 1500–1700*, ed. David H. Dye and Ronald C. Brister, 38–63. Mississippi Department of Archives and History Archaeological Report 18. Jackson.

1989 Protohistoric and Historic Native Americans. In *Archeology and Bioarcheology of the Lower Mississippi Valley and Trans-Mississippi South in Arkansas and Louisiana*, by Marvin Jeter, Jerome C. Rose, G. Ishmael Williams, Jr., and Anna M. Harmon, 221–48. Arkansas Archeological Survey Research Series 37. Fayetteville.

Jeter, Marvin, Jerome C. Rose, G. Ishmael Williams Jr., and Anna M. Harmon
1989 *Archeology and Bioarcheology of the Lower Mississippi Valley and Trans-Mississippi South in Arkansas and Louisiana*. Arkansas Archeological Survey Research Series 37. Fayetteville.

Johnson, Jay K.
n.d. Soto and the Chickasaws in Mississippi. In *Historiography of the Hernando de Soto Expedition*, ed. Patricia Galloway. Lincoln: University of Nebraska Press, forthcoming.

1990 Protohistoric Chickasaw Settlement Patterns and the De Soto Route in Northeast Mississippi. Interim Performance Report for National Endowment for the Humanities Grant No. RO-21879-89. Unpublished manuscript in author's possession.

Johnson, Jay K., Patricia Galloway, and Walter Belokon

1989   Historic Chickasaw Settlement Patterns in Lee County, Mississippi: A First Approximation. *Mississippi Archaeology* 24 (2) : 45–52.

Johnson, Jay K., and Geoffrey R. Lehmann

1990   Sociopolitical Devolution in Northeast Mississippi and the Timing of the De Soto Entrada. Paper presented at the 59th annual meeting of the American Association of Physical Anthropologists, Miami FL.

Johnson, Jay K., Geoffrey R. Lehmann, James R. Atkinson, Susan L. Scott, and Andrea Shea

1991   Protohistoric Chickasaw Settlement Patterns and the De Soto Route in Northeast Mississippi. Final report, National Endowment for the Humanities Grant No. RO-21879–89 and National Geographic Grant No. 4006–89.

Johnson, Jay K., and John T. Sparks

1986   Protohistoric Settlement Patterns in Northeastern Mississippi. In *The Protohistoric Period in the Mid-South: 1500–1700*, ed. David H. Dye and Ronald C. Brister, 64–81. Mississippi Department of Archives and History Archaeological Report 18. Jackson.

Joutel, Henri

[1684–88]   *Joutel's Journal of La Salle's Last Voyage, 1684–7*, ed. Henry R. Stiles. Albany:
1906   Joseph McDonough.

Kernion, George, trans.

1925   Documents Concerning the History of the Indians of the Eastern Region of Louisiana. *Louisiana Historical Quarterly* 8:38–39.

Ketcham, Herbert E.

1954   Three Sixteenth Century Spanish Chronicles Relating to Georgia. *Georgia Historical Quarterly* 38:66–82.

Kidder, Tristram R.

1988   The Koroa Indians of the Lower Mississippi Valley. *Mississippi Archaeology* 23 (2) : 1–42.

Kimball, Geoffrey

1994   Making the Connection: Is It Possible to Link the Koasati to an Archaeological Culture? In *Perspectives on the Southeast: Linguistics, Archaeology, and Ethnohistory*, ed. Patricia B. Kwachka, 71–80. Athens: University of Georgia Press.

Knight, Vernon J., Jr.

1984   Late Prehistoric Adaptation in the Mobile Bay Region. In *Perspectives on Gulf Coast Prehistory*, ed. Dave D. Davis, 198–215. Gainesville: University of Florida Press.

1986   The Institutional Organization of Mississippian Religion. *American Antiquity* 51:675–87.

1988   *A Summary of Alabama's De Soto Mapping Project and Project Bibliography*. Alabama De Soto Commission Working Paper 9. Tuscaloosa: Alabama De Soto Commission.

1989   Symbolism of Mississippian Mounds. In *Powhatan's Mantle: Indians in the Colonial Southeast*, ed. Peter H. Wood, Gregory A. Waselkov, and M. Thomas Hatley, 279–91. Lincoln: University of Nebraska Press.

Krech, Shepard, III, ed.

1981   *Indians, Animals, and the Fur Trade: A Critique of Keepers of the Game*. Athens: University of Georgia Press.

Kuipers, Benjamin

1978   Modeling Spatial Knowledge. *Cognitive Science* 2:129–53.

la Harpe, Jean-Baptiste Benard de

[1831] 1971   *The Historical Journal of the French in Louisiana*, ed. Glenn R. Conrad. Lafayette LA: Center for Louisiana Studies.

Lankford, George E.

1977   A New Look at De Soto's Route through Alabama. *Journal of Alabama Archaeology* 23 (1): 11–36.

1987   *Native American Legends: Southeastern Legends: Tales from the Natchez, Caddo, Biloxi, Chickasaw, and Other Nations*. Little Rock: August House.

1993   Legends of the Adelantado. In *The Expedition of Hernando de Soto West of the Mississippi, 1541–1543*, ed. Gloria A. Young and Michael P. Hoffman, 173–91. Fayetteville: University of Arkansas Press.

Lanman, Charles

1856   *Adventures in the Wilds of the United States and British American Provinces (Collected 1846–1856)*, Vol. 2. Philadelphia.

Larson, Lewis H.

1972   Functional Considerations of Warfare in the Southeast during the Mississippi Period. *American Antiquity* 37:383–92.

1980   *Aboriginal Subsistence Technology on the Southeastern Coastal Plain during the Late Prehistoric Period*. Gainesville: University Presses of Florida.

la Salle, Nicolas de

[1682?] 1898   *Relation of the Discovery of the Mississippi River*, ed. Melville B. Anderson. Chicago: Caxton Club.

Las Casas, Bartolomé de

1951   *Historia de las Indias*, 3 vols. Mexico City: Fondo de Cultura Económica.

Lauro, James

1986   The Deer Island Site and Coastal Archaeology. *Mississippi Archaeology* 21 (2): 50–61.

Leman, A. D., Barbara Straw, Robert D. Glock, William L. Mengeling, R. H. C. Penny, and Erwin Scholl, eds.

1986   *Diseases of Swine*. 6th ed. Ames: Iowa State University Press.

Leonard, Irving A.

1936   The Spanish Re-Exploration of the Gulf Coast in 1686. *Mississippi Valley Historical Review* 22:547–57.

1974   Pensacola's First Spanish Period (1698–1763): Inception, Founding and Troubled Existence. In *Colonial Pensacola*, ed. James R. McGovern, 7–48. Pensacola: Pensacola News-Journal.

Leone, Mark P.

1982   Some Opinions about Recovering Mind. *American Antiquity* 47:742–60.

Le Roy Ladurie, Emmanuel

1982   Amenorrhoea in Time of Famine (Seventeenth to Twentieth Century). In *The*

   Territory of the Historian, trans. Ben Reynolds and Siân Reynolds, 255–71. Brighton, Sussex, England: Harvester Press.

Levasseur, Charles

1981 A Voyage to the Mobile and Tomeh in 1700, with Notes on the Interior of Alabama, ed. Vernon J. Knight and Sheree L. Adams. *Journal of Alabama Archaeology* 27 (1): 32–56.

Levine, Lawrence W.

1989 The Unpredictable Past: Reflections on Recent American Historiography. *American Historical Review* 94 (3): 671–79.

Lewis, G. Malcolm

1986 Indicators of Unacknowledged Assimilations from Amerindian *Maps* on Euro-American Maps of North America: Some General Principles Arising from a Study of La Verendreye's Composite Map, 1728–29. *Imago Mundi* 38:9–34.

Lincecum, Gideon

1861 Traditional History of the Chahta Nation, Translated from the Chahta. Manuscript at the University of Texas, Austin, Center for American History.

1904 Autobiography of Gideon Lincecum. *Publications of the Mississippi Historical Society* 8:443–519.

Lockhart, James M.

1972 *The Men of Cajamarca*. Austin: University of Texas Press.

Lockhart, James M., and Stuart B. Schwartz

1983 *Early Latin America: A History of Colonial Spanish America and Brazil*. Cambridge: Cambridge University Press.

López de Gomara, Francisco

[1552] 1932 *Historia general de las Indias*. Madrid: Espasa-Calpe.

Lorenz, Karl G.

1990 Archaeological Survey and Testing within a Five Kilometer Radius of the Old Hoover Platform Mound in the Big Black River Valley. *Mississippi Archaeology* 25 (1): 1–42.

Lyon, Eugene

1974 *The Enterprise of Florida: Pedro Menéndez de Avilés and the Spanish Conquest of 1565–1568*. Gainesville: University Presses of Florida.

1993 The Cañete Fragment: Another Narrative of Hernando de Soto. In *The De Soto Chronicles: The Expedition of Hernando de Soto to North America in 1539–1543*, ed. Lawrence A. Clayton, Vernon James Knight Jr., and Edward C. Moore, 1:307–10. Tuscaloosa: University of Alabama Press.

MacLeod, William C.

1928 Priests, Temples, and the Practice of Mummification in Southeastern North America. *Proceedings of the International Congress of Americanists* 2:207–30.

Mann, Cyril B.

1988 An Archaeological Classification of Ceramics from the Pearl Mounds (22-Lw-510), Lawrence County, Mississippi. Master's thesis, University of Southern Mississippi.

Margry, Pierre, ed.

1879–88 *Découvertes et établissements des français dans l'ouest et dans le sud de l'amérique septentrionale*, 6 vols. Paris: Maisonneuve.

Marshall, Richard A.

1977   Lyon's Bluff Site (22 OK 1) Radiocarbon Dated. *Journal of Alabama Archaeology* 23 (1) : 53–57.

1982   *A Report on Archaeological Test Excavations at Goode Lake, Jackson County, Mississippi*. Mississippi Department of Archives and History Archaeological Report 10. Jackson.

1986   The Protohistoric Component at the Lyon's Bluff Site Complex, Oktibbeha County, Mississippi. In *The Protohistoric Period in the Mid-South: 1500–1700*, ed. David H. Dye and Ronald C. Brister, 82–88. Mississippi Department of Archives and History Archaeological Report 18. Jackson.

1988   *Preliminary Archaeological Testing near Mound A, Buford (22 TL 501) Site, Tallahatchie County, Mississippi*. Cobb Institute of Archaeology Report of Investigations 5. Starkville MS.

Martin, Calvin

1978   *Keepers of the Game*. Berkeley: University of California Press.

——, ed.

1987   *The American Indian and the Problem of History*. Oxford: Oxford University Press.

Martin, Jack

1992   Modelling Linguistic Prehistory in the Southeastern United States. Paper presented at the 26th meeting of the Southern Anthropological Society, St. Augustine FL.

McCrady, Edward

1901   *The History of South Carolina under the Proprietary Government, 1670–1719*. New York: Macmillan.

McKee, Jesse O., and Jon A. Schlenker

1980   *The Choctaws*. Jackson: University Press of Mississippi.

McNeill, William H.

1977   *Plagues and Peoples*. New York: Doubleday Anchor.

Meyer, William E.

1928   Indian Trails of the Southeast. *Forty-Second Annual Report of the Bureau of American Ethnology*, 727–857.

Middleton, John

1982   Lugbara Death. In *Death and the Regeneration of Life*, ed. Maurice Bloch and Jonathan Parry, 134–54. Cambridge: Cambridge University Press.

Milanich, Jerald T., and Charles H. Fairbanks

1980   *Florida Archaeology*. New York: Academic Press.

Milanich, Jerald T., and Charles M. Hudson

1993   *Hernando de Soto and the Indians of Florida*. Gainesville: University Press of Florida.

Millares Carlo, Agustín

1986   *Cuatro estudios biobibliográficos mexicanos*. Mexico City: Fondo de Cultura Económica.

Milner, George R.

1980   Epidemic Disease in the Postcontact Southeast: A Reappraisal. *Mid-Continental Journal of Archaeology* 5 (1) : 39–56.

Milner, George R., Thomas E. Emerson, Mark W. Mehrer, Joyce A. Williams, and Duane Esarey

1984   Mississippian and Oneota Periods. In *American Bottom Archaeology*, ed. Charles J. Bareis and James W. Porter, 158–86. Urbana: University of Illinois Press.

Minet

1684–85   Voiage fait du Canada par dedans les terres allant vers le sud dans l'anne 1682. MS MG 18, B 19, Archives françaises, Public Archives Canada, Ottawa.

Mooney, Timothy

1991   Many Choctaw Standing: An Inquiry into Culture Compromise and Culture Survival Reflected in Seven Choctaw Sites in East-Central Mississippi. Manuscript.

1994   Many Choctaw Standing: An Archaeological Study of Culture Change in the Early Historic Period. Master's thesis, University of North Carolina at Chapel Hill.

Morgan, David

n.d.   The Mississippi De Soto Mapping Project. Mississippi Department of Archives and History Archaeological Report, forthcoming.

Morris, Ian

1987   *Burial and Ancient Society: The Rise of the Greek City-State*. Cambridge: Cambridge University Press.

Morse, Dan F., and Phyllis A. Morse

1983   *Archaeology of the Central Mississippi Valley*. New York: Academic Press.

Munro, Pamela

1987   Introduction: Muskogean Studies at UCLA. In *Muskogean Linguistics*, ed. Pamela Munro, 1–6. UCLA Occasional Papers in Linguistics 6. Los Angeles: UCLA Department of Linguistics.

Nairne, Thomas

1988   *Nairne's Muskogean Journals*, ed. Alexander Moore. Jackson: University Press of Mississippi.

National Park Service

1990   *De Soto Trail: National Historic Trail Study*. Atlanta: National Park Service, Southeast Regional Office.

Neitzel, Robert Stuart

1965   *Archaeology of the Fatherland Site: The Grand Village of the Natchez*. American Museum of Natural History Anthropological Papers 51 (1). New York.

1985   *The Grand Village of the Natchez Revisited*. Mississippi Department of Archives and History Archaeological Report 12. Jackson.

Neuman, Robert

1984   *An Introduction to Louisiana Archaeology*. Baton Rouge: Louisiana State University Press.

Núñez, Alvar [Cabeza de Vaca]

1542   *Los Naufragios*. Valladolid.

1972   *The Narrative of Alvar Núñez Cabeza de Vaca*, trans. Fanny Bandelier. Barre MA: Imprint Society.

O'Hear, John W., Clark Larsen, Margaret M. Scarry, John Phillips, and Erica Simons

1981   *Archaeological Salvage Excavations at the Tibbee Creek Site (22Lo600), Lowndes*

County, Mississippi. Mississippi State: Mississippi State University Department of Anthropology.

Orton, Clive
1980   *Mathematics in Archaeology.* London: Collins.

O'Shea, John
1981   Social Configurations and the Archaeological Study of Mortuary Practices: A Case Study. In *The Archaeology of Death,* ed. Robert Chapman, Ian Kinnes, and Klavs Randsborg, 39–52. Cambridge: Cambridge University Press.

Oviedo y Valdés, Gonzalo Fernández
[1526] 1959   *Natural History of the West Indies,* trans. and ed. Sterling A. Stoudemire. University of North Carolina Studies in the Romance Languages and Literatures 32. Chapel Hill: UNC Department of Romance Languages.

[1851] 1944   *Historia general y natural de las Indias, Islas y Tierra-Firme del Mar Océano,* ed. José Amador de los Rios, introduction by J. Natalicio González. Vol. 2. Asunción del Paraguay: Editorial Guaranía.

[1851] 1959   *Historia general y natural de las indias,* ed. Juan Pérez de Tudela Bueso. Vol. 2. Madrid: Real Academia Española.

1924   The Expedition of Panfilo de Narváez, Chapter 2, ed. Harbert Davenport. *Southwestern Historical Quarterly* 27:217–41.

Padgett, Thomas J., and David M. Heisler
1979   *Predictive Model of Archaeological Site Location in the Central Leaf River Basin, Mississippi.* Hattiesburg: University of Southern Mississippi Department of Sociology and Anthropology.

Parker, James W.
1982   Archaeological Test Excavations at 1Su7: The Fort Tombecbé Site. *Journal of Alabama Archaeology* 28 (1).

Parker-Pearson, Michael
1984   Economic and Ideological Change: Cyclical Growth in the Pre-state Societies of Jutland. In *Ideology, Power, and Prehistory,* ed. Daniel Miller and Christopher Tilley, 69–92. Cambridge: Cambridge University Press.

Pearson, Fred Lamar, Jr.
1968   Spanish-Indian Relations in Florida: A Study of Two Visitas, 1657–1678. Ph.D. dissertation, University of Alabama.

Peebles, Christopher S.
1971   Moundville and Surrounding Sites: Some Structural Considerations of Mortuary Practices II. In *Approaches to the Social Dimensions of Mortuary Practices,* ed. James A. Brown, 68–91. Society for American Archaeology Memoir 25. Washington DC.

1974   Moundville: The Organization of a Prehistoric Community and Culture. Ph.D. dissertation, University of California at Santa Barbara.

1978   Determinants of Settlement Size and Location in the Moundville Phase. In *Mississippian Settlement Patterns,* ed. Bruce D. Smith, 369–416. New York: Academic Press.

1979a   *Excavations at Moundville, 1905–1951.* Ann Arbor: University of Michigan Press.

1979b   Moundville: Late Prehistoric Sociopolitical Organization in the Southeastern

United States. Paper presented at the annual meeting of the American Ethnological Society, Vancouver, B.C., Canada.

1983a   Summary and Conclusions: Continuity and Change in a Small Mississippi Community. In *Prehistoric Agricultural Communities in West Central Alabama*, Vol. 1: *Excavations in the Lubbub Creek Archaeological Locality*, ed. Christopher S. Peebles, 394–407. Mobile: U.S. Army Corps of Engineers, Mobile District.

1986   Paradise Lost, Strayed, and Stolen: Prehistoric Social Devolution in the Southeast. In *The Burden of Being Civilized: An Anthropological Perspective on the Discontents of Civilization*, ed. Miles Richardson and Malcolm C. Webb, 24–40. Athens: University of Georgia Press.

1987   The Rise and Fall of the Mississippian in Western Alabama: The Moundville and Summerville Phases, A.D. 1000 to 1600. *Mississippi Archaeology* 22 (1) : 1–31.

———, ed.

1983b   *Prehistoric Agricultural Communities in West Central Alabama*, 3 vols. Mobile: U.S. Army Corps of Engineers, Mobile District.

Peebles, Christopher S., and Susan M. Kus

1977   Some Archaeological Correlates of Ranked Societies. *American Antiquity* 42: 421–48.

Pelletier, Monique

1982   Les Globes de Louis XIV: Les sources françaises de l'oeuvre de Coronelli. *Imago Mundi* 34:72–89.

Penicaut, André

[1723] 1953   *Fleur de Lys and Calumet*, ed. and trans. Richebourg Gaillard McWilliams. Baton Rouge: Louisiana State University Press.

Penman, John T.

1977   *Archaeological Survey in Mississippi, 1974–1975*. Mississippi Department of Archives and History Archaeological Report 2. Jackson.

1978   Historic Choctaw Towns of the Southern Division. *Journal of Mississippi History* 40:132–41.

1983   Archaeology and Choctaw Removal. In *Southeastern Natives and Their Pasts: Papers Honoring Dr. Robert E. Bell*, ed. Don G. Wyckoff and Jack L. Hofman, 283–99. Norman: Oklahoma Archeological Survey.

Pennington, Edgar L.

1931   Some Ancient Georgia Indian Lore. *Georgia Historical Quarterly* 15:192–98.

Peterson, John, Jr.

1972   Review of Debo 1961, DeRosier 1970, Gibson 1971. *Ethnohistory* 19(2): 175–78.

1985   H. S. Halbert's Contribution to Choctaw History and Ethnography. Paper presented at the annual meeting of the American Society for Ethnohistory, Chicago.

Phillips, Philip

1970   *Archaeological Survey in the Lower Yazoo Basin, Mississippi, 1949–1955*, 2 vols. Papers of the Peabody Museum of Archaeology and Ethnology 60. Cambridge MA.

Phillips, Philip, James A. Ford, and James B. Griffin

1951   *Archaeological Survey in the Lower Mississippi Alluvial Valley, 1940–1947.* Papers of the Peabody Museum of Archaeology and Ethnology 25. Cambridge MA.

Powell, Mary Lucas

1988   *Status and Health in Prehistory: A Case Study of the Moundville Chiefdom.* Washington DC: Smithsonian Institution Press.

Priestley, Herbert Ingram

1936   *Tristán de Luna, Conquistador of the Old South: A Study of Spanish Imperial Strategy.* Glendale CA: Arthur H. Clark.

———, ed. and trans.

1928   *The Luna Papers*, 2 vols. Deland: Florida State Historical Society.

Quimby, George I.

1942   The Natchezan Culture Type. *American Antiquity* 7:255–75.

Ramenofsky, Ann F.

1982   The Archaeology of Population Collapse: Native American Response to the Introduction of Infectious Disease. Ph.D. dissertation, University of Washington.

1985   The Introduction of European Disease and Aboriginal Population Collapse. *Mississippi Archaeology* 20 (1) : 2–19.

1987   *Vectors of Death: The Archaeology of European Contact.* Albuquerque: University of New Mexico Press.

Ramenofsky, Ann F., and Patricia Galloway

n.d.   The Soto Expedition as a Disease Vector. In *Historiography of the Hernando de Soto Expedition*, ed. Patricia Galloway. Lincoln: University of Nebraska Press, forthcoming.

Redfield, Robert

1956   *Peasant Society and Culture: An Anthropological Approach to Civilization.* Chicago: University of Chicago Press.

Renfrew, Colin

1982   *Towards an Archaeology of Mind.* Cambridge: Cambridge University Press.

Renfrew, Colin, and John F. Cherry, eds.

1986   *Peer Polity Interaction and Socio-political Change.* Cambridge: Cambridge University Press.

Ricard, Robert

1966   *The Spiritual Conquest of Mexico*, trans. Lesley Byrd Simpson. Berkeley: University of California Press.

Robinson, Arthur H., and Barbara B. Petchenik

1976   *The Nature of Maps: Essays toward Understanding Maps and Mapping.* Chicago: University of Chicago Press.

Romans, Bernard

[1772] 1961   *A Concise Natural History of East and West Florida.* New Orleans: Pelican.

Rose, Jerome C., Murray K. Marks, and Larry L. Tieszen

1991   Bioarchaeology and Subsistence in the Central and Lower Portions of the Mississippi Valley. In *What Mean These Bones? Studies in Southeastern Bioarchaeology*, ed. Mary Lucas Powell, Patricia S. Bridges, and Ann Marie Wagner Mires, 7–21. Tuscaloosa: University of Alabama Press.

Bibliography

Ross-Stallings, Nancy
　1989　　　　Treponemal Syndrome at the Austin Site (22-Tu-549): A Preliminary Report. *Mississippi Archaeology* 24(2): 1–16.

Rowland, Dunbar, and Albert G. Sanders, ed. and trans.
　1927–32　　*Mississippi Provincial Archives: French Dominion*, Vols. 1–3. Jackson: Mississippi Department of Archives and History.

Rowland, Dunbar, Albert G. Sanders, and Patricia Galloway, ed. and trans.
　1984　　　　*Mississippi Provincial Archives: French Dominion*, Vols. 4 and 5. Baton Rouge: Louisiana State University Press.

Rowlands, M. J.
　1979　　　　Local and Long Distance Trade and Incipient State Formation on the Bamenda Plateau in the Late Nineteenth Century. *Paidewma* 25:1–19.

Sahlins, Marshall D.
　1968　　　　*Tribesmen.* Englewood Cliffs NJ: Prentice-Hall.
　1972　　　　*Stone Age Economics.* Chicago: Aldine.

Salley, Alexander S., Jr., ed.
　1911　　　　*Narratives of Early Carolina, 1650–1708.* New York: Charles Scribner's Sons.

Sanson d'Abbeville, Nicolas
　1693　　　　*Introduction à la géographie.* Paris: Veuve Mabre Cramoysi.

Santander, Pedro de
　1557　　　　Santander to Philip II, 15 July 1557. In *Colección de documentos inéditos para la historia de España*, ed. Fernández de Navarrete et al., 36:340–65. Madrid: Viuda de Calera.

Saucier, Roger T.
　1974　　　　*Quaternary Geology of the Lower Mississippi Valley.* Arkansas Archeological Survey Publications on Archeology Research Series 6. Fayetteville.

Sauer, Carl Ortwin
　1971　　　　*Sixteenth Century North America.* Berkeley: University of California Press.

Sauvole
　[1699–1701]　*The Journal of Sauvole*, ed. Prieur Jay Higginbotham. Mobile: Colonial Books.
　1969

Scarry, C. Margaret
　1980a　　　Plant Procurement Strategies in the West Jefferson and Moundville I Phases. In The Moundville Archaeological Project, ed. Margaret Scarry, 70–81.
　1986　　　　Change in Plant Procurement and Production during the Emergence of the Moundville Chiefdom. Ph.D. dissertation, University of Michigan.
　——, ed.
　1980b　　　The Moundville Archaeological Project. Symposium summary draft from the 37th annual meeting of the Southeastern Archaeological Conference, New Orleans.

Scarry, John F.
　1990　　　　The Rise, Transformation, and Fall of Apalachee: A Case Study of Political Change in a Chiefly Society. In *Lamar Archaeology: Mississippian Chiefdoms in the Deep South*, ed. Mark Williams and Gary Shapiro, 175–86. Tuscaloosa: University of Alabama Press.

Bibliography

Schwartz, Seymour I., and Henry Taliaferro
  1984   A Newly Discovered First State of a Foundation Map, "Amérique Septentrionale." *The Map Collector* 26:2–6.

Seeman, Mark F.
  1979   *The Hopewell Interaction Sphere: The Evidence for Interregional Trade and Structural Complexity.* Indiana Historical Society Prehistory Research Series 5(2). Indianapolis.

Serrano y Sanz, D. Manuel
  1912   *Documentos históricos de la Florida y la Luisiana, siglos XVI al XVIII.* Madrid: Librería General de Victoriano Suárez.

Service, Elman R.
  1971a   *Cultural Evolutionism: Theory in Practice.* New York: Holt, Rinehart and Winston.
  1971b   *Primitive Social Organization: An Evolutionary Perspective.* New York: Random House.

Shaffer, John G., and Vincas P. Steponaitis
  1983   Burial Mounds from the Big Black Drainage in Mississippi: Some New Interpretations. Paper presented at 40th annual meeting of the Southeastern Archaeological Conference, Columbia SC.

Shea, John Gilmary, ed. and trans.
  1853   *Discovery and Exploration of the Mississippi Valley.* New York: J. S. Redfield.
  1861   *Early Voyages Up and Down the Mississippi.* Albany: Joel Munsell.

Sheldon, Craig T.
  1974   The Mississippian-Historic Transition in Central Alabama. Ph.D. dissertation, University of Oregon.

Sheldon, Craig T., and Ned J. Jenkins
  1986   Protohistoric Development in Central Alabama. In *The Protohistoric Period in the Mid-South: 1500–1700*, ed. David H. Dye and Ronald C. Brister, 95–102. Mississippi Department of Archives and History Archaeological Report 18. Jackson.

Silverberg, Robert
  1974   *The Mound Builders.* New York: Ballantine.

Simpson, Lesley Byrd
  1966   *The Encomienda in New Spain: The Beginning of Spanish Mexico.* Berkeley: University of California Press.

Smith, Bruce D.
  1978a   Variation in Mississippian Settlement Patterns. In *Mississippian Settlement Patterns*, ed. Bruce D. Smith, 479–503. New York: Academic Press.
  1984   Mississippian Expansion: Tracing the Historical Development of an Explanatory Model. *Southeastern Archaeology* 3 (1): 13–32.
  1986   The Archaeology of the Southeastern United States, from Dalton to DeSoto (10,500 B.P.–500 B.P.). In *Advances in World Archaeology*, ed. Fred Wendorf and Angela E. Close, 5:1–92. Orlando FL: Academic Press.
  ———, ed.
  1978b   *Mississippian Settlement Patterns.* New York: Academic Press.

1990   *The Mississippian Emergence.* Washington DC: Smithsonian Institution.

Smith, Buckingham

1857   *Colección de varios documentos para la historia de la Florida y tierras adjacentes.* London: Trübner and Co.

Smith, Catherine Delano

1985   Cartographic Signs on European Maps and Their Explanation before 1700. *Imago Mundi* 37:9–29.

Smith, Marvin T.

1977   The Early Historic Period (1540–1670) on the Upper Coosa River Drainage of Alabama and Georgia. *Conference on Historic Site Archaeology Papers* 11:151–67.

1984   Depopulation and Culture Change in the Early Historic Period Interior Southeast. Ph.D. dissertation, University of Florida.

1987   *Archaeology of Aboriginal Culture Change in the Interior Southeast: Depopulation during the Early Historic Period.* Gainesville: University Presses of Florida.

Smith, Marvin T., and Mary Elizabeth Good

1982   *Early Sixteenth Century Glass Beads in the Spanish Colonial Trade.* Greenwood MS: Cottonlandia Museum Publications.

Snell, William Robert

1972   Indian Slavery in Colonial South Carolina. Ph.D. dissertation, University of Alabama.

Solis, Carlos, and Richard Walling

1982   *Archaeological Investigations at the Yarborough Site (22Cl814), Clay County, Mississippi.* University of Alabama Office of Archaeological Research Report of Investigations 30. Moundville.

Spaulding, Albert

1940   Archaeological Field Notes, MLe18. Manuscript on file, Natchez Trace Parkway Office, Tupelo MS.

Spoehr, Alexander

1947   *Changing Kinship Systems.* Field Museum of Natural History Anthropological Series 33 (4). Chicago.

Starr, Mary Evelyn

1984   The Parchman Phase in the Northern Yazoo Basin: A Preliminary Analysis. In *The Wilsford Site (22-Co-516), Coahoma County, Mississippi*, by John Connaway, 163–209. Mississippi Department of Archives and History Archaeological Report 14. Jackson.

Steponaitis, Vincas P.

1974   The Late Prehistory of the Natchez Region: Excavations at the Emerald and Foster Sites, Adams County, Mississippi. Bachelor's thesis, Harvard University.

1978   Location Theory and Complex Chiefdoms: A Mississippian Example. In *Mississippian Settlement Patterns*, ed. Bruce D. Smith, 417–53. New York: Academic Press.

1980   Chronology and Community Patterns of Moundville. In The Moundville Archaeological Project, ed. Margaret Scarry, 99–115. Southeastern Archaeological Conference Bulletin 24.

1981   Plaquemine Ceramic Chronology in the Natchez Region. *Mississippi Archaeology* 16(2): 6–19.

1983   *Ceramics, Chronology, and Community Patterns at Moundville, a Late Prehistoric Site in Alabama.* New York: Academic Press.

1991   Contrasting Patterns of Mississippian Development. In *Chiefdoms: Power, Economy, and Ideology,* ed. Timothy K. Earle, 193–228. Cambridge: Cambridge University Press.

Stevenson, Edward Luther

1909   Early Spanish Cartography of the New World. *Proceedings of the American Antiquarian Society* 19:369–419.

Steward, Julian

1955   *Theory of Culture Change.* Urbana: University of Illinois Press.

Stowe, Noel R.

1985   The Pensacola Variant and the Bottle Creek Phase. *Florida Anthropologist* 38 (1–2,pt.2) : 144–49.

1989   The Pensacola Variant and the Southeastern Ceremonial Complex. In *Southeastern Ceremonial Complex, Artifacts and Analysis: The Cottonlandia Conference,* ed. Patricia Galloway, 125–32. Lincoln: University of Nebraska Press.

Stowe, Noel R., and Richard Fuller

1993   The Bottle Creek Mounds: History of Archaeological Research prior to 1990. In Bottle Creek Research: Working Papers on the Bottle Creek Site (1Ba2), Baldwin County, Alabama, ed. Ian W. Brown and Richard Fuller. *Journal of Alabama Archaeology* 39(1–2): 10–29.

Struever, Stuart

1968   Woodland Subsistence-Settlement Systems in the Lower Illinois Valley. In *New Perspectives in Archeology,* ed. Sally R. Binford and Lewis R. Binford, 285–312. Chicago: Aldine.

Streuver, Stuart, and Gail L. Houart

1972   An Analysis of the Hopewell Interaction Sphere. In *Social Exchange and Interaction,* ed. E. Wilmsen, 47–79. University of Michigan Museum of Anthropology Anthropological Papers 46. Ann Arbor.

Stubbs, John D., Jr.

1982a   The Chickasaw Contact with the La Salle Expedition in 1682. In *La Salle and His Legacy: Frenchmen and Indians in the Lower Mississippi Valley,* ed. Patricia Galloway, 41–48. Jackson: University Press of Mississippi.

1982b   A Preliminary Classification of Chickasaw Pottery. *Mississippi Archaeology* 17(2): 50–57.

Swanton, John R.

1911   *Indian Tribes of the Lower Mississippi Valley and Adjacent Coast of the Gulf of Mexico.* Bureau of American Ethnology Bulletin 43. Washington DC.

1915   Introduction to *A Dictionary of the Choctaw Language* by Cyrus Byington, ed. John R. Swanton and Henry S. Halbert, vii–xi. Bureau of American Ethnology Bulletin 46. Washington DC.

1922   *Early History of the Creek Indians and Their Neighbors.* Bureau of American Ethnology Bulletin 73. Washington DC.

1928a   Aboriginal Culture of the Southeast. *Forty-Second Annual Report of the Bureau of American Ethnology, 1924–1925*, 673–726. Washington DC.

1928b   Social and Religious Beliefs and Usages of the Chickasaw Indians. *Forty-Fourth Annual Report of the Bureau of American Ethnology, 1926–1927*, 169–74. Washington DC.

1928c   Social Organization and Social Usages of the Indians of the Creek Confederacy. *Forty-Second Annual Report of the Bureau of American Ethnology, 1924–1925*, 25–472. Washington DC: Bureau of American Ethnology.

1931   *Source Material for the Social and Ceremonial Life of the Choctaw Indians.* Bureau of American Ethnology Bulletin 103. Washington DC.

1937   Comments on the Delgado Papers. *Florida Historical Quarterly* 16:127–29.

1939   *Final Report of the United States De Soto Expedition Commission.* Washington DC: Government Printing Office.

1946   *The Indians of the Southeastern United States.* Bureau of American Ethnology Bulletin 137. Washington DC.

Tainter, Joseph A.

1988   *The Collapse of Complex Societies.* Cambridge: Cambridge University Press.

Tanner, Helen Hornbeck

1989   The Land and Water Communication Systems of the Southeastern Indians. In *Powhatan's Mantle: Indians in the Colonial Southeast*, ed. Peter H. Wood, Gregory A. Waselkov, and M. Thomas Hatley, 6–20. Lincoln: University of Nebraska Press.

Tesar, Louis D.

1974   *Archaeological Assessment Survey of the Tallahala Reservoir Area, Jasper County, Mississippi.* Mississippi State: Mississippi State University Department of Anthropology.

Thornton, Russell

1987   *American Indian Holocaust and Survival: A Population History since 1492.* Norman: University of Oklahoma Press.

Tonti, Henri de

1684   Memoir of 4 November 1684. Bibliothèque Nationale, MSS Clairambault 1016, fols. 220–266v and 267–79.

1846   Memoir of 1691. In *Historical Collections of Louisiana*, ed. B. F. French, 1:52–98. New York: Wiley and Putnam.

Toth, Alan

1988   Early Marksville Phases in the Lower Mississippi Valley: A Study in Culture Contact Dynamics. Ph.D. dissertation, Harvard University, 1977. Mississippi Department of Archives and History Archaeological Report 21. Jackson.

Trickey, E. Bruce

1958   A Chronological Framework for the Mobile Bay Region. *American Antiquity* 23:388–96.

Trickey, E. Bruce, and Nicholas H. Holmes Jr.

1971   A Chronological Framework for the Mobile Bay Region. Revised, 1970. *Journal of Alabama Archaeology* 17 (2): 115–28.

Bibliography

Trigger, Bruce G.

1976   *The Children of Aataentsic: A History of the Huron People to 1660*, 2 vols. Montreal: McGill-Queen's University Press.

1981   Ontario Native People and the Epidemics of 1634–1640. In *Indians, Animals, and the Fur Trade: A Critique of Keepers of the Game*, ed. Shepard Krech III, 21–38. Athens: University of Georgia Press.

1983   American Archaeology as Native History: A Review Essay. *William and Mary Quarterly* 40:413–52.

Turner, Frederick Jackson

[1894] 1961   The Significance of the Frontier in American History. In *Frontier and Section: Selected Essays of Frederick Jackson Turner*, 37–62. Englewood Cliffs NJ: Prentice-Hall.

Tusser, Thomas

1878   *Five Hundred Pointes of Good Husbandrie*, ed. W. Bayne and Sidney J. Herrtage. English Dialect Society 21. London: Trübner and Co.

Usner, Daniel H., Jr.

1992   *Indians, Settlers and Slaves in a Frontier Exchange Economy*. Chapel Hill: University of North Carolina Press.

van Gennep, Arnold

1960   *The Rites of Passage*, trans. Monika B. Vizedom and Gabrielle L. Caffe. Chicago: University of Chicago Press.

Vansina, Jan

1973   *Oral Tradition: A Study in Historical Methodology*. Harmondsworth, England: Penguin.

Villiers du Terrage, Baron Marc de

1922   Documents concernant l'histoire des indiens de la région orientale de la Louisiane. *Journal de la Société des Américanistes* n.s. 14:127–40.

Voss, Jerome A.

1985   Recent Advances in Choctaw Archaeology. Paper presented at the annual meeting of the American Society for Ethnohistory, Chicago.

Voss, Jerome A., and John H. Blitz

1983   An Archaeological Survey in the Choctaw Homeland. *Mississippi Archaeology* 18 (2):49–56.

1988   Archaeological Investigations in the Choctaw Homeland. *American Antiquity* 53:125–45.

Voss, Jerome A., and Cyril B. Mann

1986   Stylistic Variation in Historic Choctaw Ceramics. *Mississippi Archaeology* 21 (1):43–58.

Wailes, Benjamin L. C.

1852   Field Notebooks. Benjamin L. C. Wailes Collection, z0076.01s, Mississippi Department of Archives and History.

Wallerstein, Immanuel

1980   *The Modern World-System*, Vol. 2: *Mercantilism and the Consolidation of the European World-Economy, 1600–1750*. New York: Academic Press.

Bibliography

Walthall, John A.

1980   *Prehistoric Indians of the Southeast: Archaeology of Alabama and the Middle South.* Tuscaloosa: University of Alabama Press.

Ward, Rufus

1984   Nineteenth Century Choctaw Indian Reservation Sites in Lowndes County, Mississippi. *Mississippi Archaeology* 19 (2) : 39–45.

Waring, Antonio

1968   The Southern Cult and Muskogean Ceremonial. In *The Waring Papers*, ed. Stephen Williams, 30–69. Papers of the Peabody Museum of Archaeology and Ethnology 58. Cambridge MA.

Waselkov, Gregory A.

1989   Indian Maps of the Colonial Southeast. In *Powhatan's Mantle: Indians in the Colonial Southeast*, ed. Peter H. Wood, Gregory A. Waselkov, and M. Thomas Hatley, 292–346. Lincoln: University of Nebraska Press.

Webb, Malcolm C.

1982   Preliminary Report on Excavations at an Early Troyville Period Site (16 ST 6) on the West Pearl River, Louisiana. *Louisiana Archaeology* 9:205–50.

1989   Functional and Historical Parallelisms between Mesoamerican and Mississippian Cultures. In *Southeastern Ceremonial Complex, Artifacts and Analysis: The Cottonlandia Conference*, ed. Patricia Galloway, 279–93. Lincoln: University of Nebraska Press.

Weddle, Robert S.

1973   *Wilderness Manhunt: The Spanish Search for La Salle.* Austin: University of Texas Press.

1985   *Spanish Sea: The Gulf of Mexico in North American Discovery, 1500–1685.* College Station: Texas A&M University Press.

1991   *The French Thorn: Rival Explorers in the Spanish Sea, 1682–1762.* College Station: Texas A&M University Press.

Weddle, Robert S., Mary Christine Morkovsky, and Patricia Galloway, eds.

1987   *La Salle, the Mississippi, and the Gulf: Three Primary Documents.* College Station: Texas A&M University Press.

Weinstein, Richard A.

1985   Some New Thoughts on the De Soto Expedition through Western Mississippi. *Mississippi Archaeology* 20 (2) : 2–24.

1987   Development and Regional Variation of Plaquemine Culture in South Louisiana. In *The Emergent Mississippian: Proceedings of the Sixth Mid-South Archaeological Conference*, ed. Richard A. Marshall, 85–106. Cobb Institute of Archaeology Occasional Papers 87-01. Starkville MS.

Welch, Paul D.

1980   The West Jefferson Phase: Terminal Woodland Tribal Society in West Central Alabama. In The Moundville Archaeological Project, ed. Margaret Scarry, 14–25. Southeastern Archaeological Conference Bulletin 24.

1990   Mississippian Emergence in West Central Alabama. In *Mississippian Emergence*, ed. Bruce D. Smith, 197–226. Washington DC: Smithsonian Institution Press.

1991   *Moundville's Economy.* Tuscaloosa: University of Alabama Press.

Wenhold, Lucy L.
1936   *A Seventeenth Century Letter of Gabriel Diaz Vara Calderón, Bishop of Cuba, Describing the Indians and Indian Missions of Florida.* Smithsonian Miscellaneous Collections 95 (16). Washington DC: Smithsonian Institution.

White, Hayden
1978   *Tropics of Discourse: Essays in Cultural Criticism.* Baltimore: Johns Hopkins University Press.
1987   *The Content of the Form: Narrative Discourse and Historical Representation.* Baltimore: Johns Hopkins University Press.

White, Richard
1983   *The Roots of Dependency: Subsistence, Environment, and Social Change among the Choctaws, Pawnees, and Navajos.* Lincoln: University of Nebraska Press.

Williams, Stephen
1963   The Eastern United States. In *Early Indian Farmers and Villages and Communities,* ed. William G. Haag, 267–325. Washington DC: National Park Service.
1991   *Fantastic Archaeology: The Wild Side of North American Prehistory.* Philadelphia: University of Pennsylvania Press.

Williams, Stephen, and Jeffrey P. Brain
1983   *Excavations at the Lake George Site, Yazoo County, Mississippi, 1958–1960.* Peabody Museum of Archaeology and Ethnology Papers 74. Cambridge MA.

Williams, Stephen, and Tristram R. Kidder, eds.
n.d.   *Coles Creek and Its Neighbors.* Mississippi Department of Archives and History Archaeological Report, forthcoming.

Willis, James
1985   Choctaw Village Scenes. In *A Choctaw Anthology III,* ed. Jane Anderson and Nina C. Zachary, 1–10. Philadelphia MS: Choctaw Heritage Press.

Willis, William S.
1963   Patrilineal Institutions in Southeastern North America. *Ethnohistory* 10:250–69.

Witkowski, Stanley R., and James W. Springer
1979   Language and Archaeology in Eastern North America. Unpublished paper in author's possession.

Wolf, Eric R.
1982   *Europe and the People without History.* Berkeley: University of California Press.

Wood, Peter H.
1984   La Salle: Discovery of a Lost Explorer. *American Historical Review* 89 (2) : 294–323.
1989   The Changing Population of the Colonial South: An Overview by Race and Region, 1685–1790. In *Powhatan's Mantle: Indians in the Colonial Southeast,* ed. Peter H. Wood, Gregory A. Waselkov, and M. Thomas Hatley, 35–103. Lincoln: University of Nebraska Press.

Woodburn, James
1982   Social Dimensions of Death in Four African Hunting and Gathering Societies. In *Death and the Regeneration of Life,* ed. Maurice Bloch and Jonathan Parry, 187–210. Cambridge: Cambridge University Press.

Worth, John E.

1994   Exploration and Trade in the Deep Frontier of Spanish Florida: Possible Sources for Sixteenth-Century Spanish Artifacts in Western North Carolina. Paper presented at the 51st annual meeting of the Southeastern Archaeological Conference, Lexington.

WPA

n.d.   WPA Files for Kemper County, Mississippi. Mississippi Department of Archives and History.

Wright, Alfred

1828   Choctaws Religious Opinions, Traditions, Etc. *Missionary Herald* 24:178–83, 214–16.

Wright, J. Leitch, Jr.

1964   Spanish Reaction to Carolina. *North Carolina Historical Review* 41:464–76.

1981   *The Only Land They Knew: The Tragic Story of the American Indians in the Old South.* New York: Free Press.

Yarnell, Richard A.

1976   Early Plant Husbandry in Eastern North America. In *Culture Change and Continuity: Essays in Honor of James Bennett Griffin*, ed. Charles C. Cleland, 265–318. New York: Academic Press.

Yearous, Jenny

1991   Report on Burials at the Meadowbrook Site, Lee County, Mississippi. Paper presented at the annual meeting of the Mississippi Archaeological Association, Cottonlandia Museum, Greenwood MS.

Index

Note: *Also* cross-references to alternate names or alternate spellings of names are made only where research indicates that both names refer to the same entity.